Engineers
Far from Ordinary:

The U.S. Army Corps of Engineers in St. Louis

Damon Manders and Brian Rentfro
Ordnance and Technical Services Branch
St. Louis District
U.S. Army Corps of Engineers
September 1, 2011

Foreword

In 2007, the state of Missouri adopted as its motto, "Close to Home, Far from Ordinary." The title of this volume – "Engineers Far from Ordinary" – builds on this motto. To some this may seem presumptuous, maybe even arrogant, but it closely reflects the fact that St. Louis has been home to some of the nation's greatest civilian and military engineers and that it has been a central hub for exploration and civil engineering almost since U.S. assumption of the Louisiana Territory. Some of the nation's leading topographical and civil engineers have called St. Louis or Missouri their home at some point in their career, including William Clark, Joseph N. Nicolette, Henry M. Shreve, James B. Eads, Henry and Edward Flad, Robert E. McMath, John A. Ockerson, Edward A. Glenn, Claude Strauser, Jack Niemi, and many others. Explorers include Lewis and Clark, Zebulon Pike, John C. Fremont, Kit Carson, and Manuel Lisa departed from St. Louis. Many leading U.S. Army Corps of Engineers officers received tutelage from the Mississippi River near St. Louis. Chief of Engineers Col. Charles Gratiot was a St. Louis citizen. Col. Stephen H. Long became the Chief of the Corps of Topographical Engineers after exploration of the Missouri River and improvements to the river at St. Louis and other locations. One of Confederate General Robert E. Lee's first assignments as an engineer officer was to improve the St. Louis Harbor. Brig. Gen. William H. Bixby was at one point simultaneously the St. Louis District Engineer, Western Division Engineer, and Chief of Engineers. No less than seven St. Louis District Engineers served as members of the Mississippi River Commission, five of them as its president, including some of the most brilliant officers that organization has known.

Likewise, the history of St. Louis is filled with some of the most important engineering accomplishments in the nation. At the beginning of the American occupation of St. Louis, the city served as a starting point for exploration and mapping of the Northwest. Topographical engineers working for the Corps of

Engineers helped make important scientific discoveries and create maps of the region. Civil engineers and engineer officers helped make the earliest improvements to the Mississippi River and established transportation routes to the west that allowed its expansion. These accomplishments include the earliest experiments to reengineer the difficult Middle Mississippi River with snag removal, wing dams, notched and permeable dikes, dredges, and other technologies. In many ways, the district served as the laboratory for the rest of the river. Some of the city's leading businessmen, biologists, and engineers worked hand in hand with the Corps, leading to some of the most productive civilian-military knowledge exchanges the nation has known. By the twentieth century, the Corps was building one of the greatest lock and dam systems in the world, constructing levees and floodwalls to protect the region from flooding, and establishing reservoirs at several tributary lakes and streams. Later environmental river engineering innovations such as chevron dikes, bendway weirs, tree screens, and environmental pool management were developed or implemented at St. Louis District as a result of their detailed studies and modeling. Such efforts demonstrate the great knowledge and innovative attitude of district engineers and planners, not only with regards to navigation and flood control, but also to environmental mitigation and restoration.

The activities of the Corps of Engineers in St. Louis always preceded its growth and change. As the Corps has improved the rivers and made it safe from flooding, the city has grown from a frontier town and French colony, to a river town and trading center, to a railroad hub and industrial giant. The population of the city grew from a few thousand in the 1820s to the fourth largest city in the U.S. by 1900. Although the population of the city itself declined after World War II, the surrounding metropolitan area has grown and the harbor of St. Louis, now stretching 70 miles along the river, continues to contribute to the well being of the metropolitan area. Reflecting the concerns of the nation about the impact of industrialization and river improvements on the environment, the Corps worked closely with other agencies and local government to maintain a balance between nature and the activities of man by restoring the river system to its former state. These connections and their impact on the city itself form an important thread in the stories that follow.

The history more or less follows a topical approach, which, although written as independent essays or units, still follows something of a chronological outline. The first section discusses the role of the Corps in westward expansion through St. Louis, its use of the city as a base of exploration, and its involvement in building the transportation routes that made the city during the first 50 to 70 years in the U.S. The second section provides an overview of Mississippi River navigation improvements, from the earliest attempts to clear the river of snags in 1825 through various attempts to maintain a channel through permanent and temporary improvements in the 1880s, to the construction of slack water dams north of St. Louis from 1934 to 1965 maintaining a nine-foot depth, through other studies and innovations up to modern day. Section three discusses flood control efforts from the growth of federal responsibility from 1917 to 1936, the construction of urban flood control projects after 1950, the development of reservoirs from the 1950s to the 1980s, major flood fights since World War II, and response to Hurricane Katrina in 2005. Section four briefly discusses the involvement of the St. Louis District in military construction, focusing mostly on World War II but including major deployments in twentieth and twenty-first century conflicts. Section five focuses on the modern era and the changes the district underwent to respond to new environmental requirements. It includes a description of the two major construction projects, one completed and the other eventually deauthorized, and their environmental impact. It also chronicles the development of major environmental technologies and programs to restore the river's natural regimen. Thus, while discussing the major responsibilities of the district topically, the history progresses from the early republic period for exploration, to the prewar era for navigation, to the twentieth century for flood control and military construction, to the late twentieth century and early twenty-first century for environmental projects.

The authors wish to extend their thanks to the St. Louis District and its support, without which this volume would not have been possible. The Ordnance and Technical Services Branch, for which the authors themselves work, provided much of the preliminary research, visited archives, collected and digitized sources, and conducted employee interviews. In particular, the authors wish to mention Jon Daly and Donna Zoeller, who put in considerable labor in paving the way for the writers to take up their task. The authors also thank Thomas A. Freeman, Rochelle Hance, Randy Curtis, Laurel Lane, and the entire branch for their support and help. The authors appreciate the participation of the more than 27 employees and military personnel who participated in interviews, as well as past interviews conducted by Michael Ruddy and others. Special thanks go to Charles Camillo, the Mississippi Valley Division historian, for his considerable expertise and guidance throughout all phases of the project. Finally, the authors wish to thank their families and friends for their support during this project, and I thank God for this opportunity to write about the city that has become my second home.

Damon Manders
September 2011

Table of Contents

Foreword iii

Part I. Gatekeepers of the West: The U.S. Army Corps of Engineers and Westward Expansion. 1
1. St. Louis: Base for Exploration 2
2. Opening the Gateway to the West 16

Part II. Engineering the Middle Mississippi: The U.S. Army Corps of Engineers and River Navigation. 29
3. Snag Removal on the Mississippi 30
4. The St. Louis Harbor and Channel Regulation 39
5. Dredging and Channel Maintenance 62
6. Canalization of the Upper Mississippi 82
7. Navigation Improvements in the Modern Era 106

Part III. Where the Rivers Run: The U.S. Army Corps of Engineers and Flood Control 134
8. Federalization of Flood Control 135
9. Urban Flood Control 148
10. Flood Control Reservoirs in the St. Louis District 166
11. Flood Fighting and Flood Management .185
12. Task Force Guardian and Hurricane Response. 209

Part IV. Serving the Nation: The U.S. Army Corps of Engineers and Military Construction 222
13. Military Construction and the Industrial Complex 223
14. War Mobilization on the Mississippi River 234
15. Deployments and Combat Engineering 242

Part V. Conservation and Controversy: The U.S. Army Corps of Engineers and the Environment **252**
16. Growing Environmental Responsibilities 253
17. The Meramec Dam Controversy 290
18. Replacement of Lock and Dam No. 26....................... 319
19. Environmental River Engineering 355
20. Environmental Pool Management 371

Conclusion. 381

Appendices
Appendix A. St. Louis District Commanders.................... 383
Appendix B. St. Louis District Chronology 385
Appendix C. Notable Engineers in the St. Louis District 393
Bibliography 406

View of St. Louis, 1835, by Leon Pomarede, Courtesy St. Louis Art Museum

Part I.
Gatekeepers of the West: The U.S. Army Corps of Engineers and Westward Expansion

In 1967, St. Louis opened the Gateway Arch to the public. Designed by Eero Saarinen and Hannskarl Bandel, the 630-foot arch quickly became an iconic symbol of the city. As part of the Jefferson National Expansion Memorial museum, the arch is a monument to the role of St. Louis as the "Gateway to the West." For many decades, St. Louis was the last civilized stop before entering the western wilderness. Dozens of explorers and thousands of settlers went through the city on their way to their own destinies in the West as the United States expanded across the continent. The arch celebrates this fact. What is less well known is the role the U.S. Army Corps of Engineers played in opening and maintaining this gateway. By first occupying the city, by leading early exploration of the northwest, and by opening and maintaining transportation routes west, the Army enabled westward expansion. Without the Army, and the Corps in particular, the route to the West may have taken decades longer to become established, or it may have taken a different route entirely. Through the perseverance and vision of the U.S. government, the Army, and the Corps, the way to the West through St. Louis opened for generations of Americans seeking a better life.

1

St. Louis: Base for Exploration

Even before the U.S. assumed possession of the Louisiana Purchase in 1804, St. Louis served as a base for exploration of the Northwest. The previous governors of St. Louis had organized several small trade journeys, but it was the expedition led by Capts. Meriwether Lewis and William Clark in 1803 that launched a period of exploration of the Missouri River, Upper Mississippi River, Arkansas River, Red River, and what would become Arkansas, Missouri, Kansas, Nebraska, Iowa, Minnesota, and the Dakotas. This exploration continued until well after Missouri became a state in 1821. As the last major city on the frontier where expeditions could purchase supplies and obtain information and where the U.S. Army maintained a presence for many years, it was the logical starting and ending point for exploration. Starting with Lewis and Clark, including Capt. Zebulon Pike and Maj. Stephen Long, and culminating in the journeys of the renowned French mathematician Joseph N. Nicollet for the Corps of Topographical Engineers, the Army and the Corps of Engineers pushed into the western frontier from St. Louis. In the process, they made important discoveries while improving maps and knowledge of the region, which enabled settlement and further exploration. At the same time, by the explorers using St. Louis as a base of operations, the city itself grew into the "Gateway of the West."

When the first U.S. Army officers arrived in St. Louis in 1803, it had already been a prominent French colony in the American West for 40 years. After initial exploration of the Mississippi River by Louis Jolliet and Jacques Marquette in 1673, permanent occupation of the colony began with the founding of Biloxi in 1698 by Pierre Le Moyne d'Iberville, and in 1707 Robert Cavelier, Sieur de La Salle named the territory Louisiana. As early as 1682, there had been a fort with the name St. Louis on the Illinois River, later rebuilt near Peoria, Illinois. It was primarily a mission and Native American trading center, never numbering more than 100 or so persons. Among the tribes it evangelized were the Tamaroas, whose principal village, Cahokia, lay across the Mississippi from modern St. Louis. Once the largest Native American city in North America,

Cahokia had been vacant for several hundred years until occupation by the Tamaroas. Including Canadian traders, the mission at Cahokia grew to about 60 by 1705. Soon overshadowing it was a Jesuit mission to the Kaskaskias, which missionaries built originally in 1700 near the River Des Peres on the south side of modern St. Louis and later moved to the mouth of the Kaskaskia River when the tribe relocated to escape Iroquois jurisdiction. The Kaskaskia mission became "something of a capitol of the Illinois country for a long time." Located near rich soil adaptable to agriculture, the mission quickly grew to more than 100 persons by 1715 with several mills as it became peopled by Canadian and Louisiana merchants attracted by close proximity to salt springs and tin and lead mines. Encouraged by Scottish financier John Law, the French established Fort de Chartres 15 miles from Kaskaskia in 1720, Fort Orleans near the Missouri River in what is now Carroll County in 1723, and lead mines near the Meramec River in 1723, which led to settlement of Ste. Genevieve. Even at this time, "these French outposts in the Illinois country quickly became western-oriented," historian James Primm observed. Trade with France's wealthy southwestern holdings kept the colony alive for a generation.[1]

Following the French and Indian War, Louisiana Gov. Jean Jacques D. Abbadie granted a trade monopoly with the Missouri tribes to Gilbert Antoine Maxent. In August 1763, his partner Pierre de Laclede left to scout a site for the endeavor. The company started permanent occupation in 1764 of the colony Laclede named St. Louis. He designed it after New Orleans in a gridiron pattern with public square, common fields, and a tow path for boats. Since the Treaty of Paris ending the war ceded French holdings east of the Mississippi to the British, the colony received many immigrants from Illinois, including at least 40 families from Fort de Chartres and Cahokia as well as Capt. Louis St. Ange de Bellerive

Pierre de Laclede

---

[1] Marcel Giraud, *History of French Louisiana*, Vol. 1 (Baton Rouge: LSU P, 1953): xi-10, 27-31, 50-69, 337-348, quote on 340; James N. Primm, *Lion of the Valley: St. Louis, Missouri* (Boulder, Col.: Pruett, 1981): 1-7, quote on 5; James B. Musick, *St. Louis as a Fortified Town* (St. Louis: R.F. Miller, 1941): 1-5; Calvin R. Fremling, *Immortal River: the Upper Mississippi in Ancient and Modern Times* (Madison: U of Wisconsin P, 2005): 101-122; Frederick J. Dobney, *River Engineers on the Middle Mississippi: A History of the St. Louis District, U.S. Army Corps of Engineers* (St. Louis: U.S. Army Corps of Engineers, Mississippi Valley Division, St. Louis [MVS], 1978): 1-7.

1683 Map of French Colonial America

Ste. Genevieve, Missouri, 1735

and his garrison. The Spanish, who had obtained Louisiana prior to the 1763 Treaty of Paris, finally exerted authority over the colony in 1767 with construction of Fort Don Carlos south of the Missouri River in 1768. In 1770, St. Louis Gov. San Pedro Piernas established garrisons and militia at St. Louis and Ste. Genevieve. With the growth of the fur trade, by 1772, the population of St. Louis was 577 and Ste. Genevieve was 691. The city grew to include a range of occupations, incomes, education, and life styles; other than the occasional ship from New Orleans, it was mostly self-sufficient. Since the Spanish opposed the British, the residents of Spanish Illinois supported the American Revolution, aiding Virginia Gen. George Rogers Clark, defeating a British and Native American attack on St. Louis in 1780, and raiding a fort at St. Joseph in 1781. Following the war and especially after passage of the Northwest Ordinance in 1787, American settlement of Illinois spurred continued trade and growth across the river. As one of the largest towns in Illinois, Cahokia became the seat of St. Clair County and the territorial government in 1790. James Piggot established the first ferry from what became East St. Louis across the river. Despite Spanish closure of the lower Mississippi to American trade, St. Louis residents remained friendly to the Americans, and the city grew to a population of 1,168 in 1792 and by 1800 formed several satellite villages with populations ranging from 181 to 614. At the same time, St. Louisans started pushing farther west in search of new trade

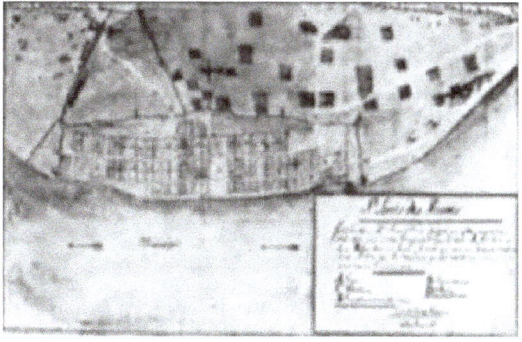

August Chouteau's 1780 map of St. Louis, MHS

Marquette and the Indians 1869 by William Lamprecht, St. Louis Art Museum

routes. From 1794 to 1796, Zenon Trudeau sponsored three expeditions up the Missouri in hopes of finding a way to the Pacific, but because of opposition from Native American tribes reached no farther than North Dakota.[2]

Early American Exploration

France reacquired Louisiana in 1801, but facing war with Great Britain, Napoleon Bonaparte offered to sell the territory to the United States for $15 million in 1803. President Thomas Jefferson accepted despite reservations that doing so violated the Constitution, and after the Senate ratified a treaty approving the sale, Gen. James Wilkinson took possession of Louisiana at New Orleans on December 20, 1803. On March 10, 1804, Lt. Gov. Carlos de Hault de Lassus officially signed over St. Louis and Fort Don Carlos to Capt. Amos Stoddard, the Revolutionary soldier and later hero of the War of 1812. From this point forward, there was a frequent if not near continuous presence of Army officers responsible for the city's protection and well-being. Stoddard served as acting governor until the arrival of William Henry Harrison in the fall of 1804. There was some apprehension and economic hardship as the territory transitioned to U.S. government with the appointment of judges and adoption of U.S. law. By showing great flexibility and deference to local government, Stoddard and Harrison maintained civil authority until Jefferson appointed Wilkinson as the territorial governor in 1805. Although initially received favorably by Creole citizens, Wilkinson was surrounded by rumors of scandal, and the rejection by Wilkinson officials of several land grants made prior to 1803 sparked calls for his removal. Jefferson ordered him to New Orleans to head up defenses there, and assigned Capt. Meriwether Lewis as governor in 1807. Lewis served as governor until his departure for Washington in 1809 to straighten out his personal accounts, and he committed suicide soon afterwards. Brig. Gen. Benjamin Howard of Kentucky then served as governor until 1812. With reorganization of the Territory of Missouri in 1812, President James Madison named Lewis' former partner William Clark the new governor.[3]

After becoming U.S. property, St. Louis quickly became a base for exploration and expansion. Although Jefferson had been planning a western expedition

---

[2] Primm, pp. 9-67; Musick, pp. 5-104; Dobney, pp. 5-10; James W. Bond, *The East St. Louis, Illinois, Waterfront: Historical Background* (St. Louis: National Park Service Division of History, 1969): 1-10. The population of St. Louis declined somewhat by 1800 to 1,039 as populations shifted to these new villages.
[3] Primm, pp. 71-86, 104-105; Fremling, pp. 122-124. William Clark was the brother of George Rogers Clark.

for years and submitted a request for funding in January 1803, he did not officially commission the scientific and military expedition up the Missouri River, led by Capts. Meriwether Lewis and William Clark, until after negotiations with France for Louisiana were completed in June 1803. The Lewis and Clark expedition has received frequent treatment in recent years in celebration of its 200-year anniversary. Suffice to state here that St. Louis played an important role in the journey, providing necessary supplies, personnel, and information prior to the expedition's departure up the Missouri. The official beginning of the expedition was August 31, 1803, when Lewis left Pittsburg, Pennsylvania. The initial crew sailed down the Ohio River through Cincinnati, Ohio, Clark joining it from Louisville, Kentucky. They then rowed up the Mississippi to St. Louis. There, Lewis found outgoing Lt. Gov. Carlos Delassus had not heard of the expedition and, despite Lewis having valid passports, would not let them enter Spanish Louisiana. Lewis returned to Cahokia, and the expedition wintered on a camp by the Wood River. By the following January, Delassus had heard from the governor in New Orleans to let the expedition proceed, and Lewis spent months in St. Louis hiring river men, copying maps, and gaining information from traders. After a long delay due to his involvement in disputes with the Osage and other tribes, Lewis assigned the military governor, Stoddard, as his agent and then joined the expedition, which departed up the Missouri River by June 3, 1804. On November 7, 1805, the expedition reached the Pacific Ocean and returned by two different routes and reunited on the Missouri River in August 1806, collecting valuable data on geography, mineralogy, anthropology, botany, zoology, and other fields. The expedition returned to St. Louis on September 23, 1806, and the subsequent publication of their accounts quickly catapulted Lewis and Clark to fame.[4]

Another less recognized but important explorer of the West – whom one author has called the "Lost Pathfinder" – was Capt. Zebulon M. Pike, who became famous for discovering Pike's Peak and the headwaters of the Arkansas River. In 1805, Wilkinson ordered then Lieutenant Pike up the Mississippi River, ostensibly to locate the source of the Mississippi, but also to negotiate

---

[4] David Lavender, *The Way to the Western Sea: Lewis and Clark Across the Continent* (NY: Harper and Rowe, 1988): 1-94, 190-191, 356-389; Dobney, p. 6; Letter No. 86, Lewis to Jefferson, Wheeling, Sept. 8, 1803; No 89, Lewis to Clark, Cincinnati, Sept. 28, 1803; No. 97 Delassus to Juan Manuel de Salcedo, St. Louis, Dec. 9, 1803; No. 100, Lewis to Jefferson, Cahokia, Dec. 28, 1803; No. 106, Gov. to Delassas, Jan. 28, 1804; No. 121, Lewis to Stoddard, May 16, 1804; No. 123, Clark to William Croghan, St. Charles, May 21, 1804; No. 124, Stoddard to Henry Dearborn, St. Louis, Jun. 3, 1804; No. 207, Lewis to Jefferson, St. Louis, Sept. 23, 1806 in Donald Jackson, *Letters of the Lewis and Clark Expedition with Related Documents, 1783-1854* (Urbana: U of Illinois P, 1962).

with local tribes to establish forts or trading posts at St. Pierre River and St. Anthony Falls. Pike left St. Louis on August 9, 1805, with 20 enlisted soldiers and an interpreter. He went as far north as what was later named Lake Cass, Minnesota, which he incorrectly identified as the headwaters of the Mississippi. He had neglected in the throes of winter to follow the course another 25 miles to its true source, Lake Itasca, discovered more than 25 years later by Henry Schoolcraft. He returned April 30, 1806. A few months later, Wilkinson tasked Pike to transport Osage prisoners from the Missouri military cantonment to their tribe, help to negotiate peace between the Osage and Canzes, and then with the aid of the Osage travel to meet the chief of the Comanche tribe at the headwaters of the Arkansas and Red rivers. Along the way, he was to collect information on the rivers, Native American tribes, flora, and fauna. According to Secretary of War Henry Dearborn, another object was to gather information on the Spanish, and Wilkinson warned Pike to move circumspectly. He departed on July 15, 1806. Accompanying him were Lt. James B. Wilkinson (son of the general), 21 enlisted soldiers, and a doctor and interpreter. While Lieutenant Wilkinson found the headwaters of the Arkansas, Pike discovered the mountain named for him but was unable to locate the head of the Red River. Captured by the Spanish, he was held prisoner in New Mexico over the winter, but returned to Natchitoches, Louisiana, in July 1807 and thence to Washington, D.C. Wilkinson communicated to Washington the information Pike sent on the rivers and particularly their navigation, the general country, the native tribes, and what Pike believed was the source of the Mississippi River, which, Dearborn wrote him, "met with approbation of the President" and were "held in high estimation."[5]

As these Army explorers opened up the West, additional explorers soon followed. Soon after the return of the Lewis and Clark expedition, Manuel Lisa of St. Louis established the Missouri Fur Company and established a fort on the Missouri River. He sent a series of expeditions into the Northwest: John Colter to the Yellowstone River in 1808, Andrew Henry to the Three Forks

---

[5] W. Eugene Hollon, *The Lost Pathfinder: Zebulon Montgomery Pike* (Norman: U of Oklahoma P, 1949): 30-73, 81-89; Donald Jackson, ed., *Journals of Zebulon Montgomery Pike with Letters and Related Documents* (Norman: U of Oklahoma P, 1966): Vol. 1, pp. 6, 131, 162; Vol. 2, Letter No. 39, Dearborn to Wilkinson, Feb. 28, 1906; No. 117, Pike to Jacob Kingsbury, Natchitoches, Jul 20, 1807; No 121, Pike to Pike, Natch., Aug. 12, 1807; quote from U.S. Cong., "Compensation to Persons Engaged in the Several Exploring Expeditions under Captain Pike," H.D. 259 (10th Cong., 2nd Sess.); John O. Afinson, *The River We Have Wrought: A History of the Upper Mississippi* (Minneapolis: U of Minnesota Press, 2003): 1-22. Many have commented on the suspicion of Pike's involvement in the Wilkinson-Aaron Burr plot to establish a nation in the Southwest, but there is no direct evidence of his knowledge and, as Hollon observes, "An examination of Pike's career makes it hard to believe that he could have plotted treason" (170).

in 1810, and H.M. Brackenridge of Kentucky up the Missouri in 1811. These expeditions all departed from St. Louis or St. Charles. In 1808, British naturalist and botanist John Bradbury received permission from the Jefferson administration to conduct a research expedition in the Northwest. He arrived in St. Louis in December 1809, and after exploring the Ozarks, departed from St. Charles up the Missouri on March 12, 1810, returning later that year. In 1811, John Jacob Astor's Pacific Fur Company commissioned an expedition by Wilson Price Hunt and Donald McKenzie to blaze a trail from St. Louis to the Pacific, only the fourth crossing of the continent. Lisa and Henry accompanied them on part of the journey. By 1812, an expedition led by Robert Stuart had explored the Snake River, Green River, and skirted the Continental Divide. By this time, traders knew the region from the Missouri to the Snake River Valley fairly well. Although these expeditions were not connected with the Army, they had been made possible in part by the Lewis and Clark and Pike expeditions, whose members aided other explorers.[6]

The War of 1812 suspended for a time exploration of the Northwest. In 1812, General Howard resigned his post as governor to serve as a commander. He later led an attack on the Illinois tribes aligned with the British and established Fort Clark near Peoria, named for Governor Clark. The threat of war, primarily with Native American allies of the British, resulted in building fortifications in St. Louis. Two companies from Louisiana led by Capts. Robert Spencer and James Musick built and garrisoned Fort Lookout near Portages des Sioux in St. Charles County, supplemented by volunteers from St. Louis led by Capt. Charles Lucas. For the most part, there was little action. When rumors arose of British intrigue among upper Missouri tribes, Clark assigned Manuel Lisa as an agent to counter this activity, and Lisa quickly bought the loyalty of several leading tribes, including the Sioux and Omaha. In 1814, Clark led an expedition of 140 volunteers to Prairie du Chien, Wisconsin, to counter Native American activities disrupting trade routes and established Fort Shelby at an advantageous vantage. However, soon after Clark's departure, the British captured the fort as well as the relief force sent a few months later. The British paroled the volunteers but held the town until the end of the war. Despite peace being declared at the end of 1814, fighting continued with local tribes until 1816, when Clark negotiated a treaty with 10 tribes near Portage du Sioux.

---

[6] Reuben G. Thwaits, *Early Western Travels, 1748-1846* (NY: AMS, 1966); Vol. V., "Bradbury's Travels in the Interior of America, 1809-1811"; Vol. VI., "Breckenridge's Journey up the Missouri, 1811"; William H. Goetzmann, *Army Exploration in the American West, 1803-1863* (New Haven, Yale UP, 1959): 1-32.

Although hounded by the St. Louis *Gazette* for showing favoritism to the tribes, Clark went on to serve as superintendent of Indian affairs and surveyor general of Illinois.[7]

Mapping the Northwest

With the conclusion of the war, the Corps set about to chart the Northwest frontier. Lewis, Clark, and Pike had received only minimal training as surveyors, as all Army officers were expected to perform some topographical duties, and they produced several maps, but of limited scope. In 1816, the Corps sent topographical engineer Maj. Stephen H. Long to aid in building defenses at Fort Clark on the Illinois River and to survey the Mississippi River. Educated at Dartmouth College, Long was already a gifted mathematician, surveyor, and inventor when he joined the Army in 1815, and he served initially as an instructor at the U.S. Military Academy at West Point, New York. Traveling to and from St. Louis, he spent 1816 improving Fort Clark and 1817 mapping the Illinois Valley to Chicago and northern Indiana to Fort Wayne. He gathered information on the width, depth, and navigability of the streams he crossed and recommended connecting the Illinois River to the Great Lakes via a canal and constructing a public road from Ohio to the Mississippi River. After a brief trip to Washington, D.C., in 1817 he made an inspection trip up the Mississippi to St. Anthony Falls,

Stephen Harriman Long from a portrait by Titian Ramsey Peal, Independence National Historical Park Collection

near modern St. Paul, Minnesota, during which he gathered data on fortifications and possible sites for new posts. He returned to Fort Belle Fontaine north of St. Louis on August 15. Although his mission was military in nature and required greater speed of travel, he nevertheless collected new information about the region. Soon after, he received orders to accompany Maj. William Bradford and a rifle company up the Arkansas River to establish Fort Smith.

---

[7] Musick, pp. 108-111; Primm, pp. 105-107.

He explored south as far as the Red River and returned to Belle Fontaine in December 1817.[8]

During the hiatus after this expedition, Long returned to Washington and learned of Secretary of War John C. Calhoun's planned Yellowstone Expedition. This was a mission to establish a chain of installations on the Missouri to the Yellowstone River, eventually reduced to just forts at the Mandan villages in the Dakota Territory and Council Bluffs, Nebraska. Long had earlier proposed a scientific expedition up the Missouri, and he again proposed exploration by a steamboat of his own design to precede the military expedition. Calhoun accepted in June 1818. Long spent most of the next year obtaining supplies, selecting scientists and officers, and designing the ever-larger steamboat, *Western Engineer*, which ended up 75 by 13 feet with a 19-inch draft. The final party numbered 24, including Capt. Thomas Biddle, Lt. James D. Graham, Indian Agent Maj. Benjamin O'Fallon, botanist William Baldwin, geologist Augustus Jessup, zoologist Thomas Say, and artist Titian Peale – Baldwin, O'Fallon, and Biddle would later leave the expedition. They left Pittsburg in April 1819 and arrived in St. Louis on June 9 to coordinate with the military expedition and collect supplies. They departed St. Louis on June 19, made stops at St. Charles and Franklin, arrived at the Missouri Company's Fort Lisa in September, and established a cantonment just upriver to spend the winter. Despite the poor performance of the *Western Engineer*, which faced frequent delays due to engine troubles caused by sludge from the Missouri, the steamboat was the first to make it so far upriver. Long returned to Washington and received new orders to travel overland to the Rocky Mountains and locate the source of the Platte, Arkansas, and Red rivers. He returned to St. Louis in April 1820 and departed in June, but struggled with obtaining provisions after budgetary cutbacks. Facing hunger, the expedition split up and returned to Cape Girardeau, Missouri, in October 1820. Despite later criticism of the expeditions, they generated an enormous amount of scientific data: two maps, 274 drawings, and discovery of more than 700 species of plants and several hundred species of insects and mammals that generated dozens of articles and books. The largest criticism of the expedition – Long calling the Great Plains

---

[8] Roger L. Nichols and Patrick L. Halley, *Stephen Long and American Frontier Exploration* (Newark: U of Delaware P, 1980): 1-60; Dobney, p. 7.

the Great American Desert – was in fact a description made by numerous contemporaries familiar with the region.[9]

Even as Long departed on his journeys, other expeditions were also going forward. From 1818 to 1819, geologist Henry Schoolcraft explored the interior of Missouri. He departed from Potosi, about 60 miles southwest of St. Louis, on November 6, 1818, and returned on February 4 the following year, during which he indentified coal and other mineral deposits. Schoolcraft would later become famous for accompanying Lewis Cass and Capt. David Douglass in exploring the Michigan territory in 1820, exploring the Middle Mississippi Valley in 1825, and identifying the true source of the Mississippi River at Lake Itasca, Minnesota, in 1832. In 1820, Maj. Stephen W. Kearny and four other officers traveled west to explore a route from Council Bluffs to Fort Snelling at the confluence of the Mississippi and St. Peter's rivers. Only three years later, Long would return to the Northwest to explore from Fort Snelling to the northern border of the U.S. at the 49th parallel, and eastward to the Great Lakes. For the most part, these explorations were commercial to identify potential mine locations or to scout routes for canals or roads. In the 1830s, the Army Topographical Department funded several new expeditions to the Northwest. The most important of these were led by George W. Featherstonhaugh (pronounced Fanshaw). During two journeys through Arkansas and up the Mississippi River to Fort Snelling in 1834 and 1835, he took notes on geography and located mineral deposits before returning to St. Louis in November 1835.[10]

Brigadier General Charles Gratiot

Exploration of the Northwest reached its zenith with the expeditions of Joseph N. Nicollet. Born and educated as a mathematician in Savoy, France, Nicollet served as astronomer at the Paris Observatory under the restored Bourbon monarchy only to lose support in the Revolution of 1830. On immigration to the U.S., he met Chief of Engineers Col. Charles Gratiot and Auguste Chouteau in Washington, D.C., who encouraged him to go to St. Louis and explore the Mississippi River. After

---
[9] Nichols and Halley, pp. 61-180; Edwin James, *Account of an Expedition from Pittsburg to the Rocky Mountains* (Ann Arbor: University Microfilms, Inc., 1966): Vol. 1, 1-75, 146, 404; Vol. 2, 282.
[10] Schoolcraft, *Journal of a Tour into the Interior of Missouri and Arkansaw* (London: Richard Phillips, 1831): 3-7, 93; Nichols and Halley, pp. 181-216.

briefly exploring the Appalachians, he left for St. Louis in 1834, traveled up the Tennessee River, and then took a detour to visit New Orleans and Florida. He arrived in St. Louis in 1835 and established a measurement station to collect meteorological and astronomical observations with which he calculated the elevation above sea level. He eventually made six other trips to the city over the next four years, usually between expeditions or trips to Washington. In 1835, he explored up the Missouri River to Council Bluffs, again making careful geographic observations. In 1836, funded by Chouteau, he made an expedition to the source of the Mississippi to gather more precise data.

Auguste Chouteau, MHS

In 1838, Col. John J. Abert, chief of the newly formed Corps of Topographical Engineers, agreed to purchase the extensive geographic data and maps compiled by Nicollet for $5,000. However, Nicollet argued that there were still gaps in knowledge about the Dakota Territory, and Abert authorized a new expedition to the triangle between the Missouri and Mississippi rivers. Accompanied by Lt. John C. Fremont and botanist Charles A. Geyer, Nicollet made expeditions in 1838 and again in 1839 on board the *Antelope*, a steamer owned by the American Fur Company of St. Louis. In 1839, Nicollet departed St. Louis for good to complete his maps in Washington. Over the next three years, he worked on the map and a report of his findings with the aid of Fremont, and in 1843, within months of his death, Congress published what was the most accurate hydrographical map of the Northwest published to that time, to include Illinois, Wisconsin, Minnesota, South Dakota, Iowa, Missouri, and Nebraska. Praised by Abert as "an extremely accurate map," by Lt. Gouverneur K. Warren as "one of the greatest contributions ever made to American geography," and by former Smithsonian Institute Assistant

Fremont 1852 William Jewette

Secretary Spencer F. Baird as "highly prized," the map appeared in numerous atlases. His incomplete journal, also published in 1843, included detailed descriptions of the geography, flora and fauna, anthropology, and history of his exploration from 1836 to 1839, as well as the first detailed history of St. Louis he compiled while visiting the city, with which he had built such a strong connection.[11]

Throughout this time of exploration, St. Louis quickly grew to something more than a frontier town. Americanization of the city, with all its virtues and vices, started early. From 1803 to 1816, 80 percent of families moving to St. Louis were American. In 1807, the first Baptist congregation moved across the river, in 1811 the first Presbyterian church, and in 1821 the first Methodist, although the Catholic Church remained strong with the establishment of St. Louis as the first head of the Louisiana diocese. The city gained its first jail in 1806, first newspaper in 1808, first grammar school in 1809, first fire company in 1810, first overseer of roads in 1811, first market house in 1812, and first bank in 1816. Industry grew rapidly, and "by 1832 St. Louis was the unchallenged capitol of the American fur trade," biologist and river historian Calvin Fremling observed. Used by Army officers as a base of operations for exploring the wilderness, St. Louis was officially incorporated in 1809 and grew quickly. With the influx of residents after the War of 1812, St. Louis grew to 4,598 by 1820, with the county growing to 9,850, an increase of 77 percent. Only a year later, when Missouri became a state, the population of St. Louis and outlying towns had reached 9,732. From 1810 to 1820, Illinois had also grown from 12,282 to more than 55,000 citizens, many of whom maintained connections across the river. It became a state in 1818, with the capitol at Kaskaskia. Army officers and engineers had led exploration of the West from St. Louis. As a result, the city had gained a prominence that would only grow in the decades that followed.[12]

---

[11] Martha Coleman Bray, *Joseph Nicollet and His Map* (Philadelphia: American Philosophical Society, 1980):12-63, 127-293; J.N. Nicollet, *Report Intended to Illustrate a Map of the Hydrographical Basin of the Upper Mississippi River*, S.D. 380 (26th Cong., 2nd Sess.): 1-94; Abert, Warren, and Baird quotes from Frank N. Schubert, *Vanguard of Expansion: Army Engineers in the Trans-Mississippi West, 1819-1879* (Wash., D.C.: Historical Division, OCE, 1980): 12-13. The Corps of Topographical Engineers existed as a parallel engineer organization with the Corps of Engineers under the War Department from 1838 to 1863, after which the two merged.

[12] Primm, pp. 86-112; Fremling, p. 125; Dobney, pp. 11-13.

St. Louis and the Oregon Trail

By 1840, "Manifest Destiny" was in full swing among Americans, and with glowing descriptions of the Pacific Coast by settlers and travelers from California and Oregon, some in Congress sought to find an overland route to the new Promised Land. Among these were Sens. Thomas Hart Benton and Lewis F. Linn of Missouri, who saw St. Louis as key to any overland route. As historian Frank Schubert noted, "Benton's St. Louis, transformed from a sleepy French outpost to a frontier metropolis at the hub of the Missouri River and Santa Fe trade routes, faced westward to Oregon and New Mexico."

Thomas Hart Benton

Benton sought out Joseph N. Nicollet, but since his health was failing, he turned to his faithful assistant, Lt. John C. Fremont of the Topographical Corps, soon to earn the nickname "Pathfinder." Benton secured funding and support from Chief Topographical Engineer Col. John J. Abert while Fremont organized an expedition that included German map-maker Charles Preuss. After marrying Benton's daughter, Fremont set out in May 1842 for St. Louis, where his family settled.

Traveling by steamer up the Missouri River, on which Fremont recruited famed trapper Kit Carson, the expedition set out from Chouteau's Landing near Kansas City. They travelled to the American Fur Company outpost of Fort Laramie on the Platte River. There the party split and explored the North and South Platte River to the Rocky Mountains, but regrouped at the South Pass, where the North Platte and Big Horn basins met the Green River. On August 15, he climbed the Wind River Range and planted a U.S. flag. He had found the gateway to Oregon. He returned and quickly published his report in "a brilliant tour de force."

In a second expedition in 1843, he again departed St. Louis and Chouteau's Landing, following his route through the South Pass along the Green River and Bear River to the Great Salt Lake by September 6, 1843. From there, he followed the Snake River to the Columbia River, which he reached on October 25. He then floated downriver to Fort Vancouver, which he reached by mid-November. After exploring northern California, Fremont returned in 1844. His second report and the maps of Preuss became the single most important source for information about what became the Oregon Trail, which established St. Louis and later Independence, Missouri, as the gateway to the West.[13]

---

[13] Schubert, pp. 19-34.

2

Opening the Gateway to the West

When Joseph Nicollet first arrived in St. Louis in 1835, he observed that it was actually two cities: the historic French city of his heart and the thriving "Queen city of the river." This was another way of saying that the city was quickly growing from its historical origins as a French colony and frontier town to a city of industry and river commerce, through which flowed thousands of souls migrating westward. It also recognizes that, more than any other factor, what enabled the transformation of St. Louis from frontier town to "Gateway to the West" was the development of safe and reliable transportation routes. In this, the Corps of Engineers played important, though at times conflicting, roles. From the establishment of St. Louis in 1764 until 1817, transportation relied mostly on slow and precarious river barge and flatboat traffic. With the advent of the steamboat and its advance north of the Ohio River, the Mississippi River became a major highway to St. Louis and the West, although navigation remained dangerous for many years until its improvement by the Corps. As traffic grew, so did the city. During the Civil War, the closure of the lower river crippled river traffic for many decades. It was at this point that the overland route to St. Louis and the growing development of railroads became more important for westward migration. It was the combination of these transportation methods – the Mississippi River and the railroad – that opened St. Louis as a gateway westward.[14]

Growth of River Transportation

Even before European settlement of the Mississippi Valley, Native Americans had used the river as a highway with simple canoes and longer pirogues. With a colony spanning the length of the valley, the French used the river to send supplies to St. Louis and furs to New Orleans. Traffic was slow, however. Most used flatboats up to 60 feet long, smaller Kentucky boats, or ribbed keelboats up to 70 feet long. Using poles and sometimes aided by small sails, these vessels

Type of small flatboat used on Mississippi

---

[14] Nicollet quoted in Bray, p. 133.

could make no more than 20 miles per day upriver with great labor. Shipping barges similar to longboats with sails and oars could make four or five miles per hour. The development of steamboats greatly increased the speed of travel and reduced the amount of labor, thereby reducing costs by a third, according to one estimate. In 1807, Robert Fulton first navigated a river with the steamship *Clermont* sporting a Boulton and Watt engine and reached Albany, New York, up the Hudson River in a record 32 hours. Working with Robert R. Livingston, in 1810 Fulton obtained from C.C. Clairborne, the governor of Orleans Territory, sole rights to operate steamboats on the Mississippi River. Their steamboat, the *New Orleans*, sailed from Pittsburg, Pennsylvania, to New Orleans from October 11, 1811, to January 10, 1812, piloted by Nicholas Roosevelt. Not including stops, it took only a little less than 11 days of continuous running time to make the entire journey. The vessel carried 300 tons and 60 passengers and made five to six miles per hour. Nevertheless, despite its speed, its deep draft led to it being snagged and sinking in 1814 near Baton Rouge, Louisiana, while their second vessel, the *Vesuvius*, embarrassingly became lodged on a sandbar and was unable to complete a widely advertised 1,500-mile trip north of Natchez, Mississippi. Although 10 steamboats operated on the river between 1811 and 1816, the river was still dangerous to navigate.[15]

Two factors enabled the growth of steam traffic that eventually made St. Louis the port it became. One was development of a steamboat that could safely navigate the river. The disaster of the *New Orleans* and the precarious trips of the *Vesuvius* and other vessels intimidated many pilots, and for many years the majority of traffic on the river above Natchez, Mississippi, continued to be pole-pushed barges. What changed this was the development of a shallow draft steamboat by boat captain and War of 1812 blockade runner Henry M. Shreve. His first steam vessel, the *Enterprise*, made it up the Red River and from Pittsburg to New Orleans and back, but Shreve did not trust it to continue to make the journey. His second vessel, the *Washington*, placed a much smaller engine on the deck with passengers on a second deck above it, thus eliminating a large hold and allowing for a shallower draft. This design, widely imitated, allowed steamboats to travel over sandbars and other obstacles more easily than past steamboats. As Fremling observed, "The hackneyed old claim about the western steamboat that could run over a field after a heavy dew was

---

[15] William J. Petersen, *Steamboating on the Upper Mississippi* (Iowa City: State Historical Society of Iowa, 1968): 1-67; Edith McCall, *Conquering the Rivers: Henry Miller Shreve and the Navigation of America's Inland Waterways* (Baton Rouge: LSU P, 1984): 19-80.

not too wild an exaggeration." The *Washington* made its first trip from Louisville, Kentucky, to New Orleans in 13 days in 1816 with a return trip in 1817 in a record 24 days. By the 1850s, steamboats made the trip from St. Louis to New Orleans on average in six days, the record, made by the *Robert E. Lee* in 1870, being under four days. With improvements in steamboats and the end of the Fulton-Livingstone monopoly after legal challenge by Shreve, by 1819 there were more than 60 steamboats operating on the river, including ocean-going vessels. In 1821, 247 steam vessels registered in New Orleans.[16]

The other factor that enabled growth of St. Louis as a port of call was improvement of the river to the point where all river traffic became reasonably safe and reliable, a process that took many years. As early as 1784, Pierre L'Enfant, a French engineer serving in the Revolutionary Army, had recommended maintaining a permanent Corps of Engineers that could develop transportation routes, among other duties. Secretary of the Treasury Albert Gallatin was the first to propose a federally funded program of roads and canals in 1808, arguing that, faced with a lack of development and far-flung populations, "The General Government can alone remove these obstacles." Although his focus was roads and canals, he envisioned the Mississippi and other rivers as part of a general system of transportation connected by canals. Both Thomas Jefferson and James Madison also expressed support for canals and a National Road, but because of their desire to limit spending, the scope of government, and "internal improvements," it was not until the Monroe administration that any effort proceeded to improve the Mississippi. After the War of 1812, Secretary of War John C. Calhoun, in compliance with a request from Congress, submitted a new report on roads and canals in which he wrote, "The experience of the late war amply proves in the present state of our internal improvements the delay, the uncertainty, the anxiety, and the exhausting effects" of calling up the militia. "It is of the utmost importance to prevent a recurrence of a similar state of things, by the application of a portion of our means, to the construction of such roads and canals, as are required." Such roads and canals would benefit communication, commerce, and defense. He also recommended improvements to rivers, although he noted that many improvements could be made by local government. Particularly in the West, the swiftness of the Mississippi, "which is no less the cause of its security, than that of its commerce and wealth," made transportation easy enough that "little remains to be done

---

[16] Petersen, pp. 68-74; McCall, 96-179; Dobney, 17-19; Fremling, 168-169, quote on 168; Anfinson, 1-22.

by roads and canals." At the time he submitted his report, a military survey of the valley was under way.[17]

As a result of Calhoun's recommendations, in 1820 Congress authorized a survey of the Ohio and Mississippi rivers with an eye toward improvement of navigation. That report, completed by Col. Joseph Totten and Brig. Gen. Simon Bernard in 1821, was the first survey of its kind of the Mississippi River. Among the obstacles to navigation it mentioned were sandbars at its mouth that prevented passage except during high water; rafts of fallen trees or driftwood, planters or trees and root wads embedded in the river, and sawyers or snags hidden in the water that obstructed and often damaged vessels; rapids and falls, which, though dangerous, were well known; and high water currents, which often pulled vessels out of the river during floods. To solve these problems, they recommended continual removal of snags, the increased use of steamboats, and use of dikes to manage current. They also recommended experiments with dikes to remove sandbars on the Ohio before proceeding to their adoption to clear 21 bars they identified. On receiving this report in 1823, Congress debated whether to make improvements, and some argued that it had no authority. This was settled by the Supreme Court in *Gibbons vs. Ogden*, in which the court affirmed that the federal government had power to regulate and improve navigation on interstate waters under the commerce clause of the Constitution. On April 30, 1824, Congress passed the General Survey Act, which appropriated $30,000 for the Corps of Engineers to conduct additional surveys for roads and canals. Less than a month later, it passed an act appropriating $75,000 for removal of snags on the Mississippi and Ohio as well as to conduct experiments to remove sandbars on the Ohio. In 1826, it passed the first official Rivers and Harbors Act to provide for additional improvement projects. Over the next several decades, Congress passed additional Rivers and Harbors acts appropriating hundreds of thousands of dollars to make improvements, a gradual process dependent on the views of Congress whether it could or should invest in what some saw merely as internal or local improvements.[18]

---

[17] Letter, L'Enfant to Continental Congress, Dec. 15, 1784, in Paul K. Walker, ed. *Engineers of Independence: A Documentary History of the Army Engineers in the American Revolution, 1775-1783* (Washington: Corps of Engineers History Office [CEHO], 1981): 358-9; Gallatin, *Roads and Canals*, S.D. 250 (10th Cong., 1st Sess.): quote p. 725; Calhoun, "Report of the Sec. of War Relative to Roads and Canals" (Washington: De Krafft, 1819): quotes on 4, 8; Forest G. Hill, *Roads, Rails, and Waterways: The Army Engineers and Early Transportation* (Norman, U of Oklahoma P, 1957): 9-10, 17-41.

[18] U.S. Cong., "Report of the Board of Engineers on the Ohio and Mississippi Rivers," H.D. 35 (17th Cong. 2nd Sess.): 4-14; U.S. Cong., *An Act to improve the navigation of the Ohio and Mississippi rivers*, PL 18-89 (18th Cong., 1st Sess.); *Thomas Gibbons vs. Aaron Ogden*, 22 U.S. 9 Wheat. 1 (1824); U.S. Cong., *An Act making appropriations for certain Internal Improvements for the year 1832* (22nd Cong., 2nd Sess.); Hill, pp. 25-49; Dobney, pp. 18-20; Anfinson, pp. 22-28.

To oversee and plan the various civil engineering projects authorized by these acts, in 1824 the Corps of Engineers established the Board of Engineers for Internal Improvements, composed initially of Totten, Bernard, and civil engineer John L. Sullivan. The board continued in existence until the formation of the Bureau of Topographical Engineers in 1831. One of the first acts of this board was to execute a snag removal program. As Bernard and Totten noted, snags were very common and were the primary cause of damage to ships on the rivers. The history of the river was replete with stories of ships damaged by snags. The board advertised payment of $1,000 for the best plan and design for a snag-removing vessel, and after review of several submissions awarded a $60,000 contract to John Bruce of Kentucky, an experienced navigator, as the Superintendent of Western River Improvements. In 1825, Maj. Samuel Babcock, the assigned Corps officer, reported significant progress, but complaints from William M. Poyntz and other boat captains that Bruce had made fraudulent claims led to an investigation by Capt. William H. Chase that fall. Evidently, Bruce believed that his contract's instructions requiring "cutting them off at the bottom of the river, or at least ten feet below extreme low water" meant that he only had to remove snags from the low-water channel, leaving the most dangerous snags in sandbars and high-water channels. The result was suspension of Babcock and the contract, although Bruce continued to fight to receive payment until the Civil War. One of Bruce's assistants served as a temporary replacement until a permanent superintendent could be found. Although he made some progress by 1826, it would take many more years before snags were under control, and continual maintenance to keep it that way.[19]

The second set of planned improvements was the removal of sandbars on the Ohio. Although there had been some experiments in Europe using dikes to narrow and increase the velocity of rivers and scour sandbars, there was little experience with such methods in the U.S., which was why Bernard and Totten suggested experiments before proceeding with permanent changes. For this work, the Corps sent Maj. Stephen Long. Unable to start the experiments in

---

[19] U.S. Cong., *Condition of the Military Establishment*, 1824, H.D. 262 (18th Cong., 2nd Sess.): 699-700, 713-714; *Annual Report of the Sec. of War, 1825*, H.D. 284 (19th Cong., 1st Sess.): 109-110, 136, 139; *Annual Report of the Sec. of War, 1826*, H.D. 334 (19th Cong., 2nd Sess.): 361; *Annual Report of the Sec. of War, 1828*, H.D. 390 (20th Cong., 2nd Sess.): 14; *Report of Chief Engineer Relative to the Application of Appropriation for Removing Obstructions to the Navigation of the Ohio and Mississippi Rivers*, S.D. 14 (19th Cong. 1st Sess.): 3-28, quote on 7; Todd Shallat, *Structures in the Stream: Water, Science, and the Rise of the U.S. Army Corps of Engineers* (Austin: U of Texas, 1994): 143-144; Hill, pp. 49-78, 153-165; Dobney, pp. 20-21; Anfinson, pp. 22-28.

1824 because of high water, he did not complete the installation of wing dams near Henderson, Ohio, until 1825. This proved successful, but no effort was made on the second experiment to allow time to judge the effect of the first. By 1828, a contractor had cleared bars near the mouth of the Ashtabula Creek, Black River, and Huron River. These experiments suggested that engineers could make similar improvements on the Mississippi. By 1832, Congress had extended appropriations to include similar improvements on the Missouri, Arkansas, Red, and Upper Mississippi rivers, even as it continued to fund improvements on the Ohio.[20]

In August 1817, the *Zebulon M. Pike*, a converted keelboat, was the first steamboat to arrive at St. Louis, followed shortly by the *Constitution*. This launched an era of St. Louis being a leading port of call on the Mississippi. By 1819, when Stephen Long entered the harbor in the *Western Engineer* on his way up the Missouri, steamboats were a common sight. By 1823, when the *Virginia* made the first trip by steamboat from St. Louis to Fort Snelling, they were more so. By this point, two years after Missouri became a state, the population in the vicinity of St. Louis exceeded 10,000. River transportation only continued to grow over the next decade. From 1831 to 1837, the number of steamboats registering in St. Louis grew from 60 to 195 per year, most of these

St. Louis Harbor 1840s

[20] *Annual Report of the Sec. of War, 1824-1828*; Hill, pp. 49-78, 153-165; Dobney, pp. 20-21; Anfinson, pp. 22-28.

St. Louis 1850

Steamboats in St. Louis Harbor 1850s

Flatboat

making 10 or more landings per year. The official number of passengers arriving by steamboat annually grew from 432 to 1,607, and the amount of tonnage unloaded grew from 7,796 to 22,794 tons. Major products being shipped initially included lead and other ore, fur, and lumber, but agricultural products became increasingly popular after 1850. Total packet boats operating on the river grew from 230 in 1834 to more than 1,000 in 1849, moving 250,000 tons. There remained many dangers for steamboat travel. The fire started onboard the *White Cloud* that destroyed 23 steamers in St. Louis harbor and 15 city blocks in 1849 and the repeated ice floes that damaged ships from 1857 to 1885 demonstrate the difficulties. There was, nevertheless, growth in travel because of the improvements to the river and the riverboat.[21]

Railroads and the Eads Bridge

While the greatly improved river channel became the primary means for transportation upriver to St. Louis, overland traffic also grew. During St. Louis' first years in the Union, roadways from the East Coast were practically nonexistent. The usual route was to travel overland to Pittsburg and then ride by boat down the Ohio River. In 1808, Congress authorized work on the National Road from Cumberland, Maryland, to Vandalia, Illinois, a project which the Corps surveyed and oversaw. Although not completed until 1841, the surveyed route was in use prior to paving. By 1817, an overland route was firmly established from Philadelphia, Pennsylvania, across Ohio to Lexington and Louisville, Kentucky, and thence to Kaskaskia, Illinois, and East St. Louis. From there, travelers could take Wiggins Ferry (formerly Piggot's Ferry) across the river, or call for a boat to be sent over from St. Louis – at that time, the Mississippi was still narrow enough to hear across it. By 1820, a stagecoach line made the trip from Vicennes, Indiana, to East St. Louis in three days, and by 1839 there was a direct connection from the National Road at Vandalia to East St. Louis, for which St. Louis lobbied in 1836. Although river travel remained cheaper on average than traveling by stage, one estimate is that some 80,000 persons made this trip over the winter of 1839 when the river was frozen and closed to traffic.[22]

In 1826, Corps work on railroad surveys started. Although Army engineers had experimented some with railroads and Gallatin had mentioned them in his report, before 1825, most railways were short mining trams or steam carriages. By 1826, Congress became more interested in railroads and authorized a survey for routes of canals and railways to connect the Roanoke, James, and Kanawha rivers. The following year, work started on surveying the eastern end of the Baltimore-Ohio Railroad. This became one of the largest surveying efforts of the Corps prior to the Mexican War. Among the engineers to work on the project were Long, William Howard, Maj. William G. McNeill,

---

[21] Fremling, p. 166, 181-183; Petersen, pp. 75-106; Primm, pp. 138-139; Anfinson, pp. 1-22; "One Hundred Years on the Mississippi River," pamphlet (Memphis: MVD, 1967): 1-2.
[22] Hill, p. 37; Bond, pp. 21-25; U.S. Cong., "Missouri-National Road," H.D. 140 (24th Cong., 1st Sess.).

Lt. George W. Whistler, and Jonathon Knight. McNeill, Whistler, and Knight travelled to England to study railroads and became three of the leading railroad experts in the U.S. By 1831, the Corps had conducted surveys for a dozen other railroad lines on the East Coast and then turned to railroad lines in the South and in Ohio after 1832. As Chief of Engineers, Colonel Totten considered railroads critical for transporting troops and munitions to proposed fortifications. By 1836, there was a railroad line running from East St. Louis to Illinoistown – about six miles – to carry coal. The owners would later extend this to Caseyville and Brooklyn, Illinois, in 1857 to carry passengers and freight. By this time, the Mississippi and Ohio Railroad was complete connecting East St. Louis to the Baltimore-Ohio Railroad, making East St. Louis the western terminus of a line that extended to the East Coast. By the following year, there were 10 lines connecting to East St. Louis. In 1851, construction began on a Pacific Railroad line from St. Louis to the Western border of Missouri, with additional lines added over the next decade. The first western train left St. Louis in 1852.[23]

Because of ferry costs, it was critical to build a bridge across the Mississippi. The Rock Island Railroad completed the first railroad bridge across the river at Davenport, Iowa, in 1855. As a result, most western traffic went through Chicago. As early as 1836, St. Louis citizens had suggested a bridge, including John A. Roebling and Pittsburg engineer Sylvanus Lothrop, who built the Allegheny Bridge. However, the cost was prohibitive for the number of investors interested. In 1855, Josiah Dent started a bridge company, but with criticism from some engineers, "the project died of fright," as one historian noted. Finally, in 1866, the St. Louis-Illinois Bridge Company obtained permission from Missouri to build the bridge, but permission from Illinois was tenuous because of opposition from the Wiggins Ferry and Chicago interests. Nevertheless, Missouri was able to get approval from Congress for the bridge in the 1866 Rivers and Harbors Act. Soon after, James Eads obtained an interest in the company and became its chief engineer. Eads was a civil engineer who had made his reputation as a salvager and inventor; he had invented a diving bell for salvage work and had designed the first U.S. iron gunships during the Civil War. He developed a unique steel bridge design incorporating arched trusses with 500-foot spans. The following year, bridge designer L.B. Boomer of Chicago and his Illinois-St. Louis Bridge Company obtained permission to build a bridge from the Illinois legislature. The Illinois Company worked to oppose

---
[23] Hill, pp. 96-132; Bond, pp. 20-21, 27-31, 34-35; Primm, pp. 211-231; on Totten's views, see U.S. Cong., *National Defense and National Foundries*, H.R. 206 (26th Cong., 1st Sess.): 123-127.

Construction of Eads Bridge

Eads by calling a conference of leading engineers to criticize his design. Eads started construction of the bridge on August 20, 1867, and Boomer tried to have workers arrested. Finally, Eads met with David Garrison, the Illinois Company president, and proposed merging the companies and letting an independent panel decide on the design. The companies merged in early 1868, and a panel selected Eads' design. Eads laid the cornerstone on February 25, 1868. The most difficult part of the work was excavating the riverbed to place the foundations for the piers on bedrock. Using pneumatic caissons fed by compressed air – an idea he adopted after a trip to England – he started work on the East Pier on October 25, 1869, and the West Pier on January 15, 1870. Even after a tornado destroyed an abutment in 1871, he completed the masonry in 1872 and started on the steel work in 1873.[24]

In 1873, John McCune, E.W. Gould, J.R. Pegram, and James Collins of the Keokuk Steamboat Line complained to Secretary of War William Belknap that the new bridge obstructed navigation. That summer, Belknap authorized a board of review to suggest modifications to the bridge in Special Order 169. The Corps convened a board to include Col. James H. Simpson, Maj. Gouverneur K. Warren, Maj. Godfrey Weitzel, Maj. William Merrill, and Maj. Charles Suter in St. Louis on September 2, 1873, while Eads was in Europe. Bridge company vice president William Taussig and assistant engineer Henry Flad appeared before the board with their attorney. However, the board would not allow sworn testimony since it was not a trial and would not allow a continuance for the company to produce additional witnesses. Charges that the board did not provide adequate notice later proved false. The board reported on September 12 that the bridge was less than 50 feet above high water – not enough space for ocean-going steamboats to pass – with spans too far apart for lights or hooks to be used for navigation. It recommended construction of a bypass channel around the bridge for a cost of $1.7 million. On his return from Europe, Eads wrote a scathing review in which he questioned the expertise of the board, objected to the board's belief the bridge was too short based on the testimony of 13 riverboat captains, and rejected the board's remedy. He and Taussig traveled to Washington to appeal to President Ulysses S. Grant, who told Belknap to drop the case. The board reconvened January 14, 1874, on order of the Chief of Engineers Brig. Gen. Andrew A. Humphreys to reconsider its opinion in light of the remarks of Eads and others. A second report on

---

[24] Bond, pp. 32-33, 51-68; Primm, pp. 291-303; Dobney, p. 41; Dorsey, *Road to the Sea: The Story of James B. Eads and the Mississippi River* (NY: Rinehart, 1949): 96-146, quote on 99.

January 31 argued that board members had been reviewing bridges for many years, that the 13 riverboat men mentioned by Eads either had no recent riverboat experience or experience limited to the St. Louis area, and that both a list of recent ships visiting St. Louis and authorities on shipbuilding proved the bridge was too low. They continued to insist on a bypass channel, but since this was "distasteful" proposed several other changes to the bridge design. However, having already gained presidential approval, Eads ignored the findings of the board. His bridge opened to pedestrian traffic on May 24 and vehicles on June 3, with the first train crossing it on June 9, 1874. By this time, there was no talk of or need for making any changes, as Eads envisioned. "The bridge will exist just as long as it continues to be useful to the people who come after us," Eads said at the dedication, and so far, it has.[25]

Thus, by 1840 river traffic was secure, and by 1874 St. Louis was second only to Chicago as a railroad junction in the Northwest. Development of these transportation routes had enduring effect on migration through St. Louis to the West. Before the Civil War, the majority of immigrants to the Upper Mississippi Valley came by steamboat "for all or part of their journey." By 1859, steamboats were navigating as far west as Montana, requiring overland travel only on the last stage of a journey. By 1857, St. Louis was receiving 3,400 steamers per year, and by 1850 it exceeded New Orleans as the largest port of embarkation on the Mississippi. It had already surpassed it in the number of steamboats originating from there. "By 1847, St. Louis had become the base of navigation for the Upper Mississippi River and its tributaries," Fremling wrote. As a result, St. Louis had reached a population exceeding 16,000 by 1840 and 35,000 by the following decade. Missouri grew to more than 350,000. These

---

[25] Dorsey, pp. 146-165; Primm, pp. 303-308; Dobney, pp. 41-42; U.S. Cong., *St. Louis and Illinois Bridge across the Mississippi River*, H.D. 194 (43rd Cong., 1st Sess.), quote on 17; Eads, "Review of the U.S. Engineers' Report on the St. Louis Bridge," in McHenry, pp. 77-88; John Barry, *Rising Tide: The Great Mississippi Flood of 1927 and How it Changed America* (NY: Simon and Schuster, 1997): 55-66. Recent historians, including Barry, have portrayed this episode as a feud between Humphreys and Eads that pitted progressive civilian engineers against a conservative Corps over control of the river. But the record suggests Humphreys was only marginally involved, and that the matter was handled routinely, despite complaints. That there may have been personal jealousy involved is certainly possible, but the board in general praised the design, and several members worked with Eads on other matters. A better grounded criticism of the Corps was its support of well-connected navigation interests. The original complaint came from ship captains friendly to Belknap, and the board seems to have accepted their testimony over that of the bridge company. In general, the Corps was favorable to river navigation over railroad – it had not been heavily involved in railroad surveys since 1853 – and it opposed several other bridges for similar reasons. After the Rock Island and Quincy Railroad bridge collisions in 1856 and 1870 and with the passage of new railroad bridge requirements in the Rivers and Harbors Act of 1866, the Corps started bridge inspections and in 1870 developed bridge design standards to protect navigation. Seen in this context, the actions of the Corps were part of a long-term review of bridges, not a vindictive act against a single engineer. See *Annual Report of Chief of Engineers, 1870*, pp. 229-249; Henry Abbot, "The Physics of the Mississippi River," *Van Nostrand's Engineering Magazine* 20:130 (Jan. 1879): 1-6. While navigation interests generally opposed bridges and railroads, "they did not dominate St. Louis," where city boosters were dominant (Primm, p. 235).

Steamers Robert E. Lee and the Natchez race from New Orleans to St. Louis

were the direct results of the improvements in steamboats and river navigation. Once the Civil War began, however, with access to the Lower River cut off, St. Louis declined as a port, but recovered only decades later. During this lull, more and more immigrants turned to railroads, which were not only more direct and thus often faster, but also far cheaper once bridges across the Mississippi replaced expensive ferries. The Eads Bridge and Union Station were monuments to this era. Chicago remained the first link in the transcontinental railroad, but "St. Louis became a rail center." By 1880, its population had increased to 350,000, behind only New York, Philadelphia, Brooklyn, and Chicago. With improvements to river navigation made by the Corps after 1880, including four-foot and six-foot channels, St. Louis became once more one of the leading ports in the nation. By this time, migration westward had more or less stabilized, while St. Louis had emerged as a commercial power house in Middle America.[26]

---

[26] Fremling, pp. 187-210, quotes 187, 198; Primm, p. 128-139, 147, 167-173, 270, 287-288; Dobney, pp. 39-43; Anfinson, pp. 1-22.

Part II.
Engineering the Middle Mississippi: The U.S. Army Corps of Engineers and River Navigation

The Mississippi River has always been king of St. Louis, and, as one visitor observed, St. Louis was its queen. The river provided the life blood of the city. It provided the primary means of transportation, a vehicle of trade, and a source of income. But it was also a source of danger for those who did not know the river. When Missouri became a state in 1821, the Mississippi and other rivers being used for transportation contained serious impediments to navigation: snags, sandbars, rapids, ice floes, and shallow waters. For decades, these prevented navigation during long stretches of the year. In 1825, the Corps began efforts to improve the river through removal of dangerous snags and obstacles and to clear out good harbors in major cities. In 1872, it began work on permanent improvements intended to increase the depth of the river. However, those who worked these projects observed that the Middle Mississippi River – generally defined as the stretch from the Illinois to the Ohio rivers – was particularly difficult to engineer. It had a lower velocity and sediment content that the lower river, but greater sediment than the relatively clear upper river. Only as the Corps of Engineers experimented with dams, dikes, revetment, dredging, and other improvements was the river made permanently navigable, but the improvements were slow in coming, and the cost was great. Long term, the impact on the river of these improvements has created controversy that has continued to present day.

3

Snag Removal on the Mississippi

In 1824, the Corps of Engineers established the position of Superintendent of Western River Improvement to oversee improvement of the Ohio and Mississippi rivers. Based on the recommendation of Brig. Gen. Simon Bernard and Col. Joseph Totten in 1821, Congress had finally authorized and funded improvements in *An act to improve the navigation of the Ohio and Mississippi rivers*, signed by James Monroe on May 24, 1824. The Board of Engineers for Internal Improvements had selected John Bruce as the first superintendent. However, despite representations he made of his success between Pittsburg, Pennsylvania, and Louisville, Kentucky, an investigation initiated after complaints on the quality of his work revealed in 1825 that he had made fraudulent claims. A second superintendent, one of Bruce's assistants, assigned to complete the work died soon after the 1826 season. Although he made some progress on the Ohio River, the program appeared doomed to failure in late 1826. To turn it around, the Corps needed to select a man of great invention and drive. The Report of the Secretary of War for 1827 noted: "A gentleman of Kentucky, who was highly recommended for his knowledge of the difficulties

Artist's representation of St. Louis harbor around 1850s

Snagboat Macomb

in the navigation on those rivers, as well as for his zeal and activity, has been chosen to superintend the removal of the obstructions." That man, Henry Miller Shreve, developed a snag-removing vessel and oversaw improvements to the Mississippi River and its tributaries for more than a decade, greatly improving navigation on the rivers surrounding St. Louis.[27]

Henry Shreve had led an ideal capitalist's life to that time. Born in New Jersey in 1785 as the son of the Revolutionary officer Col. Israel Shreve, Henry grew up in Brownsville, Pennsylvania, near the Ohio River and spent his youth working in a mill and then as a laborer on flatboats. In 1807, he entered the roaring business of merchant-boat captain by building his first keelboat. For four years, he worked the trade between Pittsburg and St. Louis and grew close to August Chouteau, Silas Bent, and other prominent St. Louis businessmen. In 1811, the same year he married, he built a second keelboat to travel to New Orleans. In 1814, he entered the steamboat craze by building the *Enterprise*, which

Henry Shreve

---

[27] *Report of Sec. of War, 1826*, p. 361; quote from U.S. Cong., *Showing the Condition of the Military Establishment and Fortifications during the Year 1827*, H.D. 360 (20th Cong., 1st Sess.): 631. Maj. Stephen Long in 1843 identified Maj. Samuel Babcock as having followed Bruce, but he did not die until after 1826.

St. Louis Riverfront 1867

was the first steamboat to travel from Pittsburg to New Orleans and back. Later that year, Brig. Gen. Andrew Jackson commandeered the *Enterprise* and its captain to carry supplies and personnel during the War of 1812 – at the time it was the only steamboat available because both the *New Orleans* and *Vesuvius* of the Fulton-Livingston company had capsized earlier that year. Shreve served Jackson enthusiastically, delivering supplies to Fort St. Phillip and other locations, running the British blockade, helping evacuate New Orleans, and becoming the first steamship to make it up the Red River to the famous raft of trees. After the war, in 1816 Shreve designed the first shallow draft steamship – the *Washington* – to allow navigation in the shallow inland river waters. By placing the engine above deck and including an additional deck for passengers and cargo, it did not need a deep hold below the waterline. When the Fulton-Livingston company sued him to prevent his operating on the Mississippi River, Shreve won a court battle that ended the company's monopoly both for himself and other steamboat operators.[28]

An avid tinkerer, Shreve had in 1821 developed an idea for a vessel to remove snags and even corresponded with Secretary of War John C. Calhoun about it in 1824 after the passage of the *Act for the Improvement of the Ohio and Mississippi Rivers*. Later that year, however, when the Board of Engineers

---
[28] McCall, pp. 1-51, 96-163; Petersen, pp. 36-74.

for Internal Improvements offered $1,000 for a snag-removing vessel in an advertisement, Shreve did not submit his plans because he felt the money was not just compensation. With the failure of Bruce to clear the Ohio and continued clamor to remove snags from the Mississippi, Secretary of War James

Early snagboat on Mississippi

Steamboats on the Mississippi

Barbour requested help from Calhoun, then vice president. Calhoun recalled Shreve's ideas and recommended him for the position. On December 10, 1826, President John Quincy Adams offered a commission to Shreve as the new superintendent. Having worked for nearly 20 years as a ship captain, Shreve understood the pressing need for river improvement. Snags, sawyers, and planters growing or embedded in the banks and bed of the river caused severe damage to vessels. According to calculations he made in 1827, since 1822 at least 14 steamboats worth $560,000 had sunk after damage from snags and 10 others had received some level of damage amounting to $115,000. Considering there were only 134 steamboats operating on the Mississippi at the time, snags impacted just under one in five vessels. Further, more than 150 flatboats and keelboats worth $360,000 had sunk, for a total of more than $1 million in losses. Other obstacles, such as sandbars, rapids, and large rafts of trees, prevented navigation for much or all of the year. Given the growth of commerce on the Mississippi – 537,000 tons in 1827 – it was an intolerable situation. For this reason, Shreve accepted the position in January 1827 for a mere six dollars a day, although he would fight for years to receive additional compensation. Because of high water, he could not commence operations until the fall, after which he removed snags, roots, and shipwrecks from sandbars and chutes on the Mississippi from the Ohio River to the St. Francis River, and snags in the main low-water channel as far north as New Madrid. It was, nevertheless, still very experimental. As with Bruce, he initially used a twin-hulled barge outfitted with manual winches and cutters to conduct the work, but found it difficult. Still, as he and his crew gained experience, he was able to increase their progress to about six miles per day focusing mostly on snags on sandbars.[29]

Based on this early experience, he made two recommendations. One was to remove trees within three or four hundred feet of the riverbank to prevent them from falling in the river or collecting as driftwood. The other recommendation was to build a steam-powered snag-removal vessel such as he had proposed in 1821. He estimated the cost at $20,000 plus $2,000 per month operating costs, which nevertheless would be half the expense of manual methods. "In fact I do believe that it will be found impossible to remove many of the most formidable snags and planters by any other means that can be applied." He submitted his own design to the Chief of Engineers that fall, and, after receiving approval

---

[29] U.S. Cong., "Letter from Henry M. Shreve to the Hon. C.A. Wickliffe on the Subject of Navigation on the Mississippi River," H.D. 11 (20th Cong., 1st Sess.): 5-6; *Condition of Military Establishment, 1827*, p. 631; McCall, pp. 180-185.

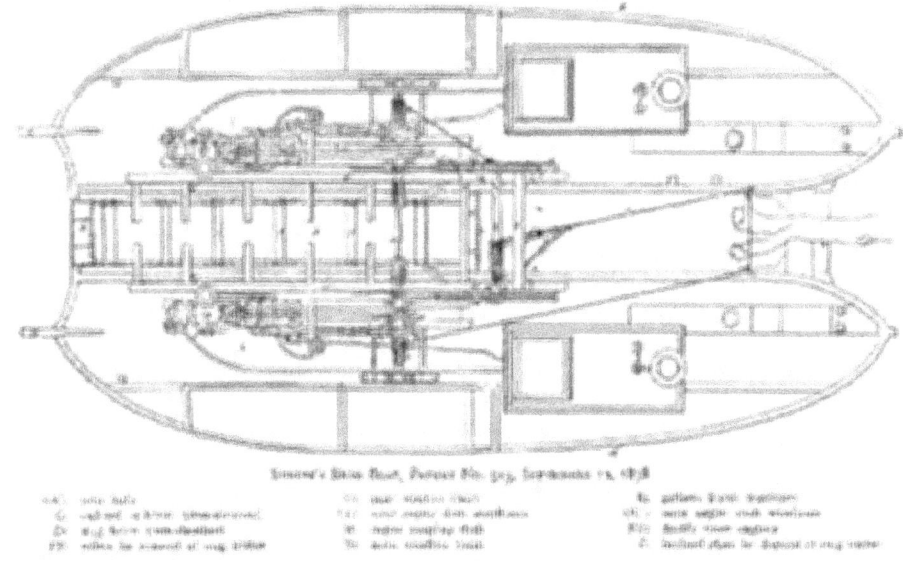

Shreve's snagboat design

from the Secretary of War in July 1828, completed construction of the ship at New Albany, Indiana, in time for the 1829 operating season. This first vessel, the *Heliopolis*, was a twin-hulled steamer, 125 feet long and 25 feet wide, with a windlass, cables, and chains for pulling up the snags. This was somewhat similar to designs submitted by Bruce and David Prentice. What separated his design was that the windlass was steam-powered, unlike that of Bruce, and that a wedge-shaped beam at the front of the vessel provided greater leverage in pulling up the snags, unlike all previous designs. Altogether, it took a crew of 40 to operate. The vessel proved so successful, Shreve built a second, the *Archimedes*, in 1831, and two more, the *Eradicator* and the *H.M. Shreve*, in 1836. Several other Corps of Engineers vessels operating on the Cumberland and other rivers also adopted Shreve's design.[30]

Shreve started work on clearing snags using the *Heliopolis* in late 1829. Typically, he would operate from late summer to early spring each year, spending flood months at St. Louis or Louisville. By 1836, he lived in St. Louis and managed Mississippi River operations from the city, although he continued to maintain an office in Louisville, from which he submitted most reports. During

---

[30] "Letter from Shreve to Wickliffe," p. 4; U.S. Cong., "Henry M. Shreve – Snag Boat," H.R. 272 (27th Cong., 3rd Sess.); "Henry M. Shreve, Jun. 7, 1844," H.R. 538 (28th Cong., 1st Sess.); *Annual Report of the Sec. of War, 1829*, H.D. 410 (21st Cong., 1st Sess.): 169; *Annual Report of the Sec. of War, 1831*, H.D. 485 (22nd Cong., 1st Sess.): 735; *Annual Report of Sec. War, 1836*, H.D.745 (25th Cong., 2nd Sess.): 689; Dobney, pp. 21-23.

the initial operating year of the *Heliopolis*, 1829-1830, Shreve removed 1,307 snags along 850 miles on the Ohio, 859 snags on the Mississippi as far north as the Missouri River, and then later another 227 snags on the Ohio. The largest snag removed was a 160-foot tree; the most snags removed were 47 on a single day. At the same time, three flatboats continued removing snags from sandbars and chutes and experimented with removing trees from the river banks. In 1831, the *Heliopolis* turned south, while the newly completed *Archimedes* turned north and removed 204 snags above the Ohio. By 1832, the vessels had removed most snags on the Ohio – those remaining were only accessible during low water, which limited the work season. Together, they removed more than 1,000 snags on the Mississippi for the first time and also felled just under 5,000 trees along the banks. In the 1833 season, the vessels removed 1,960 snags and felled 10,000 trees, while the flatboats cleared sandbars from St. Louis to the St. Francis River. In 1834, Lt. T.S. Brown and the *Heliopolis* turned to removing snags on the Arkansas River while the *Archimedes* removed 1,385 snags and logs along the waterline at 14 locations, including the mouth of the Ohio, Missouri, and St. Francis rivers and 1,622 trees from the Missouri to Natchez, Mississippi. Work continued at a high pace, as the crews removed 1,462 snags and 2,599 trees between the Missouri and Ohio in 1835 and 1,491 snags and 3,434 trees in 1836. By this point, Shreve had started clearing the Mississippi north to the Des Moines Rapids. With two additional vessels added in 1836, the crews made significant progress in 1837 – 1,894 snags and 18,141 trees removed – this despite the sinking, recovery, and repair of the *Archimedes*. In 1839, the crews turned up the Missouri and removed 1,198 snags and 1,544 trees along 335 miles and removed 1,047 snags and 64 trees on the Osage River.[31]

By 1841, incoming steamboat captain John W. Russell replaced Shreve as the new superintendent. Although Russell, a character of giant stature and legendary reputation, continued to oversee snag removal periodically until 1853, in 1843 the Corps assigned Col. Stephen H. Long as superintendent, a position he held on and off until the Civil War. By then, the Office of Western River Improvements, relocated to Cincinnati, Ohio, actively employed seven civilian engineers and superintendents who oversaw work by hundreds of laborers

---

[31] U.S. Cong., "Letter from the Sec. of War transmitting copies of the Reports of H.M. Shreve and R. Delafield on the improvement of navigation on the Mississippi and Ohio rivers," H.D. 9 (21st Cong., 2nd Sess.); "Henry M. Shreve–Navigation on the Ohio River," H.D. 74 (21st Cong., 2nd Sess.); Annual Reports of the Sec. of War, 1830-1841; Operations of the Topographical Bureau during the year 1839, S.D. 58 (26th Cong., 1st Sess.); Supplement to the Annual Report of the Chief Engineer, S.D. 125 (26th Cong., 1st Sess.); Dobney, pp. 23-24.

and contractors on specific projects or river systems. The office operated anywhere from one to five snag-boats of Shreve's design, each accompanied by a manually operated machine boat to pull up snags in shallow waters and a quarter boat to house personnel clearing banks and sandbars. It also operated dredge boats and smaller mud-scows to aid in removal of bars and other obstructions. These were steam-powered ladder dredges, which used mechanical and manual methods for removing sediment. In addition, by 1855 the office was working with the Eads and Nelson Company to remove wrecked steamboats and submerged obstructions to navigation using a diving bell invented by James Eads. Work continued on and off on removal of the Red River Raft, as well as improvements to harbors, construction of dams and jetties, and similar projects. However, the primary focus of the office remained snag removal, mainly on the Mississippi River, but also on the Arkansas, Missouri, Illinois, Osage, Red, and other river systems. After 1856, the office focused on clearing the passes of the Mississippi, not turning to snagging and dredging again until after the Civil War, when it tested and adopted a scraper dredge invented by Long that removed sandbars by pulling up sediment for redistribution downstream. Meanwhile, snag removal would continue sporadically into the twentieth century to maintain navigation on the rivers.[32]

The impact of snag removal on Mississippi River navigation cannot be underestimated. As early as 1830, Shreve noted that because of his improvements there had been only a single recorded wreck, and that was a flatboat. Snags sank five or more steamboats from 1831 to 1833, though all of questionable condition. In 1834, there were only three wrecks. 1835 was the first year in which the risk of wrecks due to collision was higher than that due to snags, and 1836 was the first year there were no known snag-related wrecks of steamboats on the river. At the same time, due to the other improvements he made, "the most dangerous passes" of the Mississippi "present now only smooth sheets of water, which may be traversed with perfect safety," Kentucky residents noted, and the full length of the Ohio and Red rivers were passable for the first time. The result of these improvements was a decline in the chances of sinking to roughly 50:1, which in turn led to a decline in the cost of insurance by 75

---

[32] *Annual Reports of the Sec. of War, 1843, 1857, 1868*. Russell, who stood over six-foot-six, beat pirate Jean Lafitte in a brawl and pulled a building into the river in Natchez with his steamboat over theft from a passenger; see Leland R. Johnson, *The Falls City Engineers: A History of the Louisville District, U.S. Army Corps of Engineers* (Wash.: CEHO, 1974): 89-101. For a description of later snag-removal operations, see *Annual Report of the Chief Topographical Engineer, 1855*, pp. 287-385. Long sometimes reported from St. Louis and Alton, Illinois.

percent. This combined with shorter travel times significantly reduced the cost of shipping goods and traveling by boat to and from St. Louis, New Orleans, and other cities. The river was not completely safe – the *Ozark* sank in the St. Louis harbor in 1841 and a snag tore open the *Shepherdess* within miles of Market Street in 1844 – but it was safer. As Shreve lay dying at his estate, Gallatin Place, outside St. Louis on March 6, 1851, he supposedly listened to the steamboat whistles of ships approaching the Port of St. Louis and remarked, "When it reaches you from somewhere in the distance, a steamboat whistle is the sweetest music in the world." He no doubt reflected on the vast improvements in the Mississippi River, increases in steamboat traffic, the growth of the Port of St. Louis, and his own role, at great expense to himself, in bringing it to fruition.[33]

---

[33] Quote from U.S. Cong., "Ohio and Mississippi River," H.R. 337 (21st Cong., 1st Sess.); "Shreve to Wickliffe"; "Henry M. Shreve, 1836"; Henry M. Shreve, 1844"; *Annual Reports of the Sec. of War, 1830-1841*; Primm, p. 155; Shreve quoted in McCall, p. 249.

4

The St. Louis Harbor and Channel Regulation

When Pierre de Laclede established the city of St. Louis in 1764, one of the reasons for selecting the site was the potential harbor at a convex curve in the Mississippi River. A bluff overlooking the river protected the site from flooding, while a narrow channel from the bluff allowed easy access to the river, which was reasonably clear at that location and far enough from the Missouri River to be impacted by its currents. It was here that he located the tow path that became the first port. This harbor served the city for 70 years without issue, and in 1836 St. Louis became a port of entry for ocean-going ships. Yet the harbor changed over time as sandbars formed both up and downriver, eventually becoming islands. By the early 1830s, it appeared the river was starting to shift to the east. Already, there had been significant investment in port facilities, ferries, and other utilities, which the city would have to move at considerable cost if the river shifted. If it moved far enough, it would lead to decline in the harbor altogether. In December 1833, the city of St. Louis requested federal support to clear the harbor, and the Corps of Engineers took action over several years. However, river training works were still experimental. It had been less than a decade since the experiments of Maj. Stephen H. Long using wing dams on the Ohio River to remove sandbars. It was unclear in 1834 when the first examinations occurred of the St. Louis Harbor whether the same technique would work on the larger Mississippi River or whether some other approach to clearing the obstructions and maintaining the harbor was possible. The methods finally used, however, not only had great impact on the St. Louis Harbor, but on the Mississippi as a whole. It was at St. Louis that engineers made the first attempts on the Mississippi River at channel regulation through permanent works.

Clearing the St. Louis Harbor

In the eighteenth century, the St. Louis Harbor could accommodate most river traffic of the time, and there were no islands in the immediate vicinity of the port. Across the river from the port was a strip of bottomland bounded by Cahokia Creek, which eventually joined a slough to form a narrow island.

Artist's representation of St. Louis harbor in 1875

After 1800, however, two sandbars had started to form in the river. One developed across from and slightly north of the harbor, and within a few years grew to more than a mile long and became populated with cottonwood and willow trees. It eventually earned the name Bloody Island because of the number of duels fought there, including nationally reported duels between Sen. Thomas H. Benton and Charles Lucas in 1817 over Benton's voting eligibility, and between Maj. Thomas Biddle and U.S. Rep. Spencer Pettis in 1831 over the National Bank. Over time, more and more of the river diverted between Bloody Island and the Illinois shore. The other bar, Duncan's Island, grew to about 200 acres and denied access to several blocks south of Market Street. The narrow channel west of the island became narrower and narrower, threatening to connect to the mainland. Together, the islands forced the channel toward Illinois and eventually eroded Cahokia Island while widening the channel between Bloody Island and Illinois until only half of the river flowed along its original course. At the same time, severe shoaling east and north of Duncan's Island created a long sandbar that presented a severe obstacle during low water by the mid-1830s. It appeared that the river was shifting toward the eastern shore and would, in time, make St. Louis an inland city. Such shifts happened frequently, as when the river later cut off Kaskaskia – the one-time capitol of Illinois – from the rest of the state, placing it on the same side of the river as Missouri.[34]

---

[34] Primm, pp. 117, 141-157; Bond, pp. 34-50; Toni Flannery, "How Young Robert E. Lee Helped Save the St. Louis Waterfront," News Clipping (MVS Archives).

Recognizing in particular that the sandbar blocking the harbor would be a detriment to commerce, in 1832 the city of St. Louis paid John Goodfellow $3,000 to remove it using a primitive dredge. During low water, he used a team of oxen to plow up the bar in order to allow the current to remove the sediment. Unfortunately, the bars quickly reformed and were not measurably smaller. By the end of 1833, the city council voted to send a memorial to Congress asking for aid in clearing the harbor, which the Missouri legislature forwarded to its congressional delegation in January 1834. The same year, St. Louis requested that the Superintendent of Western River Improvements, Henry M. Shreve, make a preliminary survey. After a brief examination, he recommended the use of wing dams to clear the channel. He had used similar means to clear numerous bars on the Ohio River and believed the same principles would work here. Based on this testimony, Chief of Engineers Brig. Gen. Charles Gratiot, a St. Louis citizen, personally investigated the site in 1834. He proposed a dam extending from the Illinois shore to Bloody Island to direct the channel toward Missouri and wash out Duncan's Island or possibly a wing dam on the Missouri shore between Chouteau and Cascarot islands to force the channel toward Illinois, which would then tend to push westward after clearing Cascarot Island. Failing these, he recommended a wing dam at the southern end of Bloody Island to push the channel toward Missouri. He estimated the total cost at $40,000. His plan also met the approval of Capt. John Symington of the St. Louis Arsenal. As a result of Gratiot's recommendations, Congress appropriated $15,000 in 1836 for harbor improvements, although this was far less than what he recommended and what was ultimately necessary.[35]

The proposed project faced immediate difficulties, including a legal challenge. As soon as Robert Duncan, for whom the island was named, heard about the proposal of the city council and recognized the value of the island if it were adjacent to the port, he built a hut on the island to claim title to it, and then filed a preemption claim at the Surveyor's Office in New Madrid, Missouri. Complicating matters, Duncan sold land on the island to surveyor general Elias T. Langham, A.W. McDonald, and A.H. Evans, who then filed a petition to block the bill, arguing that the city had no right to destroy the property and home of its citizens without due process simply for the benefit of the city. The city council filed a counter petition accusing the owners of claiming the property to

---

[35] U.S. Cong., "Memorial of the Legislature of Missouri," H.D. 21 (23rd Cong., 1st Sess.); "Harbor at St. Louis," H.R., 14 (23rd Cong., 2nd Sess.); Robert R. Brooks, "Robert E. Lee – Civil Engineer," *Civil Engineering* 10:3 (Mar. 1940): 167-169.

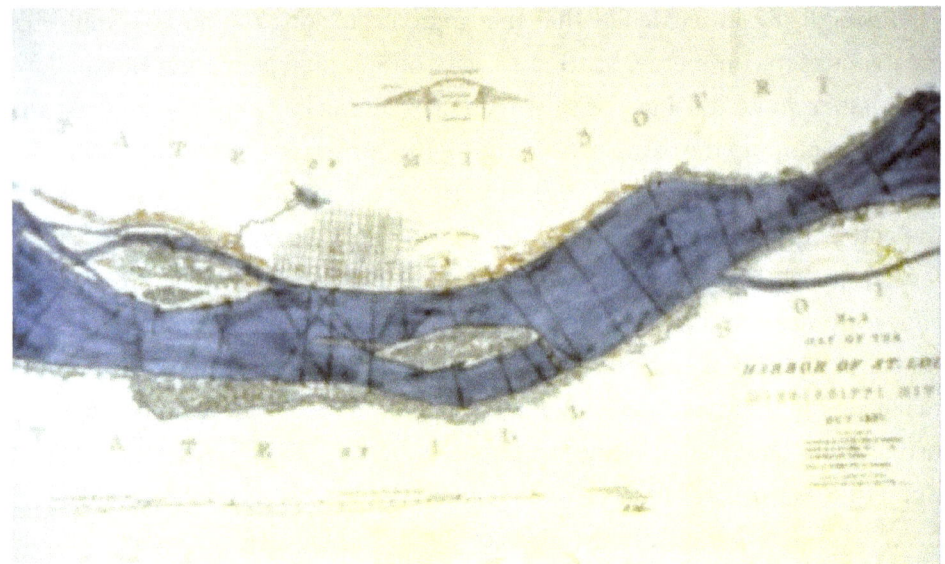

Lee's map of St. Louis Harbor

Robert E. Lee

drive up its value. Duncan's claim was based on Spanish law, which held sway over the region until 1804, but the city noted that even according to Spanish law islands belonged to riparian landowners. In any case, an investigation by Congress into Duncan's claims found that he had not previously filed for a title, but only for the preemption at the end of 1835, and therefore had no legal claim to prevent removal of the island. A later suit by Illinois interests also tried to prevent work on Bloody Island, but ultimately to no effect.[36]

Gratiot assigned Shreve to make the improvements in October 1836, but he was unable to commence the work because of prior commitments on the Red River. He stressed to Gratiot and to St. Louis mayor John F. Darby the need for more money than Congress appropriated, which would barely cover preparations. In his estimation, at least $50,000 was necessary. The city submitted a memorial requesting more money for the work, and Congress increased the

---

[36] U.S. Cong, "Memorial of E.T. Langham and A.W. McDonald," H.D. 278 (24th Cong., 1st Sess.); "Pre-Emption to the Sand Bar, in Front of St. Louis," H.D. 197 (24th Cong., 1st Sess.); "Relative to the Title to the Island Opposite St. Louis," H.D. 1539 (24th Cong., 1st Sess.).

total to $50,000 in 1837, which the city supplemented by another $15,000. In Shreve's place, Gratiot sent young engineer officer Lt. (soon Capt.) Robert E. Lee to manage the work. After arriving in St. Louis and finding housing for his family in August 1837, Lee obtained the services of Lt. Montgomery C. Meigs and civil engineer Henry S. Kayser. By December, he had completed a survey and established a plan to build a dam from Illinois to Bloody Island, bank protection on the western side of the island, and a dike extending from its southern tip for $160,000, although he admitted the work was experimental. This was essentially the same plan proposed by Gratiot but at four times the price. Later, he would change the planned works to a set of dikes from just south of Venice, Illinois, to Bloody Island and, after receiving approval, set to work building them. By 1840, however, the Corps had reassigned Lee to New York to work on harbor fortifications. Kayser continued construction on the St. Louis dikes as city engineer for the next 10 years. At the time Lee left, the dikes were still not complete despite expending all federal funds by the end of 1840. They had completed about 940 feet on the upper end of Bloody Island, but had not completely closed off the channel east of the island. It was left to St. Louis to complete it and build the 2,000-foot dike at the foot of the island. Despite their uncompleted state, the works did achieve a measure of success. Duncan's Island started to erode, the distance between Bloody Island and Illinois lessened, and within two years there was a 13-foot channel into St. Louis Harbor, which continued to grow. The only problem resulting from the works was shoaling at the end of the dike on the south end of Bloody Island. [37]

By 1843, the situation had started to deteriorate again as sandbars trapped ships or forced them to take a two-mile detour, prompting a new survey by Lt. Col. Stephen H. Long. His preliminary report noted that Lee's dike extended along the Illinois shore for some distance, but left a large gap east of Bloody Island for boat traffic, through which flowed a stream the size of the Missouri River. The completed dike was creating a sandbar north of St. Louis harbor that extended toward Missouri, while the Illinois shore north of the dike was eroding. The dike at the foot of Bloody Island was causing the island to narrow and

---

[37] U.S. Cong., "Sand Bar—Harbor of St. Louis," H.D. 124 (24th Cong., 2nd Sess.); "Harbor of St. Louis," H.D. 298 (25th Cong., 2nd Sess.); "A report of the Chief of Engineers upon the proposed improvement of the Mississippi River from Alton to the Meramec River," S.D. 50 (41st Cong., 3rd Sess.): 11-15; Primm, pp. 155-158; Flannery, "How Lee Helped Save Waterfront"; Horace J. Sheely, Jr., "Lee Serves in the West," Research Report (Jefferson Expansion Memorial); Brook, "Robert E. Lee—Civil Engineer." St. Louis has long claimed Lee – Mayor Darby once said that "Lee brought the Father of Waters under control" (Sheely, p. 3) – yet Lee, although a competent engineer, merely started a plan proposed by others and never actually completed the work.

extend southward. Chief of Topographical Engineers Col. John J. Abert, while agreeing that correction of the situation was necessary, believed the Corps could complete the work for less than Lee's original estimate. The same year, St. Louis obtained two additional surveys by Shreve and city assistant engineer Clement C. Coote. Shreve added that the base of the dike had eroded considerably and urged completion of a dam to Bloody Island and construction of wing dams on its western shore at a cost at $150,000. He also observed severe erosion of the Illinois shore opposite the Missouri River. Coote recommended a similar plan for $155,000, with additional protection of the Bloody Island, Kerr's Island, and the Illinois shore near Venice, as well as elimination of Bissell's Point, which pushed the current toward Illinois. As a result of these surveys, St. Louis submitted a new memorial in January 1844 for funds to improve the harbor, renew snag removal, check erosion across from the Missouri River, lower tolls on the Ohio Canal, and improve the Des Moines Rapids.[38]

In February 1844, Long assigned Capt. Thomas J. Cram to develop a plan of action. Cram provided an additional level of specificity in the status of the project, noting that only 42 of Lee's upright posts remained, that only 124 feet of dike existed with another 350 feet underwater, and that the St. Louis dike had washed away or was partially underwater, having separated from Bloody Island. He recommended abandoning the works to remove Duncan Island; because the harbor had since expanded northwards, there was no commercial reason to try to improve the harbor south of Market Street. The greater danger in his mind was the Missouri River eroding the Illinois shore, which might allow the Mississippi to divert down Long Lake and Cahokia Creek, shifting it far to the east and away from St. Louis. He proposed several possible works: revetment along the Missouri and Illinois shores, a crib dam to increase flow east of Cascarot Island, building a dam from Illinois to Bloody Island, building three wing dams north of Bloody Island, and cutting a canal bound by a snag dam to channel the Missouri River toward a rocky portion of the Illinois shore. He recommended the revetment and snag dam for somewhere between $300,000 and $500,000 depending on the materials and methods used.[39]

However, both Long and Abert rejected Cram's plan as too experimental and expensive. Long doubted the proposed revetment would work since there had been no experiments with them, while Abert wrote, "While I am willing to

---

[38] *Report of Chief Topographical Engineer, 1843*, H.D. 2 (28th Cong., 1st Sess.): 134-136; "Memorial of a Number of Citizens of St. Louis, Missouri," S.D. 185 (28th Cong., 1st Sess.): 36-45; Primm, p. 156.
[39] U.S. Cong., *Harbor of St. Louis*, H.R. 203 (28th Cong., 1st Sess.).

award him all imaginable credit for his acquirements and for his ingenuity, I yet must acknowledge that I could not agree with him in the plans proposed," primarily because the plan did not directly attack the problem of the harbor but concerned issues north of it. To review the plan, he assigned a board of review composed of Long and Lt. Col. James Kearney. They recommended building a dam from the Illinois shore to Bloody Island with a causeway on top and protection of the shores of Bloody and Kerr islands to prevent erosion for $190,000. Cram made some preparations for the work in 1845 using remaining funds, but with U.S. entry into the Mexican War, no action ensued for several years. By 1849, Long had nearly completed a dam to Bloody Island, and although the Flood of 1850 demolished what is now East St. Louis, eroded Cahokia Island until Cahokia Creek was the Illinois shore, and destroyed a huge section of the dam, the works had been effective in enlarging the channel into St. Louis harbor and starting to scour Duncan's Island once more. The Corps repaired the dam in 1852 and completed the causeway from Illinois to the island. From that point until after the Civil War, Congress provided no additional appropriations to complete the work, so no further progress was made on the project, despite a small amount of funds remaining unused.[40]

It was not until after the Civil War that the Corps renewed its attention to the harbor. By this time, the predictions of Shreve and Cram on the Missouri River scouring the banks of the Mississippi and impacting the harbor were coming to pass. In particular, the harbor at Alton, Illinois, just north of the confluence of the Missouri and Mississippi, was starting to silt, with a large sandbar blocking access to the port. The Missouri had shifted about a mile south, and the Illinois shore across from the river had eroded some 3,500 feet since 1862. Because of the drought of 1863, navigation on much of the river between the Missouri and the Ohio was more treacherous, with many shoals, sandbars, and shallow places that blocked passage during part or all of the year and impaired traffic to and from St. Louis. The central harbor had stabilized as Bloody Island became attached to the Illinois shore, and a somewhat smaller Duncan's Island became attached to Missouri, eventually becoming the new shoreline of the wharf. Other than city dikes protecting Kerr Island and Cahokia Bend, there were no new works completed. In 1866, Congress authorized 49 projects and

---

[40] *Harbor of St. Louis*, pp. 2-3; *Report of Chief Topographical Engineer, 1844* (28th Cong, 1st Sess.): 272; *Report of Chief Topographical Engineer, 1845* (28th Cong., 2nd Sess.): 368-373; *Report of Chief Topographical Engineer, 1851* (32nd Cong., 1st Sess.): 429; "Report on Mississippi River improvement, 1870," pp. 12-13.

Levee, St. Louis, Missouri (LOC)

26 surveys, but none specifically in St. Louis. By then, the federal government had appropriated $75,000 of more than $900,000 spent on the improvements. After complaints about the Alton harbor, Congress authorized a survey in 1868. Lacking funds, Maj. Gouverneur K. Warren arranged for the city of Alton to pay for civil engineer Henry C. Long to make some basic measurements. He determined that in some places the river was no more than three feet in low water, and that a large bar was forming south of the harbor, quickly becoming an island. He proposed a dam for $112,000 to close off the channel west of Ellis Island to funnel water against the Illinois shore at Alton, plus more detailed surveys. At the same time, St. Louis paid Col. William E. Merrill to complete a new survey of its harbor, which he did by 1869. He revealed that, while the middle harbor near Market Street was of sufficient depth, the harbor north of Biddle Street and the southern harbor at Carondolet, recently added to St. Louis, were too shallow in low water to allow development of the wharf.[41]

---

[41] *Report of the Chief of Engineers, 1867-1870*; "Report on Mississippi River Improvement," pp. 1-2, 11-14; Anfinson, pp. 33-37.

Stereo by T.W. Ingersoll, Mo. - St. Louis - View of Levee looking toward Eads Bridge, 1899 (LOC)

Establishment of the St. Louis Engineer Office

In 1870, work on the harbors received a boost when the Office of Western River Improvements relocated from Cincinnati, Ohio, to St. Louis with the reassignment of Lt. Col. William F. Raynolds as officer in charge. An 1843 West Point graduate, Raynolds was an experienced topographical engineer, who had made improvements on the Ohio River, explored the Missouri and Yellowstone Rivers, oversaw lighthouse construction, and served in the Mexican and Civil wars, including the defense of Harper's Ferry in 1863. Since the time of the superintendency of Henry M. Shreve in the 1830s, the work of the Office of Western River Improvements had been divided between the Ohio River on one hand and Mississippi, Arkansas, Red, and Missouri rivers on the other. Shreve often worked from a project office in St. Louis to oversee projects on the Mississippi while still maintaining an office in Louisville, Kentucky. Stephen H. Long had moved the main office to Cincinnati after 1843, but in practice, engineer officers in the Corps of Topographical Engineers maintained temporary offices

Horse-drawn shoe wagons flooded levee, St. Louis (LOC)

Busy St. Louis Levee (LOC)

near each project to oversee work, including one in St. Louis or Alton. After the Civil War and the reunification of the Topographical Engineers and Corps of Engineers, there were separate offices overseeing work on the Ohio River and Western Rivers, each reporting separately to the Chief of Engineers. Most of this work remained snag removal, for which the Corps had built numerous snag-removal vessels. It was only logical to relocate the office closer to the projects being managed by moving the Office of Ohio River Improvements to Cincinnati and Western River Improvements to St. Louis. This was, in essence, the first step taken from a project-based Corps office in St. Louis to what became a district office overseeing regional projects. By 1872, Raynolds was reporting from the Engineer Office in St. Louis with responsibility from the Illinois to the Ohio River rather than from the Office of Western River Improvements, which had ceased to exist.[42]

In 1870, Congress approved a new detailed survey of the St. Louis and Alton harbors. This survey, completed in 1871 by Raynolds and Capt. Charles Allen, provided the additional detail the 1868 surveys lacked. They agreed with previous surveys that a dam from Missouri to Ellis Island would force the river against the Alton Harbor and thus increase the harbor depth, recommended clearing snags west of Maple Island and opening Mobile Chute to divert part of the Missouri away from the Illinois shore, and suggested clearing sandbars and snags east of Cabaret (previously Cascarot) Island to reduce scour in Sawyer's Bend and the northern St. Louis Harbor. They also called for more soil borings and surveys on which to base future decisions and noted in general the problems encountered in the past in trying various works without knowing the effect. In essence, Raynolds argued that "the only safe method of proceeding is to follow nature as closely as practicable" by encouraging the river to follow known or established paths and not diverting it where it would not naturally go. The following year, Chief of Engineers Brig. Gen. Andrew A. Humphreys formed a board of review composed of Raynolds, Allen, Warren, Merrill, and Lt. Col. John Newton. The board recommended adoption of the plans to close the channel west of Ellis Island and to open Mobile Chute, but believed revetment of the banks and building or extending parallel dikes along both shores in Sawyer's Bend would be more effective than opening Cabaret Slough. They

---

[42] Compare *Annual Reports of the Sec. of War, 1832-1836* with the *Reports of the Chief of Engineers, 1869-1872*; George E. Cullum, *Biographical Register of the Officers and Graduates of the United States Military Academy at West Point, New York, since its establishment in 1802*, Vol. II, pp. 155-156 (http://penelope.uchicago.edu/Thayer/E/Gazetteer/Places/America/United_States/Army/USMA/Cullums_Register/, Jan. 19, 2011); Anfinson, pp. 33-49. The first districts established were St. Paul in 1866 and Rock Island in 1869.

also recommended completing surveys from St. Louis to the Ohio River, an area on which navigation to St. Louis depended. Total suggested funding was $409,000.[43]

In June 1872, Congress appropriated $125,000 to start work on the improvements and another $200,000 in March 1873. During this time, Raynolds was able to make preparations for the harbor improvements in addition to making improvements on the Missouri, Cuivre, Fourche La Faive, Bayou Bartholomew, Black, White, and Onachita, Arkansas, Osage, and St. Francis rivers, to include snag removal, dredging, damming chutes, and wing dams to improve rapids or scour sandbars. On January 1, 1873, Col. James H. Simpson took over as the officer in charge. An 1832 West Point graduate, Simpson had gained experience with harbor improvements, although he had also surveyed numerous roads and railroads, including a new route from Salt Lake City, Utah, to the Pacific Coast in 1859. After service in the Civil War, he returned to oversee improvements to the Susquehanna, Tombigbee, and Coosa rivers and Cape Fear, Mobile, Pensacola, and Tampa harbors, among other projects. As the St. Louis Engineer, he started the planned works on the Mississippi with gusto, raising the dike at Ellis Island, removing obstructions in Mobile Chute, protecting Sawyer's Bend using dikes and retaining walls, and overseeing work by contractors extending and raising the Venice and Long dikes within the St. Louis Harbor. Most of this work was complete by 1875 other than periodic repairs. After receiving additional funds, Simpson added a dam blocking the western channel of Piasa Island across from Alton in 1875, and in 1879, Congress authorized the closure of the channel west of Maple Island, again with the idea of forcing more flow against the Illinois shore and thus scouring sandbars. In 1878, St. Louis requested an additional dike from Bloody Island to Venice to improve access to the northern wharf, but Simpson refused to endorse the plan barring relocation of the wharf some 600 feet where the channel was sufficiently deep. Simpson also continued execution of improvements on the Osage River such as the removal of Shipley's, Dixon's, Round Bottom, Bard's, Locket's, and General Bolton's shoals and snag removal on the Little Missouri, White, and St. Francis rivers, although the latter projects were later transferred to other officers. By 1874, Humphreys would note of the contraction works that "the system of construction is no longer experimental, but can be applied

---

[43] "Report on Mississippi River Improvement," pp. 2-4, quote p. 2; *Report of the Chief of Engineers*, 1872, H.D. 1, Pt. 2 (42nd Cong., 3rd Sess.): 54-55, 358-36; Dobney, pp. 44-47.

View of completed St. Louis Bridge with steamboats in Mississippi River and views of stages of bridge construction, based on photographs taken in 1874 by R. Benecke, sections of pier and machinery, and portrait of Capt. James B. Eads. 11437 U.S. Copyright Office, Copyright by Compton & Co. (1874) LOC

generally with assurance of success if skill, care, and forethought be exercised in the location of works and management of construction."[44]

While Simpson built the approved projects, he also completed a survey from the Missouri to the Ohio to locate obstacles to navigation and identify improvements. The Corps briefly surveyed Kimswick to Cairo, Illinois, in 1873, followed by an in-depth triangulation survey of the river through 1875. This was the most detailed and scientific study of the river to that date and included a general description of characteristics, detailed maps and cross-section surveys, discharge and velocity measurements, depth soundings, sediment transport evaluations, and sediment analysis. In his analysis, Simpson proved his brilliance in understanding basic hydraulic theories and application. "A permanent improvement must of necessity be designed and executed in entire harmony with the natural laws of the river. A mighty river is impatient under restraint – can be led, not driven." Good navigation required depth and width

---

[44] *Cullum's Register*, Vol. 2, pp. 515-516; *Report of the Chief of Engineers*, 1872-1880, quote from 1874, p. 61.

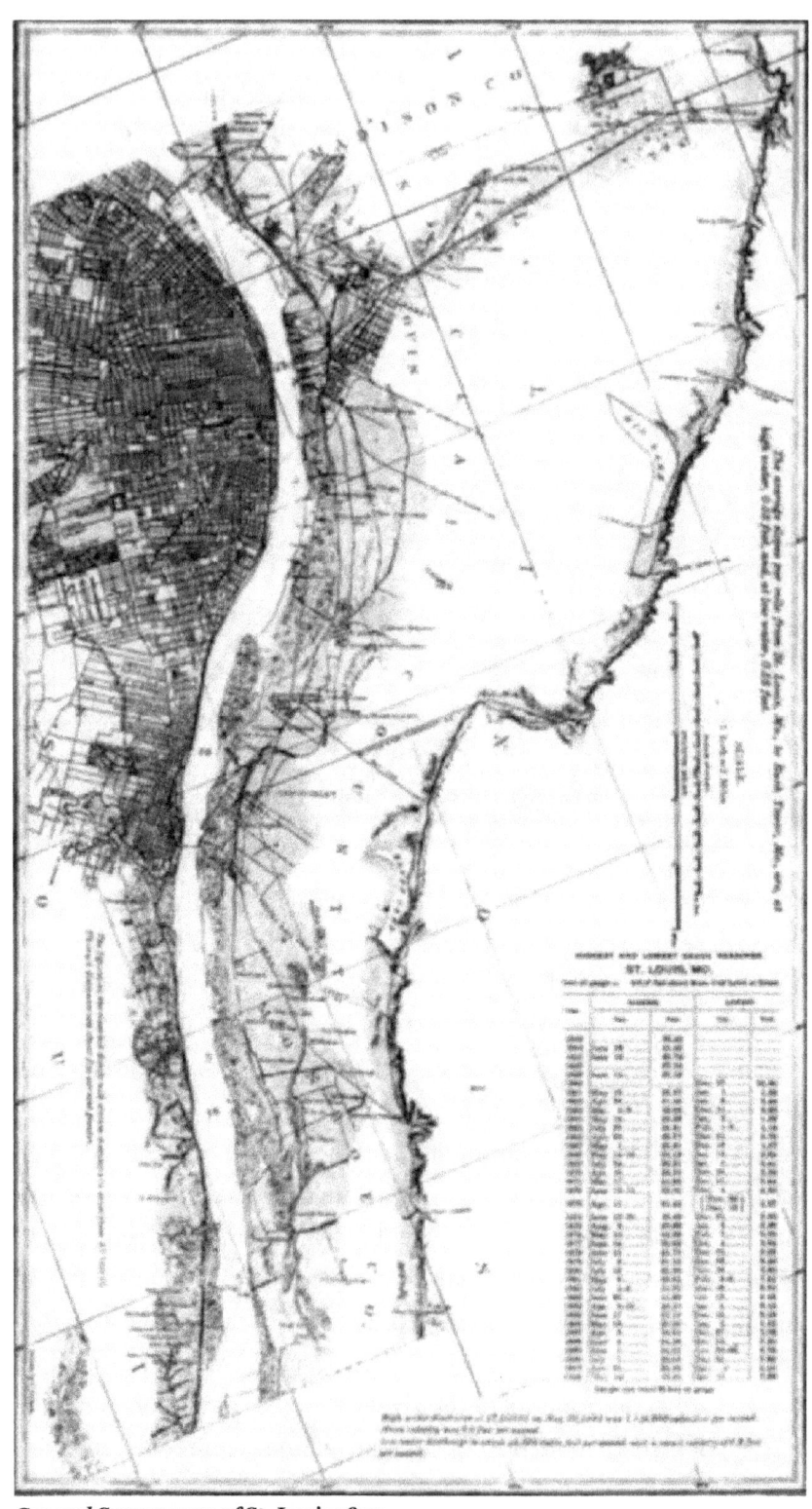
General Survey map of St. Louis 1892

of water and moderate velocity, with easy access to ports. By contracting width through permanent works such as dikes or hurdles and chute closures, engineers could increase the depth. Undue straightening and cutoffs could cause dangerous increases in velocity, and it was difficult and expensive to change the channel's direction or maintain unstable bends. In his view, most improvements were more a matter of politics and finances than engineering – many riparian landowners opposed closing chutes and other contraction works, it would take many years of improvements to see results, and sufficient funding was necessary to pursue the desired end over time until met. He seemed to ask for patience among lawmakers to allow the improvements time to work. Once improved, temporary improvements such as dredging and low-water dams could help maintain the river, but at greater expense and less effect. And although he noted that the current object of improvement was navigation, he also recognized the need to protect landowners from bank erosion and flooding, a statement prescient of future problems faced by the Corps. [45]

The result of this survey, which identified a total of 21 locations requiring improvement from the Illinois to the Ohio, was a series of projects authorized by Congress over the next decade that greatly increased the work of the office. The first of these projects was construction in 1874 of dikes and jetties along the shore from Carondelet to the foot of Carroll's Island to remove Horsetail Bar, a particularly difficult sandbar and shoal that reduced the depth of the river just south of St. Louis to less than four feet. By the following year, the works had increased the depth to about eight feet, although an additional dike became necessary in 1876 when the flood of 1875 eroded part of Arsenal Island, which

Wing dams on Mississippi, 1891

---

[45] *Report of the Chief of Engineers, 1874-1875*, quote from 1875, p. 485; Dobney, pp. 48-52.

formed a bar about a mile and a half above Horsetail. The same year, Congress had also authorized closure of Cahokia Chute, which was the apparent cause of the erosion of the island. Because of the rate of erosion, he invested most appropriations in protecting both shores of the island in 1877 and completed the closure by 1879. In 1875, Simpson completed work on dams to block chutes near Fort Chartres, Towhead, and Turkey islands and started construction of a dam at Liberty Island and Devil's Island and a dike and revetment in Missouri Chute to widen that channel. In 1876, Congress authorized protection of the banks of Dickey's Island and the mouth of the Ohio River as well Kaskaskia Bend, which was quickly eroding. By 1877, he had identified more than 20 locations on the river where banks were caving that required protection. Work at several of these locations, including Kaskaskia, Liberty Island, and Dickey's Island, faced continual problems with erosion. Efforts to revet these locations failed because of lack of funding. By 1879, he concluded that lack of progress was due to inadequate funding, and that, at the rate of $200,000 a year, it would take a century to complete all of the works contemplated. "Enlarged operations will leave more unfinished works at the end of each year and subject the government to greater loss from their destruction by the failure of appropriations the following year."[46]

In March 1880, Capt. (later Maj.) Oswald H. Ernst relieved Simpson as the St. Louis Engineer. Ernst had graduated from West Point in 1864, served briefly in the Civil War, returned to West Point as an instructor through most of the 1870s, and replaced Allen as Simpson's junior officer in 1878. He would later serve as superintendent of West Point and be promoted to major general in the Spanish-American War. As historian Frederick Dobney observed, "While Simpson came to St. Louis at the end of his career, Ernst arrived when his had just begun." This difference in age demonstrated itself in a noted difference in style. Although he adhered to Simpson's preference for permanent improvements, Ernst was more open to new methods, for example, the application of hurdles – permeable dikes that held up better against the ravages of current while forming new bank by trapping sediment. After experiments with hurdles in 1879 in Horsetail Bar, he applied them widely in the St. Louis area. Unlike previous engineers, he believed that erosion of the banks was the cause of the deteriorating conditions. He observed that surveys confirmed the river had materially widened to the detriment of navigation, but less so in wooded

---

[46] *Report of the Chief of Engineers, 1874-1880*, quote 1879, p. 1032.

locations. As a result, he encouraged use of hurdles combined with planting willow trees to prevent widespread bank caving. He also first implemented telephones, hydraulic excavators, and steam pile drivers. In addition, he was less concerned with local businesses than he was with ensuring that money was available for general improvements. Simpson tended to be more responsive to local pressure, for example, making expensive surveys or improvements at the request of congressmen or local interests, particularly at ship landings. However, Ernst argued:

> *The money, having been appropriated for improvement of the Mississippi between the Illinois and Ohio rivers, must, I think, be applied so as to benefit the greatest number of persons interested in navigation of the entire stretch of river lying between those limits. There is no doubt that one important feature of an improved river is convenient access to landings; but the **most** important result to be obtained by the improvement, and the one to be first aimed at, is cheap **through** transportation for freight.*

He tended to use general improvement funds for the river channel unless Congress specifically authorized and appropriated funds for harbor improvements. Agreeing with Simpson that riparian landowner rights were damaging engineering efforts, he proposed legislation to make the federal government owner of the riverbed to high water, since federal ownership of land was critical for his reclamation projects.[47]

Ernst completed the dam closing Cahokia Chute, neared completion of new dikes at Horsetail Bar, reinforced protection of Kaskaskia Bend, and expended the remaining funds on Dickey's Island. However, he refused further work on Kaskaskia or the mouth of the Ohio and requested separate funding for these projects if they were to continue. Instead, he sought to spend general funds on improvements near Piasa Island to rectify rapids caused by previous works. He completed a survey in 1881 and received approval to proceed, but pulled funds to improve Alton Harbor, which had started to silt once again, as required by the Rivers and Harbors Act of that year. He completed a dike near the harbor by 1883 and cleared the harbor by 1884. The hurdles at Horsetail Bar made significant progress in reclaiming the bank despite some minor setbacks, and Ernst started to apply the technique to Cahokia Chute other locations. Several

---

[47] Dobney, p. 52; *Report of the Chief of Engineers, 1876, 1879-1880*, quote from 1880, pp. 1359-1360.

times after 1880, ice severely damaged many of the works, causing significant repair spending. Ice also caused serious damage to ships, which is why Congress approved in 1880 construction of an ice harbor in St. Louis, a protected harbor where ships could moor when the river froze, but after the plan met with indifference among St. Louis steamboat captains, Ernst recommended suspension of construction. In 1881, Congress established a standard of maintaining an eight-foot channel and standardized 2,500-foot width in the Middle Mississippi and approved projects to improve the Cape Girardeau Harbor and the river between Carroll's Island and the Meramec River. Ernst completed surveys in 1882 and recommended projects to include hurdles on the east bank and revetment on the west bank of Twin Hollows, hurdles near Pulltight to prevent enlargement of a chute near Beard's Island, closure of the west channel of Chesley Island, and hurdles and revetment to build up the banks of Jim Smith's and Foster's islands. By 1884, he had completed work on Twin Hollows, Jim Smith's, and Cape Girardeau and spent additional funds on repair and maintenance even as he pushed to complete the remaining projects.[48]

The District under the Mississippi River Commission

At this point, the St. Louis Engineer Office came briefly under the authority of the Mississippi River Commission. Congress had created the Mississippi River Commission in 1879 to "correct, permanently locate, and deepen the channel and protect the banks of the Mississippi River; improve and give safety and ease to the navigation thereof," and "prevent destructive floods." With the growing impact of severe flooding in the Lower Mississippi Valley, flood control proponents had proposed a commission early in the year, but it met with stiff opposition from those who viewed flood control as essentially a local issue that did not fall under the commerce clause of the Constitution. Only after Rep. Randall L. Gibson of Louisiana proposed a compromise bill that reduced emphasis on flood control and eliminated spending for levees did the bill pass. After passage of the act, the coalition broke apart, and for many years navigation proponents opposed funding for levees while fiscal conservatives opposed excessive spending, forcing the commission to focus primarily on minimal contraction works south of Cairo to improve navigation. The newly

---

[48] *Report of the Chief of Engineers, 1880-1884.*

appointed commission included St. Louis civil engineer James B. Eads, future president Benjamin Harrison, former Louisiana Chief Engineer Benjamin M. Harrod, Henry Mitchell of the Coast and Geodetic Survey, and Bvt. Maj. Gen. Quincy A. Gillmore, Bvt. Brig. Gen. Cyrus B. Comstock, and Bvt. Brig. Gen. Charles R. Suter of the Corps of Engineers. Since it was ostensibly responsible for the entire river, one of its first resolutions in 1879 was to make St. Louis – the halfway point on the river – the location for the commission headquarters, where it would remain until 1929. Several St. Louis engineers, civil and military, played a role in the commission over the years.[49]

In the face of congressional funding constraints, the commission voted to concentrate its limited funding on the more hazardous lower Mississippi River, although it completed an assessment of the middle river in 1881. "The success of Captain Ernst's works thus far justifies in our opinion the methods he has employed, and we are of the opinion that it should be pushed toward completion under liberal appropriations," it concluded. It not only endorsed the work of the St. Louis Engineer Office; it adopted the same methods for the lower river, which it made its sole focus of improvement. Eads, however, disagreed both with endorsing Ernst's works, which he had not seen, and with turning over management of the river from the Missouri to the Ohio. "I do not believe the public expectation will be met by exempting so extensive and important section of river as this two hundred miles from the supervision of the commission," which he noted had by law responsibility over the whole river. He would later disagree with and leave the commission over his belief that levees and closure of all outlets from the river would increase the river's scouring capability and deepen the channel. Using what resources it had, the commission started construction in 1881 of dikes and revetment at the Plum Point and Lake Providence reaches of the river, but, lacking a force of laborers, made little progress. It was for this reason that in 1882 Congress gave the commission supervision and initiative authority over the Corps offices south of Cairo, which the commission divided into four districts to carry out its work – another step toward geographic districts. North of that point, the commission coordinated

---

[49] Charles A. Camillo and Matthew T. Pearcy, *Upon Their Shoulders, A history of the Mississippi River Commission from its inception through the advent of the modern Mississippi River and Tributaries Project* (Vicksburg, MS: MRC, 2004): 25-84, quote on C1; "[MRC] History," N.D. (NARA-KC, RG 77, Ent. 521, Box 22).

with but did not manage or fund river improvements, which the Corps carried out through existing offices.[50]

In the Rivers and Harbors Act of 1884, Congress placed work north of Cairo under commission oversight by providing funds under commission control to continue the same projects. At the direction of Chief of Engineers Brig. Gen. John Newton, Ernst suspended work, furloughed workers, and spent several months transferring property to the commission, although he did spend just under $6,000 on maintenance. After receiving commission funding late in the year, he was able to conduct little or no work. He added new hurdles near Carroll's Island and repaired work at Twin Hollows, Pulltight, Chesley Island, and Jim Smith's, but did little else because of winter and high water, though what he did accomplish was particularly effective. By August 1886, however, Congress had decided to move the St. Louis office back under the Chief of Engineers and provided $375,000 in funding to continue improvements. Soon after, Ernst left the office, having been transferred to Texas on November 22, 1886. Replacing him in St. Louis was Maj. Alexander M. Miller. Although some level of coordination continued, and the commission and Corps shared resources and employees such as Robert E. McMath and several district engineers, the St. Louis office would remain responsible for Mississippi River navigation improvements between the Illinois and Ohio rivers.[51]

By the end of Ernst's administration, the St. Louis Engineer Office had more or less entered the modern era. Prior to the Civil War, the Office of Western River Improvement and Corps of Topographical Engineers oversaw most navigational projects in the region. After the Civil War, regional offices evolved that managed numerous projects in a specific geographic region, in this case, from the Illinois to the Ohio River. Improvement of the St. Louis Harbor and surrounding area, which continued sporadically from 1833 into the twentieth century, spanned these organizations and provided a measure of federal activity. At the beginning of the project, Corps methods were experimental. Using wing-dams to increase river velocity and scour sandbars, first applied in 1825, was still new, as was use of revetment to protect riverbanks. These works were expensive, and given the *laissez faire* philosophy that dominated the federal government, funding was often not forthcoming to complete the

---

[50] *Report of the Mississippi River Commission, Nov 25, 1881*, H.D. 10, (47th Cong. 1st Sess.): 1-20, quote on 20; "Communication, of the 12th instant, from Mr. James B. Eads, a member of the Mississippi River Commission," H.D. 10, Pt. 2 (47th Cong. 1st Sess.): 11; Camillo and Pearcy, pp. 42-83.
[51] U.S. Cong., *Report of the Chief of Engineers, 1885-1887; Report from the Mississippi River Commission*, H.D. 38 (49th Cong., 1st Sess.): 15-17; Dobney, pp. 52-57.

many projects it began. The limited improvements made through 1852 were nevertheless effective in clearing the middle harbor, although other projects suffered from frugal financing. By 1886, however, the role of the federal government had changed. To improve navigation in the upper St. Louis Harbor, in Alton Harbor, and the Mississippi River between the Illinois and Ohio, the government had to invest considerably more in river improvements to maintain a navigable channel. Although the debate continued for decades as to the utility and authority to make many improvements and the methods used were often prone to impermanence, it was nevertheless the beginning of modern water resources development.

River Regulation to the Twentieth Century

In an article in 1921, Maj. Dewitt Jones of the St. Louis District noted, "the methods employed in the regulation of the Mississippi River are based on experience extending over many years." In fact, the strategies for river regulation had changed little since the 1880s, and would not change for many decades, although the materials and methods used continuously improved.

Snag Removal – The Corps continued snag removal annually to maintain the river, for which Congress authorized in 1888 expenditures of no more than $100,000 per year. Into the 1920s, St. Louis District was responsible for snag removal on the Middle and Lower Mississippi and Atchafalaya. It used the *H.G. Wright* and *J.N. Macomb*, built in 1880 and 1874, which required 40 to 45 personnel from July to March. Both vessels were of the Shreve design with dual hulls, a winch, and a leverage beam.

Stone Dikes – This was the first form of channel constriction, typically consisting of a foundation of brush held in place by piles, on which stone was placed until it reached 10 or 15 feet below low water. However, the district had largely abandoned the method by the 1880s because of the expense and difficulty in maintaining them.

Hurdles – Hurdles or permeable dikes were the preferred method of strengthening convex banks and chutes and side channels. The district greatly improved them by using double versus single pile rows to hold the mattresses, driven up to 15 feet deeper using pile-driving machinery. In addition, the district spaced the hurdles up to 1,000 feet apart versus no more than 300. Piles, preferably cypress or white oak, were 18 inches in diameter and up to 65 feet long. Brush mattresses, later lumber, were 12 to 30 feet long and six inches thick, held together by steel wire. Mattresses typically ended 20 feet below low water. Hurdle plants included four to eight pile drivers, derricks, one to two steamships to carry shops and construction units, and quarter boats to house the 100 to 200-man workforce.

Revetment – Use of revetment to protect convex banks probably improved the most of all strategies. Initially, revetment consisted of a dike extending six feet above low water, grading of banks, and paving with stone above water, but rock was subject to considerable erosion. From 1875 to 1881, for subaqueous protection, the district introduced woven willow or cottonwood mattresses roughly 40 by 700 feet, later

Matress construction along Mississippi for river bank protection

Timber piling clump dike, Chester to Ste. Genevieve, Mo, 1947

expanded to 125 feet wide to increase effectiveness. As willow trees became scarce, the district substituted lumber. The district constructed mattresses and then sank them using ballast so that they ended at the low water line and overlapped downstream, with stone paving on the exposed bank. It took a crew of 86 to build and lay the mattresses, including grading and clearing crews. With improvements to concrete technology, by 1914, the Mississippi River Commission was experimenting with 10 or 12-foot concrete slabs, and in 1915 with mattresses of 3- to 4-foot articulated concrete blocks connected by galvanized steel cable, although these were not universally accepted until after 1930.

Matress revetment between St. Louis and Cairo

Portable Jetties – After experiments to determine the best angle and distance to achieve results, the district drove a line of sheet piles to support 10 to 20-foot corrugated sheet-metal panels riveted to a three-inch thick frame, using mattresses to reduce erosion on the bed. Although temporarily effective, the district abandoned their use as too labor-intensive in 1898 after development of the dredge.

Dredging – The Mississippi River Commission started experiments with hydraulic dredges beginning in 1893, while the district built the first jet-type dredge in 1896 and completed the first three suction dredges the following year. While the jet dredge was no longer in service by 1906, Dredges No. 3 and 4 (christened *Selma* and *Thebes*), and two others completed in 1907 (*Ft. Gage* and *Ft. Charles*) were still in service after World War I. These required crews of 37 to 39.[52]

---

[52] Jones and James Skelly, "Regulation of Middle Mississippi River," *TME* 13 (1921): 197-204, 272-274; Raymond Haas, "Development of Concrete Revetments on the Lower Mississippi," *Concrete* (Apr./May 1947): 1-10.

5

Dredging and Channel Maintenance

Through 1886, the primary mission of the St. Louis Engineer Office was to improve navigation on the Mississippi by maintaining an eight-foot channel on the Middle Mississippi through permanent improvements – dams to close chutes, dikes and jetties to contract the channel, hurdles to build up the banks, and revetment to protect the banks. Such maintenance work that occurred consisted of removal of snags, wrecks, or other obstacles. While Col. Stephen H. Long and others had experimented with dredges or scrapers to physically deepen the channel, since the time of Col. James H. Simpson, most considered these temporary measures as merely supplementary to more permanent works. They might improve navigation for a time by removing silt, but they did not correct the causes of the siltation as permanent improvements sought to do. In addition, because of limitations in technology, dredging could only help maintain the channel once lowered but not improve it without considerable cost. Although there were some successful experiments with jet- and suction-type dredges as early as 1881, these were not perfected until the Mississippi River Commission performed a series of experiments and developed several working prototypes after 1892. By 1896, the commission was promoting the use of dredging as the primary means of improvement because of the higher cost of permanent improvements. At the recommendation of the newly formed Board of Engineers for Rivers and Harbors, in 1905 Congress adopted dredging as the primary method for maintaining a navigable channel of sufficient depth for the entire river. These recommendations gripped the St. Louis District in a debate that lasted a decade about the effectiveness of temporary versus permanent improvements.

Col. James H. Simpson DE
January 1, 1873 - March 30, 1880

Maj. Alexander M. Miller had taken over the St. Louis office in November 1886 and more or less continued the program of Maj. Oswald Ernst of building

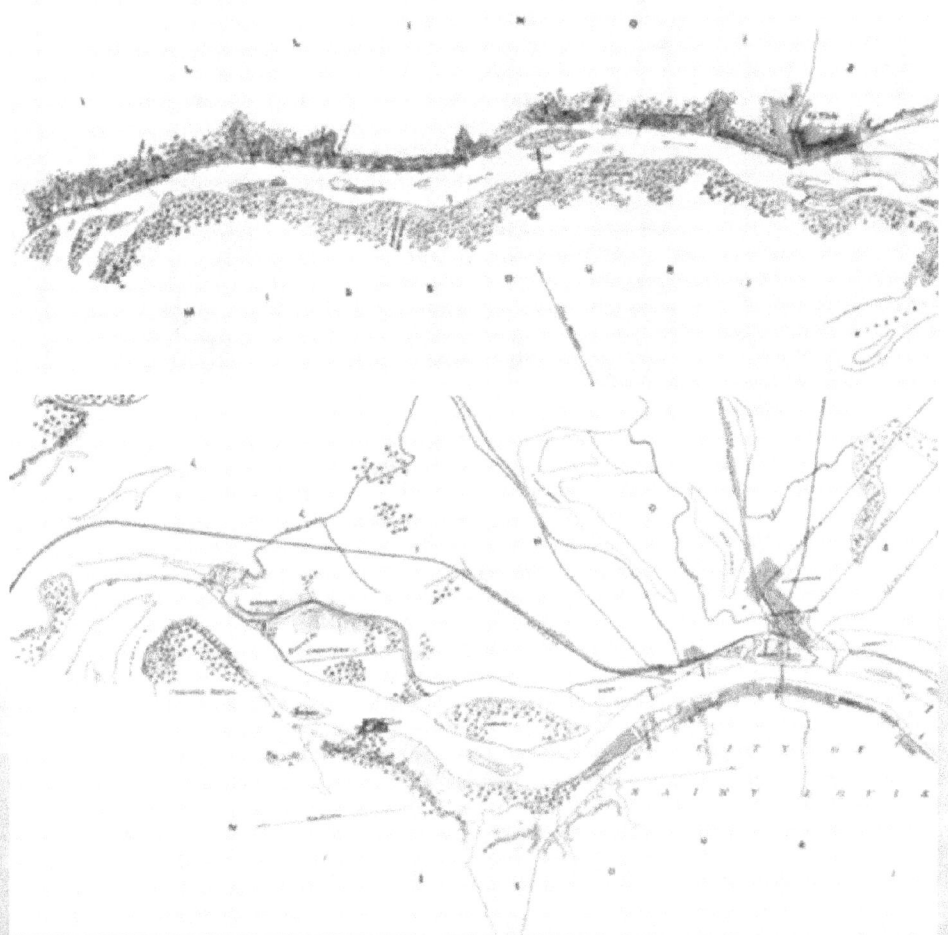

Simpson Charts - These are maps of the Mississippi River between the mouth of the Ohio River showing successive shore lines and topography. 1870-1878

hurdles and revetment to maintain an eight-foot deep, 2,500-foot wide regularized channel as required by 1881 guidance from the Chief of Engineers. Miller continued the projects at Piasa Island, Horsetail Bar, Twin Hollows, Pulltight, Jim Smith's Island, and Chesley Island. He also started new improvements, including an extension of the Jim Smith hurdles to Sulphur Springs; bank protection at Cairo, Illinois; hurdles to contract Lucas' Crossing, a chute behind Calico Island; hurdles at Bruce Island near St. Charles, Missouri; protection of the bank on the Illinois side of the Ste. Genevieve Bend; hurdles at Rush Tower on the east side of James Landing; and hurdles near Venice, Illinois, to narrow the river north of the Eads Bridge. Each of these projects required periodic repair and additions to see long-term improvement, and they often saw

Maj. Alexander M. Miller

year-to-year setbacks as ice or floods destroyed the works or caused new problems. To these responsibilities, the Corps had added snag removal on the Missouri and Mississippi rivers and responsibility for the Missouri, Gasconade, and Kaskaskia rivers. Formerly, another office headed by Col. Charles R. Suter in St. Louis was responsible for snag removal on the Mississippi and improvement of these other rivers, but this office merged with the St. Louis office after its separation from the Mississippi River Commission in 1886. There were only two snag removal vessels available, the *H.G. Wright* and *J.N. Macomb*, which usually divided work between the Missouri and Mississippi or used borrowed equipment. The work on the Kaskaskia was the first improvement to this river and consisted of removing Nine-Mile Shoal. In 1889, the Corps made another step toward modern organization by establishing five divisions in charge of multiple Corps offices. The St. Louis office operated initially under the Southwest Division headed by Col. Cyrus B. Comstock, who also served as president of the Mississippi River Commission.[53]

Miller continued as engineer until March 4, 1893, when replaced by Maj. Charles J. Allen. While Miller was known best as a scholar – he had graduated third at West Point in 1865 and translated a French work on Egyptian irrigation during his time in St. Louis – Allen had a reputation for hands-on experience with the river, having served as assistant to both Col. William F. Raynolds and Col. James H. Simpson. The period of 1894 to 1896 was one of widespread drought – at one point in 1895 the river between St. Louis and Cairo, Illinois, was closed to navigation for 56 days. With limited success with hurdles clearing a channel to the required eight feet, Allen began using new methods to aid in removing silt. One was the application of portable jetties. These were iron panels ten or so feet high that engineers could place temporarily in the channel to focus the current toward a shoal or bar and aid in clearing it. Once the channel was clear, they could remove the jetties for placement elsewhere. In 1894, Allen successfully used them to aid in clearing the channel near Fort Chartes and removing a bar at Devil's Island, and in 1895, it took 22 men four days to drive pile and set up a 1,200-foot jetty near Danby Landing. He also experimented

---

[53] *Annual Reports of the Chief of Engineers, 1887-1893*; Dobney, pp. 56-57.

with a jet dredge in Ste. Genevieve Bend. He attached two large two-cylinder pumps on the deck of the towboat *Gen. H.L. Abbot* capable of pumping 5,000 gallons per minute through a metal pipe to scour away sandbars. On January 13, 1896, Maj. Thomas H. Handbury replaced Allen. Handbury had previously worked as assistant division engineer under Suter before overseeing rivers and harbors work on the Columbia, Willamette, Ohio, and White rivers. As a student of Suter, who later headed the Mississippi River Commission's Committee on Dredges and Dredging, Handbury was the first major proponent of using temporary improvements to clear the river near St. Louis. From 1896 to 1902, he promoted his views as a member of the Mississippi River Commission, which argued strongly after 1896 for increased funding for dredging in preference to other methods of improvement.[54]

As early as 1896, Handbury was arguing that "movable dikes, dredges, and other temporary expedients will be necessary" to help maintain a navigable channel. The problem, he observed, was that there were times when the Missouri River pumped too much sediment into the Mississippi, resulting in "engorgement of the improved channel" as the sediment settled. In 1879, for example, analysis of sediment content of the water and along the bottom at St. Charles showed that the sediment at that location would fill a square mile to a depth of 400 feet in one year. He asserted for the first time, "That [the river] will be able to maintain itself at that depth at all times without dredging and other temporary expedients cannot be asserted with positive certainty." He quickly took up Allen's experiments and advanced them beyond his isolated attempts. By 1897, Handbury had improved the *Abbot* by placing the jets in the aft, completed construction of another steam-powered jet dredge, and had three hydraulic suction dredges under construction, which went into service the following year. While continuing construction of hurdles and other permanent works, he increasingly used temporary improvements as the primary means of improvement. At Lucas, Ste. Genevieve, and Seventy-Six Landing, he

Maj. Thomas H. Handbury

---

[54] *Annual Reports of the Chief of Engineers, 1893-1896*; Dobney, pp. 57-58; *Cullum's Register*, Vol. III., pp. 35-36, Vol. IV, p. 150; "Discouraging River Report for '95," *Waterways Journal* (Sept. 19, 1896): 6.

used dredging in combination with revetment or hurdles to achieve a navigation depth of eight feet; at Harrisonville and Philadelphia Point, he used dredging alone to maintain the channel.[55]

Development of Dredging

Dredging had been a means of improving navigational depths in water for thousands of years. The word dredge derives from the French term for "drag," and most early dredging technologies were nothing more than wooden or metal scoops, buckets, or plows dragged manually across the bottom or banks, typically at low water. The most complicated manual methods involved buckets or shelves attached to hand-cranked ropes, conveyor belts, or chains forming a ladder to rapidly move earth. After 25 years of experimentation, the first successful steam-powered ladder dredge, designed by George Dutton, came into use in 1829 at Ocracoke Inlet, North Carolina, for a Corps harbor project. By the 1850s, ladder dredges on steam-powered vessels were in common use throughout the U.S. for Corps river and harbor work. They were slow, however, had minimal effectiveness, and required large crews of laborers to operate and aid in clearing a channel. After the Civil War, development of dredges proceeded in four different lines. First was the scraper or agitator, whose purpose was to stir up sediment for the current to move downstream. This was particularly important given the hard crust that often formed on sandbars. Col. Stephen H. Long had designed a scraper in 1860 that included a metal frame with a harness that attached with chains to a ship's bowsprit. Tested from 1867 to 1869 under Maj. Gouverneur Warren on the Upper Mississippi River near St. Paul, Minnesota, the scraper came into wide use the following decades. Another scraper tested in 1867 under Maj. M.D. McAlester was a screw-type, which used an enlarged propeller to cut up the bottom. Inventors in the years that followed designed various submarine excavators, plows, drums, and booms, most of which had limited use. The most successful of the agitator type was the circular dredge – a rotating wheel with teeth to break up the earth – designed in 1878. This was later used in conjunction with suction-types in cutterhead dredges.

---

[55] *Annual Reports of the Chief of Engineers, 1896-1899*, quotes from 1896, p. 1723; Dobney, pp. 57-58.

Dredge Alpha

Dredge Beta

By themselves, scrapers were only moderately successful, capable of removing a foot or two of sediment at most after considerable labor.[56]

Another line of development involved redirection of current to dredge out a channel, which, although not technically dredging per se, was often used with other methods with great success. In its most basic form, this involved placement of trees or rocks at strategic locations, and most permanent works were designed using this principle. As early as 1879, engineers developed metal

---
[56] Frank Snyder and Brian Guss, *The District: A History of the Philadelphia District, U.S. Army Corps of Engineers, 1866-1971* (Phil.: USACE, 1974): 64-5; *Annual Report of the Chief of Engineers*, 1867, pp. 367-376; 1868, 317-340; John A. Ockerson, "Dredges and Dredging on the Mississippi River," *ASCE Transactions* 40 (1898): 215-348.

triangular boxes with movable sides that could be dropped and adjusted to effect maximum scour, then removed at the end of a season. This was essentially a precursor to the large metal plates adopted by Allen in 1894. Another device was the marsh jetty, a sinkable barge with flat sides that could be dropped into place. These temporary expedients could be used anywhere jetties were effective but were reusable and lower cost. Another type was the Adams flume, developed in 1879, which was essentially a pipe that redirected the current. A third line of development was the jet dredge, which used jets of concentrated water to scour sediment. These typically included pipes or hoses and nozzles attached to a boom, frame, or the vessel itself through which a pump pushed water, either pumped directly from the river or filtered to remove sediment. The earliest test of a jet dredge mounted on a pile driver was by Maj. Oswald Ernst at Horsetail Bar in 1881, and the earliest test of a vessel-mounted jet was in 1896 by Handbury. There were also experiments with using explosions to remove sediment, but these were mostly unsuccessful. In general, redirection was highly successful in removing deep bars, but only for a short distance; a redirected channel would lose velocity, and lengthy bars or obstacles tended to render jets ineffective.[57]

Finally, there were hydraulic suction dredges, which used pumps to suck water and sediment either down a pipe to the riverbank or, in the case of hopper dredges, into the vessel itself to be deposited at a designated location. The first suction dredges were of the dipper type. Developed in 1870, these dredges included a long arm with a suction head that operators dipped into the river onto sediment. Used widely on the Illinois River and Upper Mississippi after 1883, they were highly successful under favorable conditions with little sediment. In 1871, Maj. Quincy Gillmore developed the first hopper dredge in the U.S. based on a model developed by French engineer Henri-Emile Bazin in 1867. By storing sediment inside, it could operate in open waters where deposit was not possible or desirable, such as existed in shallow Florida waterways or the mouths of rivers. James Eads designed a similar hopper type in 1877, the Dredge *Bayley*, to aid in clearing the Mississippi River passes near its mouth. In 1888, the Corps built the *Menge* and *Pah-Ute*, combined suction-ladder dredges that pumped silt brought up by a ladder into scows or sluice boxes on the shore. More successful were dredges that used output pipes, such as the

---

[57] Ockerson, pp. 231-242.

Dredge Ram, designed by Capt. John Millis for use on the Red and Atchafalaya rivers.[58]

Perhaps what most promoted and enabled use of dredges was their development and endorsement by the Mississippi River Commission after 1892. In 1891, a delegation of ship captains operating below St. Louis raised concerns that conditions on the river had deteriorated to the point where they impaired navigation. As a result, the commission created the Committee on Dredges and Dredging in 1892 to research, prototype, and deploy dredges in the Lower Mississippi River. Suter and St. Louis civilian engineer Henry Flad were the initial committee members, which eventually included Benjamin Harrod and Handbury. By the following year, the committee had developed the Dredge *Alpha*, which featured a pump and drag system and discharge pipe extending aft. A mooring spud kept the dredge in place, allowing it to move back and forth over a bar. First used near Cape Girardeau in 1894 to clear a 1,600-foot bar, the dredge was a huge advance in technology, but lacked sufficient power. A second model introduced in 1896, the Dredge *Beta*, used two pump engines and improved the discharge pipe. After the 1896 Rivers and Harbors Act provided funding to build additional prototypes, the committee completed the Dredge *Gamma* later that year, which included more sophisticated pumps and two intake lines and heads. A jet provided agitation to increase the effectiveness of the suction, and a 1,000-foot outtake line maximized distance to deposit areas. In 1897, the committee introduced the Dredge *Delta*, which used a mechanical cutter on the suction head to break up soil. This was followed by the dredges *Epsilon* and *Zeta*, which used jet and scraping agitation to break up soil prior to suction. While experimenting with design, the committee also tried various combinations of crew numbers and operation. With completion of these prototypes, dredging entered maturity of design and operation.[59]

The result of these tests was unqualified endorsement of dredging by the Mississippi River Commission. In 1896, the commission passed a resolution stating:

> *The general and permanent improvement of the Mississippi River by means of bank protection and contraction work will involve an outlay and difficulties of obtaining materials so*

---

[58] Ockerson, pp. 242-246, 295-298; Charles Prelini, *Dredges and Dredging* (NY: Van Nostrand Co.: 1911): 94-115.
[59] Ockerson, 246-295; Herbert S. Gladfelter, *Fifty-Five Years of Dredges and Dredging on the Mississippi River in the Memphis District*, Vol. 1, Pt. A (Memphis: USACE, 1952): a-j.

> much greater than was originally estimated, that the Commission should inform Congress thereof, and submit to it the question of its continuance, particularly as it is of opinion that the practical results contemplated by the Act organizing the Commission of deepening the channel of the river for navigation ... can be attained with greater economy and probability of success in less time by dredging of obstruction bars in low water and maintenance.[60]

The costs of buying willows, lumber, and rock; the wages for large crews to install them; and the continual repair and replacement of hurdles and revetment was far more expensive than building a boat, after which the only cost was annual payment for fuel, small crews, and upkeep of the vessel.

The Great Dredging Debate

On March 21, 1899, Capt. Edward Burr relieved Handbury, bringing with him a renewed faith in permanent works and thus departing somewhat from the commission. In his mind, the only thing preventing completion of the permanent project was application of sufficient funds. Since 1896, when Congress appropriated $2.6 million over three years, the only significant appropriation was for $100,000 in 1900, requiring Burr to conserve funds to ensure emergency funding was available. "Unless pressed with such appropriations as [the project's] magnitude warrants," he wrote in 1900, "satisfactory results either as to progress or economy cannot be expected." Incomplete works could not provide effect, and completed works faced problems such as ice damage or erosion of earth behind hurdles that would require periodic repair. He believed $1 million per year for five years was necessary to complete the project. In addition to repair or extension of hurdles and revetment at Ste. Genevieve, Rush Towhead, Penitentiary Point, Devil's Island, and others and continued dredging at Sulphur Springs, Staton Towhead, and several new locations, he added hurdles on the Illinois shore across from the St. Louis harbor north of the Eads bridge and revetment of the Illinois shore near Beechridge just north of Cairo to prevent the river from cutting across to the Cache River. He also started to add buoys to mark navigation channels.[61]

---

[60] Gladfelter, pp. g-h.
[61] *Annual Reports of the Chief of Engineers, 1899-1902*, quote from 1900, p. 2639; Dobney, pp. 67-68.

The next district engineer, Maj. Thomas L. Casey, was more amenable to the recommendations of the commission after he took office on November 7, 1901. Initially, he continued a balance of permanent works and dredging as funding allowed. Congress did not appropriate more funds until 1902, when it provided $2 million over three years. High water the following year made dredging unnecessary other than at Okaw Crossing, but he was able to make some repairs to hurdles. By 1904, however, he changed course when he received the recommendation of the Board of Engineers for Rivers and Harbors. The Rivers and Harbors Act of 1902 established the board to review Corps projects for cost-efficiency and technical correctness prior to implementation. One of the first projects it reviewed was improvement of the Mississippi River between the Missouri and Ohio rivers, which it did at the request of Congress rather than a project report submitted by district or division engineers as was usually the case. In 1902, board members made a survey of the river between the Missouri and Ohio and reviewed data such as previous reports of district engineers. In his testimony before the board, submitted by correspondence, Casey noted that permanent works were helpful in many locations, but were often destroyed by flood or the river changing course. "It has frequently occurred to me to question the propriety of continuing much further along the present lines." Permanent works would cost more than $22 million, while dredging alone would cost

Construction of early mattress revetment

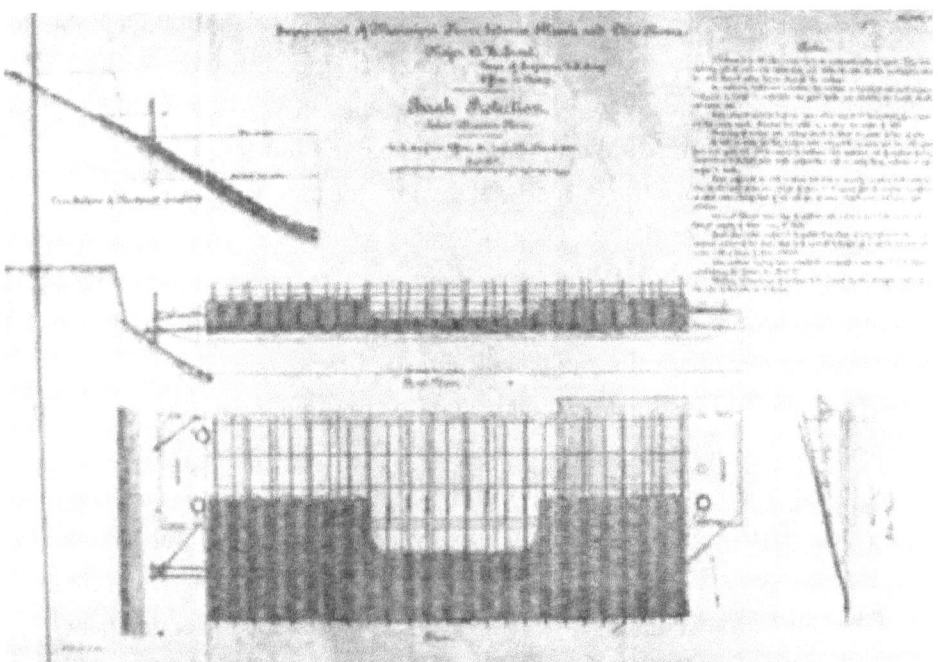

Diagram of early mattress revetment

$500,000 per year – only $200,000 more than annual dredging costs required whether or not one implemented permanent improvements.[62]

On November 12, 1903, the Board of Engineers made its report. It recommended continuation of the eight-foot channel from the Ohio to St. Louis and a six-foot channel above St. Louis, which it believed would require $20 million in contraction works and bank protection plus annual maintenance. But "this cost can be materially reduced by a use of dredging more extensive than is made at the present time." This would require spending $1.2 million on dredging plant and $300,000 per year for operation. The only dissent came from then Major Burr, who was an instructor at the Engineer School and member of the board. While admitting improvements in dredging technology and efficiency, he nevertheless argued that "permanent improvement is feasible from a technical standpoint, and that such improvement will

Maj. Thomas L. Casey

---

[62] *Annual Reports of the Chief of Engineers, 1901-1905*, quote from 1905, p. 1590; *History of the Board of Engineers for Rivers and Harbors* (Fort Belvoir, Va.: CEHO, 1980): 1-34, 47-48; Dobney, p. 69

produce a low-water barge channel so superior in location, width, permanence, and certainty to any temporary dredged channel that it is much to be preferred to the latter even at a conceded greater cost." In his experience, the greater discharge and alluvium below the Ohio that made dredging more effective than permanent improvements did not exist above the Ohio, and dredging alone would not maintain the channel. Some combination in methods was necessary. Based on these findings and with permanent works taking too much time and money, Congress adopted dredging as the primary means of improvement in the Rivers and Harbors Act of 1905. Casey greeted the change enthusiastically, observing that hurdles and revetment "may be considered auxiliary and subsidiary to dredging, which ... is authorized as the chief means of maintaining the channel." Since Congress approved spending remaining funds on projects, he continued some work on hurdles and revetment, particularly revetment of Sawyer Bend and contraction of the river at Cahokia Ferry, but he considered these as supporting efforts to dredge the channel rather than the converse. Using $650,000 appropriated by Congress, he dredged throughout the district to maintain and increase the channel to eight feet and completed design of the two dredges authorized by Congress, which cost a total of $330,000.[63]

Meanwhile, dredging had increased dramatically over the entire Mississippi River. Below Cairo, the Mississippi River Commission took charge of dredging operations. The Committee on Dredges and Dredging, led by Handbury and later John A. Ockerson, continued its experiments and in 1902 made a series of recommendations on dredge construction. Once the committee had developed dredges, the commission established the position of Superintendent of Dredging in 1894, which operated out of the office of the Secretary of the Commission in St. Louis. The first superintendent was Col. Carl W. Sturtevant. He was followed by F.B. Maltby in 1898, William Gerig in 1904, and Foster H. Hilliard in 1905. These superintendents managed all dredging operations on the lower river and coordinated closely with St. Louis personnel, who continued to build and experiment with dredges. In 1918, the commission established a separate Dredging District, relocated to Memphis, Tennessee,

Col. Clinton B. Sears

---

[63] *Annual Report of the Chief of Engineers, 1904*, quotes from 1904, pp. 2145-2150 and 1905, p. 1589; Dobney, pp. 68-69.

which was responsible for dredging as far north as St. Louis. In 1928, dredging responsibilities would be distributed throughout all of the districts on the Mississippi River.⁶⁴

By the time that Col. Clinton B. Sears relieved Casey on August 9, 1906, Congress had authorized expenditure of the balance of funds on permanent improvements, although the vast majority of funds were still used for dredging and construction of the two authorized new dredges. At first dredging seemed to be working. The channel had increased from consistently above six feet to above eight. In the Rivers and Harbors Act of 1907, Congress reiterated use of dredging alone other than excess funds to maintain permanent works already built, but it also cut the overall budget by 40 percent by providing a mere $1.5 million for five years. Only a balance of $250,000 was available to maintain permanent improvements. Part of the reason for this cut in spending was the request by Congress for a survey in 1907 to determine the feasibility of a 14-foot channel. On January 28, 1908, Capt. Gustave R. Lukesh took over as St. Louis district engineer. The same year, the Corps reorganized, placing the Mississippi River and great Lakes districts under a single Western Division. Although engineers had used the term district for at least a decade, from this point the Corps officially applied the term to the geographic regions under engineer offices. Lukesh observed that "the interpretation" of the 1905 act "virtually stopped all construction work for the permanent improvement of the river in the district" and that funding constraints limited repair of existing works. Despite the small level of funding, in his brief tenure Lukesh was able to dredge four miles of channel at 12 locations throughout the district in 1908 and repair or extend permanent works at James Landing, Crain Island, Willard Landing, Devil's Island, and Eliza Towhead. He used the dredges only about three months out of the year, which he explained as the result of efficiency improvements rather than the funding cuts that likely inhibited their use.⁶⁵

Col. William H. Bixby

---

⁶⁴ Gladfelter, Vol. 1, Pt. A, pp. a-j, 1-38; Vol. 2, pp. 1-14.
⁶⁵ *Annual Reports of the Chief of Engineers, 1906-1908*, quote from 1908, p. 1615.

After Col. William H. Bixby assumed command on September 30, 1908, the Corps increasingly sought to revise the dredging-only policy. An 1873 West Point graduate, Bixby studied in France before serving in district offices at Wilmington, North Carolina; Charleston, South Carolina; Newport, Rhode Island; Detroit, Michigan; and Chicago, Illinois. At the time he took charge in St. Louis, he was also the Northwestern (later Western) Division Engineer and president of the Mississippi River Commission. After being named Chief of Engineers and promoted to brigadier general on June 12, 1910, he served more than a week in all three capacities, although several times he left operations in the hands of Lt. Clarence H. Knight. In 1909, he spent only $50,000 on permanent improvements because of the budgetary constraints, but put dredges *No. 5* and *No. 6*, finally delivered in 1908 and 1909, to work maintaining an eight-foot channel. He also addressed the low-water plane for St. Louis, which was critical for establishing the legal requirements for navigation. The low-water plane is the lowest point reached by the river used to calculate channel depth for the congressionally mandated eight-foot channel. The record low-water of 1863 had previously defined "zero" on the Market Street gage, which, established in 1861, was one of the oldest gages on the river. This was the starting point for calculating channel depth. With the many improvements to navigation and several low-water years, by 1909 the low-water plane was 3.6 feet below zero, depending on the method of calculation. Bixby proposed spending $1.3 million on weirs and other works to raise the plane, and although the plan was not adopted, it was the beginning of a discussion on how to determine the channel depth for district operations. The 1915 Rivers and Harbors Act established a mean low-water depth for dredging based on a 15-day low-water mean for any given season, a much lower number – equivalent to -5.2 feet on the St. Louis gage – and much harder to maintain. In 1927, the district formally established the low-water reference plane, eventually adjusted to -3.5 feet. However, the debate between proponents of dredging and permanent improvements continued for several decades over which number was proper for the district to use in maintaining the channel.[66]

In 1909, the Board of Examination and Survey of the Mississippi River established by Congress to consider a 14-foot channel finally submitted its report. Board members included Bixby, Lt. Col. Curtis M. Townsend, Lt. Col.

---

[66] *Annual Report of the Chief of Engineers, 1908-1910*; Memo of Opinion, "Integrated River Management; Mississippi River Navigation Project Dimensions," May 26, 1993; Mr. Martin, "Low Water Reference Plane – St. Louis to Thebes," Dec. 20, 1972 (MVS Archives); Dobney, pp. 69-71.

J.G. Warren, and Mississippi Commission members Henry B. Richardson and Homer P. Ritter. Included in the report was a recommendation to return to the 1881 project of permanent improvements on the Middle River, with funding of $21 million (the original $20 million plus $1 million for repairs). They believed dredging might be able to maintain the current channel most of the time, but the only way to get a permanently deeper channel was through permanent works. In his annual report for that year, Chief of Engineers Brig. Gen. William L. Marshall argued that "the 1881 project... needs no further revision other than to add urgent recommendations for annual appropriations large enough to allow of the completion of the $20,000,000 project." It was, as Bixby noted after he became chief, a situation where Congress adopted a single recommendation of the Board of Engineers for Rivers and Harbors "to the exclusion of the others," injuring efforts to improve the river. As a result of the report of the Board of Examination and the influence of the arguments of Bixby, the Rivers and Harbors Act of 1910 restored the 1881 project, along with dredging, to make permanent the navigable depth dredging had helped the Corps achieve. It also provided $750,000, the largest appropriation since 1905 and three times the amount provided the previous year, which would allow significant progress.[67]

Lt. Col. Charles L. Potter

Col. Curtis M. Townsend

Finally, after months of temporary and multitasked personnel filling the district engineer slot, Lt. Col. Charles L. Potter assumed the position on August 22, 1910. An 1886 West Point graduate, he was assigned originally to the U.S. Cavalry in the West before transferring to the Corps of Engineers, where he served in the Spanish-American War and various civil works positions in Memphis, Vicksburg, Little

---

[67] U.S. Cong., *Report by a Special Board of Engineers on Survey of Mississippi River*, H.D. 50 (61st Cong., 1st Sess.): 1-21; *Annual Report of the Chief of Engineers, 1909*, p. 551; *1910*, p. 620; Dobney, pp. 70-71.

Dredge Potter

Rock, and St. Louis. He would later become a member of the Mississippi River Commission and was its president during the disastrous Flood of 1927. Potter took the approach of using permanent works where dredging did not work. For example, from 1910 to 1911 he closed a chute near Grand Tower Island to increase the depth of the channel over a gravel bar that dredging could not remove. On June 30, 1913, Col. Curtis M. Townsend became the new St. Louis District Engineer. He had a career similar to that of Potter, having graduated from West Point in 1879, served in the Spanish American War, and held district posts at Rock Island and the Great Lakes. Considered one of the leading experts on hydraulics in the early twentieth century, he was during the same time district engineer and president of the Mississippi River Commission and later an author of a leading textbook on rivers and harbors work. He believed that when correcting the river by regulation, "the dredge becomes a necessary adjunct to the improvement" while the river adjusts its slope, and that just because dredging was successful in the lower river did not mean it would be successful in other locations. Although the debate continued into the modern era as to whether dredging or permanent improvements were of greater importance or efficiency, from this point forward, both were considered only part of the solution for maintaining a navigable channel.[68]

---

[68] *Annual Report of the Chief of Engineers, 1910-1913*; Townsend, *The Hydraulic Principles Governing River and Harbor Construction* (NY: MacMillan, 1922): 91.

Dredging operation at Cape Girardeau, Dredge Ste. Genevieve, 1935

The result of these and other improvements was what St. Louis historian James Primm called "spectacular growth" in St. Louis in the 1890s and 1900s. The St. Louis World's Fair and Exposition of 1904, celebrating the 100-year anniversary of the Louisiana Purchase, and the hit song "Meet Me in St. Louis" demonstrated the degree to which residents' pride in their city had grown. The city's population had increased to 575,000 by 1900 and 687,000 by 1910, making it the fourth largest city in the U.S. The number of businesses in the city had doubled from 1880 to 1890 to 6,148, and the value of manufactured goods rose to $229 million per year. It rose another 79 percent to $430 million per year by 1910 despite the hard-hitting Depression of 1893. St. Louis was a leader in the production of tobacco, beer, whiskey, whole sale goods, and groceries. For the latter, the development of refrigerated railroad cars was critical, and in general the growth of railroads played an increasing role in the prosperity of the city, for despite the improvements in the navigation channel, shipping had actually started to decrease.[69]

By 1913, just before the start of World War I, shipping on the Mississippi River had declined greatly over the previous decade. From 1901, when more

Dredge operations north of St. Louis, 1935

---

[69] Primm, pp. 345-353, quote on 418.

than 600,000 tons had been shipped by river to St. Louis, it had declined to 266,000 tons in 1912. Receipt of goods from the upper river had also declined precipitously, e.g., a 50 percent reduction in corn and wheat and greater than 90 percent reduction in flour and rye. Part of the reason for this decline was a series of low-water years, including 1910, which was the most severe drought since 1864. There was no June rise, and the river north of St. Louis was closed for much of the year, shutting down freight lines. At Dubuque, Iowa, people could wade across the river. "In fact, the difficulty seems to be to find a place where the river cannot be waded," *The Waterways Journal* observed. Through dredging and other works, Potter and Townsend had increased the lowest mark on the river from four to eight feet by 1913, but several freight lines were irreparably harmed, in part because of a decade lost with congressional spending reductions and overemphasis of dredging. Yet the greater reason for the decline was the lower cost of shipping goods by rail and by automobile, which were far cheaper than river navigation at that time. From all appearances, Mississippi River shipping was on the decline. What changed this was World War I, which led to the need for an even greater channel.[70]

---

[70] "Fleeting shadow of the Mississippi," *Waterways Journal* (Jul. 30, 1910): 3; *Annual Report of Chief of Engineers, 1901-1913*; Dobney, p. 73; Anfinson, pp. 101-114.

The Sinking of the *Dredge Ste. Genevieve*

Newspapers called her "beautiful." Those who worked with her said, "She got to you; she was different." "Understandably, she was the object of many love affairs," historian Cecily Jones said. The *Dredge Ste. Genevieve*, fondly called Genny by nearly everyone in the district, was a fixture in St. Louis for more than 50 years and the last of the steam-powered stern-wheel dredges.

The district contracted Dravo Corporation of Pittsburg, Pennsylvania, to build the *Ste. Genevieve* in 1932 for $413,236, along with a twin vessel, the *Grafton*. Named after the historic city 65 miles south of St. Louis, the *Ste. Genevieve* was 267 feet long, 48 feet wide, and weighed 947 tons. Two Norberg steam engines powered the oak paddle wheel. It took a crew of more than 50 personnel working three shifts to operate the dredge.

For 52 years, Genny helped to clear more than 200 miles of the Mississippi River, the lower Illinois, and on contract part of the Missouri and Ohio rivers. The dredge was a cutterhead, in which a series of blades like an egg beater broke apart the soil to allow the suction dredge or a dustpan dredge to remove sediment. At times, the cutterhead ran into debris, including cars, sunken vessels, and, on one occasion, an old dock wagon. Yet even at 52, the *Ste. Genevieve* was tough but sleek, with pristine white and orange lines.

Dredge Ste. Genevieve

After retirement of the vessel in 1984, most wanted to see her turned into a museum. The city of Davenport purchased her but later turned her over to the General Services Administration. The Marine Learning Institute of Portage des Sioux, Missouri, acquired her in 1990, but the vessel sunk near the Ohio River after a collision while being towed. After a month in dry dock for repairs, the *Ste. Genevieve* sunk again in deep water outside Cape Girardeau, Missouri, only to be sold for salvage in 1994.

Captain Geroid Lix of the *Dredge Potter*, the last master of the *Ste. Genevieve*, grieved her loss, noting that "she made a good living for a lot of families." He had started on the vessel as a deckhand and worked on her for more than 30 years. Stephen Miller, the last pilot of the dredge, said it was like watching your house destroyed by a tornado. "The one who claimed her was the one she worked on for so many years, the Mighty Mississippi," Jones concluded.[71]

---

[71] Jones, "Dredge Ste. Gen Lost to Mississippi," *Esprit* (Jul. 1996): 11-12.

6

Stair-Steps on the Upper Mississippi River

Aerial view of Melvin Price Locks and Dam

After a series of droughts and extreme low-water years from 1890 to 1910, the Upper and Middle Mississippi River no longer provided a reliable route for navigation. Corps dredging was able to carve out a four-, six-, or eight-foot channel as authorized, but only after a long season of work following annual high waters that placed new sediment and changed the channel. For long stretches of the year, numerous locations in the channel were lower than this, and some sandbars required constant attention to keep the channel open. Even then, barges often had to travel half-full to navigate all portions of the river. Railroads, which faced no such constraints, were much more reliable and saw incredible growth during the same period. The time to market was much faster for agricultural products using railroads instead of barges from the Midwest to either the East or West coasts. Completion of the Panama Canal in 1914 cut even deeper into Mississippi barge traffic since it was suddenly faster and cheaper to ship goods directly from one coast to the other via the canal than it had been to use a combination of river and trains. During World War I, however, with troop supplies, military construction, and food provision for Europe, traffic began to increase once more, but it faced constant problems with the river depth. Navigation boosters argued that if only the channel was deep enough to allow newer barges to move fully loaded, traffic (and profits) would be restored to their former levels. The only way this was possible was to make the river itself into a canal with locks and dams to ensure there was enough water in the channel to pass all traffic.

The Federal Barge Line and a Nine-Foot Channel

The navigation industry in St. Louis finally saw signs of improvement during World War I after decades of decline, although it did not return to previous levels of commerce. With the increased demand for food, both to supply troops and a war-torn Europe, the amount of agricultural products shipped on the Mississippi was once again on the rise. The lumber industry on the Upper Mississippi continued to decline with the deforestation of the Northwest, but new industries grew up, including Muscatine buttons made from mussel shells, introduced in the late nineteenth century. By 1914, there were 114 button factories along the upper river. Commerce through St. Louis increased from

Steamer Mississippi, 1935

$11 million to $18 million by 1918. At the same time, the railroad industry, which grew to dominate inland navigation, was showing signs of strain. The "bridge arbitrary," a tax on railroads using the Eads Bridge, increased shipping costs by a third, leading to widespread criticism of the St. Louis nouveaux rich, known as the Big Cinch, whom author Kate Chopin once described as "short, round, blond, and bald." A free bridge movement resulted in construction of a city bridge by 1917, but a city toll kept the cost high for more than a decade. Several times in the early twentieth century, including 1907-1908, 1916-1918, and 1921, railroad car shortages prevented prompt delivery of goods. Rates increased as a result, but not until 1925 did the Federal Trade Commission standardize on these higher prices. Low-cost bulk agricultural products in particular suffered from high shipping rates. With high volumes keeping prices low, high shipping rates kept farmer profit margins thin, whether they used higher cost railroads or shipped less per load on barges. The adoption after 1900 of diesel engines and screw propellers on barges reduced costs, as did the practice of driving lines of six or eight barges per tug, but these could not operate in very shallow water or tight bends.[72]

With the unreliability and cost of transportation injuring the war effort, in 1917, President Woodrow Wilson created the Railroad Administration to improve the efficiency of interstate transportation, primarily railroads but also waterways and marine commerce. In 1918, Congress created a federal barge line under the administration to help relieve overburdened railroads and provided $8 million to purchase or lease vessels. The line ran from St. Louis to New Orleans and along the Warrior River. By the end of the year, the line had purchased or leased three tugs and 19 barges. It proved so successful, Congress continued the line after the war, placing its 25 tows and 69 barges in the Department of Commerce in 1920 and in the Department of War under the Inland Waterway Commission in 1924. The line had great impact on commerce. Between 1919 and 1921, river commerce in St. Louis more than doubled to $47.4 million. In 1924, Congress authorized the barge line to operate on the upper river, but it was not until the Twin Cities Real Estate Board and other navigation boosters convinced the commission in 1926 to lease equipment from the new Upper Mississippi Barge Line Company that the line started regular service north of St. Louis. Yet, while the extension of the line promised to increase navigation and profits, the limited channel depth, which still had not

---

[72] *Annual Report of the Chief of Engineers, 1914-1918*; Primm, pp. 422-425, Chopin quote on p. 424; Anfinson, pp. 175-195; Dobney, p. 73.

reached the authorized six feet in the miles south of Minneapolis, continued to prevent the full use of barges in the upper river. The response, as it had been the previous half-century, was to increase the authorized channel depth, this time to nine feet.[73]

The Civil War had demonstrated the need for consistent depths to allow barges to navigate the river above the Illinois, and river boosters had lobbied Congress to establish a minimum depth of four feet in 1866. This spurred the Corps to create its first district offices at St. Paul, Minnesota, and Rock Island, Illinois, to manage the resulting increase in work. As traffic increased over the following decade, promoters lobbied for a deeper channel. The Granger movement – a series of agricultural improvement organizations established after the Civil War – and Chambers of Commerce from major cities led the effort to increase the channel depth. In the 1878 Rivers and Harbors Act, Congress established a 4.5-foot channel. Because of the greater ease in maintaining a channel in the middle river, in 1881 the Corps established a six-foot channel north of St. Louis to the Missouri River and an eight-foot channel south to the Ohio. South of Cairo, Illinois, the Rivers and Harbors Act of 1896 established a nine-foot channel to the Gulf of Mexico, but this had not been possible north of St. Louis. Nevertheless, by 1900, the Upper Mississippi River Improvement Association and shipping companies were pushing for a six-foot channel north of the Missouri and found widespread support from the Corps, particularly Col. Curtis M. Townsend, then serving as the Rock Island District Engineer. Congress authorized the six-foot channel in the 1907 Rivers and Harbors Act, but even at that time, a six-foot depth was too shallow for most barges. In 1907, Congress requested that the Corps investigate the possibility of a 14-foot channel from Chicago to the Gulf of Mexico. A board headed by Col. William H. Bixby found in 1909 that, while south of St. Louis this was possible using dredging and contraction, it did not recommend it because the existing depth was sufficient for navigation. It did, however, recommend a nine-foot channel north of St. Louis.[74]

Calls for a nine-foot channel continued to increase in the years that followed, particularly after 1925. The problem was that there were places where

---

[73] U.S. Cong., "United States Railroad Administration," S.D. 275 (65th Cong., 2nd Sess.): 1-11; "Inland Water Transportation: Hearings on the subject of Inland Water Transportation," Dec. 13, 1918 (65th Cong., 1st Sess.): 1-5; *Annual Report of the Chief of Engineers, 1919-1921*; Anfinson, pp. 197-219; Dobney, p. 73.
[74] Anfinson, pp. 53-144; William P. O'Brien et al, *Gateways to Commerce: The U.S. Army Corps of Engineers' 9-Foot Channel Project on the Upper Mississippi River* (Denver: NPS, 1992): 17-20; U.S. Cong., *Report by a Special Board of Engineers on Survey of Mississippi River from St. Louis, Mo., to its Mouth*, H.D. 50 (61st Cong., 1st Sess.): 1-26; Dobney, pp. 93-94.

it was difficult to maintain even the authorized six-foot channel using traditional dredging and contraction. In the St. Louis District, decreases in funding because of the war had impacted the ability of engineers to maintain the channel, and the river had widened considerably since 1914 as a result. Maj. DeWitt C. Jones, who took over as district engineer on June 1, 1920, after several years of service at West Point and the Engineer School, would write after his first year, "Because of the small and insufficient appropriations for this district in recent years the regulation works have deteriorated rapidly, many sections having been entirely destroyed, and their repair and restoration is deemed urgent." As funding increased over the next several years under Jones and Maj. Lunsford E. Oliver, who served from 1922 to 1924, they were able to make many repairs, but there were still problem areas north of St. Louis. Particularly in the 30 miles south of St. Paul, Minnesota, the Corps was unable to achieve a six-foot depth despite dozens of wing dams and continuous dredging. This led the Corps to install a lock and dam complex at Hastings, Minnesota, from 1928 to 1930. In the Rivers and Harbors Act of 1927, Congress authorized a nine-foot channel from St. Louis to the Ohio River. War hero and former Alaska Engineer Commission member Maj. John C. Gotwals, who became district engineer on May 5, 1924, would note that this was the minimum operational depths for many barges, making the nine foot channel critical for navigation. Yet, some in the Corps doubted if the amount of commerce in the upper river justified a deeper project. In contrast with St. Louis, the upper river saw little to no recovery from the decline of navigation, and Corps leaders such as Chief of Engineers Maj. Gen. Harry Taylor did not believe that commerce would increase with a deeper channel.[75]

The Corps was not alone in its opposition to the project. By 1925, there was sizable opposition from conservationists, who reached their zenith of influence the previous decade. Conservationism evolved initially as a response to the Desert Land Act of 1888 that sought to "conserve" water for multiple uses. "Conservation," historian Samuel P. Hays wrote, " was a scientific movement," in which scientists and government administrators sought to maximize use of natural resources, by efficiency improvements, dual-use facilities, and protection of resources from overuse. As such, it was primarily a top-down movement – only later did it include a popular element. Restoration of wilderness was important to the movement, but mainly in support of sportsmen

---

[75] Jones quote in *Annual Report of the Chief of Engineers, 1921*, p. 1201.

or commercial fisheries or furrier industries. Conservationists had been concerned about the effect of Mississippi River improvements for some time. Although the impact of human activities was slight at first, snagging, bank clearing, dredging, contraction, and finally damming the river had changed its natural regimens. Denuding forestlands near the river had increased soil erosion and bank caving, polluting the river. Dredging had reduced mussel crops or fish spawning grounds in some locations. Removal of sandbars or shallows and reclamation of wetlands had reduced the size of traditional hunting and fishing grounds. Most had no objection to navigation, but wanted to see it balanced with other activities, and they were just as critical of industries that polluted the river or fished species to near extinction. By the late nineteenth century, lumber mills dumped 1.6 million feet of sawdust into the river each year, and many cities dumped garbage and sewage directly into open water, garnering the grave concern of conservationists.[76]

Over several years, conservationists had worked to create government oversight and pass laws to manage the environment. In 1871, Congress created a Commission of Fish and Fisheries, which reorganized as the Bureau of Fisheries in 1903, to promote the fisheries industry. It would eventually merge with the Bureau of Biological Survey to create the Fish and Wildlife Service in

Dipper dredge St. Paul removing trailer dike near Lock and Dam No. 26

---

[76] Samuel P. Hays, *Conservation and the Gospel of Efficiency: The Progressive Conservation Movement, 1890-1920* (Cambridge, Mass.: Harvard UP, 1959): 2.

1940. By 1889, it had developed fish rescue and propagation programs on the Mississippi River designed to relocate fish from endangered areas to side pools and tributaries where spawning could take place. A series of biological stations established along the upper river from 1908 to 1922 rescued more than 100 million fish. In the 1890 and 1899 Rivers and Harbors Acts, Congress first limited and then established a permitting program for dumping or altering navigable waters to reign in pollution. There were several efforts to create a national park or refuge to place parts of the river outside of navigational improvements. Iowa, for example, called for a national park in 1908 that resulted in a positive report in 1917. Finally, in 1924, after several years of lobbying by the conservationist organization the Izaac Walton League, Congress agreed to create a wildlife refuge at the Winesheik Bottoms with the approbation of the Corps, the first such refuge on the Mississippi, which eventually expanded to more than 233,000 acres.[77]

Slack-Water Dams

All of these concerns came to a head when Congress requested a study of using slack water dams to create a nine-foot channel, first from St. Paul, Minnesota, to Lake Pepin in 1925, then to the Missouri River in 1927. The concept of slack water dams had been around for a century, and the Corps had successfully applied the method on the Ohio River. Essentially, dams built every few miles created pools or slack water that deepened the channel, while locks allowed access to the higher-elevation pools like climbing steps. After design and construction of the first dams by Col. William E. Merrill from 1874 to 1885, the system on the Ohio River grew to include 51 dams. These were movable dams – dams that included gates or wickets that could open during high water to allow passage of vessels or increased flow – and included the first concrete dam in the U.S. However, there had been no attempt to build a similar system on a river the size of the Mississippi. In 1894, the Corps started construction of a small dam between St. Paul and Minneapolis, which it replaced by 1917 with a higher dam and hydroelectric plant after passage of the six-foot channel in 1907, but these did not impede navigation because they were so close to the headwaters. From 1903 to 1914, after receiving the approval of the Corps and Congress, the Keokuk and Hamilton Water Power Company built a dam near

---

[77] Anfinson, pp. 145-173; Fremling, pp. 155-156, 218-219, 230; Hays, pp. 1-143.

the Des Moines Rapids to generate power for the two Iowan towns. It was the first non-navigable dam below the Twin Cities, but since fewer and fewer vessels tried to pass through the rapids each year and instead used a previously constructed bypass canal and lock, the reviewing engineer did not believe it was an issue. Although the Corps built locks at Moline and a bypass canal at Le Claire, these allowed open water navigation if needed and thus came under less criticism by conservationists than the Keokuk Dam. The Corps did not consider another lock and dam until construction of the Hastings Dam in 1928. There was, nevertheless, precedent for non-navigable dams on the Mississippi.[78]

The Corps initially assigned Maj. Charles L. Hall of the Rock Island District to perform the survey Congress requested, but surprisingly, in 1928, he came out against the dams, ostensibly because they were not economically justified, but also because he believed them environmentally harmful. At first, Chief of Engineers Maj. Gen. Edgar Jadwin supported Hall against what he saw as special interests, but with pressure mounting from navigation boosters and the threat looming of congressional hearings, he requested a restudy. After holding private and public meetings into early 1928, Hall declared his findings unchanged on February 27, 1929. Boosters and towns in favor of the plan conducted press campaigns against Hall and the Corps, and the Mississippi Valley Association convinced the Board of Engineers for Rivers and Harbors in April that Hall had overestimated the costs because he had not completed a detailed survey as directed. In the end, the Corps assigned a special board to review the project, including Mississippi River Commission president Brig. Gen. Thomas H. Jackson, Louisville District Engineer Lt. Col. George R. Spalding, St. Paul District Engineer Lt. Col. Wildurr Willing, Hall, and Gotwals. The Corps relieved Hall from duty on the board on October 14 because he was campaigning against the project. With insufficient time to complete the survey, the board submitted an interim report on December 16, 1929, which the Secretary of the War forwarded to Congress on February 15, 1930. The special board recommended a two-phased approach building six dams and improving the three existing dams north of the Wyoming River, followed by construction of 11 other dams north of the Illinois River. The Board of Engineers for Rivers and Harbors, however, was "unable to determine upon a satisfactory plan"

---

[78] O'Brien et al., pp. 35-44; Anfinson, *River We Have Wrought*, pp. 197-222; Leland R. Jonson, *The Ohio River Division, U.S. Army Corps of Engineers: The History of a Central Command* (Cincinnati: ORD, 1992): 26-30; Anfinson, "The Secret History of the Mississippi's Earliest Locks and Dams," *Minnesota History* (Summer 1995): 254-267.

because of the incomplete surveys and tentative nature of the special board's recommendations.[79]

Conservationists, meanwhile, continued to lobby against the new rivers and harbors bill based on the plan, as did the railroads. Both the Bureau of Fisheries and Bureau of Biological Survey reviewed the bill and feared the dams would either create pools of insufficient depth below the dams or instable pools above that were not conducive to wildlife. Although they thought the dams might prove beneficial after several years of adjustment, they wanted input on the design. After meeting with the organizations on May 9, 1930, the Corps agreed to conduct a joint study of Cooper Lake below Keokuk Dam to determine the impact of dams on wildlife in return for approval of the plan. With the support of these organizations, despite continued opposition from the Izaak Walton League and other local conservationists, Congress authorized the dam projects in the Rivers and Harbors Act of 1930. The study of Cooper Lake later that year found that the dam was beneficial as long as water levels were consistent and did not isolate wildlife in backchannels and that pollution would impact only the community dumping it, not the entire chain of pools. As a result, the Corps agreed to maintain consistent water levels after the dams were in place. The railroads also lobbied against the project, and in 1931 sued to stop construction of Lock and Dam No. 4 based on changes in the plan made after the 1930 report. Although the injunction approved by the district judge was eventually overturned, Congress passed a resolution authorizing future changes in the interim plan in 1932. With these issues resolved, the Corps proceeded with construction of the project.[80]

To handle work on the new dams, the Corps reorganized its division structure in 1929, establishing an Upper Mississippi Valley Division to which St. Louis District transferred. It would remain in this division until abolished in 1954. Also in 1929, the Corps extended the district boundary from the Missouri to the Illinois River and in 1933 to Clarksville, Illinois, making district responsible for more than 250 miles of river, including areas covered by the dam project. The division completed site surveys, started designs, held public meetings in 1930, and on December 9, 1931, released the final report on the dams. The system would include 26 locks and dams, incorporating existing structures but

---

[79] Anfinson, *River We Have Wrought*, pp. 222-237; O'Brien et al., 27-32; U.S. Cong., *Mississippi River between Mouth of Missouri River and Minneapolis, Minnesota (Interim Report)*, H.D. 290 (71st Cong., 2nd Sess.): 1-7.
[80] Anfinson, *River We Have Wrought*, pp. 239-269; Dobney, pp. 94-95.

also 24 new structures below Hastings that would essentially turn the upper river into a navigation canal. Three of these dams would be inside the enlarged St. Louis District: Nos. 24, 25, and 26. The 1931 report divided these works into four categories: A. those dams critical for commerce; B. those necessary to achieve at least a six-foot channel; C. those dams critical for a nine-foot channel; and D. those needed to achieve the nine-foot channel in areas that could potentially be maintained through heavy dredging. All of the dams in St. Louis District were the lowest priority. By 1931, design of the first dams was complete and construction started, with a third of the dams completed by 1934. In St. Louis, design of the first dam started in 1933. Maj. William A. Snow established a Lock and Dam Section, which included one officer, four engineers, two draftsmen, and a clerk. An experienced combat engineer with degrees from West Point and MIT, Snow understood the need for a robust organization to manage large construction projects. Capt. William A. Wanamaker headed the section, and Lawrence B. Feagin served as senior engineer. After initial design by division engineers William A. McAlpine and Frederick Griffin, Feagin was responsible for engineering on all three dams in the district. Feagin, who later received a commission as a colonel and served as district engineer during World War II, conducted tests on the behavior of piles under changing and static loads that led to a change in design with the adoption of concrete struts. Like the Ohio River locks and dams, the dams were all movable. Most early designs used roller gates – large metal tubes that could be lowered or raised – to control water flow, but by 1933 designs were incorporating lower-cost tainter gates, large wedge-shaped gates, to some degree. Lock and Dam No. 25 and 26 used a combination of roller and tainter gates; Lock and Dam No. 24 used exclusively tainter gates. Once design was complete under Snow, Maj. Barley M. Harloe (1933-1935) oversaw early construction, which Maj. Paul S. Reinecke (1935-1940) completed.[81]

Dam 25 construction, 1938

---

[81] U.S. Cong., *Survey of Mississippi River between Missouri River and Minneapolis*, H.D. 137, Pt. 1 (72nd Cong., 1st Sess.): 1-10; *Annual Report of the Chief of Engineers, 1929-1933*; Anfinson, *River We Have Wrought*, pp. 255-256; O'Brien et al., pp. 47-51, 63-97, 190; "William Arthur Snow," *ASCE Annual Report* (Jun. 10, 1941): 333-341; Dobney, pp. 93-95.

Although with 1930 appropriations and other funds the Corps had more than $13.8 million available to start the project, this barely covered surveys, design, and purchase of easements on the first three dams. Fortunately, the projects came at the advent of the New Deal programs initiated by President Franklin D. Roosevelt in response to the Great Depression. This included the Emergency Relief and Construction Act of 1932, the National Industrial Recovery Act of 1933, which established the Public Works Administration (PWA) and included $3.3 billion in public works, and the Emergency Relief Appropriations Act of 1935, which established the Works Progress Administration (WPA). The projects received $7.2 million in 1932, $71 million in PWA funds in 1933, and $25 million in 1935, $27 million in 1936, and $28.6 million in 1937 from WPA funds for a total funding of $170 million. As the earliest dam built in the district, Lock and Dam No. 26 received mostly PWA funds, while Nos. 25 and 24 received mostly Emergency Relief Appropriations Act or WPA funds. These programs ensured the project was flush with money; work started within a month of Snow receiving PWA funds in September 1933. Yet because these programs were designed to provide maximum employment rather than efficiency, the projects faced problems with untrained workers and hiring delays, unions expressed concerns about worker safety, and there were inevitably conflicts with local program administrators. Dealing with these and similar issues within the tight schedules demanded by the projects required decentralization of real estate and contracting functions to local offices. In one case, when Alton WPA chairman John D. McAdams wrote in the *Alton Evening Telegraph* that the Corps should reconsider objections to a recreation area for the Alton Dam, Reinecke publically agreed, but observed privately to McAdams,

> *A W.P.A man is said to be a man who knows a great deal about very little and who goes along knowing more and more about less and less until finally he knows practically everything about nothing.... An engineer starts out knowing practically everything about everything, but ends up knowing nothing about anything, due to his association with editors and W.P.A men.*[82]

It was a humorous reminder of the bureaucratic chaos that resulted from conflicts among these "alphabet soup" agencies at multiple levels.

---

[82] Anfinson, *River We Have Wrought*, pp.269-274; O'Brien et al., pp. 55-62; Dobney, pp. 89-93, Reinecke quote on p. 97; on the PWA and WPA, see, e.g., William E. Leuchtenburg, *Franklin D. Roosevelt and the New Deal, 1932-1940* (NY: Harper and Row, 1963): 55-58, 124-130.

Construction of the Dams

The first lock and dam built in St. Louis District was Lock and Dam No. 26 at Alton, Illinois, 23 miles above St. Louis. Originally intended for Grafton, 15 miles upriver, the Corps changed the location, at least in part, because of the limited space for equipment storage in Grafton versus Alton. McAlpine completed design of the dam in 1934, which included two locks, one 110 by 600 feet, the other 110 by 350 feet. The 1,724-foot dam included three roller gates and 30 tainter gates. The Corps awarded the construction contract for the locks to Griffiths and Son for $3.2 million, and the company started construction on the coffer dams in February 1934. As with all of the locks and dams, the contractor

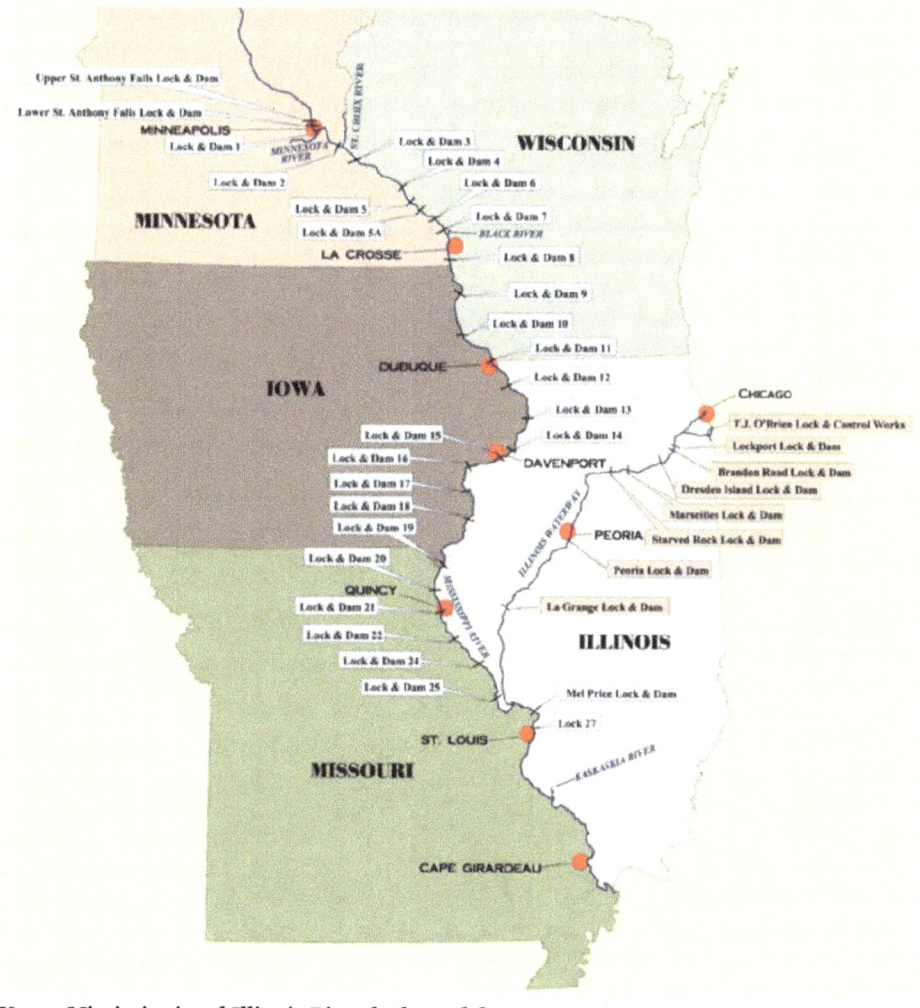

Upper Mississippi and Illinois River locks and dams

first built a coffer dam to keep water out of the construction area, and construction proceeded on the lock first to leave the river open for navigation until its completion. Griffiths started draining the area by May and started work on driving piling and setting foundations in June. The contract ran consistently behind schedule, primarily because of the contractor's use of a conveyor belt to deliver concrete, which, although labor-saving, was much slower than manual transportation of the concrete. Because of this, erection of steel work did not start until February 1935. Work was 65 percent complete in June 1935, and the company completed the main lock in September 1935. Griffiths started construction on the auxiliary lock in October, but had to stop construction in mid-December because of ice. As a result of continued frozen weather, the coffer dam broke on February 29, 1936. When the contractor refused to complete the lock because of its losses, the Corps terminated the contract in April 1936. The Corps had to hire a separate contractor to remove the remains of the coffer dam and complete the lock. At the same time, it awarded a $4.9 million contract to Engineering Construction Company for the dam. The contractor installed the three coffer dam sections, started draining the enclosed area by August 1935,

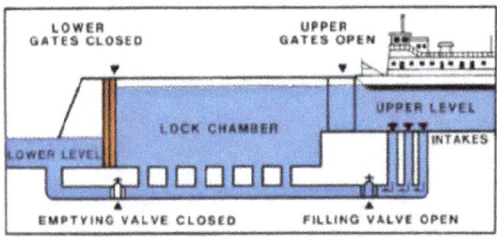

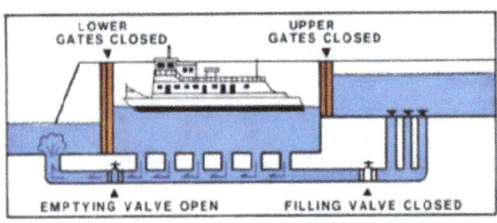

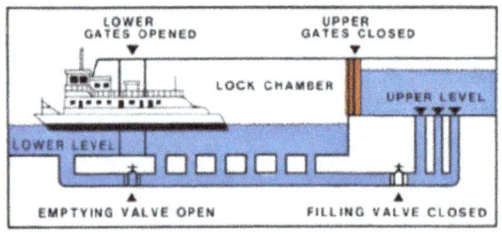

and was laying concrete by October using cranes, pumps, and barges. The company completed the first section in February 1936, and the gate fabricator – American Bridge Company – started installing the gates by June. Work was 50 percent complete by June 1936. Work on the third section was complete in April 1937. All that remained on the two structures was connection of utilities, completed in 1938, and the addition of a recreation area abutting the reservoir, completed in 1940. The total cost of the dam was $13.1 million.[83]

---

[83] U.S. Cong., *Report of the Chief of Engineers, 1934-1940*; O'Brien et al., pp. 105-125, 197; "Concrete Report: First Coffer Dam, Dam No. 26" (St. Louis: St. Louis District [MVS], 1936): 1-7; Dobney, pp. 95-99.

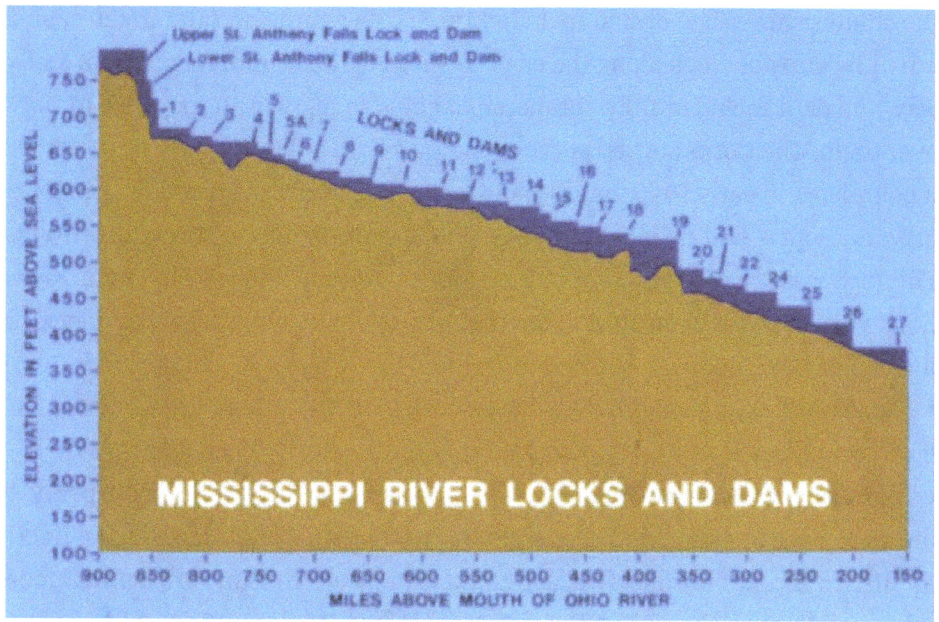
Locks and Dams, 9-foot Channel project

Construction on the other two locks and dams in St. Louis District, designed by Griffin, started after 1935. The Corps next built Lock and Dam No. 25 at Winfield, Missouri, near Bradley Island, 241 miles above the Ohio. It included a 1,296-foot dam to the island and a 2,566-foot earthen dike from the island to

Towboat Crimson Duke towing 42 barges, 1986

the Illinois shore. The design included three roller gates, 14 tainter gates, and a 110- by 600-foot lock along the eastern shore of the island. Instead of a spillway, the dam included fully submersible gates to allow water and ice to flow over them. The Corps started surveys and purchase of land in July 1935, which it completed in early 1936, but the contractor – United Construction Company of Minnesota – had proceeded to construction of the lock at the end of 1935. The lock was 35 percent complete by June 1936 and finished by June 1937. Construction of the dam started on May 21, 1937, was 66 percent complete by the end of 1938, and was finished in 1939.

Lock and Dam 24, although lower cost than the other three, was much more complicated in design. Located 93.5 miles above St. Louis near Clarksville, Missouri, the dam was difficult to design because of the flood plain – the river is ordinarily 1,650-feet wide but expands to 3,800 feet during flood events. To account for this, Griffin designed a 1,340-foot dam with a 2,720-foot submersible dike. Coming at the apex of tainter gate design, No. 24 included 15 tainter gates, making the design much lower cost. It also is the only of the three locks built on gravel instead of piling. This was due to the shale foundation, which prevented driving piling. The contractor, Central Engineering Company of Iowa, started construction in 1936. The lock was 65 percent complete by June 1937 and finished by 1938. Construction on the dam started February 26, 1938, was seven percent complete by June 1938, 62 percent by June 1939, and finished by 1940. Thus, original construction on all of the dams was complete by American entry into World War II.[84]

There were some minor modifications to all of the dams, such as enhancement of the dam pools for use as recreation areas. At the insistence of local residents, when construction of Lock and Dam No. 26 was completed, the Corps added a recreation area with a landscaped scenic drive. It had also added a picnic area near Lock and Dam No. 25. By the 1960s, in line with Corps efforts to include recreation areas in its reservoirs, the district initiated construction of recreation and public access areas at all three dam pools. In 1961, the Corps approved district designs for a boat ramp, parking lot, and comfort station complete with running water and sewage at Alton (No. 26). In 1963, the Corps approved designs for boat ramps, parking lots, comfort stations, and additional picnic areas at Winfield and Norton Woods, Missouri (No. 25), and

---

[84] U.S. Cong., *Report of the Chief of Engineers, 1934-1940*; Anfinson, *River We Have Wrought*, p. 274; O'Brien et al., pp. 192-195; Dobney, pp. 99-101.

Model of Lock and Dam 25

in 1968 approved designs for a boat launch, parking area, comfort station, and reforestation near Clarksville, Illinois (No. 24).[85]

There were also some major modifications to the dam system near the Chain of Rocks. Located 190 miles above the Ohio River, the Chain of Rocks is a seven-mile stretch of rapids caused by a series of rock ledges that extend at times almost the width of the river. After completion of the other 26 dams, the Chain of Rocks was the only remaining area on the river in which navigation was often below nine feet and sometimes as shallow as 5.5 feet. Because of the rapids, which moved up to 12 feet per second, it was extremely hazardous to navigate. There had been discussion of building a bypass canal as early as 1903, but Congress did not request a plan until 1938, which the Corps submitted in December the same year. In it, the Division Engineer Lt. Col. Malcolm Elliott proposed several plans, including a bypass canal and a lock and dam on the river. Unfortunately, although Congress approved the plan, President Roosevelt vetoed the rivers and harbors bill because of the war. He finally approved it when resubmitted in 1945 at the war's end. The design was for an 8.4-mile, 550-foot wide, 32-foot deep canal following Cabaret Chute bypassing the worst of the rocks, the north end just south of the Missouri River and the south end

---

[85] USACE, *Alton Navigation Pool, Mississippi and Illinois Rivers*, DM 2Cc1 (St. Louis: MVS, 1962): 1-12; *Winfield Navigation Pool, Lock and Dam No. 25, Mississippi River*, DM 2Cc1 (St. Louis: MVS, 1963): 1-16; *Clarksville Navigation Pool, Lock and Dam No. 24, Mississippi River*, DM 2 (St. Louis: MVS, 1967): 1-14.

Old Lock and Dam 26

Lock and Dam 26 construction, 1935

Lock and Dam 26 construction, 1938

near Granite City, Illinois. It included two locks – 110 by 1,200 feet and 110 by 600 feet – about a mile above the lower terminus, with six control towers, the most of any lock in the system. The main lock was the first 1,200-foot lock in the system. The use of double vertical-lift gates on the north end instead of miter gates allowed flow of ice down the canal during cold weather. The contract, issued to River Construction Corporation, started in 1947 under the oversight of Col. Rudolph E. Smyser, Jr. Most of the early work consisted of moving roads and utilities, which continued through 1950. Particularly difficult was movement of Highway 66, which required construction of a 17-span bridge over the canal. The contractor started work on the locks on July 1, 1947. In November 1948, work started on the canal using dredges and placement of

Col. Rudolph E. Smyser   *Col. Beverly C. Snow*   *Col. Fred E. Ressegieu*

protective levees along the canal. Included in the design was a 6,750-foot harbor facility near the southern end. The canal opened to traffic in February 1953.[86]

Although the original Chain of Rocks design considered a small wicket dam, Congress did not authorize it, and the district did not construct it. By 1955, however, the Corps recognized that increases in slope due to scouring below the Alton Dam were inhibiting navigation. In one 98-day period from 1955 to 1956, the depth was too shallow for the dam to operate. In response to request for a study, the district conducted public hearings and submitted a preliminary report to Congress in 1957. St. Louis District Engineer Col. George C. White recommended either altering the Alton Dam or building a low-water dam at the Chain of Rocks. Authorized in the Rivers and Harbors Act of 1958, the dam was a 10.5-foot high, 3,240-foot long rock dam 950 feet south of the Chain of Rocks Bridge with a 700-foot spillway to allow ice to flow

Col. George E. White, Jr.

Col. Charles B. Schweizer

downstream. This was the first dam completely cutting off the river with no lock on the river itself. Similar to a design used above Niagara Falls, the dam

---

[86] U.S. Cong., *Mississippi River between Ohio River and Mouth of Missouri River*, H.D. 231 (76th Cong., 1st Sess.): 1-47; *Annual Reports of the Chief of Engineers, 1947-1953*; *Mississippi River – Chain of Rocks Project* (St. Louis: MVS, 1947): 1-7; O'Brien et al., pp. 127-129, 201; Dobney, pp. 113-117; Col. Clark Kittrell, "Navigation Improvement at Chain of Rocks," *TME* (Dec. 1948): 556-557; Col. F.E. Ressegieu, "The Chain of Rocks Canal," *TME* (Mar.-Apr. 1953): 128-130.

used alternating zones of small and intermediate stones instead of large rock as originally contemplated. The contractor started construction of the dam in February 1959 under the leadership of Col. Charles B. Schweizer without coffer dams using a cableway to place stones directly onto the rock foundation in a specific order to prevent water from disturbing them. This made the cost of the dam less than half of other designs contemplated. Revetment on the east bank prevented erosion where the dam did not sit on rock. Construction was practically complete in 1963, with some additional work and improvements to the lock stretching into 1964.[87]

A final change occurred in the dam system in 1990 – the replacement of Lock and Dam No. 26 with the Melvin Price Locks and Dam (See Section V.). At the time the first of the locks in St. Louis District came online, it passed 1.4 million tons of traffic. By 1967, it was passing more than 40 million. The 600-foot lock as well as its alignment with the channel greatly constrained traffic, and there were often long delays in locking through to the upper river. Given the amount of traffic, year-round versus seasonal use, and its key position as gateway to the Upper Mississippi and the Illinois River, the Corps considered this a national

View south from Chain of Rocks canal

---

[87] U.S. Cong., *Mississippi River between St. Louis, Mo., and Lock and Dam No. 26*, S.D. 7 (85th Cong., 1st Sess.): 1-17; *Annual Reports of the Chief of Engineers, 1947-1964*; *Mississippi Low Water Dam between St. Louis, Mo., and Lock and Dam No. 26*, GDM 2 (St. Louis: MVS, 1958) 1-30; O'Brien et al., pp. 127-129, 201; Dobney, pp. 113-117.

issue. There were also additional problems with the foundation; insufficient piling had allowed greater movement in the foundation – up to ten inches – that caused cracks in the auxiliary lock, causing a spike in maintenance costs. The numerous attempts to repair the facility in the 1950s were impermanent, buying only another estimated 10 years of life. As the situation continued to

Tow leaving Chain of Rocks canal

Chain of Rocks

deteriorate, in 1968, the district conducted a study of replacing the lock and recommended a plan of building another dam with two larger locks slightly downstream from the original. It would, however, take another two decades for the project to be authorized and constructed, in part due to opposition from environmental groups and the long planning time required by the National Environmental Policy Act, which required coordination with dozens of agencies and groups. It was, nevertheless, constructed and the old dam decommissioned and removed in 1990. Despite opposition, the nation would continue to approve using the slack water dam system to maintain navigable depths, although somewhat modified to meet the new environmental imperative.[88]

Before World War I, navigation on the Mississippi River had declined to just over 250,000 tons being shipped to St. Louis. At that time and as late as 1925, with the growth in railroads and trucking, Corps leaders believed that the Upper Mississippi River in particular would no longer be used for commercial navigation. A combination of improvements in barges, high railroad fares, and the development of a federal barge line helped improve navigation. The line would continue to operate until after World War II, with continued increases in tonnage. However, it was the nine-foot channel, achieved through a series of locks and dams north of St. Louis, that truly restored navigation to earlier levels and eventually surpassed them. In 1938, more than a million tons shipped through the completed Lock and Dam No. 26. By 1956, tonnage shipped through the lock exceeded 15 million tons and was anticipated to top 26 million by 1963. The system as a whole was passing more than 2.6 million

---

[88] USACE, *Report on Replacement, Lock and Dam No. 26, Mississippi River, Alton, Illinois* (St. Louis: MVS, 1968); "Locks and Dam No. 26, Mississippi River – Alton, Illinois," report on failure (St. Louis: MVS, [1977]); O'Brien et al., pp. 130-132, 199.

tons by 1940, which increased to 27 million tons by 1960 and 46 million tons by 1970. There can be no doubt that the nine-foot channel had vastly increased waterborne commerce, as navigation boosters had predicted, but it also had many environmental impacts, most of which were unanticipated. Unlike the claims of the Izaak Walton League and other conservationists, wildlife initially teemed in the new pools created by the dams. Yet, pollution from fertilizers has become a problem, some migrating species of fish were cut off from spawning waters, and the lack of sediment in the river created complex problems, such as a decline in delta creation in Louisiana. Most of these issues were complex and had multiple causes. They would, nevertheless, become a rallying cry for the environmental politics that embraced the nation after 1970.[89]

---

[89] "Merchant Marine of the Middle West," *Literary Digest* 124 (Jul. 3, 1937): 36-38; *Mississippi River between St. Louis, Mo., and Lock and Dam No. 26*, pp. 6-7; Anfinson, *River We Have Wrought*, pp. 276-286.

Architecture of the Mississippi River Locks and Dams

The locks and dams constructed on the Upper Mississippi River contained many new technologies, which reflected the latest engineering. The use of tainter gates instead of traditional roller gates after 1936, the transition from submersible to non-submersible and open-frame to solid gates, the improvements to miter gates on locks, and the extensive testing of concrete, piling, and other structures all demonstrate the evolution of technology. However, as with all engineering projects, the locks and dams built as part of the nine-foot project also reflected the evolving architectural tastes of the designers and of the times.

William McAlpine and Lenvik Ylvisaker designed all of the locks and dams prior to 1934, most of which the Corps built before 1936. These designs were mostly utilitarian with neoclassical influences. They typically included large industrial windows, arched or alcoved window sills, buttress detailing, and hipped roofs. Lockmaster houses were traditional colonial two-story homes. As O'Brien et al. note, "In all cases, simplicity was the hallmark of design."

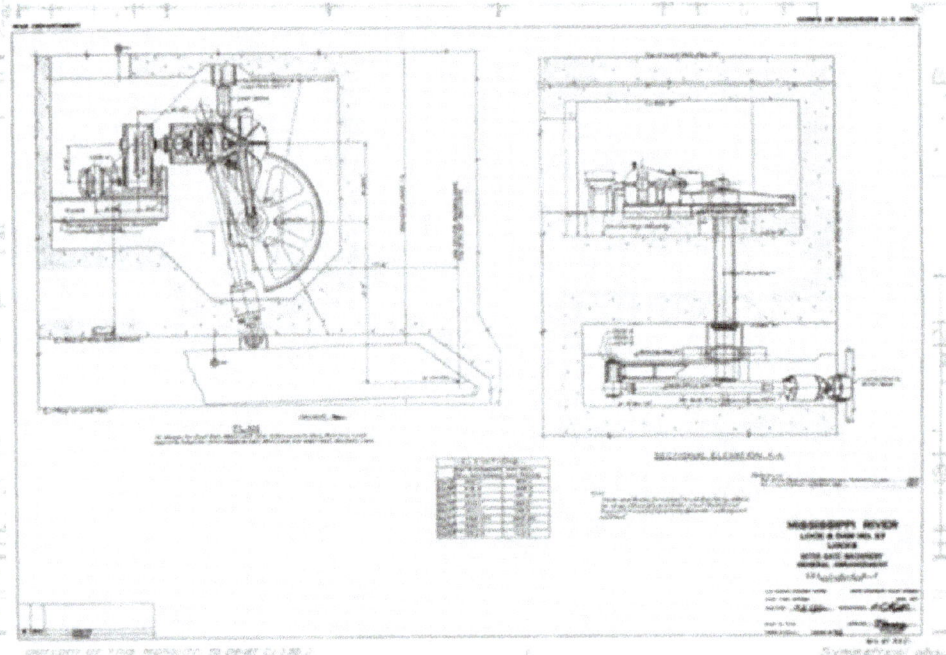

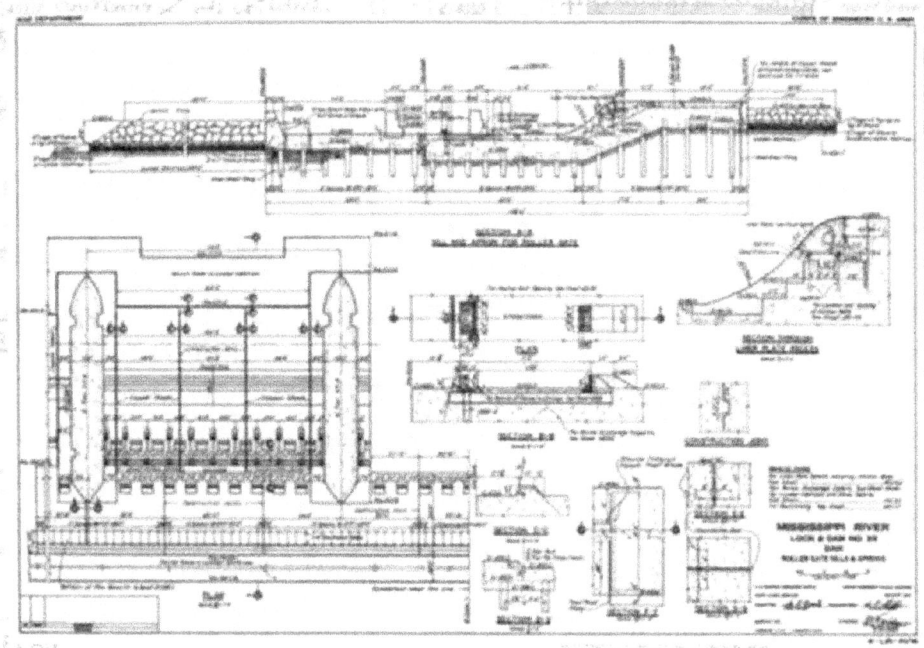

After 1934, Edwin Abbot took over design of the dams, constructed after 1936. By this time, the influence of the Modern Art style became prominent. The result was unbroken planes and surfaces, flat roofs, slits instead of windows, inset or gear-like gate structures, curved lines, and sweeping arches. Particularly influential were the international designs and technology presented at the 1933 Century of Progress Exposition in Chicago. There were many parallels in U.S. designs to German roller gates on the Rhine River. "The Depression-era 'message of the modern' had not been lost on America's engineers."

In St. Louis District, while McAlpine started the design of Lock and Dam No. 26, it was Frederick Griffin who completed that design and the designs for Locks and Dams Nos. 24, 25, and 27 after initial design by the Upper Mississippi Valley Division. Thus, one can see more utilitarian block designs in Lock and Dam No. 26, such as the central control station, yet also more gentle curves on the tainter gate assemblies and roller gate piers. The other dams have even more prominent modern designs, although there is still simplicity of design for the locks.

Such nuances in design remind observers that engineering is both an art and a science. While most historians focus primarily on the science, on new technologies such as gates and adaptations to the engineering realities of geography, the structures as art are an oft overlooked but critical aspect of design.[90]

[90] O'Brien et al., pp. 63-102.

7

Navigation Improvements in the Modern Era

River traffic continued to increase after World War II. During the ten-year period from 1953 to 1963, commerce on the Middle Mississippi River grew 124 percent, nearly five times the river as a whole. Tonnage handled by the port of St. Louis also increased as a result. It had tripled from the end of World War II to 1956. This did not always result in greater employment, and the late 1950s and early 1960s were periods of economic stagnation for St. Louis in general – unemployment was high, and there were areas of urban flight as more than 100,000 left the city. Nevertheless, there can be little doubt that navigation increasingly contributed to the prosperity of the city as more and more goods were transported on the river versus over means. This was due in large part to the continual efforts to maintain and improve navigation on the Mississippi River. By World War II, the permanent project of hurdles, wing dams, closing chutes, and revetment was 75 percent complete. As long as there was at least 75,000 cubic feet per second of water flowing in the channel, the permanent project could maintain a nine-foot depth along 90 percent of the channel below

Early photo of shipwreck on the Middle Mississippi

Lock and Dam No. 26, requiring only minimal dredging, although in drought years more dredging became necessary. Yet as the district continued work on these and other navigational projects, issues new and old continued to change the way the district conducted business. Concerns about the environment and cost greatly impacted the shape of new projects, even as engineers worked to update aging infrastructure and reduce project costs. As a result, they developed innovative techniques to improve efficiency and lower cost while maintaining optimal environmental conditions.[91]

Progress on the permanent project or channel improvement program continued in the decades following World War II. With damages to navigational works from the Floods of 1944 and 1947 and additional works added, the district reported an estimated completion of 68 percent in 1950. By 1960, the program was only 78 percent complete, primarily because of damage to revetment resulting from heavy ice in 1951 and 1958, but the channel itself was greatly improved. After reaching 81 percent completion, in 1974 the district completed a study to determine changes needed to maintain a nine-foot channel, which resulted in authorization of an additional 170,000 linear feet of dikes and revetment, greatly increasing the program size. The district completed about

Early river training structure

---

[91] Dobney, pp. 113-114; U.S. Cong., *Mississippi River between Coon Rapids Dam and Mouth of Ohio River*, H.D. 669 (76th Cong., 3rd Sess.): 26-27.

a quarter of the remaining program to reach 69 percent completion by 1980 and 79 percent by 1990. A rock removal contract issued in 1988 removed some 100,000 cubic yards of rock from the channel by 1990. Despite expenditures of more than $2 million per year on average, the program never reached more than 85 percent completion because of continued refinement, repair, and addition of dikes and revetment to improve the channel. Nevertheless, the program was able to maintain a channel depth of 10 feet during high water in most locations, making dredging required only during low water.[92]

Fighting Droughts

The exception was during drought years, when excessive dredging became necessary to counter the hazards of low water. Over time, the district greatly improved its response to droughts. The primary response to past droughts, such as that of 1910 or 1939, was to increase dredging to keep a channel clear. By the first major drought after World War II in 1964, Corps response expanded to include working with other agencies to maintain the channel. From 1952 to 1964 during the long dry spell, precipitation in St. Louis was 42 inches below normal and seven inches below normal in 1964. Dry conditions extended into Minnesota, Montana, and the Dakotas. Other than briefly on March 10, 1964, water levels were between zero and -5.5 feet on the St. Louis gage for months on end, including 130 consecutive days since November 2, 1963 – the longest since the 1939-1940 drought (166 straight days). In addition to reducing channel depths below nine feet, low water contributed to silting in many locations, closing numerous side channels and reducing the depth of the St. Louis Harbor from 28 feet to around seven. The harbor was closed for 36 consecutive days while barges moored all along the 11-mile waterfront waiting to offload cargo so as to achieve a five-foot draft and proceed upriver. In addition to its usual dredging, the Corps worked with the Coast Guard daily to survey and mark open channels with buoys and coordinated release of water from reservoirs on the Upper Mississippi by the end of March 1964. Other suggestions that the Corps never implemented included one by St. Louis District Engineer Col. James Meanor, Jr., to build a dam near Jefferson Barracks in an attempt to back water up to the Chain of Rocks Dam and increase channel depths.[93]

---

[92] *Annual Report of the Chief of Engineers, 1950-2008.*
[93] "Old Man River in Trouble Here: Low Water at St. Louis," *Post-Dispatch* (Sun., Mar. 22, 1964): 1-5.

The most extreme drought in the history of the Mississippi River occurred from 1988 to 1989. It impacted all major tributaries of the Mississippi, many of which saw record low stages and flows more than 50 percent below normal, unlike the drought of 1964, during which the Ohio and other tributaries were near normal stages. In St. Louis, flow was at or below 50 percent of normal from May to October 1988. Stages at St. Louis started to decline in April 1988 and continued to go down until July, normally a period of high water. Throughout the low water season, the gage stayed near or below zero, reaching only -5.2 feet on December 23 and 26. The drought also set numerous daily record lows and had the lowest 210-day flow. By June, numerous channels were shoaling, and there were 26 channel closures between St. Louis and Baton Rouge, some lasting as long as three days. One of these near Ste. Genevieve kept nearly 500 barges waiting from June 23 to 26. The Corps and Coast Guard restricted tows to 20 barges and an 8.5-foot draft, later increasing the number to 25 barges. As with previous low water periods, the district started emergency dredging and snagging and working with the Coast Guard to survey and mark the channel. The Corps shortened the navigation season for the Missouri, dredged the river for the first time since 1979, and surveyed and marked the channel. Such activities continued until October. Aiding the channel depth was the release of water from Corps reservoirs, particularly the Gavins Point Dam on the Missouri. After determining that it would have little impact on low water, the Corps did not time release at the reservoirs with low water elsewhere, but the reservoirs' seasonal release nevertheless added 36,000 cfs or 50 percent of the Mississippi flow at St. Louis, which amounted to approximately four feet. Navigation remained fairly normal above St. Louis because of the locks. When the district discovered that Lock and Dam No. 26 was passing excessive flow, potentially draining the navigation pool, it implemented emergency repairs to roller gates at Locks and Dams Nos. 24, 25, and 26. All of these measures had some success, as demonstrated by consistently high tonnage moved despite the obstacles.[94]

The drought also presented new challenges. For the first time, the states of Illinois and Missouri requested relief under PL 84-99 and the Stafford Act to address water supply issues. Several wells and water intakes on rivers and reservoirs went dry or were threatened by low water or later ice. The Illinois

---

[94] IWR, *Surviving the Drought: Corps of Engineers Response to Drought Conditions in 1988* (D.C.: USACE, 1989): iii-8; James R. Tuttle, "Overview of Hydrometeorology Subbasin Flow Contributions and Water Levels, Mississippi RiverDrought '88'," *American Public Works Association* (Vicksburg: LMVD, 1988): 1-12; "Low Water Wreaks Havoc on the River," *Esprit* (July 1988): 8-9.

Matress revetment

Early photo of stone revetment

Emergency Management Agency instituted permits to use reservoir water. Numerous small communities and farmers or ranchers along the Missouri River requested assistance with their water supply, leading to several field investigations. Papineau, Illinois, requested emergency water after 56 of 70 wells went dry, and the Corps provided a temporary piping system until regular deliveries started. After Blandinsville, Illinois, requested support to transport water to the town, the district provided an emergency permit to open a new well. At other locations outside the district, the Corps installed pumps or worked with the National Guard to deliver water. Overall, critical communication during the event was much improved. The Lower Mississippi Valley Division collected and distributed water level information throughout the event. As with floods, the Corps established a River Industry Executive Task Force Committee that included the Corps, Coast Guard, and river industry, which helped distribute information and guided the federal government on decisions impacting navigation.[95]

Tow navigating Mississippi River under icy conditions

---

[95] *Surviving the Drought*, pp. 8-28; Tuttle, pp. 13-17.

The Environment, Aging Infrastructure, and Cost Constraints

By 1970, a combination of new national imperatives and new technologies were radically changing the navigation mission of the Corps. The environmental movement (see Section V.) became a force impacting nearly all Corps projects by the late-1960s and resulted in numerous statutory and regulatory requirements that changed the way the Corps did business. Cols. Edwin R. Decker, Carroll N. LeTellier, and Guy E. Jester led the district during this period of change as it adjusted its operations to meet these new demands. As a result of the new requirements, most Corps projects started to include elements to mitigate their environmental impact, while other projects originated primarily for the purpose of environmental restoration. Coordination among stakeholders, to include federal environmental agencies such as the U.S. Fish and Wildlife Service or Environmental Protection Agency and state agencies such as the Missouri Department of Conservation, increased greatly as river engineers cooperated on ways to improve habitat on the Mississippi River while improving the channel. By planning dredging locations, altering existing dikes and revetment, and applying new environmental river engineering techniques, the district was able to recreate diversity of habitat even as it maintained a stable navigational channel. A primary concern was maintaining wetland areas rather than converting the river to dry land, as had been the goal of past reclamation projects, and the district worked to maintain or recreate shallow pools and side channels by reducing sedimentation, notching dikes to allow water behind diked areas, and building pools that incorporated fast and slow water using rock interfaces. In these ways, the day-to-day operations of the district addressed new environmental goals.[96]

Ecological concerns also impacted projects with no specific environmental content, such as the Kaskaskia River Dam, whose construction spanned passage of environmental law. The Kaskaskia River runs approximately 325 miles from central Illinois to the Mississippi River about 118 miles north of the Ohio River. Prior to 1896 the Corps had made minor improvements to increase the river depth and remove snags in the lower 22 miles, especially at Evansville, but river depths remained as low as two feet in low water, with widths 60 to 75 feet. Because of these limitations, Chief of Engineers Maj. Gen. Lytle Brown

---

[96] Jon Daly and Donna Zoeller, Interview with Claude Strauser, Jul. 28, 2010 (MVS Archives).

reported in 1933 based on district analysis "the river is clearly not suitable for improvement for modern barge traffic." He did not recommend a plan submitted to Congress that year to build a slack-water system of six locks and dams, but in 1954 the Senate requested a reevaluation. The district examined channel improvements in the lower 50 miles only. In general, residents were favorable to the project, other than opposition by the railroads. A major factor in promoting the plan was the fact that 1.8 billion tons of coal lay in the ground within 15 miles of the river as far north as Fayetteville, Illinois. The plan submitted by the district in 1961 included a lock and dam at mile four to ensure deeper water in the lower river, a nine-foot deep and 200-foot wide channel created through straightening and deepening of the river, increases in water supply from upstream reservoirs, and various bridge and road alterations. Supported by the Board of Engineers for Rivers and Harbors, Acting Chief of Engineers Maj. Gen. Keith R. Barney recommended the project for $58 million. With savings of $5 million in transportation costs, the benefit-cost ratio was 1.9. Congress approved it in the Rivers and Harbors Act of 1962.[97]

Preconstruction work started in 1964; the district awarded the first contract on the canal from mile 19 to mile 23 in April 1966; and construction started in June. Another contract awarded in 1967 covered channel correction, and the district awarded a contract for the lock and dam on September 22, 1968, with an original completion date of 1972. Actually completed in 1974, the lock was 600-feet long and 84-feet wide, and the reinforced concrete dam included two 60-foot wide bays controlled by six tainter gates. With its completion, the project was 70 percent complete overall. It was fully operational in 1977 and complete in 1978. By the time construction ended, costs for the project had increased to $119.6 million, with $7.6 million local. By this time, there had also been born a new environmental consciousness. In 1978, the Illinois Department of Transportation (IDOT) published the Kaskaskia River Project Master Plan, which a contractor had developed to plan land use in the project area. In the weeks after publication of the plan and at a public meeting that September in New Athens, in which the state presented the plan to 250 attendees, several new issues arose. The largest complaint among local boater associations and residents was that the plan limited recreational boating in the canal. The Sierra Club and Audubon Society sought more wildlife areas and wanted to limit multi-use areas they believed would fall victim to economic development

---

[97] U.S. Cong., *Kaskaskia River, Illinois*, S.D. 44 (87th Cong., 1st Sess.): i-47; USACE, "Kaskaskia River Fact Sheet," (St. Louis: MVS, 1964).

such as strip mining. Biologists from the Illinois Department of Conservation criticized the entire project for its impact on wilderness areas. IDOT considered alterations to the plan and published the final version in January 1979, which, although it accommodated additional recreational aspects, did not meet all demands for wilderness areas and limitations on economic activity.[98]

Col. James B. Meanor, Jr.

Spurred by this belated criticism of the canal, local papers and organizations launched investigations that questioned the benefits of the projects. Changes in railroad shipping, the sale of an option for a Kaiser Aluminum plant, and increases in construction costs due to shoreline erosion had reduced the benefit-cost ratio to 1.1, which would likely not have earned congressional approval. Further, the coal mining anticipated did not develop in the first several years of the project, with the primary developer remaining Peabody Coal Company, one of the original boosters of the project (many called it "Peabody's Ditch"). For Peabody's customers, the canal did provide a sav-

Col. Edwin R. Decker

ings of a $1 per ton of coal shipped, but the customer base was rather limited in 1978. Nevertheless, District Engineer Col. Leon E. McKinney argued it was too early to judge benefits, which would come over the next 20 years. As it turned out, he was correct. By 1997, industries had shipped 50 million tons of cargo on the canal worth $1.75 billion, and new cargo docks had opened. Among goods shipped were grain at a significant savings, which injected more cash into the local economy. One report estimated the canal had created more than 4,000 jobs, including 600 in the coal mining industry. Equally important was the growth in recreational boating – more than 8,000 vessels used the lock in 1997

---

[98] USACE, "Navigation Project: Kaskaskia River, Illinois" (St. Louis: MVS, 1968); "Kaskaskia River Navigation" (St. Louis: MVS, 1974); Shirley Flood, "Tempers `Flare' at the Kaskaskia River meeting," New Athens, Ill., *Journal-Press* (Sept. 7, 1978): 1, 3; Bill Anderson, "Kaskaskia River land use plan faces difficulty," St. Louis *Globe-Democrat* (Aug. 29, 1978): 1-2; Timothy Middleton, "Kaskaskia River Canal: A facelift or a death mask?" *Southern Illinoisan* (Thurs., Aug. 17, 1978): 24.

Col. Carroll N. LeTellier

alone. Some criticisms of the environmental impact of the project continued, but most were satisfied as to its final shape. Although environmental challenges to the project came mostly after its completion, such issues demonstrate the difficulties of meeting both environmental and navigational objectives in the modern era.[99]

Addressing environmental goals in navigational projects came at a cost, however. Many projects saw delays as the Corps sought additional coordination with other agencies and the public, prepared documentation, and developed mitigation plans. At times, delays were lengthy. Unlike Lock and Dam No. 26, which was designed and built in the 1930s in seven years, it took more than 20 years after 1970 to get approval and build the Melvin Price Dam as its replacement. Other projects did not advance at all, such as the 12-foot navigation channel. The 1944 Flood Control Act had authorized a 12-foot channel below Cairo, Illinois. Resolutions had authorized study from Cairo to Minneapolis in 1945, but the Korean War delayed action on the 1949 survey. Congress approved a restudy of the issue in 1968. Barge lines argued that a consistent channel depth would lower commodity costs – most barges had to either carry less cargo or reload after entering the lower river – by increasing the tonnage shipped per load up to 1,600 tons. Since some pools in the river were already 12 feet, the North Central Division estimated only 25 percent of the channel would require adjustment through dredging or increased dam heights. The St. Louis District participated in these studies. It had already been experimenting with maintaining a nine-foot channel with a 1,200-foot width in prototype sections, and applied the data to the 12-foot study. Railroads opposed the channel, as they had the nine-foot channel, and they found ready allies in the environmental movement then blossoming. Environmental interests found neither dredging nor raising lake levels acceptable – one could destroy river bottom fish habitats, the other could flood wetlands and destroy waterfowl and plant habitat. Release of the

---

[99] Timothy Middleton, "Cost analysis shows Kaskaskia Canal loser," *Southern Illinoisan* (Aug. 15, 1978): 24; "Kaskaskia River Project called 'Peabody's Ditch,'" Centralia, Ill., *Sentinel* (Fri., Aug. 25, 1978): 3; Timothy Middleton, "Big boost for area hasn't been realized," Edwardsville, Ill., *Intelligencer* (Aug. 15, 1978): 1; Bob Lockhart, "Kaskaskia celebrates 25th anniversary," *Esprit* (Nov. 1998): 1, 7.

preliminary draft of the Upper Mississippi River Comprehensive Basin Study in 1972, which contained language favorable to the channel, greatly alarmed environmental interests, and this spilled over to opposition to the St. Louis District study of replacing Lock and Dam No. 26 as a first step to building the 12-foot channel. In the end, the final draft published in 1973 recommended against the channel above Grafton, Illinois, as not cost-effective, and the Corps deferred further study on the middle river.[100]

Aside from the costs of lost revenue of economic benefits and the added costs of environmental project features, high inflation combined with delays to increase the cost of many projects by more than 10 percent over several decades. This impacted both the district and its customers. Large budget cuts and increased spending scrutiny from 1980 to 2008 sometimes forced the district to choose among options or to delay projects until funding was available. Since 1983, the district had lost about 280 employee slots through attrition or conversion to temporary positions, and this impacted district operations. In April 1990, District Engineer Col. James Corbin established strict cost controls over the Operations and Maintenance budget because of cost overruns at maintenance-intensive projects such as the reservoirs. He assigned a team to review all spending decisions. One challenge they faced was high dredging costs, and Mike Dace, Dave Busse, and others worked to improve forecasting of water levels to determine dredging requirements. Typically, dredges operated using a 28-day weather forecast and dredged for the worst case scenario, but this was often inefficient because the forecasts were inaccurate and did not provide enough lead time to bring on additional crews. Busse developed a low-stage probability model or "low-cast" that determined the chance a certain river stage would be reached 30 to 120 days out based on local and tributary forecasts.

Dave Busse receives Chief of Engineers Design Environmental Award

---

[100] Raymond H. Merritt, *The Corps, the Environment, and the Upper Mississippi River Basin* (Wash.: Historical Division, OCE, 1984): 65-72; Michael Ruddy, Interview with David Comfort, Mar. 17, 1980; Memo, Remarks of Jack Niemi to LMVD, Apr. 14, 1975 (MVS Archives).

This helped to reduce dredging by predicting months in advance the number of dredges required. The team also introduced the use of global position system-based channel sweeps to more accurately determine where dredging was required.[101]

By 1991, under incoming Commander Col. James Craig, the team had evolved into what he termed Integrated River Engineering or later Integrated River Management (IRM), an interdisciplinary steering committee under William Sutton to improve operations and reduce costs for managing the river. Craig would note soon after its formation:

In the past, the attitude has been you have "x" dollars to dredge the river and you use that money dredging the river until the money is gone. Well, that is not necessarily the smart way to do it. There's a lot of energy out in the river just with the water moving along, and we ought to tap into that to help us dredge the river, keep that navigation channel open.[102]

The team would review issues such as dredging or flood forecasts as well as work with outside agencies such as the Soil Conservation Service to address siltation or Fish and Wildlife Service to look at environmental issues. At times, operating as a team caused some tensions. In 1993, for example, the IRM reviewed the low-water reference plane to reduce dredging requirements. The district had established a low-water reference plane (LWRP) of -5.0 feet on the St. Louis gage (equivalent to 40,000 cubic feet per second or cfs) in 1927. The district periodically updated the LWRP, for example to 54,000 cfs in 1933 to account for upstream reservoirs. The most recent review had been in 1993, which continued to maintain the -3.5 LWRP. For dredging, however, the district followed the mean low-water depth established by the Rivers and Harbors Act of 1915 of 15 consecutive low-water days in a year, which was equivalent to -5.0 feet St. Louis gage or a nine-foot channel at a design flow of 40,000cfs. The dispute between dredging and engineering depth proponents went so far as a legal review of the issue by the district Office of Counsel, with the different authorities under which the district operated indicating that the district had discretion under the authority of the Chief of Engineers to adjust depths "to admit of such increase ... as may be necessary to allow of the free movement of

---

[101] Daly and Zoeller, Interview with Michael Dace, May 25, 2010; Interview with Dave Busse, May 26 and July 26, 2010; Ruddy, Interview with Col. James Corbin, Jan. 4 and Nov. 3, 1989, Dec. 14, 1990 (MVS Archives).
[102] Ruddy, Interview with Col. James Craig, Nov. 20, 1991 (MVS Archives).

boats" but to maintain the maximum depth where "feasible and justified." This opened the district to reduce dredging in locations where it was not justified, although in practical application total dredging remained near or above five million cubic feet per year.[103]

The increased cost of federal projects also presented problems to local communities as sponsors struggled to raise necessary cost-share funds. The most prominent project facing such challenges was the construction of new works to protect the St. Louis harbor. Despite improvements made throughout the nineteenth century, the St. Louis harbor continued to face navigation problems during low water. Congress had authorized additional study of the problem in 1964 and 1971. Based on a feasibility study completed in 1982, Congress approved the project in the Water Resources Development Act of 1986. However, a model study conducted at the Waterways Experiment Station on the L-dike in March 1986 recommended its replacement with a Prototype River Access Improvement Structure (PRAIS), essentially an outer wall for the docks that would divert the current and scour sediment. The Municipal Dock was favorable to the PRAIS project, but the Tri-City Regional Port near the Chain of Rocks wanted a smaller (1,800-foot) harbor to be built first with completion of the project 10 years later to reduce maintenance costs. 1991 costs for the project were $12 million federal and $23 million nonfederal. When a value engineering study in 1987 suggested using coffer dams would save $200,000, the district completed a letter report revising the benefit-cost analysis. As a

Col. James D. Craig *Col. Thomas C. Suermann* *Col. James E. Corbin*

[103] Ibid.; Memo, District Counsel to CELMS-PM-M (Sutton), Legal Opinion on the Mississippi River Navigation Project Dimensions, May 28, 1993 (MVS Archives).

Col. Thomas J. Hodgini Col. Michael R. Morrow Col. Kevin C. Williams

result, the Chief of Engineers requested a General Evaluation Report. The district started work on this in 1996. In 1998, the Tri-City Regional Port requested modification of the project to change the harbor location and size to avoid dependence on the dam. By this time, the cost of the project had increased to more than $30 million nonfederal, and in 2001 the St. Louis Municipal Port stated it could no longer support the PRAIS. Because of the smaller benefit-cost ratio and safety concerns for the Tri-City Port plan, the district did not recommend it, more or less ending work on both projects.[104]

Environmental issues also touched another major area of concern for the district – renewal of aging infrastructure. One challenge faced by the Corps after 1970 was that most structures built prior to World War II were reaching the end of their 40 or 50-year design lifecycle, such as Lock and Dam Nos. 24-27 in the St. Louis District. In addition to structural issues, the increased size of tows and smaller capacity of older locks increased the wait time required for locking through these facilities. In the Flood Control Act of 1970, Congress approved an operational study of existing navigational facilities. From 1975 to 1988, the Corps or its contractors developed various studies on operational improvements, small craft locks, year-round navigation, mooring, hydropower, and lock capacity. These generally confirmed that an average 15-barge tow, typically 1,200 feet in length, had to lock through 600-foot locks in two stages, causing a delay of up to two hours on all Upper Mississippi locks other than No. 26 and No. 19, which had 1,200-foot locks. The Corps had been researching mitigation plans for the locks since it first developed environmental impact statements, and environmental proponents sought to tie mitigation to the

---

[104] *Annual Report of the Chief of Engineers, 1991-2005*; USACE, *General Reevaluation Report: St. Louis Harbor Missouri and Illinois Project* (St. Louis: MVS, 2004).

navigational upgrades. By 1988, the Corps completed initial assessments of the need for upgrading the facilities and proceeded to a reconnaissance study. Rather than treating the locks separately as it had in the past, the North Central Division combined the studies of all locks so as to better understand the impact of the entire system, a novel but complex approach. After completing the reconnaissance study in 1991, the Corps combined the Upper Mississippi River Navigation System with a similar study of the Illinois River in 1991 for the feasibility study. The St. Louis District was deeply involved in this effort.[105]

The feasibility study proceeded in 1993, but by 1998 encountered several delays. It was taking longer than expected to develop the engineering, economic, and environmental data for requirements identified during public meetings. In particular, the complex economic models used to project lock usage over 50 years proved very difficult. With the study running behind schedule, Col. James V. Mudd of the Rock Island District, which led the project, pressured the team to complete the study. In early 2000, St. Louis District economist Donald C. Sweeney submitted an affidavit through the Office of Special Counsel charging that the Corps had falsely developed economic data to win approval of the project. This resulted in an Inspector General investigation,

Chevrons near side channel

---

[105] USACE, *Integrated Final Feasibility Report and Programmatic Environmental Impact Statement for the UMR-IWW System Navigation Feasibility Study* (N.P.: MVD, 2004): 1-19.

Shallow pool on Kaskaskia River

congressional hearings, and an independent review of the study by the National Research Council. Although the Office of Special Counsel found the charges had merit, leading to reprimand of several persons, and Sweeney was widely lauded as a whistleblower, especially in the environmental community, ultimately there were no charges of fraud, and incoming Chief of Engineers Lt. Gen. Robert Flowers maintained that the impression of impropriety came as a result of trying to complete the study on time. "We had workers, Dr. Sweeney among them, who were trying to do the right thing," Flowers would later state. In the end, the 2001 National Research Council report, while acknowledging the difficulties of predicting economic activity, found that the economic model developed by Sweeney was untenable. "It was this emerging realization that caused much of the tension between the parties involved in the allegations," Flowers testified before Congress, and he later noted that "if the IG, in the time they did their investigation on the whistleblower allegation, would have had the National Academy of Sciences report, it might have been a different outcome." The National Research Council recommended improvements in the economic model, greater consideration of nonstructural approaches, and better integration of environmental factors.[106]

---

[106] Sweeney quotes from Matt Sorrell, "Flowers Talks on Waterways Issues," *Esprit* (Apr. 2002): 7-8 and "US Army Corps Responds to Navigation Study Critics," Wed. Feb. 28, 2001 (*http://www.mvr.usace.army.mil/PublicAffairs Office/InternetNews/TopStory/CorpsResponds.htm*, June 29, 2011); NRC, *Inland Navigation System Planning: The Upper Mississippi River-Illinois Waterway* (Wash., D.C.: National Academy Press, 2001): 61-87; "Affidavit of Donald C. Sweeney" (*http://www.mvr.usace.army.mil/PublicAffairsOffice/NavStudy/SweeneyAffidavit.htm*, June 29, 2011); Kellie Lunney, "Army Corps employee receives whistleblower award," *Government Executive*, Mar. 7, 2001 (*http://www.govexec.com/dailyfed/0301/030701m1.htm*, June 29, 2011).

The feasibility study completed in 2004 analyzed six different alternatives ranging from no action to a combination of new locks, lock extensions, mooring and switchboat facilities, and increased fees with five different ecological alternatives to include structural changes, pool management, channel restoration, fish passages, and island building. In the end, it recommended a dual-purpose integrated plan encompassing minor structural improvements, nonstructural improvements, and lock extensions on locks 20 to 25 for $2.4 billion and a long-term intermediate ecological plan to include habitat creation, water level management, fish passages, and floodplain restoration for $5.3 billion. The federal government would pay for all of the design and engineering and 65 percent of construction. Congress approved the overall plan in the Water Resources Development Act of 2007 and scheduled General Investigation funds starting in 2005 for Preconstruction Engineering and Design. As of 2010, the Corps had spent more than $61 million on designing 30 site-specific ecological and small-scale navigation projects. It had prepared more than $57 million in shovel-ready construction projects, but as of 2011 none of the projects had proceeded while waiting on final decision on local funding.[107]

At the same time, the St. Louis District did proceed with major rehabilitation of locks 24, 25, and 27. The district submitted rehabilitation reports on 24 and 25 by 1992, and planning started on the projects after receiving funding in 1994. Starting in 2001, the district closed Lock No. 24 over the winter for three years to repair piers and concrete walls and replace gates, valves, and electrical equipment for $35 million. During the first year, the district replaced the auxiliary gates, the second year it dewatered the lock for the first time in a decade to replace the machinery and culvert valves, and in the third year it dewatered the lock again to break up and carefully remove deteriorated concrete and replace with precasted concrete panels. Spotters would shut down operations if any endangered bald eagles came within 500 feet of the lock. It also allowed an opportunity to remove the zebra mussel from the walls, an invasive species harmful to lock operation. The district completed repairs to lock 25 by 2002 for $24 million, including a new control computer, miter gates, pedestrian bridge, and gate operating equipment and motor. In 2007, the district shut down Lock No. 27 for two 55-day periods over 16 weeks to refurbish lift-gate machinery and counter weights, install new computer controls, and repair concrete for

---

[107] *UMR-IWW System Navigation Feasibility Study*, pp. i-xv; Project Fact Sheet, Upper Mississippi River System Navigation and Ecosystem Sustainability Program, Jan. 1, 2011 (*http://www2.mvr.usace.army.mil/projects/ dsp_ factsheet.cfm?ProjID=F5C2680A-9D38-8690-BF35D7AB9AA74F7C*, June 29, 2011).

Chute on Kaskaskia

Kaskaskia Lock and Dam

$13 million in first the main lock and then the auxiliary lock, leaving one lock operational at a time.[108]

Evolving Navigation Technology

Even as the St. Louis District struggled to balance environmental requirements with spiraling project and maintenance costs, it worked to incorporate new technologies that helped reduce the environmental footprint and maintenance costs of many projects. Although the district had been leasing an IBM 650 mostly for administrative purposes since 1949, its first application of a computer to an engineering project came in the late 1950s on the St. Louis floodwall project. Afterwards, it used computers for a variety of projects. Innovations such as the use of channel sweeps, global positioning systems, and the Internet to automatically upload data saved considerable funds on dredging. Over several years, the district adopted or developed numerous other technologies that aided navigation on the Mississippi or other rivers. For example, the addition of mooring buoys south of Lock and Dam No. 27 in 1991 allowed

L-Dike north of St. Louis

---

[108] "St. Louis District's Lock 24 Gets a Renewed Lease on Life," *Esprit* (Feb. 2003): 1-6; "Lock and Dam 24's deteriorated concrete walls get a facelift," *Esprit* (Jan. 2004): 1-4; "Lock 27 Machinery Rehabilitation Nears Completion," *Esprit* (Feb. 2006): 1-5; USACE, "Lock and Dam No. 25 Major Rehabilitation, Mississippi River, Illinois and Missouri: Closeout Report" (St. Louis: MVS, 2004).

barges to moor midstream while waiting for lockage, thereby avoiding wake damage to the shore or mooring to and damaging trees, as was often the case. While the district developed technologies such as notched and step-up dikes, notched closure structures, and off-bankline revetment primarily to achieve environmental goals, it developed several others that had dual purposes. Hard-point structures were short rock dikes that extended into the side channel from the riverbank. When the flow encountered a hard point, it directed the flow downward into the riverbed, creating scour holes beneath the structures that deepened the channel. The construction after 2005 of chevron dikes – horseshoe-shaped rock dikes in the middle of the river bordering the main channel with the ends downstream – redirected flow and aided in scouring the channel. This reduced the more than $925,000 per year dredging requirements near St. Louis. The district implemented three chevron dikes near St. Louis to help to scour the channel, which promised to greatly reduce or possibly eliminate dredging. It promised to pay for itself within six years. "This is river engineering at its best," Leonard Hopkins, the chevron dike project manager, said.[109]

Two major innovations developed in St. Louis were riparian corridors and bendway weirs. St. Louis District engineer Jerry Rapp developed the concept

Closure structure

---

[109] Dohney, pp. 129, 134; "River industry's prototype mooring buoy," *Esprit* (April 1998): 1, 4-5; Alan Dooley, "Arches in the river aid navigation, save money and support the environment," *Esprit* (Oct. 2007): 7, 12; "River Engineering," Web page (*www.mvs.usace.army.mil/arec/basics.html*, June 30, 2011).

Construction of chevron dikes

Thompson Bend riparian corridor

Tow navigating river bend

Bendway wier

of riparian corridors as a solution to a potential cutoff at Dry Bayou-Thompson's Bend. This narrow loop just south of Cape Girardeau had been experiencing severe erosion that risked cutting a new channel and impacting navigation for several years. The district assigned Rapp to solve the problem in 1986. After trying stone revetment and various other solutions and facing setbacks after the 1993 and 1995 floods, Rapp and others developed the concept of a tree screen or riparian corridor – a buffer strip of fast-growing, water-resistant hardwoods planted between the riverbank and the flood plain to prevent erosion. They worked through the Real Estate Office with landowners associations to strategically plant and harvest cottonwood and other trees, making the concept at once navigationally beneficial, environmentally friendly, and financially lucrative, the concept earned numerous conservation awards.[110]

One of the most important and highly acclaimed innovations that the district introduced was bendway weirs. These were submerged rock structures that extended upstream at a 30 degree angle from the outside bank of a river bend that widened the channel by taking the spiraling and secondary flows from the outside of

---

[110] Terrie Hatfield, "DE Visits Thompson Bend Riparian Corridor Project," *Esprit* (Apr. 2000): 1, 8-10.

the river bend and redirecting them into the inner portion of the bend. The redistributed flow greatly reduced sediment accumulation and widened the river to create a safer and more navigable channel, revolutionizing the way river engineers address the problem of river bends. River bends had long been the most troublesome and treacherous stretches of the river. One problem arose because the Mississippi's meandering tendencies, which eroded the banks of bends, threatening the existing channel. The usual method of countering this problem was to revet the outer riverbank, but this tended to redirect the river's energy away from the bank and into the riverbed, scouring an excessively deep channel. Another problem was that sediment accumulated on the inside of the bend, causing channel narrowing and point bars to develop. These deep and narrow channels produced spiraling currents that forced tows to navigate the channel using a flanking movement by moving sideways while entering the bend. The maneuver was extremely complex and difficult, and not all tows could perform it successfully. On average, these treacherous bends caused 20 groundings each year between St. Louis and Cairo, Illinois. These groundings, combined with the slow movement around bends, caused bottlenecks and traffic delays that cost the navigation industry between $13 and $26 million annually. The Corps spent more than $5 million annually dredging bends in the region to keep them from narrowing. For more than a century these problems plagued river engineers until the development of bendway weirs.[111]

The district river engineers began developing the weirs in the late 1980s. To better understand the river mechanics at river bends, the district worked with the U.S. Army Engineer Waterways Experiment Station (WES) in Vicksburg, Mississippi, to develop physical models of two particularly troublesome bendways, Dogtooth Bend and Prices Bend. After testing and evaluating a number of different structures, engineers concluded that a never before used structure called a bendway weir was the best solution. However, these were only model tests, and engineers still needed to test the new structures on the river itself. The district began constructing the first bendway weir on the river in June 1989, and by December 1990, it had completed a field of 13 bendway weirs at Dogtooth Bend. The field cost only around $1 million and yet almost

---

[111] USACE, "Bendway Weirs," brochure (St. Louis: MVS, 1993); "District receives Presidential Design Award," *Esprit* (June 1994): 3; Daly and Zoeller interview with Busse; USACE, *Bendway Weirs on the Mississippi River* (St. Louis: MVS, 1992): 15-50. The district submitted the latter to ASCE as a nomination for the Outstanding Civil Engineering Achievement Program. For a detailed discussion of engineering principles in bendway weirs, see Robert Davinroy, "Bendway Weirs: A New Structural Solution to Navigation Problems Experienced on the Mississippi River," *PIANC Bulletin*, No. 69 (1990). While WES claims credit for the final bendway weir design, the district developed the initial concept; see Interview with Busse.

Aerial of riverbend

immediately the weirs began widening the channel. Within two months of the project's completion, Dogtooth Bend, which had been a challenge to engineers and the navigation industry for more than a century, was widened by more than 200 feet. The widened channel's current slowed sufficiently enough that tows could now navigate the formerly treacherous bend with relative ease. The weirs improved navigation so much that within just five months of the construction of the first weir field, tows could navigate Dogtooth Bend without using flanking maneuvers. There was a dramatic decrease in accidents and delay times at river bends, saving shippers millions annually. Moreover, the weirs eliminated the need for costly dredging in these areas. By 1998, the district installed the weirs on 16 bends, including Price, Cape Rock, and Red Rock. There were 125 individual weirs on this stretch of the river alone. In recognition for this innovation, the district and its personnel received numerous awards, including the Presidential Award for Design Excellence, the American Society of Civil Engineers Award of Merit, the Permanent International Association of Navigation Congresses Gustave Willems Award, and the Chief of Engineers Design and Environmental Awards Program's Award of Excellence.[112]

---

[112] "Arches in the river aid navigation"; "River Engineering," Web page; "Bendway Weirs," brochure; USACE, *Bendway Weirs Design Manual* (St. Louis: MVS, 1990); *Bendway Weirs on the Mississippi River*, pp. 38-49; "More recognition for bendway weir project," *Esprit* (Dec. 1991): 4

Micro-Modeling

The development and use of several of these innovations came as a result of micro-modeling — or Hydraulic Sediment Response modeling — conducted at the St. Louis District in the Applied River Engineering Center. Physical hydraulic models are scale replicas of water channels based on Isaac Newton's principle of similitude – that liquids will behave in a similar manner at different scales. First developed by hydraulic engineers at universities and laboratories in the late nineteenth century, physical models became a popular method of testing hydraulic structures prior to construction. A movable bed model includes sedimentation processes using materials imitating real sediment.

Applied River Engineering Center

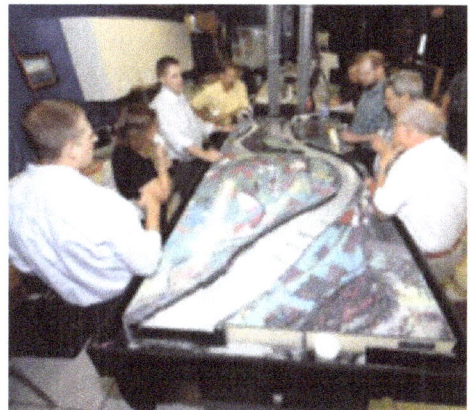
HSR (Micro) Model

In 1993, Rob Davinroy of the district Potamology Section tested a hypothesis that a small-scale model of a section of the Mississippi was as accurate as larger models. District engineers were intrigued, so Davinroy entered a master's degree program at the University of Missouri-Rolla to test his hypothesis. He chose to test a 20-mile section of the Mississippi that included Dogtooth Bend. Engineers at WES constructed a large-scale model of this section of the river to serve as the prototype for the smaller model. This "micro-model" had a scale of approximately 1:15,000 horizontal and 1:1,200 vertical, about the size of a tabletop. After constructing, calibrating, and analyzing the micro-model, Davinroy concluded that "the micro model overall displayed similar bed configurations as compared to both the larger WES model and the Mississippi River hydrographic surveys." Not only did results reveal that micro-modeling was a viable solution for analyzing and predicting sediment flow, it could do it for a fraction of the cost and time required for large-scale models and field experiments. The micro-model needed only one month to yield results, as opposed to the years it sometimes took to obtain results from field experiments. The overall impact of micro-models revolutionized river engineering.[113]

To implement the concept, the district established the Applied River Engineering Center. The center opened in 1994, and river engineers immediately went to work refining micro-modeling and applying it to the river's most complex problems, such as sediment transport. One reason why scientists and engineers had been skeptical of using small-scale models in the past was that the technology needed to calibrate and measure them simply did not exist. However, advances in technology allowed engineers to improve micro-modeling by employing advances such as laser technology and electronic automation. To create accurate models, engineers at the center teamed with the district's Geospatial Engineering Branch to collect data on the existing physical condition of the river. Engineers used bathymetric surveys, side scan sonar, vessel mounted LIDAR, and water velocity vector surveys to collect critical data that allowed them to accurately evaluate the existing physical conditions of the river. They then used the accumulated data to create a bathymetric survey, similar to a topographic map of the riverbed. Next, they combined this survey with data

Macro Model at the U.S. Army Engineer Research and Development Center (ERDC)

---

[113] "Davinroy gets patent," *Esprit* (Feb. 1998): 1, 4; Davinroy, *Physical Sediment Modeling of the Mississippi River on a Micro Scale* (Master's thesis, University of Missouri-Rolla, 1994): 49-90, 136-137; USACE, "Micro Modeling," Applied River Engineering Center brochure (St. Louis: MVS, 2000).

on flow patterns and velocities to calibrate the micro model. After constructing the model, engineers used the data from the actual river and compared it to the model to ensure that it was an accurate replication. They did this by scanning the model using laser technology, which collected flow data and created a bathymetric survey of the model's riverbed. Lastly, engineers compared the data to determine if there was any need for further calibration. Once calibrated, they used computers to control the simulation of flow and sediment loads. With an accurate simulation in place, they used their knowledge and intuition gained from years of studying and observing the river to implement and test structural modifications to the river. They then collected data from the experiments and used this to make a qualitative assessment about the effects of a proposed design alternative.[114]

The numerous successful projects and various awards associated with micro-modeling exemplify how revolutionary the technology was. Between 1980 and 1995 more than 40 barge accidents occurred on a specific stretch of the Mississippi near Locks and Dam No. 24 because of dangerous crosscurrents that caused barges to become misaligned and break apart. Engineers knew the cause of the current, but there was no practical method for them to determine a permanent solution. Micro-modeling allowed engineers to study more than

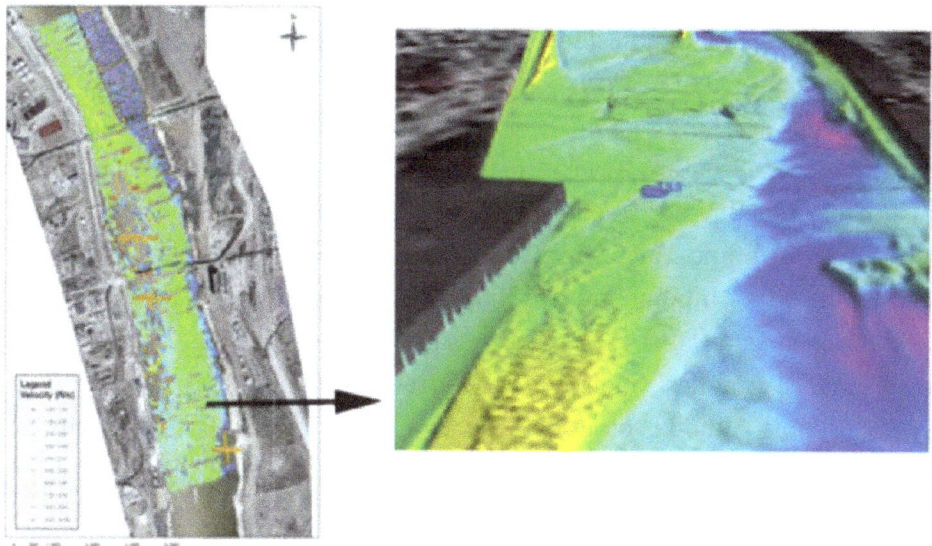

Bathymetric image of a section of a river

---

[114] "Micro Modeling," brochure; "Davinroy gets patent"; "Applied River Engineering Center," Web pages (www.mvs.usace.army.mil/eng-con/expertise/arec and www.mvs.usace.army.mil/arec/riverengineering_data.html, May 26, 2010). For a more detailed discussion of the process of collecting data for and calibrating micro models, see Davinroy, "River Replication."

30 structural alternatives. Once engineers found the best solution – four underwater weirs – they implemented it, and this section of the river was soon safe to navigate without harm to the environment. This technology also allowed the district to test structures to ensure that the natural energy of the river did the work of moving sediment out of the main channel. In an important commercial section of the river located 45 miles upstream of St. Louis, sedimentation was a chronic problem. The region, known as Bolter's Bar, often required dredging twice a year. However, the center was able to find a solution that eliminated the need for dredging and saved the Corps millions of dollars. The center solved numerous other potamological questions such as soil and sediment deposition and developing plans for bendway weirs, chevron dikes, or other structures at locations such as Marquette Island, Santa Fe and Picayune chutes, and the Southeast Missouri Port. In recognition of micro-modeling, the district and its employees received numerous awards and honors, including the Chief of Engineers Design and Environmental Program Award. In 1997, the U.S. Patent Office granted the district a patent on micro modeling.[115]

Davinroy receives 1994 Presidential Design Award from President Clinton

In the meantime, the navigation mission of the St. Louis District continued to affect the shipping industry in St. Louis. The port of St. Louis, which Primm called "gateway to the world," was in 1980 the largest port in the nation by area, with facilities ranging 70 miles from St. Charles, Missouri, to Kaskaskia, Illinois. Although other ports led by volume, and the Port of Southwest Louisiana surpassed it in size, the port nevertheless remained critical for the region, directly employing more than 21,000 workers and affecting the jobs of

---

[115] *Environmental River Engineering*; Davinroy, "Managing sedimentation using micro modeling," *Esprit* (Sept. 1996): 7-8; Davinroy, "River Replication"; David Gordon, "A Remedy for the Chronic Dredging Problem," *Engineer: Professional Bulletin for the Army Corps of Engineers* (Oct.-Dec. 2004); "Micro Modeling Wins Honor Award," *Esprit* (Mar. 2001). "Applied River Engineering Center," brochure (St. Louis: MVS, 1997); Claude Strauser, "Davinroy gets patent"; Strauser, "Environmental River Engineering," *Esprit* (Sept. 1996):6; "Strauser named Civilian of the Year," *Esprit* (Sept. 1997): 4.

43,000 others. It was the central facility for shipping everything from food to low-sulphur coal from Wyoming. Its 86 docks transported more than 24 million tons per year. This despite the general decline in population and industry, for while outlying towns and the county grew somewhat, St. Louis, with its fixed borders, declined in population to less than 550,000 by 1980, twenty-fourth in the nation. This decline has continued to present day, with the 2010 census showing St. Louis with only a population of 319,000 with St. Louis County declining somewhat to 998,000. Manufacturing also declined, although there was growth in specific industries such as transportation equipment, fabricated metals, aerospace, and chemical products. Even with such decline, 30 companies with annual sales more than $100 million were headquartered in St. Louis in 1980 and 24 of the top 25 companies in the U.S. had operations in the city, and many of them relied on or used port facilities. Thus, as the city dwindled, navigation became even more important, not just for the city but for the entire region. Yet, at the same time, flood control grew increasingly important for protecting these industrial assets.[116]

Santa Fe Chute

---

[116] Primm, pp. 472-518; Press Release, "U.S. Census Bureau Delivers Missouri's 2010 Census Population Totals, Including First Look at Race and Hispanic Origin Data for Legislative Redistricting," Feb. 24, 2011 (*http://2010.census.gov/news/releases/operations/cb11-cn49.html*, May 31, 2011).

Part III.
Where the Rivers Run:
The U.S. Army Corps of Engineers and Flood Control

St. Louis is situated near the confluence of the Missouri and Mississippi rivers. Separately, these two form the thirteenth and fourteenth longest rivers in the world, the first and second longest in the United States. Together, they form the longest system in the world. By volume, the Mississippi and Missouri are among the five largest rivers in the United States. The state of Missouri is itself a great junction of the rivers of the U.S. heartland. The Mississippi River forms its eastern border. The Arkansas, White, Black, and St. Francis basins drain most of its south. The Osage drains the central and western end of the state. The Missouri forms part of the western border and, with the Grand and Chariton, drain much of the north and west. Further, the Kansas, Platte, Des Moines, and Ohio rivers border Missouri. It is no wonder that Missouri once adopted as its motto, "Where the Rivers Run." As these rivers sometimes rise, Missouri has often suffered from severe flooding from numerous locations. For most of the nineteenth century, the federal government considered flood control as mostly a local issue, and the state worked to minimize flooding, primarily through the use of levees. With several floods after 1850, the government established the Mississippi River Commission in 1879 to help plan flood control, and in 1917 started funding flood control works. After the Great Floods of 1927 and 1936, the federal government assumed responsibility for large flood control programs, particularly on the Lower Mississippi River. Today, the Corps of Engineers is responsible for various flood control programs including works to minimize flooding on the Mississippi and other river basins, urban flood planning, and flood and hurricane response.

Aerial view of the confluence of the Mississippi and Ohio rivers during the 1993 Flood

8

Federalization of Flood Control

Since before the founding of St. Louis, the Middle Mississippi River faced periodic floods and drainage problems. The Corps of Engineers had been deeply involved in navigational improvements to rivers and harbors since 1824, but until the twentieth century it supported flood control only indirectly. Because the Supreme Court ruled in *Gibbons vs. Ogden* that Congress could regulate navigation under the commerce clause of the Constitution, for most of the nineteenth century a majority in Congress believed that navigational improvements were constitutional but that flood control was essentially a local matter. After 1850, Congress provided some funding for flood control indirectly to local organizations, periodically paid for surveys that made flood control recommendations, and empowered the Mississippi River Commission to provide guidance and support building dual-purpose levees, but it was not until 1917 that it specifically authorized direct funding of works for flood control. As a result, flood control was mostly a state and local responsibility for most of the early history of St. Louis. With the growth of large, multi-state flood control programs, it became increasingly clear that local authorities lacked the resources and authority to complete works necessary for the protection of their communities, requiring greater and greater response from the federal government. As the preeminent authority over engineering on rivers that flooded, it fell to the Corps to propose solutions for flood control problems.

The Middle Mississippi, as with the rest of the river, experienced annual high waters and was prone to bank overflow every two to three years. Some of these floods were very severe. The first recorded flood of any size near St. Louis was in 1724. Prior to U.S. control of Missouri, the largest flood was "L'anée des grandes eaux" (Year of Great Water) in 1785, which reached what would be 40.7 feet on the St. Louis gage according to later estimates. The largest flood on record in the nineteenth century was in 1844, which reached 41.4 feet in St. Louis and extended from St. Charles, Missouri, to Thebes, Illinois. According to one account, waters were so deep in St. Louis that the steamboat Lightner moored in front of a store on Front Street, and most of Kaskaskia, Illinois, was under 20 feet of water. Other disastrous floods included 1851, 1858, and 1892, which all reached more than 36 feet in St. Louis, although the floods of 1811, 1828, 1854, 1856, 1881, and 1883 also caused some damage. Because St. Louis sat mostly on a limestone bluff, the impact area was usually limited to those regions adjacent to the river or extended low ground south of the Chain of Rocks, north of Arsenal Street, and north of River des Peres. On the east bank, the American Bottoms was particularly flood-prone. Running south of the Illinois Bluffs, the region was a stretch of alluvial valley running nearly 10 miles wide, with numerous lakes and rivers and some of the most fertile land in the region. It encompassed most of Madison, Monroe, and St. Clair counties from Alton to Chester, Illinois, including notably the towns of East St. Louis, Cahokia, Brooklyn, Venice, Madison, and Granite City. As both of these areas grew in population – by 1900 St. Louis had a population over 550,000 and the American Bottoms more than 50,000 – floods had become more and more costly as they impacted more industry and homes.[117]

The Earliest Levees

The earliest and most common way of protecting against floods was construction of levees. As early as 1823, St. Louis started improvement of its wharf through the construction of levees to protect the bank from annual rises, and the city extended and partially paved these in 1845 and 1854. They were, however, of limited scope and size, being no more than a few miles in length. Other than railroad embankments built after 1850 and a few private levees of uneven quality and height, there were few levees on the Middle Mississippi, and none built by the government, until after the Civil War. In 1850, Congress passed the Swamp Land Act, which authorized the sale of federally owned swamp land in 12 states to pay for levees or reclamation efforts, in essence providing indirect federal payment for local flood control. Illinois received more than 1.5 million acres, and Missouri received more than 3.3 million through the act, most of which was prairie wetlands. It took a decade or more to identify the land, turn it over to the counties for sale, and then arrange for its transfer, with railroads being the leading purchasers. Little of this land bordered the Mississippi River, so most funds were used in the interior of both states. The earliest state law authorizing assistance to local levee districts on the Mississippi River did not come until 1879 in Illinois, and within three years there were low levees under

---

[117] U.S. Cong., *Harbor and Approaches to St. Louis*, H.D. 772 (59th Cong., 1st Sess.): 9-11; Clarence J. Root, "Draining the American Bottoms," *Monthly Weather Review* (May 1911): 698; Primm, p. 418; Dobney, pp. 30-32.

construction at Chouteau-Nameoki, Venice, and Columbia. By 1890, these and adjacent communities had raised about a 50-mile stretch of levees to a level of 36 feet, high enough to resist the Flood of 1892.[118]

These were exclusively state and local levees. The primary federal assistance provided during this period was advice on plans and construction standards. In 1850, Congress authorized the first major hydrographical survey of the Mississippi River, which the War Department split into two studies. The first, completed by French-educated civilian engineer Charles Ellet, Jr., in 1852, was concise, contained limited data, and recommended a combination of levees, outlets, and reservoirs to protect the Mississippi Valley from destructive floods. He was, Dobney noted, "ahead of his time—too far ahead, it turned out, to be taken seriously," though he spurred considerable discussion, and Congress later adopted a plan containing many of his suggestions. Due to an extended illness suffered by lead researcher Capt. Andrew A. Humphreys, the second study was not complete until 1861. Authored by Humphreys and Lt. Henry L. Abbot, the *Mississippi Delta Survey* provided the detail that Ellet's study lacked and was one of the most influential documents ever produced by the Corps. After extensive analysis of the river and comparison of methods, Humphreys and Abbot recommended the use of levees and maintenance of the existing bed and outlets below Cape Girardeau, Missouri, as the best method to prevent destructive floods. A second study by Humphreys after the Civil War and another by a board headed by Col. Gouverneur K. Warren in 1874 more or less echoed the findings of the *Delta Survey* that the best way to protect the valley was through a developed levee system. All of these studies stressed the need for the federal government to help fund and oversee implementation of their plans. Finally, in 1879, Congress created the Mississippi River Commission to both improve navigation and reduce flood damages on the river. The commission established its headquarters in St. Louis.[119]

Although Congress gave the Mississippi River Commission authority over the entire river, because of funding limitations and congressional strictures on using funds for flood control, the commission first focused primarily on

---

[118] Primm, pp. 122-123, 160-175, 281-282; U.S. Cong., *Mississippi River from Cape Girardeau, Mo., to Rock Island, Ill.*, H.D. 628 (63rd Cong., 2nd Sess.): 10-11, 19-21; Gary R. Dyhouse, "Chronology of Levee Construction on the Middle Mississippi River," Dec. 2009 (MVS Archives); Margaret B. Bogue, "The Swamp Land Act and Wet Land Utilization in Illinois, 1850-1890," *Agricultural History* 25:4 (Oct. 1951): 169-180.
[119] Camillo and Pearcy, pp. xiv-35; *Reports in Reference to Inundations of the Mississippi River*, S.D. 20 (32nd Cong., 1st Sess.); Humphreys and Abbot, *Report upon the Physics and Hydraulics of the Mississippi River (Delta Survey)* (Wash., D.C.: GPO, 1876): 445-450; *Report of Sec. of War, 1875*, H.D. 1, Pt. 2 (44th Cong., 1st Sess.): 536-565; Dobney, pp. 77-78, quote on 78.

navigational improvements below Cairo, Illinois. Other than a brief period from 1884 to 1886, the St. Louis District was not part of the commission, although it was under its oversight and several district engineers also served as members, including Maj. Thomas Handbury, Col. William F. Bixby, and Col. Curtis M. Townsend. At first, there was much disagreement about the proper methods of improvement. All agreed that jetties and bank protection would improve low-water navigation as they had in St. Louis, but civilian engineer James B. Eads also argued that levees would help contract the river during high water and scour the bottom, especially if the commission closed all outlets. Col. Cyrus B. Comstock disagreed that levees had any impact on low-water navigation and believed in closing outlets only when it aided navigation by reducing dangerous currents or increasing scour of the riverbed. In 1882, the commission adopted a compromise position that acknowledged that levees could aid jetties in contraction but that did not recommend closure of all outlets, and soon afterwards Eads left the commission. Because of financial constraints, the commission accomplished little with flood control other than establishing levee standards, experimenting with methods, and providing support to local levee and drainage districts, which conducted most of the work on levees. Over time, recommendations of the commission supporting levee construction convinced Congress to support levee construction for navigation improvement, so that levees became the only politically acceptable solution for both navigation and flood control proponents.[120]

By the turn of the century, the commission had overseen construction of an extensive levee system throughout much of the valley reaching up to 60 or 70 feet high. North of Cairo, the levees, being locally or privately built, were still of uneven heights and quality. This started to change only after the Flood of 1903, the second worst flood on record to date and the first since rapid growth in population. This flood exceeded 38 feet on the St. Louis gage (eight feet above flood stage), overtopped the Illinois levees, and devastated the lowlands near St. Louis and the American Bottoms as it extended more than 10 miles from bluff to bluff. It lasted from June 5 until June 19 at St. Louis, rising two feet per day until it peaked on June 11. Venice, Granite City, and Madison succumbed almost immediately to three breaches in the Madison County levees. Seventeen drowned and 70 percent of low-lying areas on the east bank was inundated – more than 320,000 acres – ruining wheat, potato, and corn crops.

---

[120] Camillo and Pearcy, pp. 37-95; Dobney, pp. 78-79.

The Madison levee commission agreed on June 6 to create another cut in the levees at Chouteau Island to relieve the Cross levee protecting East St. Louis. The city initially held on by inches, but the levee breached a few days later, flooding half the town and killing another two. About 25,000 were homeless; several hundred took refuge in St. Louis, which, other than the riverside areas, was mostly above water. By June 7, high water blocked traffic across the Eads Bridge, and railroads were unable to run, causing many to turn to steamboats to transport people and goods across the river. Preliminary damage estimates exceeded $15.8 million. Before the floodwaters subsided, the St. Louis *Post-Dispatch* asked, "How can another flood be prevented?" Robert E. McMath, a former civilian engineer for the district and president of St. Louis Board of Improvements, argued that improvements "should be undertaken boldly and with no thought of what the cost may be." Mississippi River Commission member and St. Louisan John A. Ockerson was more circumspect, noting that the cost would be high but less than the cost of a flood every decade. "If properly presented to Congress, I have no doubt that government appropriations to pay a considerable part of the best of construction would be forthcoming."[121]

Because of reports of levees, bridges, and railroad embankments contracting the river near St. Louis during the flood, in 1905 Congress authorized a survey of the approaches to St. Louis to prevent floods caused by obstructions in the river. The district engineer, Maj. Thomas Casey, took this as instruction to develop a general flood control plan. Authored by assistant engineer William S. Mitchell, what became known as the Mitchell report acknowledged that the severity of flooding was the result of contraction of the river near St. Louis, which likely raised gage readings by three feet. But rather than proposing removal of obstacles, the report recommended raising levees to 45 feet on the St. Louis gage at federal expense to counter future rises and extending the levee system along both shores and in the bottoms backcountry. It was the first major recommendation for the federal government to adopt the same flood control measures north of Cairo as it had in the lower river in line with commission standards. While Northwest Division Engineer Col. William F. Bixby, the Board of Engineers for Rivers and Harbors, and Chief of Engineers Brig. Gen. Alexander Mackenzie all endorsed the recommended measures in

---

[121] Root, p. 698; "Flood's Widespread Havoc at St. Louis," *NYT* (June 9, 1903); *The Flood of 1903* (Chicago and Alton Railway, N.D.); "The Great Madison Levee," *Post-Dispatch* (Fri., Jun. 5, 1903): A1; "Levees Dynamited to Relieve Pressure," *Post-Dispatch* (Sun., Jun. 7, 1903); "Threatening Break in Northern Levee," *Post-Dispatch* (Thurs., Jun. 11, 1903); "Flood Damage $16 Million" and "How Can Another Flood Be Prevented" *Post-Dispatch* (Sun. Jun. 14, 1903): McMath and Ockerson quoted on A1 (MVS Historical Files).

1906 as sound and called for their adoption by local authorities, they disputed Mitchell's overall plan, stating that as the levees were not for navigation they should not be a federal responsibility, that the levees could have detrimental effect on navigation and require extension of levees northward, that the cost of more than $3 million did not include relocation of railways and buildings, and

Cairo floodwall at the junction of the Ohio and Mississippi rivers during the 1927 flood

1927 flood at Cape Girardeau

that it did not really address the problem requested by Congress – the removal of obstacles on the river.[122]

Although Congress did not adopt the Mitchell plan, it did in 1906 extend the jurisdiction of the Mississippi River Commission to Cape Girardeau at the request of the commission to authorize construction of levees to protect the upper end of the St. Francis Basin from Mississippi River floods. This meant improvement of levees from Cape Girardeau to Cairo partially at federal expense. Despite the lack of federal flood control works for most of the region north of Cape Girardeau, state and local authorities made significant improvements in the levee system over the next decade. By 1913, local governments had created more than 52 levee and drainage districts north of Cairo, of which 30 were in Illinois and 16 were in Missouri. Eighteen of these were but recently formed and had either not started or were in very early stages of construction, and so had not yet provided protection. The rest had levees under construction, although most of these were of insufficient height, being no more than 10 feet high with a crown no more than 14 feet wide. By comparison, most commission levees were more than 45 feet on average. A few state levees were higher quality, including the Wood River levee, which reached a height of 32 feet for

St. Louis floodwall, 1935 (LOC)

---

[122] *Harbor and Approaches to St. Louis*, pp. 1-20.

five miles by 1915. By 1914, there were 216 miles of Mississippi River levees in Illinois and 34 in Missouri, although these were not contiguous.[123]

Finally, in 1913 Congress requested a survey by the Mississippi River Commission from Cape Girardeau to Rock Island, Illinois, to determine the flood control needs of this stretch of river. The report, completed by the following year, recommended extension of the levee system to protect the middle valley, relying on local levee districts to conduct most work. In 1916, Congress extended the jurisdiction of the commission on the Mississippi River to Rock Island as well as to some tributaries. The following year, the Flood Control Act of 1917 recognized for the first time that the levees being constructed by the commission were also for flood control and authorized considerable spending increases on levee construction provided that local interests paid for at least half of construction costs, provided all rights of way, and paid for maintenance of the levees. As a response to these increases in mission, in 1918 the commission created a Northern District, headquartered in St. Louis, to build levees north of Cape Girardeau, as well as a Dredging District in Memphis, Tennessee, to dredge throughout its jurisdiction. From that point until 1928, the Northern Commission District was officially responsible for levee construction north of Cairo, while the St. Louis District continued to be responsible for navigational improvements such as hurdles and dredging. There continued some interchange in personnel as there had previously been with the commission. Although spending levels increased initially to more than $200,000 a year by 1920 for levee construction from the Ohio River to the Missouri River, they afterwards dropped to a level of roughly $100,000 per year, where they stayed consistently until 1928. The commission planned for and invested in levees at Clear Creek, East Cape, East Side, the Alton-to-Gale reach, and the St. Louis-to-Cape Girardeau reach, among others, but most of the funding and labor still came from the local levee districts.[124]

The Flood Control Acts of 1928 and 1936

In 1927, the Mississippi Valley experienced the worst flood in its history, sparking extensive changes to both the Mississippi River Commission and the

---

[123] *Mississippi River from Cape Girardeau Rock Island*, pp. 4-12; *Annual Report of the Chief of Engineers, 1904-1906*; Dyhouse, "Levee Chronology"; Camillo and Pearcy, p. 100.
[124] U.S. Cong., *Mississippi River from Cape Girardeau to Rock Island*, pp. 1-12; *Flood Control Act of 1917*, PL65-367 (65th Cong, 1st Sess.); *Annual Report of the Chief of Engineers, 1918-1927*; Dyhouse, "Levee Chronology"; Camillo and Pearcy, pp. 103-122.

flood control program, and leading to a wholesale reevaluation of the levees-only policy, which many blamed for the disaster. After presentation of numerous plans, Congress endorsed that of Chief of Engineers Maj. Gen. Edgar Jadwin in the Flood Control Act of 1928. This plan included a controlled spillway, three uncontrolled floodways, and higher levees, including increases in levee height of up to three feet between Cairo and Cape Girardeau. The act also initiated a series organizational changes in the commission and gave responsibility for directing the plan to the Corps. Since the majority of the new project was south of Cape Girardeau and work north of that point was nearing completion, Jadwin considered the Northern District no longer necessary and coordinated with commission president Brig. Gen. Thomas H. Jackson to transfer its employees and equipment to the St. Louis and Rock Island districts, both of which managed flood control work north of Cape Girardeau under commission guidance. The districts south of Cape Girardeau also merged with Corps districts, but remained under the authority of Jackson, who served as commander of the new Lower Mississippi Valley Division. On Jadwin's order, he also transferred the Dredging District to Memphis District. Jackson then submitted a new functions statement for the commission making it an advisory body with the Corps now responsible for all investigations and execution of work. Since the work of the Mississippi River Commission was then the responsibility of the Lower Mississippi Valley Division, whose jurisdiction no longer included St. Louis, Jadwin started reviewing relocation of the commission to Memphis or Vicksburg, Mississippi. On October 7, 1929, the new Chief of Engineers, Maj. Gen. Lytle Brown, ordered the commission to move its headquarters to Vicksburg by November 30.[125]

In the seven years following the passage of the 1928 Flood Control Act, most of the flood control efforts were focused on raising or repairing existing levees, with the commission establishing a standard levee height of up to 44 feet (St. Louis gage). Devastating flooding in the Northeast in 1935 and 1936 once again brought attention to the need improved flood control legislation.

---

[125] Camillo and Pearcy, pp. 141-172; E.J. Thomas, "Flood of 1927" (MRC Tech Files 2-2-23): 1-2; U.S. Cong., *Flood Control in the Mississippi Valley*, H.D. 90 (70th Cong., 1st Sess.): 23-33; U.S. Cong., *Flood Control Act of 1928*, PL 70-391 (70th Cong., 1st Sess.): Sec. 8; Memo, Jackson to Jadwin, Abolishing the Northern District, Mississippi River Commission, Jul. 7, 1928; Jackson to Jadwin, Field Reorganization, Jul. 13, 1928; Jackson to Jadwin, Functions and Agencies of the Mississippi River Commission, July 27, 1928 (MRC Archives); Camillo and Pearcy, pp. 170-172. "History against us in flood fight bill – Col. Potter," Memphis, Tenn., *Commercial Appeal* (May 17, 1928) (NARA KC, RG 77, ENT 521, Box 22), Memo, Lt. Col. Thomas Robins to Jackson, Reorganization of Engineer Department at Large, Oct. 7, 1929; Elliott to Maj. J.H. Carruth, Nov. 25, 1929; Maj. AKB Lyman to Secretary of War, Transfers at Government expense, Oct. 22, 1929 (MRC Archives).

Near the St. Louis landing during Mississippi flood

1944 flood at Cape Girardeau

Although the floods did not impact the Mississippi Valley, the region benefited from the legislation that followed. The Flood Control Act of 1936 was one of the most sweeping pieces of legislation in the New Deal era. For the first time, Congress admitted that "flood control on navigable waters or their tributaries is a proper activity of the Federal Government" and that "improvement of rivers and other waterways for flood control and allied purposes shall be under the jurisdiction of and shall be prosecuted by the War Department under the direction of the Secretary of War and supervision of the Chief of Engineers." Once and for all, Congress established flood control as a nationwide responsibility of

View of 1903 flood at Eads Bridge

the Corps of Engineers. Flood control projects not under the direct control of the commission were now under the Corps, making the St. Louis District responsible for flood control within its boundaries. The act also outlined more than 270 flood control projects, of which 21 were in the domain of the St. Louis District. Among these were projects at Venice, East St. Louis, Prairie du Pont, Columbia, Harri-

General Jadwin

sonville, Fort Chartres, Ste. Genevieve, Perry County, Degognia, Preston, Clear Creek, East Cape Girardeau, Wood River, Grand Tower, and North Alexander. By 1940, construction was ongoing in more than 10 levee districts. Three of these projects were complete by the end of World War II with several others progressing considerably. With projects added in flood control acts passed in the years that followed – particularly the Flood Control Act of 1938 – and with continued repairs, construction on some projects has continued to present day, although most work was complete by the mid-1960s.[126]

---

[126] Joseph L. Arnold, *The Evolution of the 1936 Flood Control Act* (Fort Belvoir: CEHO, 1988): 50-71; U.S. Cong., *Flood Control Act of 1936*, PL 74-738 (74th Cong., 2nd Sess.), *Annual Report of the Chief of Engineers, 1936-1945*; Dyhouse, "Levee Chronology"; Dobney, pp. 103-108. Ironically, the record-breaking Flood of 1937 hit less than six months later, although the worst of it affected the Ohio River and Lower Mississippi; *Annual Report of the Chief of Engineers, 1928-1935*.

The Flood of 1844

The Flood of 1844 was the largest flood by volume experienced by St. Louis until late into the twentieth century. Although the 1993 Flood holds the record for flood height at 49.6 feet and number of consecutive days above flood stage at 148, unlike that of 1844, this was the height confined by the levee system.

Although the winter of 1844 was not particularly severe, the spring brought major rainstorms starting in May. The river was over bank full stages by May 1, but started to recede on May 3. Over the next two months St. Louis saw 18.11 inches of rain, 10 inches higher than normal. Other regions up the Missouri River, such as Fort Leavenworth, Kansas, saw more than 20 inches. The river began to rise again on May 10, and a week later, the Missouri *Republican* called it "a tremendous flood."

> *The waters are coming down upon us from every quarter. The Mississippi is now as high as it has been known for many years and is still rising. Just above Oak street it was last evening within 6 or 8 feet of touching the curbstone. The cellars above the wharf are filling with water....The whole of the American Bottom, from Alton to Kaskaskia, will be, we fear, submerged. The people are deserting their homes in Illinois towns.*

The flood continued to rise until it was at the doors of stores on Front Street north of Pine, and vendors had to evacuate their goods to the second story. On the Illinois side, the flood extended to the Pap house, or two and a half miles. The flood started to recede again on May 23 until it was within its banks again on June 7. But as one Corps report noted, "the flood from the Missouri was yet to come." It began to rise again on June 8. By June 17, water was six inches higher than it had reached in May, and it reached a peak at St. Louis on June 28 at 41.7 feet on the Market street gage.

View of St. Louis during 1844 flood

The water covered all of East St. Louis, with several houses overturned or sliding from their foundations. Residents of Cahokia fled to the bluffs. It covered the entire country from Weston to Glasgow, ruining thousands of acres of farmland, and Camden Bottom was six to eight feet underwater. In places, the river ran upwards of 15 miles wide. In St. Louis, the water rose to door hatches on Front and Morgan Street, allowing the steamer *Lightner* to rest her bow on Henry N. Davis' store. At Pine and Front, the water was midway up on the doors, and lower areas, such as Mill Creek, were complete submerged. Some 500 persons in the city evacuated their homes.

Based on measurements taken by Capt. Thomas J. Cram at the St. Louis Arsenal, the flood reached 30 feet (flood height) on May 17 and remained above flood stage until July 18, a total of 63 days. For the week of 24 to 30 June, the water was consistently above 40 feet. Later estimates were that the flood flow reached 1.3 million cubic feet per second, with 900,000 cubic feet per second coming from the Missouri. Although later floods overturned some of these statistics, and the U.S. Geological Survey would later downgrade the estimated flow of the flood to one million cfs, for nearly a century, the Corps deemed the Flood of 1844 a 200-year flood event used for planning flood protection works.[127]

---

[127] "Floods of Rivers within or near the St. Louis Missouri Engineer District," [1942] (MVS Archives).

9

Urban Flood Control

By 1950, the St. Louis District had made significant progress in bringing levees up to standard. Projects at Miller Pond, Kaskaskia Island, Seahorne, Meredosia Lake, and East Cape Girardeau were mostly complete; work at Clear Creek, Perry County, Columbia, East St. Louis, and Prairie du Pont were at various stages of construction; and projects at Preston, Fort Chartres, Harrisonville, Grand Tower, and Wood River, delayed by World War II and the floods of 1943 and 1944, started soon after 1945. South of Cape Girardeau, Missouri, flood control was under the authority of the Mississippi River Commission, which had been busy raising those levees to standard. Although before the war the district had started to raise levee heights to the 1935 standard, the floods of 1943 and 1944 and later the floods of 1947 and 1951 demonstrated the need for additional protection to account for confinement of floodwaters between the growing levee walls. The Corps continued to adjust levee standards, which repeatedly extended construction on existing levees into the future, yet a new problem arose – protection of urban areas where the levee system could not or had not yet reached. Beginning after World War II, the Corps started to study

Alton, IL. At the intersection of W. Broadway and State during the 1943 flood

and build additional flood protection for St. Louis, Cape Girardeau, and Ste. Genevieve, Missouri, and Alton and East St. Louis, Illinois, that protected those cities from flooding, as it had with thousands of acres of farmland since 1917. This was sometimes challenging because of the limitations of space, time, and the money needed from local government to help pay for the works, but the district made great strides to bring protection to these regions over the next half-century.[128]

High water in Cape Girardeau during 1944 flood

Evolution of Urban Flood Control Standards

In 1935, the St. Louis District had established standard levee heights of up to 44 feet, St. Louis gage, from the Illinois River to the Ohio River. Based on the 1903 Flood, this is what the Corps believed provided protection for a 50-year flood – 38 feet plus up to six feet of freeboard depending on local conditions. North of the Illinois River, the Rock Island District had established levee standards of 12 to 18 feet in 1914, although the Corps recognized the need to revise these standards after completion of the Upper Mississippi lock and dams, which had altered high water lines in some locations. By 1940, the St. Louis District had already started to adjust levee standards in urban areas to meet changing requirements for protection due to confinement of floods between the levees. Particularly near East St. Louis and Cairo, Illinois, the Corps believed the large populations of these cities and their industrial importance required even higher protection. As a result, the district had since 1935 increased levee heights two feet higher than the 44-foot standard on the eastern side of the river from East St. Louis to Prairie du Point. Because St. Louis was mostly on a protective bluff, it was not initially a concern. In 1940, Upper Mississippi Valley Division Engineer Lt. Col. Malcolm Elliott recommended, and Chief of Engineers Maj. Gen. John L. Schuley approved, these levee heights as the standard for the East Side. These levees included a one-to-three slope on the water side and one-to-five slope on the land side, depending on the type of

---

[128] *Report of the Chief of Engineers, 1941-1946.*

construction material, with a crown 10 to 12 feet across. Although maintaining these heights placed areas protected by lower levees at higher risk, Elliott recognized that a confined flood reaching the 50-year level would breach first in less developed regions, providing greater protection to the cities. His overall conclusion was that "levees appear to offer the most practicable and economical means of flood relief for lands along the main stem," a sentiment repeated by district engineers over the next three decades.[129]

The floods of 1943 and 1944 were the worst floods the district had faced in a century, exceeding all previous stage records except 1844. Although the discharge was only 660,000 cubic feet per second (cfs) or roughly 66 percent of the 1844 flood, the 1943 Flood reached 38.9 feet at St. Louis because of greater confinement of the levees, and it reached even higher in Kaskaskia. Sixteen of 19 levee districts flooded despite the improvements in the flood control system. The 1944 Flood was even greater, its 844,000 cfs reaching 39.19 feet at St. Louis and flooding 15 of 19 districts. As a result, in 1944, the district formally increased levee standards to 47 feet (St. Louis) for the East Side to cover a 200-year event equivalent to the Flood of 1844. It conducted a survey of levee heights in light of the revised standards and adjusted completion rates in the process. As the district completed these levees, confined floods continued to threaten the system. The Flood of 1947 came in three crests – April 12 to 19, April 26 to May 2, and June 9 to July 13 for a total of 50 days above flood stage. Again, despite having a flow of only 782,000 cfs, it reached a peak of 40.2 feet on July 2 – a foot higher than in 1944 – and flooded 10 of 19 districts. Although its flow was even lower at 772,000 cfs, the Flood of 1951 reached nearly the same height, cresting at 40.28 feet on July 22. This followed two crests from May 6 to 8 and June 29 to July 30, totaling 35 days. Because of improvements in the system, only three of 19 districts flooded, with the largest breaches at Degognia, Missouri. As the levees advanced and provided greater protection, confined heights grew despite lower flood flows. While flooding impacted fewer areas as the system neared completion, those areas not protected – primarily urban areas – saw severe damages.[130]

---

[129] U.S. Cong., *Mississippi River between Coon Rapids Dam and Mouth of Ohio River*, H.D. 669 (76th Cong., 3rd Sess.): 43-58, quote p. 78; Dyhouse, "Levee Chronology."
[130] Dyhouse, "Levee Chronology"; *Annual Report of the Chief of Engineers, 1941-1951*.

View north from McArthur Bridge, July 20, 1951

View south on Second from Chouteau, July 19, 1951

Cape Girardeau and St. Louis

Congressional concern about still unprotected areas grew rapidly after the floods. One of the first projects the district studied was improvement of Cape Girardeau. The district had already started levees across the river in East Cape Girardeau and in nearby Perry County and Grand Tower. In 1943, Congress requested a review of additional flood protection for St. John's Bayou Levee District to the south and also at Cape Girardeau, but the war delayed work on the survey. The floods of 1944 and 1947 impacted the town particularly hard. On May 3, the Flood of 1944 reached 40.70 feet at Cape Girardeau; the Flood of 1947 reached 41.88 feet on July 6. In both floods, about 800 acres of industrial property along the water front flooded. Average annual damages were $328,000, but these did not include potential damage to three major factories subject to 200-year flooding, which would have raised this amount to nearly $3 million. In light of the probable impact area and damage, in 1949 the district recommended about 1.5 miles of 49-foot levees (Cape Girardeau gage) and floodwalls extending from high ground on the north end of town to Cape La Croix Creek south of the city, relocation of several highways and railroads and construction of five gates for roads that could not be moved, two new pump stations, and improvements such as widening and paving sewers and

Cape Girardeau floodwall

ditches for $4.2 million. However, the Board of Engineers for Rivers and Harbors, noting that the city is on a bend, believed "a higher degree of protection is desirable," and raised levee heights to 51 feet for $5.2 million, $4.7 million of which the federal government would pay.[131]

Although Congress authorized the Cape Girardeau project in the Flood Control Act of 1950, it took several years to work out cost-sharing agreements for the $5 million project. In 1955, the local levee district provided assurances for Reach 2 in the downtown area, and construction started in February 1956. Construction was 80 percent complete by 1960 and complete by the following year other than a single section held up by difficulties in obtaining rights of way. The levee district requested that the federal government proceed with condemnation of the property on March 21, 1961. With this accomplished in 1963, construction proceeded on the section and was complete in 1964. However, the levee district never provided cost assurances on the other three reaches, which Congress de-obligated in 1978. Meanwhile, work on the East Cape Girardeau levee was mostly complete by 1959, but the district suspended further work on the project because of lack of local concern on correcting seepage issues discovered near the levees. It would take another five years to work out funding issues and complete the project. On the recommendation of the Chief of Engineers in 1984, Congress approved another project protecting the Cape Girardeau-Jackson Metropolitan Airport in the Water Resources Development Act of 1986. This included channel improvements to Cape La Croix Creek and Walker Branch, a small floodwater detention reservoir, bridge improvements, and recreation features for a total cost of $41 million, with $11.8 million in local contributions. After receiving a local cooperation agreement for the project by 1991, construction started on the channel improvements in 1993, which were complete by 1999. Construction on the reservoir started in June 2000 and was complete in 2004. After many years of settlement and wear and tear, in 2004 Congress approved reconstruction of the Cape Girardeau floodwalls. Improvements included a rock berm to stabilize the existing retaining wall; repairs to floodwalls, including joint repairs, toe drain replacement, soil stabilization, and seal replacement on closure gates; and various mechanical, electrical, and structural repairs to pump stations. Once the city signed the local cooperation

---

[131] U.S. Cong., *Mississippi River at Cape Girardeau*, Mo., H.D. 204 (81st Cong., 1st Sess.):1-18, quote on 6.

East St. Louis floodwall, 1951

agreement, from 2008 to 2010 the district contracted more than $2 million in work on the flood protection system.[132]

The Flood of 1947 devastated low-lying regions of St. Louis, and in 1948 Congress requested a new study of flood protection for the city. A hearing conducted the following year found most residents were favorable to protection. The St. Louis District completed the study in June 1953. The plan examined a combination of 47-foot floodwalls and levees (St. Louis gage), closure gates, and improved drainage structures in five reaches extending along the entire waterfront as well as part of the River des Peres. It recommended construction of Reach 3 from Maline Creek to the Eads Bridge and Reach 5b from River des Peres to Broadway Street and deferment of Reach 4 from the Eads Bridge to Chippewa Street and the rest of Reach 5 from Fillmore Street to Jefferson Barracks because of a low benefit-cost ratio. In its 1954 analysis of the plan, the Board of Engineers for Rivers and Harbors made three important modifications. First, noting that "flows considerably greater than those on record," i.e., 1.3 million cfs, "are possible of occurrence," the board argued that the levees should be 52 feet – a five foot increase over those proposed by the district.

---

[132] *Annual Report of the Chief of Engineers, 1956-1964, 1990-2004*; Dyhouse, "Levee Chronology"; "Cape Girardeau (Floodwall), Missouri," Web page (www.mvs.usace.army.mil/pm/cape-floodwall/index.html, Mar. 31, 2011).

Second, in light of these changes, a recalculation of damages revealed that Reach 4 had a positive cost-benefit ratio, and it recommended adoption of this reach. The board agreed that the other areas had experienced little flood damage and did not need the protection. Last, because local interests expressed concern that Reach 5b would interfere with new businesses in the area, the board recommended deferment of that project. Further discussion with several railroads through 1955 resulted in adjustments to the alignment that also increased the cost slightly. Altogether, the project included 11 miles of levees and floodwalls, 44 improved sewers or drainage ditches, and 28 new pump stations for $131 million, $8 million of which was local. Congress approved the project in the Flood Control Act of 1955.[133]

St. Louis Project south of Market St., 1959

St. Louis Project floodwall, 1964

St. Louis Project, aerial view NE from Humboldt St. showing levee and Baden pumping station

The biggest challenge was obtaining the funds to pay for the local share of the project. "Where were we going to get that, we knew it would be absolutely impossible, except through a bond issue," local businessman Morton Meyer observed. Yet even at that time, it was difficult to get approval for a bond issue. He and 100 other businessmen, including attorney William Crowdus, Harry Gaines of Gaines Hardware and Lumber Company, Harry C. Colwell of Terminal Railroads, and others, formed the St. Louis Flood Control Association, which was instrumental in getting approval for the project

---

[133] U.S. Cong., *Mississippi River at St. Louis, Mo.*, S.D. 57 (84th Cong., 1st Sess.): vii-11, quote on 3; USACE, *Flood Protection for City of St. Louis and Vicinity: Supplementary Detailed Cost Estimate* (St. Louis: MVS, 1954):1-11.

from 1948 to 1955. Elected in 1953, Mayor Raymond A. Tucker had pushed through a small tax increase, sought consolidation of county and city government to improve its financial situation, and was favorable to the project. Since he was proposing a $110 million bond for various other improvements throughout the city such as for transit and sewerage, the association worked to lobby to include the flood control project under the bond through parades, press and speaking campaigns, and testimony before Congress and the Corps. Citizens eventually voted six to one in favor of the bond issue and project. The association continued to push for completion of the project over the next 20 years and worked with the district engineers to resolve technical and business issues.[134]

After completing local cooperation agreements, the contractor broke ground on the project on February 24, 1959. By 1965, the walls and levees on Reach 3 were 80 percent complete and capable of providing preliminary protection, while Reach 4 was 10 percent complete. By 1968, the project was 86 percent complete for both reaches. By 1973, the project was practically complete and provided critical protection during the Flood of 1973. This flood paralleled the Great Flood of 1927 in many ways. By March 7, 1973, the river was at 37 feet in St. Louis – seven feet above flood stage. Six different flood crests followed. On April 28 and 29, the river reached 43.3 feet on the St. Louis gage at an estimated 852,000 cfs, causing 150 to evacuate along the River des Peres and breaking 35 of 36 private levees along the Mississippi. There were more than 12,000 acres of damage to urban areas not protected by Corps projects compared to 8,000 acres of damage in protected areas. One area that was protected was St. Louis. Only a single gap in the protection was incomplete, requiring placement of sandbags, but "nobody got wet, not a soul," Meyer would later

St. Louis floodwall construction, 1964

---

[134] Primm, pp. 496-506; Michael Ruddy, Interview with Morton Meyer, Aug. 22, 1980 (MVS Archives).

West Alton, MO, during the 1973 flood

note. The official dedication of the St. Louis floodwalls was on May 21, 1974. The project prevented more than $929 million of damages during the four major floods in the last quarter of the twentieth century, including 1973. As early as 1968, the city created a Riverfront Development Plan that incorporated flood protection into its architectural and engineering plans. In 1974, Congress assigned the district to develop a plan for the St. Louis metro area. Although this never resulted in new projects, it is notable as the district's primary foray into urban planning.[135]

East Side Levees and Alton to Gale

Construction of levees on the east side of the river, which was of such concern prior to World War II, also advanced to increase protection of cities in Illinois, starting with Alton. South of and adjacent to Alton, Congress had

---

[135] "St. Louis Eleven-mile flood protection: Project Moves Ahead," presentation (St. Louis, MVS, 1966) (MVS Archives); Ron Jones, "The wall that save St. Louis (again)" Esprit (Apr. 1994): 4-5; *Mississippi River and Tributaries: Post-Flood Report, 1973* (Vicksburg: LMVD, [1974]): 1-60; Quote from Ruddy Interview with Meyer; *Floods and Flood Control on the Mississippi, 1973* (N.P.: USACE, [1974]): 1-33; Dyhouse, "Levee Chronology."

approved federal levee improvements on the Wood River in 1936. As early as 1942, the district was seeking to extend these levees to provide additional protection to industrial areas north and south of the river. A separate study completed in 1953 also recommended extension of the Wood River levees northward to provide protection to the city of Alton, which had a population just over 30,000 at that time. Although partially protected by the Wood River levees, gaps in the protection allowed flooding of about 100 acres in the business district, which had caused $1 million in damages since 1943. The project flood – 650,000 cfs – would have caused closer to $3 million. The proposed project included a little over a mile of levees and floodwalls, with levees and a closure structure adjacent to the Lock and Dam No. 26 guide wall and access road, a pump station, and improvements to the city sewer system. Total cost was $4.2 million, of which the local share was $886,000. Congress approved the project in the Flood Control Act of 1954. In 1958, the district renewed recommendation of extending the Wood River levees from Alton to Hartford to protect more than 7,000 acres of industrial area. The proposed levees included extension and reconstruction of 22 miles of levees north, south, and along the fork of the river, raised to a height of 45 feet on the St. Louis gage, with riverside levees raised to 52 feet. This required more than 20 closure structures of various design. The district also recommended numerous pump stations and sewer improvements to aid interior drainage for a total of $15 million. The district added another pump station and enlargement of drainage structures in a report of 1963.[136]

In 1957, Congress requested an inquiry into what modification to flood protection was necessary for the Mississippi between the Missouri and Ohio rivers, specifically mentioning St. Clair and Madison counties, Illinois. By the time the district completed the study in 1963, the 22 miles of levees in the East Side Levee District approved in 1936 were more than 83 percent complete, with an expected completion date of June 30, 1964. There were, nevertheless, still issues with interior drainage in low areas near Blue Waters Ditch and Harding Ditch, and also near the Cahokia Creek diversion, which funneled the creek outside of the levee. The overflow in these areas impacted 18,000 acres with annual damages estimated to increase to $980,000 as industrialization of the region increased. Among the improvements the district recommended were improved

---

[136] U.S. Cong., *Mississippi River, Urban Areas at Alton, Ill.*, H.D. 397 (83rd Cong., 2nd Sess.): 1-27; *Wood River Levee and Drainage District*, H.D. 150 (88th Cong., 1st Sess.): 1-48; USACE, *Wood River Levee and Drainage District*, GDM No. 4 (St. Louis: MVS, 1958): 1-57.

ditches, a storage reservoir in Little Canteen Creek, and a new pump station for $9.3 million, of which $3.1 million was local. Congress approved the plan in the Flood Control Act of 1965. An additional interior drainage study completed in 1984 found other improvements as not economically justified because of the low property value of remaining areas prone to flooding, although Congress did authorize reconstruction and repair of the pump station, drainage works, and several bridges in the Energy and Water Development Appropriations Act of 1988 for $37 million. Additional interior flooding in the vicinity of East St. Louis from 1993 to 1996 prompted Congress to request a reevaluation in 1997. After several years of study, in 2000 the Corps proposed converting the project to an ecosystem restoration project, and started developing funding estimates. The report, which Chief of Engineers Lt. Gen. Carl A. Strock signed on December 22, 2004, included projects such as diversions, creek channel relocation, sediment retention structures, and wetlands development around eight bottomland areas that had incidental flood control benefits for a total of $208 million. Congress approved the project in the Water Resources Development Act of 2007. Once approved, the district started monitoring ecological conditions and modeling the solution but had not started construction as of 2010.[137]

As early as 1935, the district considered levees from Alton to Gale, Illinois, as a unit, despite being managed by 17 levee and drainage districts. Part of the reason was that multiple levee districts protected some urban areas, requiring coordination with various agencies to complete flood protection. Despite continuation of multiple projects in these areas, by 1950 the district discussed the system as the Alton-to-Gale levees. Significant reaches of these levees were complete by 1968, including at Prairie du Pont and the East Side levees, with the remainder complete by 1977. Even before this time, many of the levees experienced slides resulting from clay soils cracking during hot weather and partially collapsing during high water in areas where the slope was too steep. By 1961, these slides were so extensive and frequent that the district started to maintain an inventory of them. Most levee districts saw 20 or more slides over the next 48 years, with some districts – such as Grand Tower and Degognia – experiencing as many as 200 slides during this period. The slides impacted nearly 25 miles of levee along the system. Although the St. Louis District was

---

[137] *Annual Report of the Chief of Engineers, 1997-2008*; *Water Resources Development Act of 2007*, PL 110-114 (110th Cong., 1st Sess.): Tit. 1, Sec. 1001: 18; "East St. Louis and Vicinity, Illinois" (*www.mvs.usace.army.mil/pm/esl-vicinity/index.html*, Apr. 6, 2011).

able to repair most of the slides after the fact using PL84-99 funds for emergency repair, it recognized as early as 1979 that preventative measures were necessary to address the problems long-term. That year and in 1986, the district proposed repairing the levee sections by degrading the levees and rebuilding them using replacement materials. In 1997, the district submitted a draft report recommending a repair method using an injection of a lime-fly ash mixture to fill cracks and stabilize the soils for $113 million. The Memphis District had been using similar methods to repair levees since 1995. As of 2010, the project was undergoing independent peer review before final submission.[138]

Ste. Genevieve

Despite early interest in making improvements to Ste. Genevieve, it was the last prominent town in the district to see flood protection. In 1936, Congress had approved improvements to levees southeast of the town to protect

Ste. Genevieve, MO during 1973 flood

---

[138] *Annual Report of the Chief of Engineers, 1997-2008*; Dyhouse, "Levee Chronology"; Gary P. Lowe, Presentation, Alton to Gale Organized Levee Districts, Illinois and Missouri (Continuing, Deficiency Corrections) Letter Report, Jul. 15, 2010 (MVS Archives).

farmland in Ste. Genevieve Levee District No. 1, and the Corps started plans on the levees in 1941 but delayed the project because of the war other than reviewing and recommending modification of the project to cover the Common Big Field near Valle Spring Branch. In 1945, Congress requested an investigation of flood control requirements between Ste. Genevieve and St. Mary's focusing on the Cottonwoods area west of Kaskaskia, so the St. Louis District suspended further action on improvements to the Levee District No. 1 levees outside of town until it could advance a final plan. In 1948, the Corps completed this study. After reviewing three options, it recommended an extension of the Perry County levees along the waterfront, to incorporate the original Ste. Genevieve Levee District levees as well as include protection of the Cottonwood and Common Big Field areas, for $5.7 million in federal spending. All levees would be two feet higher than the 50-year flood (1903). However, none of these levees actually entered into town, and Congress never approved the project, probably because of the low cost-benefit justification – the population of Ste. Genevieve was never greater than five thousand.[139]

Although the town itself did not request protection of industrial assets, it did finally request protection of historical assets. In 1950, as part of its analysis of flood protection along the Middle Mississippi requested by Congress in 1844, the St. Louis District conducted a preliminary study recommending a detailed survey to see if flood protection was warranted, but the town never requested further study. By the mid-1960s, however, the Ste. Genevieve Tourist Bureau had developed a master plan for restoration of the town based on its historic past. Established in 1735 – nearly 30 years before St. Louis – Ste. Genevieve had several buildings older than 150 years centered on a one-mile stretch of river. The master plan proposed relocation of outlying historical buildings, restoring those that were in need of repair, reproducing historical conditions, and adding fencing, landscaping, parking, and vending to provide a tourist attraction for the city. It was only after these improvements came under the assault of the Flood of 1973 that the town requested and Congress funded the study in 1974. The flood had caused more than $1.5 million in damages and potentially threatened long-term destruction of the more than 70 irreplaceable historic buildings. Estimated flood damage for the urban design flood reaching 49 feet on the local gage was more than $7 million. In addition to the Mississippi, the town also faced periodic flash flooding from Gabouri

---

[139] Dyhouse, "Levee Chronology"; USACE, *Ste. Genevieve – St. Marys, Missouri* (St. Louis: MVS, 1948); *Annual Report of the Chief of Engineers, 1941-1948*.

and occasionally Valle Spring creeks. The plan, completed in 1979, proposed a combination of 3.5 miles of levees and three closure gates, two pump stations, drainage improvements, water detention areas, widening and deepening of Gabouri Creek, and environmental and recreational areas just under $40 million. The district reviewed five different alternatives, but none of them had cost-benefit ratios higher than 0.3. Noting that Corps regulations prohibited construction of projects that did not have at least a 1:1 ratio, yet with "sufficient merit" based on environmental and historic benefits, District Engineer Col. Leon E. McKinny argued, "it would, therefore, be up to Congress to override this policy in the interest of historic preservation," and recommended that Congress do so.[140]

The Flood of 1982 struck Ste. Genevieve worse than the Flood of 1973, and most of the historical buildings received some level of damage. With the city continuing to push for protection, the district continued to prepare data for the project, for example through completion of an archaeological assessment of the plan in early 1983, even as the town promoted its historical resources through national publications to help justify the project. Finally, in 1985 the Board of Engineers for Rivers and Harbors submitted its report on the district's 1979

St. Louis floodwall that prevented flooding of large industrial areas during the 1973 flood

---

[140] Allies Engineers and Architects, *The Master Plan for Restoration of Ste. Genevieve, Missouri* (St. Louis: Hellmuth, Obata, and Kasselbaum; Booker and Associates, 1966): 1- 44; USACE, *Ste. Genevieve Survey Report* (St. Louis: MVS, 1979): 1-95, quotes 93, 95.

survey. The board also endorsed the project based on historical value despite the lack of economic justification. By this time, the cost was $31 million, with the local share being $2.5 million. Based on this testimony, Chief of Engineers Lt. Gen. E.R. Heiberg approved the project, which Congress finally added to

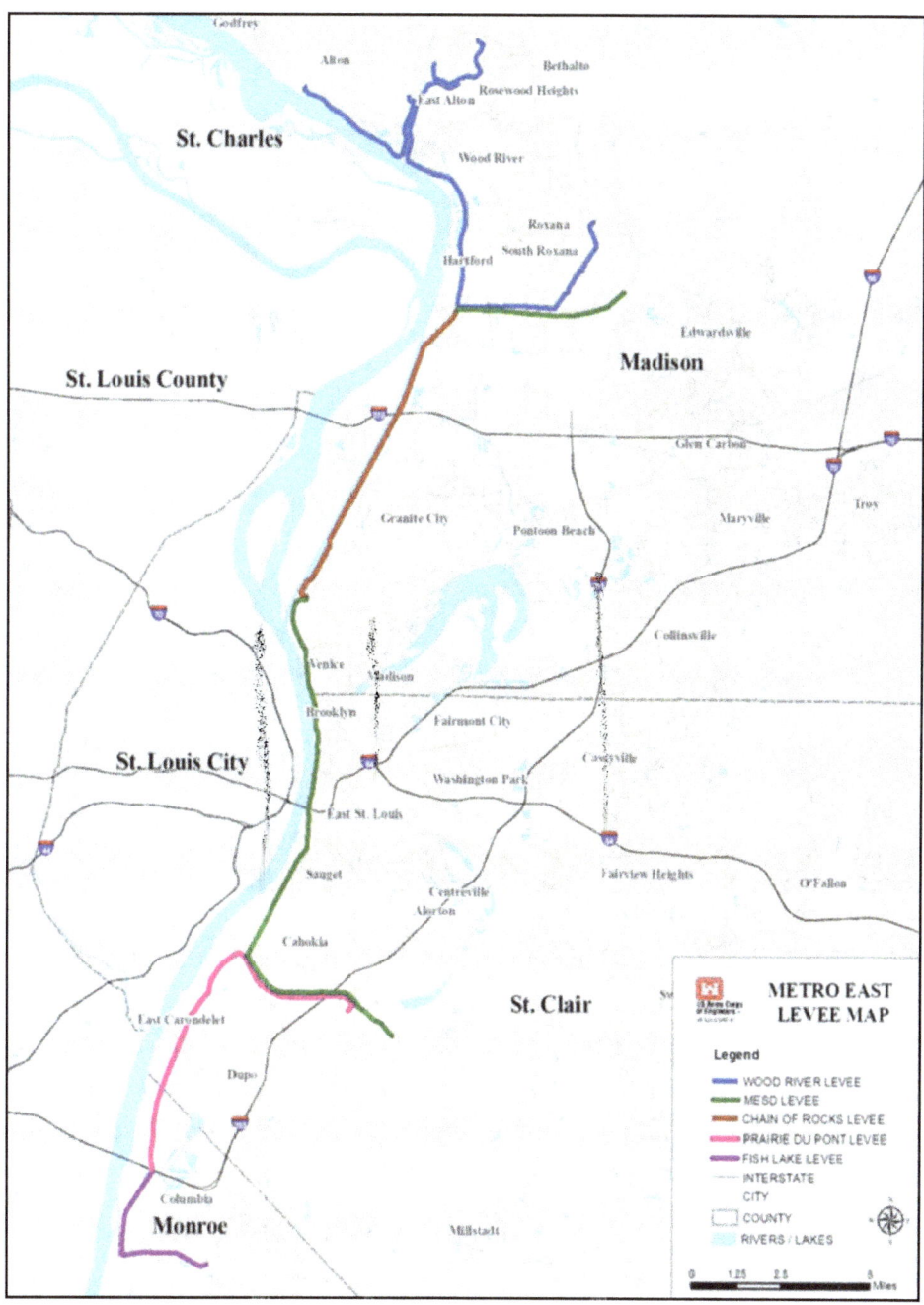

Metro East levees

St. Louis floodwall, September 18, 2008

the Water Resources Development Act of 1986. It took another decade and another major flood – the Flood of 1993 – to convince local agencies to sign the LCA and provide funding for the project. At the time it started, the project cost had increased to $48 million. The groundbreaking ceremony was on August 9, 1997, and most project features were complete by 2002. It took several additional years to complete the recreation features.[141]

---

[141] Michael J. McNerny and R. David Hoxie, *Final Report: Archaeological Resources Survey and Impact Assessment of the Ste. Genevieve Levee Project* (St. Louis: MVS, 1983); Maj. Gen. N.G. Delbridge to Chief of Engineers, Ste. Genevieve, Missouri, Apr. 16, 1985; Heiberg to Secretary of the Army, Aug. 20, 1986 (MVS Archives); Terrie Hatfield, "A new beginning for Ste. Genevieve," *Esprit* (Sept./Oct. 1997): 1, 8, 13; "Ste. Genevieve, MO – High and Dry," *Esprit* (2002): 13; for examples of city promotion, see "Ste. Genevieve: A French Legacy in Middle America," *Better Homes and Gardens Country Home* (August 1985): 58-70.

By 1978, other than annual maintenance and periodic repairs, the original federal levee projects authorized starting in 1936 were complete. The only exception was the Kaskaskia Island levees project, which ended a decade later. The urban projects at Cape Girardeau, St. Louis, East St. Louis, and Alton were also complete, despite the difficulties of construction in a congested urban area and obtaining cost assurances from smaller towns and suburban areas. In 1993, the worst flood in more than 100 years hit the valley. By July, the Mississippi Basin surpassed its average annual rainfall, and July rain was 600 percent above normal. The river was above flood stage (30 feet on the Market Street gage) for 80 consecutive days and 148 days altogether, beating the previous record of 77. It was above 40 feet for 36 days. The more than one million cfs discharge was the highest measured flow to pass St. Louis. Although the St. Louis District saw flood damages exceeding $1.4 billion, the flood control system built by the Corps over the previous 55 years prevented an estimated $5.4 billion in damages – a savings of more than 80 percent. The urban flood control projects were an integral part of this system by preventing or limiting damage to urban and industrial zones not covered by the original project. Had it not been for these projects, the Flood of 1993 and other floods would have assuredly caused even more damage to the St. Louis area.[142]

St. Louis landing, September 18, 2008

---

[142] Gary Dyhouse, "Myths and misconceptions of the 1993 flood," *Esprit* (May 1994): 6-8.

10

Flood Control Reservoirs in the St. Louis District

For more than 70 years, the Corps of Engineers opposed reservoirs as too ineffective and costly to be part of any flood protection plan for the Mississippi Valley. Although the Corps had worked with local levee districts in building flood control reservoirs, primarily at the headwaters of the Mississippi, and had even approved one reservoir for power generation on the Mississippi – at Keokuk, Iowa – it had remained opposed generally to reservoirs despite advocacy by leading engineers. In general, the Corps argued that reservoirs could only reduce flood heights a limited amount, requiring additional and expensive flood control or protection methods such as levees, and that the cost of purchasing land for building enough reservoirs to achieve needed effect was high. This attitude did not really change until the Corps faced the difficulties of resolving real estate issues to implement the Mississippi River and Tributaries Project. By this point, any method of reducing flood heights became acceptable, and in 1935 the Corps identified numerous reservoir sites and adopted a strategy of adopting these gradually mostly at local cost. Several of the reservoirs identified were in St. Louis District, including on the Kaskaskia and Big Muddy rivers, Illinois, and on the St. Francis, Meramec, and Salt rivers, Missouri. Built over several decades as local communities were able to pay for them, the reservoirs helped to reduce localized flooding while providing economic benefits such as recreation areas and power generation.

Slow Acceptance of Reservoirs

European engineers had used reservoirs since at least 1711 as a method of flood control, navigational improvement, and irrigation or water supply. The method typically involved building dams upstream on a river with a spillway to allow controlled overflow. The stream would back up and form a lake, which engineers could use for multiple purposes or release during low water. In the past, however, engineers mostly used them on small streams rather than a large basin that involved dozens of tributary rivers miles from the main stem. The first engineer to suggest using reservoirs to control floods on the Mississippi was Charles Ellet, Jr., in 1849 and then in 1852 in a widely distributed report for the War Department. He believed reservoirs were necessary to offset levees eliminating natural reservoirs on the river and up tributaries, where the river expanded during high water and stored a portion of floodwaters. By building reservoirs on the tributaries, it would not only relieve "the whole valley of the Mississippi" but "render every stream that is ever navigable permanently so." In his 1861 *Mississippi Delta Survey*, Capt. Andrew A. Humphreys, responding to Ellet, argued that such a reservoir system was impractical. While not denying that reservoirs could improve navigation and aid flood control on small rivers, he believed that "the idea that the Mississippi delta may be economically secured against inundation by such dams has been proven ... to be in the highest degree chimerical." Setting aside the question of cost, his analysis of the Flood of 1858 found that it would have been necessary to hold back more than one million cubic feet of water per second for 36 days, which would have required 90,000 square miles of storage, more than the total area available in the Ohio Valley where the majority of floodwaters originated. This made using reservoirs exclusively to prevent floods not only ineffective but nearly impossible, although he did not address the use of reservoirs to supplement other flood control methods.[143]

Later reports, including by the Mississippi River Commission, largely came to the same conclusion as Humphreys. Although the commission lacked the funds in 1880 to conduct a sufficient survey to recommend specific plans for reservoirs, it nevertheless reported favorably on the use of reservoirs at the Mississippi headwaters and on tributaries above the Wisconsin River solely to improve navigation, which it estimated could hold back more than 15,000 cubic feet per second for 100 days. Such a system, the commission argued, would have no appreciable effect below Rock Island, Illinois. Commission president Col. Curtis Townsend, formerly the St. Louis District Engineer, argued after the Flood of 1912 that "a reservoir must be close to the locality to be benefited" and that reservoirs on the Mississippi's tributaries "are too great distance for the regulation of any stream." He also argued they would not be cost-effective because of the amount of storage required to have even a minimal effect on flood levels compared to the lower cost of levees. After the Flood of 1927, the Corps conducted one of the most detailed examinations of reservoirs in its history. Civil engineer James P. Kemper would later observe that

---

[143] *Inundations of the Mississippi River*, in U.S. Cong., *Reports on the Ohio and Mississippi Rivers*, House Flood Control Comm. Doc. 17 (70th Cong., 1st Sess.): 112-120, quote p. 116; *Delta Survey*, pp. 406-411, quote on 411.

"it was a very comprehensive report, indicating much study in a short time." Chief of Engineers Maj. Gen. Edgar Jadwin appointed a board headed by Col. William Kelley, who was retiring from the Federal Power Commission. The board examined existing reservoirs in the Upper Mississippi, at Keokuk, and on the Miami River in Ohio. It also reviewed 203 additional sites. In the end, the board concluded that since it would cost $1.2 billion to build enough reservoirs to store 98-million acre feet of water, and that this would lower flood heights less than 10 feet on average, such a system was not economically justified. It further argued that it would be impossible to develop reservoirs for multiple uses since operating them for local flood control, power, or irrigation would likely conflict with the need to time the release of water specifically for Mississippi River flood control.[144]

Despite such opposition, reservoirs remained the preference of leading conservationists such as Gifford Pinchot because they believed they could be used for multiple purposes, i.e., for agriculture, water supply, navigation, and flood control. This was by no means a universal attitude, and many recognized as Kelley did the difficulties in operating reservoirs for multiple purposes while still being able to reduce floods. Power generation required a constant flow to turn turbines, irrigation or water supplies required a fairly full reservoir year-round, while flood control required low levels prior to spring rains to contain floodwaters. Other engineers argued strenuously for reservoirs to supplement levees in lieu of outlets, which were highly unpopular. Kemper, for example, drafted a plan for the Louisiana Board of Engineers based on a subset of 11 reservoirs identified by Kelley along the Arkansas and White rivers, which he believed would lower flood levels enough to eliminate the proposed Boeuf Floodway in Arkansas. Another reservoir proponent, Miami Conservancy president Arthur Morgan, doubted that the commission had seriously considered reservoirs and later proposed a series of reservoirs on the Tennessee and Ohio rivers as president of the Tennessee Valley Association.[145]

---

[144] U.S. Cong., *Report of the Mississippi River Commission, 1880*, H.D. 95 (46th Cong., 3rd Sess.): 8-14; Townsen quoted in Benjamin G. Humphreys, *Floods and Levees of the Mississippi River* (Wash.: Miss. River Ass., 1914): 141-142; *Report on the Control of Floods of the Mississippi River by Means of Reservoirs*, House Flood Control Comm. Doc. 2 (70th Cong., 1st Sess.): 1-33; Kemper quote from *Rebellious River* (Boston: Bruce Humphreys, 1949): 114.
[145] Morgan, "Flood Control by Reservoirs," *ENR* (Aug. 12, 1937): 263-268; "Reservoir Control for Mississippi Suggested by 1927 Flood Data," *ENR* (Mar. 20, 1930): 488. On differences on reservoirs, compare Pinchot in U.S. Cong., House Committee on Flood Control, *House Flood Control Hearings*, Vol. 5, (70th Cong., 1st Sess.): 3467-3486; Elmer Peterson, *Big Dam Foolishness: The Problem of Modern Flood Control and Water Storage* (NY: Devin-Adair, 1954): 93; and Luna B. Leopold and Thomas Maddock, Jr., *The Flood Control Controversy: Big Dams, Little Dams, and Land Management* (NY: Ronald Press, 1954): 36-51, 246.

As a result of continued questions about reservoirs, Congress repeatedly requested consideration by the Corps of flood plans using them, particularly after Maj. Gen. Lytle Brown became Chief of Engineers in 1929. However, he refused to commit to any plan until completion of the 308 Reports established by the Rivers and Harbors Act of 1927. House Document 308 of the 69th Congress recommended that the Corps conduct surveys to determine whether improvements for all major waterways were justified for power generation, irrigation, or flood control. Conducted by local district engineers, the surveys took many years to complete. The first report based on this data, the 1931 commission report on modification of the Mississippi River and Tributaries Project, examined 269 reservoir sites in various combinations for $547 million, but none of them eliminated the use of floodways, making them an added cost. However, the report did establish the concept that the government would need to build a system of reservoirs gradually as funding allowed rather than all at once as with most Corps projects. With the completion of 156 of the 308 Reports by the end of 1933, the Corps finally submitted its comprehensive review of reservoir sites in 1935. In the report, the commission reviewed three plans, one that proposed operation of reservoirs for Mississippi flood reduction, one for localized flood reduction, and one to achieve the greatest reduction in flood heights for the lowest price since the first two plans cost more than $1 billion. Given the cost, it recommended building and operating reservoirs for local flood reduction as local resources allowed. Although this lessened the effect on the Mississippi, it made the reservoirs inherently more desirable for local levee boards, which would then pay the majority of the cost of the reservoirs. Later, provisions in the Flood Control Act of 1944 (PL 78-534) authorized construction of recreation areas at reservoirs, increasing their local value and making them multiple-purpose. Among the reservoirs identified were four that would eventually fall in the St. Louis District on the Meramec and Salt Rivers, Missouri, and the Kaskaskia and Big Muddy Rivers, Illinois. The district would spend the next 40 years completing these, and one it never completed.[146]

---

[146] U.S. Cong., *Control of Floods in the Alluvial Valley of the Lower Mississippi River*, Vol. 1, H.D. 798 (71st Cong., 3rd Sess.): 1-15; *Comprehensive Report on Reservoirs in Mississippi River Basin*, H.D. 259 (74th Cong., 1st Sess.): 1-42; *Flood Control Act of 1944* (78th Cong., 2nd Sess.): Sec. 4.

Reservoir Construction Begins

The first reservoir built in the district was the Wappapello Dam and Reservoir on the St. Francis River in the Ozarks of southern Missouri, although it was in the Memphis District at the time of its construction. There had been long-running problems with flooding in the St. Francis Basin. Mississippi River Commission levees provided some relief after 1917, but there was still extensive flooding at its headwaters far from the levees. After passage of the Rivers and Harbors Act of 1927, the Memphis District completed the 308 reports on the St. Francis River in 1929 and 1930, focusing on the upper river and backwater area. Although the reports considered a power generation reservoir at Wappapello, Missouri, it found the reservoir more expensive than a system of levees and recommended it as not economically justified. It was not, therefore, included in the 1935 Corps reservoir report. In 1935, the St. Francis Levee District proposed a flood control reservoir at Wappapello instead of more extensive levees to protect against headwater flooding. Although the plan cost roughly the same, "it is believed to be better engineering," Memphis District Engineer Maj. William E. Hoge wrote. Approved by the commission, the reservoir was among changes to the Mississippi River and Tributaries (MR&T) Project Congress authorized in the Overton Act of 1936. The Corps started construction in 1938 and completed it in 1941. The reservoir included a 2,700-foot earthen dam with a concrete spillway and three 20-foot wide tainter gates. The resulting pool held 613,000 acre-feet, of which 23,000 was for flood reduction. Although constructed and operated by the Memphis District as part of the MR&T, since the reservoir fell within area already in the St. Louis District, the Corps transferred it to St. Louis District control in 1982, including operation of both the reservoir and recreation site. The current site, 150 miles south of St. Louis and just west of Cape Girardeau, includes 180 miles of shoreline and beaches and 44,000 acres of wilderness trails and areas. Through a memorandum of understanding with the district, The Nature Conservancy helps to monitor and maintain the unique ecology of the site, such as Deep Muck Fen.[147]

Most other reservoir projects in the district were initially included in the 1935 Corps Reservoir Report. Perhaps the largest of these were on the Kaskaskia River in Illinois. Although the Kaskaskia Basin was not a major industrial

---

[147] U.S. Cong., *St. Francis River, Mo. And Ark.*, H.D. 159 (71st Cong., 2nd Sess.): 1-3; Hoge to Div. Eng., Report on letter from Mr. H.N. Pharr, Mar. 15, 1935 (MRC Archives); "Wappapello Lake: Pride of Southeast Missouri," *Esprit* (Nov. 1996): 1, 6; Wappapello Fact Sheet (*http://www.mvs.usace.army.mil/wappapello/wap-facts.htm*, Apr. 26, 2011).

Wappapello Dam, 1945

Wappapello Dam, 2008

base – it was mostly agricultural other than a well-developed timber industry – it contained a fairly large population, with 350,000 spread over the 5,800-mile area and at least four urban areas greater than 10,000 in population. The 325-mile river flooded annually, with the flood of record being in 1943, which reached stages near 40 feet at New Athens and over 20 feet at Shelbyville. These caused average annual damages exceeding $2.5 million including urban areas. Over time, 129 levee and drainage districts tried to improve the situation through drainage ditches, and eight of them built low levees totaling 36 miles, yet flooding remained an issue. As noted previously, a survey for a system of navigation locks and dams conducted in 1933 found the project "inadvisable" because "the river is clearly not suitable for improvement for modern barge navigation." However, the Corps had proposed a reservoir near Carlyle in its 1935 reservoir report, but, without a corresponding detailed 308 report, did not provide specifics. The Flood of 1937 generated interest in the project, and after a preliminary survey Congress authorized a dam and reservoir in the Flood Control Act of 1938. The initial plan developed by 1940 was for a 2,600-foot dam and spillway at Carlyle, a reservoir to hold 860,000 acre-feet, and levees between Carlyle and New Athens to protect the basin from overflow. Like other projects approved prior to 1941, World War II delayed completion of the plans. Once the war was over, local interests formed organizations to

Aerial of Carlyle Lake

push for the project, including the Kaskaskia Industrial Development Corporation and Kaskaskia Valley Association. Among the citizens leading the effort were Emil Bugard, the president of the development corporation, association president and attorney Eldon Hazlett, development corporation secretary and realtor Albert Wilson, and publisher Henry Norcross. These organized numerous public meetings to discuss the projects, which intensified after the 1950 Flood.[148]

After several years of local organizations lobbying for the project, the Corps completed a revised report in 1957. The report included the Carlyle Dam and Reservoir more or less as previously designed. This was a 2,600-foot dam with a concrete spillway and seven 40-foot tainter gates, holding back 983,000 acre-feet in storage in a lake with 83 miles of shoreline. However, the plan also added a dam and reservoir at Shelbyville. This included a 3,000-foot earthen dam with five 40-foot tainter gates. The reservoir would hold 474,000 acre-feet with 172 miles of shoreline. Both projects would include recreation features, including campgrounds, wilderness areas, and boating and swimming facilities. Total cost was $73 million at a benefit-cost ratio of 1.3. The Shelbyville project alone was expected to increase the number of boats navigating the river to 3,000 per year, attract up to four million visitors and generate more than $13 million per year in revenue by 1971, and provide for a general increase in land values. The Flood Control Act of 1958 authorized both projects and removed the Carlyle reservoir from the Mississippi River Basin Plan to authorize it as a separate project. With its design already complete, construction on the Carlyle Dam started in 1958, was 25 percent complete by 1962, and finished in 1967 for a total cost of $42 million. Design of the Shelbyville Dam started in 1958, and work on the reservoir started in 1963 with filling in of old local mines, the location of many of which had never been recorded. The Corps opened the reservoir in 1970 with a dedication ceremony on September 12. After congressional approval, the Corps completed the local cooperation agreement for the New Athens levees in 1964 and started construction in 1965. At the recommendation of the Board of Engineers for Rivers and Harbors, the federal government assumed the total cost of the levees, including the $3.5 million in local contributions, provided the local levee organizations paid for easements

---

[148] "Emile Bugard Faithful Backer of Project," East St. Louis *Sunday Journal* (July 29, 1962): 4; U.S. Cong., *Kaskaskia River, Illinois*, H.D. 232 (85th Cong., 1st Sess.): 1-18; Dobney, pp. 138-140.

and rights of way. The project was complete by 1970 other than a $26 million upgrade to recreational facilities on both lakes approved in 2010.[149]

Both the Shelbyville and Carlyle reservoirs are operated under an approved Water Control Plan and have active upstream and downstream coalitions. Several groups organized to address issues relevant to their specific section of the Kaskaskia River. These groups worked in partnership with the St. Louis District and divided the river into four reaches. These groups came together in the mid-1990s to form a coalition that came to be called the Kaskaskia Watershed Association (KWA). District representatives meet regularly with the association's board to discuss the management of the basin. The goals of this cooperative include effective use of the basin's resources, economic development, increased recreational opportunities, sound agricultural practices, and ecosystem restoration. The collaborative between the KWA and the district increased support for corps projects in the watershed while maximizing the benefits of the projects.[150]

A second location identified in the 1935 Reservoir Report was the 155-mile Big Muddy River in Illinois. Since 1915, the 2,300-mile river basin experienced six major floods, with the flood of record in 1961 achieving 25.9 feet at Benton and 29.6 feet in Plumfield. Average annual damages exceeded $157,000. Total population of the two counties near the river – Jefferson and Franklin – was 71,600 in 1962, half of it urban, with coal, timber, and agriculture being leading industries. The region had suffered chronic unemployment since the Great Depression, making job creation an important rationale for a project. Although studies in 1925 and 1933 did not find flood control or navigation projects justified, the Corps considered the river a potential location for a reservoir, but there was no serious investigation of the site until after World War II. In 1949, Congress requested a review of flood control plans, and in response Illinois formed the Rend Lake Conservancy District in 1955 to urge creation of the reservoir. The 1957 feasibility study found navigational improvement was possible but did not address flood control. However, an Illinois study the same year favored a reservoir for recreation and water supply. A 1961 hearing on

---

[149] *Kaskaskia River, Illinois*, pp. 18-48; "Carlyle Lake," *Esprit* (Jan. 1996): 1, 6-9; Annette, McMichael, "Lake Shelbyville: Central Illinois showpiece," *Esprit* (Apr. 1996): 1, 6; MVS, "Carlyle Lake, Illinois," 1996 brochure (MVS Archives); "Thousands Witness 'Beginning of Era,'" Moultrie County, Ill., *News*, newsclipping, May 9, 1963 (MVS Archives); USACE, "Shelbyville Dam Dedication After Action Review (St. Louis: MVS, 1970); U.S. Cong., *Kaskaskia River Levees, Illinois*, H.D. 351 (88th Cong., 2nd Sess.): 1-10; Dobney, pp. 138-140

[150] Information Paper, Kaskaskia River Watershed based Pilot Budget for FY 2014 (MVS Archives, N.D.); Information paper, Kaskaskia Watershed Association, Inc. (MVS Archives, N.D.).

Aerial of Rend Lake, 2008

the issue in Benton drew more than 500, including the governor, congressmen, and local mayors, most of whom favored project. The largest concern was the number of coal mines the lake would cover, and although some companies sought compensation, Corps policy was to allow continued mining in the project area. The Corps submitted its final report in 1962 proposing an earthen dam near Benton with a 500-foot concrete spillway and vertical lift gates. The reservoir would hold 302,000 acre-feet of water, 111,000 for flood control. This would lower flooding by up to six feet. Total cost was $30 million at a benefit-cost ratio of 1.6. Approved in the Flood Control Act of 1962, construction started on the impoundment dams in 1965 and the main dam in 1968. It was complete in 1970 and operational in 1972 for a final cost of $60 million. Since its completion, the recreation features have been critical in providing jobs for the local community. Use of the wilderness area has grown annually – 27 percent in 1994 alone – generating $200,000 annually. In 2010, the Corps started a $26 million upgrade to facilities on the lake.[151]

The next reservoir completed was the Cannon Dam and Reservoir on the Salt River in Missouri. The Salt River is 192 miles long. More than 95,000 live in the 2,920 square-mile basin, more than half in urban areas. At the

---

[151] U.S. Cong., *Rend Lake Reservoir, Illinois*, H.D. 541 (87th Cong., 2nd Sess.): 1-39; Interview with Elmer F. Huizenga, N.D. (MVS Archives); Mark Meador and Maureen Curran, "Rend Lake: Gateway to Southern Illinois," Esprit (Mar. 1996): 1, 6; Dobney, pp. 140-142.

same time, more than 9,500 soybean, corn, and wheat farms dot the rural areas, which were subject to frequent flash floods. The largest flood on record, that of 1958, had a flow of up to 70,000 cubic feet per second, which resulted in flood heights of 29.9 feet at New London and 34.8 feet at Monroe City. Average annual damages were $339,000. Local residents first proposed a dam to increase river depth in 1931, but it was never built. The Corps initially included it as a potential reservoir site in its 1935 Reservoir

Map of Mark Twain Lake and Clarence Cannon Dam

Report, and the 1936 Flood Control Act authorized a study of a reservoir and levees on the Salt River. After an initial public meeting at which the 125 attendees gave approval to the project, numerous locally organized meetings followed. The district completed its initial study in 1937 but did not recommend a plan. Nevertheless, the 1938 Flood Control Act authorized a dam and reservoir near Joanna, Missouri. In a report published in 1940, the Federal Power Commission recommended revising the project to include power generation, but no action was taken because of U.S. entry into the war. Once the war was over, Chief of Engineers Lt. Gen. Raymond A. Wheeler requested a restudy of the project in 1946, but with no change in results. It was not until Congress requested a study in 1961 that the Corps finally developed a new plan for a reservoir for power generation and flood control. The study reviewed three potential sites but continued to support the site near Joanna. The design included a 1,900-foot earthen dam and a concrete spillway with seven 40-foot

Construction of Clarence Cannon Dam 12 April 1977

tainter gates. The reservoir would hold 880,000 acre-feet of storage for flood control and 437,000 for power generation. The Northeast Missouri Electric Power Cooperative would be responsible for the 50,000 to 62,000 kilowatts generated by the plant. In addition, the project included 36 miles of channel improvement for a total cost of $63 million at a benefit-cost ratio of 1.3. Since the construction of the reservoir, it has held back inflows greater than 70,000 dsf on seven occasions, and even held back over 100,000 dsf in 2008. The reservoir has been integral to flood control plans, under-promising but over-performing, it has prevented more than $1 billion in flood damages over the life of the project.[152]

The Flood Control Act of 1962 authorized the reservoir as a project separate from the Mississippi River Basin Plan. After four years of design from 1963 to 1966 and several more years of site preparation, construction on the dam started in 1971 and came to a conclusion in 1983. With the pool filled, the Corps dedicated it in 1984 as the Clarence Cannon Dam, named after the long-serving Missouri U.S. Representative, and christened the pool the Mark Twain Lake. The Corps operates the dam remotely from the Kansas City District, which is actually closer to the dam's location, with an automatic test index

Assembly of stay ring at Clarence Cannon Dam. Ring used for controlling flow of water to turbine runner, 1980

---

[152] U.S. Cong., Salt River, Missouri, H.D. 507 (87th Cong., 2nd Sess.): 1-58; "Cannon Dam and Mark Twain Lake," *Esprit* (Feb. 1996): 6; Dobney, pp. 142-144.

capability that allows users to interactively adjust turbine efficiency. Northeast Power Cooperative runs the power yard, selling electricity primarily to the Association of Missouri Electric Cooperatives Inc., with excess power sold to Southwest Power Association. The association includes 40 member-owned cooperatives across Missouri.[153]

The final reservoir recommended by the Corps was the Meramec Dam and Reservoir on the Meramec River in Missouri. There had been numerous studies of a dam on this river. The earliest study of the river in 1880 found it could not be improved and later studies for hydropower found it unsuitable for a power generation reservoir. There were, however, long-term flooding problems in the extensive basin. The 308 study of the basin, completed in 1929, recommended a flood control reservoir, the 1935 Reservoir Report included it, and Congress approved it in the 1938 Flood Control Act. Delayed by World War II, the project did not receive close attention until after the war, with a 1949 report published by a Meramec River Cooperative that recommended a plan of multiple dams and reservoirs for navigation similar to what the Corps had installed on the Ohio River and elsewhere. However, with rediscovery of parts of the basin as pristine wilderness areas, there was widespread environmental concern among

Aerial of Mark Twain Lake and Clarence Cannon Dam, 2008

---

[153] "Cannon Power Plant First in Nation," *Esprit* (Mar. 1988): 6; "Cannon Dam"; "Clarence Cannon Dam and Mark Twain Lake," brochure, MVS, 2007 (MVS Archives); "Electric Co-ops in Missouri" (*ww.amec.org/coops.html*, May 10, 2011).

local citizens who opposed the plan. The district took a cautious approach to studying the reservoir, holding frequent public meetings from 1947 to 1949, but as opposition grew, the governor of Illinois postponed further planning for the basin and requested suspension of the project. The Chief of Engineers officially suspended the project in 1951. Over the next decade, severe flooding in the Meramec Basin sparked renewed interest in the project, but environmental organizations remained opposed to it. Although planning continued on the project for the next two decades, environmental opposition prevented any action on the project other than preliminary real estate purchases. It would remain a thorny issue throughout the 1970s (see Section V).[154]

Since their construction, district reservoirs have played a critical role in reducing flood stages on both the Mississippi River and its tributaries. Taken alone, reservoirs may not seem to reduce flood stages significantly, but these reservoirs must be understood as merely one element of a system that also includes floodwalls, agricultural levees, and urban levees. The district must also balance recreation needs with flood management, as holding back too much or too little water in reservoirs can create less than desirable conditions for recreation seekers. During periods of high precipitation, reservoirs store enough water to reduce flooding downstream, with the water being released so as to minimize flood damages downstream.

The efficacy of the Kaskaskia reservoirs has been put to the test numerous times since their construction, preventing an estimated $622 million in economic losses between 1993 and 2011 alone. One of the first tests occurred in August of 1978, when torrential rains in would have caused significant flooding in the Kaskaskia River Basin had it not been for Lake Shelbyville. The inflow into the reservoir rose to 17,000 CFS, yet downstream of the reservoir the Kaskaskia remained within its banks. During the potential flood, the reservoir stored over 18 billion gallons of flood waters, preventing an estimated $1.1 million in damages.[155]

One of the greatest tests for the two reservoirs came in the spring of 2002. Rainfall 150 percent above normal saturated the region by late April 2002, yet the reservoirs still had over 100 percent of their storage capacity by the end of April. When rainfall reached 200 percent above average for the month of

---

[154] T. Michael Ruddy, *Damning the Dam: The St. Louis District Corps of Engineers and the controversy over the Meramec Basin Project from its inception to its deauthorization* (St. Louis: MVS, 1992): 1-30; Dobney, pp. 144-147; Michael Ruddy, Interview with Michael Dace, Feb. 15, 1985 (MVS Archives).
[155] "Shelbyville dam credited with preventing floods," *Clinton County News* (Aug. 30, 1978); Information Paper, Kaskaskia River Watershed based Pilot Budget for FY 2014 (MVS Archives, N.D.).

May, flooding became a major concern downstream of Lake Carlyle. If the district followed its approved Water Control Plan, recreation would have suffered greatly and farmers would not have been able to plant their crops. The control plan determines minimum and maximum releases through a combination of the time of year, pool levels, downstream conditions, and future precipitation forecasts. The plan also included a mechanism for temporary deviation which allowed Water Control Managers to deviate from the approved plan when deemed appropriate. This was just such a circumstance, as deviation was necessary to limit losses from flooding. On April 21, district Water Control Managers made an aggressive move with the pool elevation at 443.79 feet NGVD (below target elevation), deciding to make bankfull releases that would allow for as much flood control storage as possible. Rain continued to fall into late-April and early-May, with pool elevations at Carlyle reaching above 455.6 feet NGVD by May 14. On May 16, a new record pool elevation was set and eventually levels reached nearly 460 feet NGVD, just 2.5 feet from the top of the flood control pool. If downstream releases were too high, they would impact farmers well into planting season; however, if discharge was too low, recreation facilities would have to remain closed until near the end of the season. The challenge was finding a way to save both the recreation and crop season. On May 16, district personnel spent all night going over various scenarios and trying to work out a solution with members of the Kaskaskia coalition. The coalitions and the district developed a deviation from the plan that was agreeable for both farmers and recreationists, allowing downstream farmers to plant and harvest crop prior to the 4th of July so that recreation could resume by the holiday. The solution was raising discharge above maximum levels (10,000 cfs) in 1,000 cfs increments. The discharge eventually reached 13,000 cfs and flooded approximately 26,000 acres of agricultural land, but farmers were still able to plant and recreation use at Lake Carlyle reached 94 percent of what it was in 2001 and 2003.[156]

The performance of reservoirs is perhaps best exemplified by the 1993 flood. During the event, federal flood control reservoirs stored over 17 million acre feet of water, none of which reached St. Louis until after the August crest. These reservoirs are estimated to have reduced flood levels at St. Louis by three feet. Mark Twain was filled and emptied three and a half times during the 1993 flood, and average daily inflows were as high as 92,000 cfs. Yet releases never

---

[156] Joan Stemler and Jackie Taylor, "The Kaskaskia Flood of 2002: A Case Study on Cooperation and Conflicting Project Purposes" (St. Louis: MVS, 2002)

exceeded 12,000 cfs and during critical periods, releases were maintained at around 50 cfs. Water Control Managers at Mark Twain were able to ensure that the maximum release rate was observed whenever possible so that pool elevations could remain low. Yet discharge had to remain low during critical periods to reduce flood levels downstream. Thus, Water Control Managers had to constantly monitor conditions at their own reservoirs while at the same time monitoring conditions downstream as well as forecasts for future precipitation. While the 1993 flood was devastating, it could have been far worse had it not been for the reservoirs. The experience gained in the 1993 flood helped the district to prevent what could have been a devastating flood the very next year. Had it not been for Mark Twain and Truman lakes, flood stages could have reached 47.4 feet in St. Louis. Yet the stage at St. Louis reached on 36.6 feet because Truman Lake and Mark Twain Lake absorbed inflows of 400,000 cfs and 75,000 cfs respectively, while only releasing 500 cfs and 50 cfs respectively. The flood stage could have been second only to that of the 1993 flood, and yet because of the performance of the reservoirs, the 1994 flood became the disaster that never happened.[157]

Growth in District Responsibilities

The St. Louis District made several organizational changes to support new work on reservoirs. One change was enlargement of the Real Estate Office. Creation of a reservoir required purchasing thousands of acres of land – not only for building dams and spillways but also the land flooded to create the lakes. To handle these transactions, the district created an enlarged Real Estate Office. The office reached peak employment of 73 in 1967 in the Meramec project, declining to between 20 and 30 personnel for most of the 1980s and 1990s, after which it reached a low of 15 personnel in 2007. This corresponded to the number of field offices the St. Louis District Real Estate Office operated at reservoir sites – five in 1967, declining to three in 1973, all of which were eliminated after 1978 with completion of the projects. These employed the majority of the personnel in the office. Led by Elmer Huizenga for more than 38 years (1951-1973), the district's Real Estate Office had one of the best records of amicable resolution of condemnation suits in the Corps, obtaining 85 percent of land tracts through voluntary purchase. In addition, as the number of recreation

---

[157] James T. Lovelace and Claude N. Strauser, "Protecting Society from Flood Damage: A Case Study from the 1993 Flood" (*www.mvs-wc.mvs.usace.army.mil/papers/93flood/93flood.html*, Jan. 13, 2012).

facilities under Corps management grew, the district required enlarged operations. The Corps employed dozens of park rangers and other employees to manage camp grounds, wilderness areas, boat ramps, and swimming areas. It also maintained operators and technicians at each dam to manage the overflow and water levels in the lake. Prior to 1966, the district had an integrated Construction-Operations Division, but the district created a separate Operations Division by 1967 and a separate Recreation Resources Management Branch in 1970 (later renamed the Natural Resources Management Branch). A reservoir office opened at Carlyle in 1966, Shelbyville in 1970, Rend Lake in 1971, Cannon in 1975, Wappapello in 1983, and Cannon Power Plant in 1985. Each reservoir employed 30 to 40 personnel, increasing the operations total to more than 170 by 1983, where it has consistently remained until combination of the construction and operations divisions again in 1993.[158]

Despite the initial misgivings of the Corps about the cost-effectiveness of reservoirs, ultimately, the Corps embraced them because, even when operated for local flood control as most were designed, they still aided flood control to a degree on the Mississippi River. There is little doubt that the reservoirs helped local communities. From 1985, the first year after the last dam became operational, until 2010, the Shelbyville and Carlyle dams had prevented an estimated $691 million in damages, Rend Dam $550 million, Wappapello Dam $100 million, and Cannon Dam more than $2 billion. At the same time, the recreational areas built near the reservoirs generated anywhere from several hundred thousand dollars to more than $10 million in revenue annually, which provided an enormous boost to local communities. The Cannon Dam provided power used throughout the state of Missouri by many rural areas that would not likely be able to generate their own power. Such benefits often outweighed the high cost of federal investment in developing and operating these projects.[159]

---

[158] Dobney, p. 144; Interview with Huizenga; District Organization Charts (MVS Archives).
[159] *Annual Report to Congress for Flood Damage Reduction*; E-mail, Don Cool to Damon Manders, reservoir data, Apr. 26, 2011; One cubic foot of water per second amounts to 724 acre-feet per year.

Center for Dam Monitoring

The St. Louis District completed construction on the Clarence Cannon Dam in 1983. Because of its distance from district offices and to reduce overhead, by 1987 it had installed automated monitoring and management systems to allow the Kansas City District (the closest to the dam) to remotely operate the dam. Based on this experience, Headquarters tasked the district to develop guidance and conduct PROSPECT classes. In 1995, Headquarters assigned the district as the Technical Center of Expertise (TCX) for Automated Performance Monitoring of Dams. The first chief of the center was Jim Brown.

As the TCX, the district provides support for agencies requiring aid in designing, procuring, installing, integrating, training on, and maintaining systems for collecting, transmitting, and reading data for monitoring and managing dams and related structures. Because of the lack of commercially available software, the district developed the Instrumentation Database Package, which it ported to Microsoft Windows in 1996. As of 2011, version 5.0 of the software was available.

As aging monitoring systems have reached obsolescence, one of the issues the center faced was to upgrade systems. For example, in 2010, it helped upgrade hardware and software for monitoring the Chief Joseph and Howard Hansen dams in the Seattle District. It helped replace 79 legacy data loggers – including hardware and software – that had been monitoring 980 instruments at the dams since the 1970s. Another major issue faced by systems is grounding and lightning protection.

With continued downsizing of the Corps after 1990 and increased concern with the safety of civil works after Hurricane Katrina and other floods, future work for the TCX would likely increase. Based on its superior performance, the TCX was recertified in 2012.[160]

---

[160] "Clarence Cannon Dam and Mark Twain Lake," *Esprit* (Feb. 1996): 6; "TCX for APMD," *Esprit* (Mar. 1996): 3; "Automated Performance Monitoring of Dams," Web page (*http://www.mvs.usace.army.mil/eng-con/expertise/ apmd.html*, Aug. 19, 2011).

11

Flood Fighting and Flood Management

In addition to designing and building flood control works such as levees, floodwalls, and reservoirs, the Corps of Engineers has also long been involved in responding to floods and other emergencies through flood fighting, emergency response, and levee rehabilitation. Prior to World War II, these activities were mostly ad hoc. Because of widespread belief in limited government, the federal government in general was only loosely involved in emergency response, and it was only as it gained responsibility for levee construction that it aided in flood fighting activities such as sandbagging, patrolling and shoring up levees, and rescue or evacuation. This started to change only after the Great Flood 1927, one of the worst natural disasters in the twentieth century. Without an organized federal response to what was a national disaster, suffering would have been much prolonged and the death count likely much higher. With the recognition in 1936 that flood control was a federal responsibility, it was only a matter of time until Congress began to also take steps to provide for a federal response to natural disasters that overwhelmed local resources. Starting with the Disaster Relief Act of 1950, increasing with establishment of the Federal Emergency Management Agency and passage of the Stafford Act in the 1970s and 1980s, and culminating in the establishment of the Homeland Security Department and National Response Plan in 2004 and 2005, the role of Corps of Engineers and St. Louis District in flood fighting and emergency response continued to grow over the past century.

Prior to the twentieth century, the federal government had a minimal role in flood response. With the creation of the Mississippi River Commission in 1879 and a growing role in overseeing construction of levees and other flood control works, though often under the guise of navigational improvements, the Corps of Engineers also gained responsibility for protecting and strengthening these works. Using existing funding, the Corps could improve known weak areas through construction of emergency berms or dikes, sandbagging substandard height levees, and patrolling levees for signs of underseepage or other weaknesses, although local agencies often provided most of the labor and cost of these fixes as they had for many years. Other emergency response functions, such as evacuation or caring for refugees, were mostly private affairs. There was no federal agency and no legislative provision to handle such operations nationwide; most agencies operated under a patchwork of laws that were not specific to national emergencies. When events outpaced the response of individual agencies, the tendency was to create special teams to oversee these functions, as actually happened during the Flood of 1927. President Calvin Coolidge created a Special Mississippi Flood Committee headed by Secretary of Commerce Herbert Hoover that included the secretaries of war, navy, agriculture, and treasury. Because there was no funding set aside for the response and Corps funding was dependent on local contributions, Secretary of War Dwight Davis actually spent more than $7 million on nothing more than the promise of House Appropriations Chairman Martin B. Madden that he would supplement the funds when Congress was in session. Even then, the main resources provided by the Corps were for reconstruction, although they did provide boats and airplanes to search for and rescue survivors. Care for refugees fell to the Red Cross, for which Hoover helped to raise nearly $17 million. Although later Flood Control Acts provided some funds for emergency purposes, this rarely exceeded one or two million dollars, mostly for levee repair.[161]

Grand Tower, Illinois, after levee break during 1927 flood

---

[161] Pete Daniel, *Deep'n As It Come: The 1927 Mississippi River Flood* (Fayetteville, Ar.: University of Arkansas Press, 1996): 14-175; Arthur D. Frank, *The Development of the Federal Program of Flood Control on the Mississippi River* (NY: AMS, 1968): 193-198; U.S. Cong., *Congressional Record*, House, 70th Cong., 1st Sess., Pt. 1 (Dec. 1927): 217-218. As Joan Wilson noted in, *Herbert Hoover: Forgotten Progressive* (Boston: Little, Brown, 1975): 78-121, the use of the Red Cross closely fit Hoover's view of volunteerism.

Disaster Response

In 1950, Congress passed the Disaster Relief Act (PL 81-875), which provided a fund for some emergency relief activities. It also authorized the Corps to aid local authorities with planning, technical assistance, and emergency relief. Congress expanded these resources in the Emergency Flood Control Work Act of 1955 (PL 84-99), which authorized the Corps to support flood fighting and other relief activities, as well as to repair damaged civil works if requested by local government. It required a presidential emergency declaration to put the law in motion. At the same time, the White House made efforts to improve coordination of emergency response through the Office of Civil and Defense Mobilization and Office of Emergency Planning, which managed executive emergency response from 1958 to 1973. It was not really until 1979 when President Jimmy Carter created the Federal Emergency Management Agency (FEMA) in Executive Order 12127 that there was a federal agency of sufficient resources to manage national or regional emergencies. FEMA initially had a mixed record of responding to major disasters such as Hurricane Hugo in 1989 and Hurricane Andrew in 1992, but President William J. Clinton greatly improved the agency by making it cabinet-level, expanding its grant

Flood fighting efforts at Swan Drainage and Levee District, Illinois River, 1943

program, and assigning the capable James D. Witt as its administrator. The Federal Disaster Relief Act of 1974 (PL 93-288), as amended by the Robert T. Stafford Disaster Relief and Emergency Assistance Act (PL 100-707) in 1988, required the Corps to support FEMA and other agencies in planning for and

Flood fighting at Illinois River levee, 1943

Meramec flooding at Valley Park, 1945

responding to disasters and emergencies by providing public engineering tasks such as debris removal, temporary roof repairs (i.e., blue roofs), or portable public buildings as well as supporting rescue and recovery, emergency housing, oil removal, and other tasks.[162]

Throughout the period immediately after World War II, even after passage of PL 81-875 and 84-99, the primary task of the Corps during emergency response operations remained flood fighting and levee rehabilitation. Through the late 1960s, the Mississippi Valley as a whole experienced numerous low-water years in what has been termed the "long dry spell." After the Flood of 1951, it was a decade before the next large flood in 1961, and then nearly a decade after that until the next flood. The response to the Flood of 1969 was perhaps typical. In fact, there were four floods that year in January, April, July, and October, affecting mostly the Mississippi, Illinois, Salt, and Meramec basins, with river stages in St. Louis reaching just over 40 feet in April. The January and October floods were primarily flash floods, and the district minimally staffed its response during these events. St. Louis District experienced

Looking south from Eads Bridge during flood stage 39.3 feet, July 20, 1951

---

[162] U.S. Cong., *Disaster Relief Act Amendments of 1974*, PL 93-288 (93rd Cong., 1st Sess.); *Robert T. Stafford Disaster Relief and Emergency Assistance Act*, PL 100-707 (100th Cong., 2nd Sess.); ER 500-1-1; Christopher Cooper and Robert Block, *Disaster: Hurricane Katrina and the Failure of Homeland Security* (NY: Times Books, 2006): 47-73.

Kaskaskia River flood at New Athens, Illinois, May 11, 1961

more than $30 million in damages in both Missouri and Illinois. The district's response included conducting reconnaissance, providing advice to local agencies, operation of a flood fight center with the Red Cross in April and July that coordinated with other agencies and military units operating in the region, providing floating plant for rescue operations and levee patrols, and helping to shore up defenses where local agencies were incapable. Overall, the federal flood control system held up well, with the majority of levee breaches in private levees, although there were sand boils where water boiled up on the land side of the levee, slumping of levees, and bank caving requiring repair. Total repair cost was only $179,000.[163]

The next major flood, and the last before the advent of FEMA, was the Flood of 1973. Heavy rains from October 1972 to January 1973 in the Missouri and Upper Mississippi basins saturated the ground, and by February 1973 the Upper Mississippi reached flood stages. By April 1, 1973, the flood stage at Cairo, Illinois had reached 55.67 feet. The maximum discharge reached in the middle river was 850,000 cfs at St. Louis, where gages reached over 40 feet for eight straight days, and nearby Alton, Illinois, saw record discharges

---

[163] USACE, *1969 Floods* (St. Louis: MVS, 1969): 1-22 and inc. 2.

Flood fighting at Kaskaskia Island, March 31, 1973

Sandbagging at Arnold, Mo. during 1973 flood

Flood stage at St. Louis Floodwall, 1973

Crystal City, Mo. April 29, 1973

St. Louis floodwall just downstream of Eads Bridge during 1973 flood

Corps intelligence officer at flood fighting center, 1973

of more than 500,000 cfs. Operation of reservoirs in the Missouri and Upper Mississippi reduced flow at St. Louis about two feet. Most breaches in the levee system occurred above Grafton, Illinois Altogether, there were 11 breaches of federal levees that resulted in $2.1 million in damages. For once, the Ohio

Relative flood stage of 1951 flood at Alton, Mo.

River and St. Francis River saw less impact and no major breaches, although the Lower Mississippi saw extensive flooding, with a total of $1.1 billion in damages valley-wide. While the Mississippi River Commission activated the Morganza Spillway and Bonnet Carré Spillway, it ended up flood fighting at the Bird's Point-New Madrid Floodway. The St. Louis District started emergency operations on March 1 in Illinois and March 6 in Missouri, and continued to operate for more than a month. As before, the district's primary task was to patrol the levees, coordinate with and advise local officials, help man the Red Cross flood fight center at Grafton, and provide flood fighting supplies such as the 1.1 million sandbags, 30 pumps, 400 life preservers, and 350 rolls of roofing plastic. In many areas, the district also provided services for which it became well known in modern flood fights – debris removal, utility restoration, road and public building repairs, as well as levee repairs.[164]

The Great Flood of 1993

While there were floods with localized impact in 1982 and 1983, the first major flood after the institution of FEMA was the Flood of 1993. Prior to 1993,

---

[164] USACE, *Post-Flood Report, 1973* (Vicksburg, MS: LMVD, 1973): iii, 11-42, 53-71.

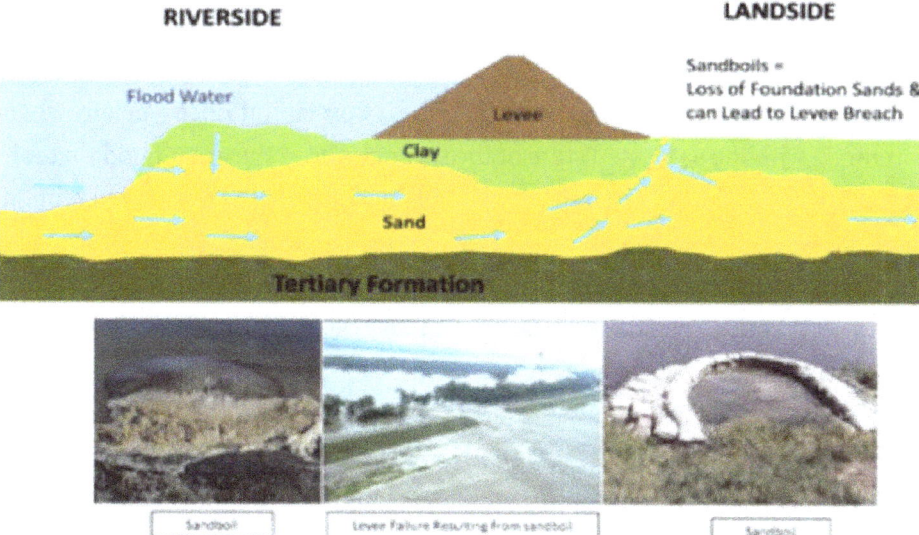

the largest flood on the middle Mississippi occurred in 1844. Although discharge from this flood was estimated to have been approximately 1.3 million cfs, modern estimates have adjusted this to approximately 1 million cfs. The 1993 flood exceeded this total by approximately 80,000 cfs. This number is even more staggering considering that reservoirs decreased peak discharge by an estimated 200,000 cfs, making the 1993 flood the greatest ever recorded on the middle Mississippi and the supreme test of the Corps flood control system.[165]

Rank, Magnitude (inches), and Date (month/year) of the Five Largest Precipitation Events Recorded on the Upper Mississippi River Basin for Selected Durations.[166]

Rank	1 month	2 months	3 months	12 months
1	8.03 (7/93)	14.76 (6-7/93)	19.62 (6-8/93)	45.00 (10/92-9/93)
2	7.30 (6/47)	11.70 (5-6/08)	17.20 (5-7/15)	39.38 (11/85-10/86)
3	7.24 (9/65)	11.52 (5-6/90)	16.10 (5-7/02)	38.98 (2/51-1/52)
4	7.05 (9/26)	11.35 (6-7/15)	15.91 (6-8/51)	38.83 (7/72-6/73)
5	7.01 (6/67)	11.28 (8-9/65)	15.70 (5-7/90)	38.51 (6/02-5/03)

---

[165] USACE, *After Action Flood Report: Midwest Flood of 1993* (St. Louis: MVS, 1993); Gary Dyhouse, "Was the Great Flood of 1993 all that great?" *Esprit* (Jan. 1999).
[166] *The Great Flood of 1993: Causes, Impacts, and Responses*, ed. Stanley A. Changnon (Boulder: Westview Press, 1996), 58.

Beginning early in the summer of 1992 and continuing into the fall, higher than average precipitation covered much of the Upper Mississippi River Basin. Then, after a normal winter, the spring rains came, producing the wettest period experienced in the upper basin in 99 years, with precipitation being 150 percent or greater in some areas. This heavy precipitation, especially when combined with the saturated state of the soil, produced the great flood that followed. On June 26, the Mississippi River reached flood stage and would remain there (except for a few hours on September 14) continuously until October 7. On August 1, the river reached its peak flood stage at the St. Louis gage, reaching 49.58 ft with a discharge of 1,080,000 cfs. Damages resulting from these flows would have been far greater were it not for the flood control system in place on the upper Mississippi. This system consisted of three components: agricultural levees, urban levees/floodwalls, and flood control reservoirs. In total, there are around 1,600 levees above St. Louis, approximately 95 percent of which are agricultural levees. These are small, mostly privately owned levees constructed to protect productive farmland from seasonal flooding. During larger floods, these levees are designed to overtop so that they can relieve pressure on the levees/floodwalls protecting urban areas. The other 5 percent are urban levees/floodwalls that protect more densely populated areas and critical infrastructure (bridge approaches, interstates, commerce, chemical plants and manufacturing, water plants, etc) from larger floods. Reservoirs hold back water in the tributaries to reduce pressure on the levees along the main channel. Each component of this system must be considered as part of a whole in order to assess its overall efficacy.[167]

The Corps had 251 levees in the five upper Mississippi basin districts, 193 of which were affected by the 1993 flood. Of those affected, 157 prevented flooding that would have inundated over 1 million acres and caused an estimated $7.4 billion in damages. The Corps' urban levees and floodwalls were especially effective, protecting vital areas with high population densities from inundation. The fact that flows did not overtop a single urban levee is a testament to the system's efficacy. Of the 36 remaining agricultural levees, 32 met their design capacity, only overtopping when this capacity had been exceeded. In fact, many levees actually withstood floodwaters above their design capacity. At the request of locals, the Corps breached the other four levees before they reached design capacity so that they would not overtop. By intentionally

---

[167] USACE, *AAR: Midwest Flood of 1993* (St. Louis: MVS, 1993); GAO, *Midwest Flood: Information on the Performance, Effects, and Control of Levees* (Wash., D.C.: GPO, 1997).

breaching the levees at the bottom, the areas were backflooded, thereby eliminating damages from scouring that would have occurred if the levees had been allowed to overtop. Breaching these levees may have flooded farmland, but it also relieved pressure on other levees and floodwalls in the system, thus giving added protection to vital urban areas such as St. Louis. In all, flooding at these levees caused an estimated $450 million in damages, and although a large sum, this pales in comparison to damages that the levee system prevented. The Corps had designed its levee system to protect vital urban areas and the system had done just that. In addition to the Corps levees, non-federal

St. Louis floodwall

agricultural levees, which represented around 95 percent of the total levees, dotted the basin. However, these levees were not Corps-operated nor were they designed to withstand major flooding events like the 1993 flood. Rather, they were designed to protect farmlands from floods ranging from a frequency of 10 to 50 years.[168]

Reservoirs, the other component of the flood control system, provided further relief during the 1993 flood, holding back more than 20 million acre-ft of water at just the right time to relieve pressure on the levee system by reducing flood stages in urban areas. For example, reservoirs at Mark Twain and Carlyle set new record pool elevations of 636.9 and 455.53 respectively. The district carefully monitored discharge from these reservoirs so that minimum release could be used when flood crests were occurring at downstream locations. Thus, the downstream movement of water held in reservoirs could be delayed so that the water would arrive after the crest. The Corps was able to use these and other reservoirs in its system to reduce the flood stage at St. Louis by 3 to 5 feet. Since the Corps designed the St. Louis floodwall for 52 ft plus two feet of freeboard, the use of reservoirs reduced the flood stage at St. Louis just enough to protect against a potential catastrophic failure. While levees did raise flood stages higher by confining the flow to a narrower portion of the floodplain, reservoirs held back the additional flow, thereby having the cumulative effect of reducing flooding.[169]

Although levees and reservoirs had the net effect of reducing flooding on the system, numerous flood fighting challenges remained. One challenge was forecasting flood stages, as the Corps forecasts consistently predicted flood stages higher than those predicted by the National Weather Service (NWS) during the 1993 flood event. Flood fighting efforts depending on accurate forecasts of flood stages, so missing the mark by even a miniscule margin could make a huge difference. In the district's engineering judgment, the river would crest at the St. Louis gage at around two feet higher than what the NWS was forecasting. The NWS and other forecasting agencies all had the river going down as of July 24. However, the district, which understood the complexities of this river system, forecast that the river had not yet crested and would reach over 49 feet on the St. Louis gage by the end of July or beginning of August. Thankfully,

---

[168] Ibid; James T. Lovelace and Claude N. Strauser, "Protecting Society from Flood Damage: A Case Study from the 1993 Flood" (*www.mvs-wc.mvs.usace.army.mil/papers/93flood/93flood.html*, Jan. 13, 2012)
[169] Lovelace and Strauser, "Protecting Society from Flood Damage: A Case Study from the 1993 Flood"; GAO, *Midwest Flood* (Wash., D.C.: GPO, 1997).

Levee overtopping during 1993 flood

Mississippi at normal stage and during the 1993 flood

District Engineer Col. James Craig trusted the judgment of district engineers and sent out word to prepare for 49 feet. Although official federal responsibility for forecasting rested with the NWS and it was not the responsibility of the Corps to contradict the NWS's public forecast, the district could compromise by advising flood fighters that it would be prudent to prepare for NWS forecast plus an additional two feet of freeboard. The district's advice allowed those flood fighting in the various levee districts to be better prepared for when the

August 8, 1993 *After flood*

actual crest did occur. Ultimately, the judgment of the district proved correct, as the river crested at 49.53 feet on the St. Louis gage.[170]

Another challenge was ensuring that the floodwalls and levees held back the massive wall of water beyond them. In densely populated urban areas like St. Louis, a failure would be catastrophic, potentially causing billions of dollars in damages. Flood fighters had to combat cracking, underseepage, and sand boils at levees and floodwalls. The St. Louis floodwall nearly gave way after experiencing severe cracking and underseepage, but the district shored up one section with rock and built ring levees around boils, preventing the wall from failing. At Ste. Genevieve, the levees leaked considerably but held after the district increased their height to 50 feet using sandbags. At Fort Chartres, because a drainage culvert would not open, local officials requested that the Corps breach a levee to allow water out of a back flooded area, which it did on August 4. Engineers leading the flood fighting efforts often had to make decisions rapidly and on the spot, relying largely on their knowledge and experience as guidance. The efforts of these flood fighters, combined with the structural flood control system of levees, floodwalls, and reservoirs, was estimated to have reduced potential flood damages by over 50 percent. Moreover, all of the levees/floodwalls built to urban design standards withstood the wrath of the river.[171]

After the flood stage peaked on August 1, the district had to begin releasing the water that it had held back in reservoirs. The challenge for the Corps was how to go about releasing the water in such a way that it restored the capacity of the reservoirs while at the same time not prolonging flood levels on the Mississippi. The navigation industry had already lost an estimated $100 million

---

[170] Interview with Dave Busse, Nov. 10, 1995 (MVS Archives); Interview with Jack Niemi, Nov. 1995 (MVS Archives).
[171] Lovelace and Strauser, "Protecting Society from Flood Damage: A Case Study from the 1993 Flood."

due to the closure of the river to commercial navigation for 36 days. The Corps needed to ensure that water was released from the reservoirs in such a way that commercial navigation could return to the river. The district carefully monitored weather forecasts, rainfall, and rainfall runoff computations, using this information to determine the optimum amount of water it should release from its reservoirs so that navigation could return to the river while at the same time minimizing any potential hazards to levees. The district's efforts allowed navigation to resume on the river at the earliest possible time, saving millions for the navigation industry and the consumer.[172]

Flood Fighting after 1993

Only two years later, in 1995, the district faced another flood fight. After twice the normal spring rainfall in the Dakotas, Kansas, and the Ohio Valley and 325 percent higher than normal rainfall in St. Louis that May, the river reached flood stages by mid- month, reaching a peak of 41.8 feet at St. Louis on May 22. It was above flood stage for 52 straight days. Peak discharge was 800,000 cfs at St. Louis and 857,000 cfs at Chester. There were numerous challenges, with local levees failing on the East Side and nearly all local levees at St. Charles, but once again no federal levees failed, although at least six levees would have overtopped had it not been for Corps reservoirs. The district operated its EOC from May 17 to June 6, managing 183 district personnel. The president declared Illinois a disaster area on May 30 and Missouri on June 3. The district provided 3 million sandbags, 36 pumps, and 2,000 rolls of plastic. The flood fight was extremely active in numerous locations, such as the Illinois River, Kaskaskia, St. Louis, and St. Charles. In 1993, sinkholes threatened to undermine the St. Louis floodwall at Riverview Blvd. In 1995 the district constructed a rock berm to prevent uncontrolled underseepage of the levee at Kaskaskia Island. As in 1993, navigation was a major challenge that the district had to closely manage. Four of five locks in the district closed, as well as the lower 80 miles of the Illinois River. When the Corps and Coast Guard established the Joint Traffic Control Center, it also included representatives of the tow industry, earning high praise from industry representatives. The center developed processes for conducting test tows with industry to get locks open

---

[172] Ibid.

quicker, and as a result navigation returned to normal within three weeks of closing.[173]

Emergency response in the Corps changed dramatically after the terrorist attacks of September 11, 2001. The creation of the Department of Homeland Security, the placement of FEMA under it, and the creation of an agency to manage grant programs required some adjustments in operation. In addition, the development of a National Response Plan in 2004 to manage all national emergencies introduced new agencies and processes. Signed by all federal agencies involved, the plan did not introduce new law but provided a structure to better meet legal requirements. The plan used the National Incident Management System – a system developed by state emergency workers in California and elsewhere – that introduced standard organizations and terminology. Upon presidential declaration of emergency and DHS declaration of incident of national significance, FEMA would establish a Joint Field Office for each region affected. Among its officials was a Federal Coordinating Officer, who helped coordinate the federal response. The plan included 15 Emergency Support Functions, each assigned a federal lead. The Corps of Engineers was responsible for No. 3, Public Works and Engineering, but had responsibilities supporting several others. Along with other agencies, the Corps would then establish Recovery Field Offices, typically near the Joint Field Office so as to coordinate with FEMA and other agencies. The Corps nevertheless also had its traditional responsibilities for flood control and repair under PL 84-99 and the Stafford Act.[174]

While there was minor flooding in 2002, it did not exceed 40 feet at St. Louis, and the flood control system mitigated its impact, although there was severe flooding at the Wappapello reservoir and other locations. "It was about a normal flood," Jake Scanlon said. The largest flood after the National Response Plan went into effect was in 2008. It was actually two major flood events. After heavy winter snowfall in Ohio and from Iowa to Wisconsin, Missouri experienced the wettest March on record and the third wettest May. Cape Girardeau and Jackson, Missouri, reached new 48-hour rainfall records. The spring flood crested at 30.7 feet at St. Louis and 41 feet at Cape Girardeau in April. Additional rainfall in Wisconsin in early June sent the Des Moines and Skunk rivers to record stages, while more rain fell in late June over the Missouri River Valley. The summer flood crested at 29.5 feet at St. Charles on the

---

[173] USACE, *After Action Flood Report: Midwest Flood of 1995* (St. Louis: MVS, 1995): 1-14.
[174] Cooper and Block, pp. 131-3; DHS, *National Response Plan* (N.P.: DHS, Dec. 2004): 8-19, 22-39

Missouri River on June 19, at 30.8 feet at Grafton on June 29, at over 38 feet in St. Louis and Chester on July 1, and at 42 feet at Cape Girardeau on July 3. The flood stretched all along the Middle Mississippi.[175]

The district EOC operated from March 18 to May 21 and then again from June 10 to July 18, 2008. During its operation, 85 employees worked at the EOC and four of the seven flood fight areas. The district distributed 630,000 sandbags and 322 rolls of plastic sheet during the spring flood and 2.1 million sandbags, 12 pumps, and 1,000 rolls of plastic during the summer flood. It was a hard-fought flood. Two levees overtopped at Miller Pond near Cape Girardeau and Vandalia near Kaskaskia, Illinois, on March 18 and 20, with numerous other slides and sand boils reported. During the summer flood, 13 levees overtopped, including at Winfield, Kuhs, Elm Point, and Columbia Bottoms, with severe scour reported at Ste. Genevieve. This inundated more than 60,000 acres. The district was able to recover from a slide at the Wood River levees and prevented scour from weakening a levee at Ste. Genevieve using rock berms, prevented breaches along the Illinois River and the East Side Levees through placing ring levees around sand boils and by constant monitoring, and investigated a leak at a gravity drain at Degognia. The spring flood briefly closed the Kaskaskia Lock, but the summer flood closed Lock 25 and 25 and the Kaskaskia Lock for more than 20 days. Lock 26 and 27 remained open. Once again, a team that included the Corp, the Coast Guard, and the transportation industry monitored events and evaluated requests for emergency movement. The president declared several counties in southern Missouri a disaster area on March 19 and on June 25 declared 22 counties in Missouri a disaster area while declaring it an

Col. Thomas E. O'Hara

Col. Christopher G. Hall

---

[175] Scanlon quoted in "Flood Fight of 2002," *Esprit* (May 2002): 1-5; USACE, *Mississippi River Spring Flood 2008 After Action Report* (St. Louis: MVS, 2008): 1-8, 15-18; USACE, *Mid-West Flood 2008 After Action Report* (St. Louis: MVS, 2008): 1-9.

incident of national significance. Aside from the major flood fights, the district spent nearly $38,000 supporting Emergency Support Function No. 3. It spent $4 million on both floods.[176]

Flood Forecasting

Part of the Corps response to the annual high waters and bi- or triennial floods included efforts to forecast the floods so as to reduce flood impact. The Corps normally forecasted all river conditions, both high and low water, in an attempt to support and manage navigation. Corps offices used such forecasts to manage a range of operational issues including annual dredging and operation of reservoirs. Prior to 1980, attempts to forecast floods with any precision faced the same challenges weather forecasters faced – manual data collection and small numbers of data points provided incomplete pictures of trends that did not allow more than 24 to 48-hour forecasts with any accuracy. This situation improved greatly in the digital age. Instead of manually collecting data from gages once or twice a day, the Corps established digital gages that broadcast data by radio wave on an hourly basis, allowing for easier and faster collection and more thorough trend analysis. The availability of satellite and radar imagery for every section of the country, especially after the

---

[176] *Mississippi Flood 2008 AAR*, pp. 9-24; *Mid-West Flood 2008 AAR*, pp. 9-38.

explosion of the Internet's popularity in 1990, made it much easier for Corps forecasters to determine weather patterns. By the late 1980s the data became accurate enough to allow long-term forecasting needed to support flood fighting. By determining how high flood water would reach in various locations, the Corps could place sandbags, teams, or other resources far in advance. The Corps developed software to integrate real-time radar, rainfall data, and river observations to create mathematical models and terrain visualizations to aid forecasting. Although data collection was automatic, users set some parameters based on engineering experience. The Flood of 1993 was the first in which Corps forecasts played a major role, with the district accurately predicting far in advance that flood heights at St. Louis would reach nearly 50 feet. Although questioned by the National Weather Service and others, the final result demonstrated the accuracy of the experienced Corps analysts. The models used to make this forecast served primarily an internal audience, but after 1993 many local agencies and the navigation industry increasingly started to request Corps forecast products, including models, maps, and visualizations, which helped to communicate the timing of flood crests.[177]

As the district worked to improve the products it provided to its customers, several other changes helped to vastly improve forecasts. From 1993 to 1997, it further refined its modeling software. The Levee Safety Program, instituted after questions arose about levee safety following Hurricane Katrina in 2005 and established as a long-term program in 2007, resulted in the most thorough inventory of levees in the St. Louis District. This allowed forecasters to have an even better understanding of which levees would overtop at what time, and how this would affect flooding. When the public complained that river forecasts provided by the federal government during the Flood of 2008 were inconsistent, unreliable, and not widely distributed, Mississippi Valley Division Commander Maj. Gen. Michael J. Walsh held a conference to investigate the issue. He discovered that most users found St. Louis District forecasts exceptional, but other agency forecasts were less so. Although the National Weather Service, U.S. Geological Service, and other Corps districts often used the same data, their assumptions and use of the data varied widely. As a result of the conference, the Corps established a fusion team of forecasters from the

---

[177] Damon Manders, Interview with Dave Busse, July 11, 2011; "Engineering Innovation in the St. Louis District," *Esprit* (Feb. 1997): 1-2.

respective agencies to work together to improve river forecasting. The result was even greater accuracy, proved most recently in the Flood of 2011.[178]

The floods of 1993, 1995, 2008, and 2011 were some of the largest floods the Middle Mississippi River and Missouri River had ever known, and though they caused several million dollars in flood damages, flood control works built by the Corps of Engineers prevented billions of dollars in additional damages. While much of this protection was due to the quality of the structures, the integrity of the structures was due in part to the efforts of the Corps in forecasting, managing, and responding to the floods through vigilance and protective measures. Additional efforts in support of FEMA and other agencies to aid in rescue, emergency engineering, and rehabilitation of public works greatly alleviated flooding and suffering that occurred as a result of overtopping or breaching of the levees. Such responsibilities had evolved since World War II, and continued to expand as federal responsibilities to respond to disasters also grew. The St. Louis District had become increasingly involved in emergency activities as a result of these requirements, both in flood fighting and aiding flood victims. Yet perhaps the greatest emergency response achievement of the St. Louis District came, not within district boundaries, but far to the south. It was this that proved its mettle in modern disaster response.

---

[178] Ibid.

The Great Flood Fight of 1993

As the spring of 1993 approached, winter snow began to melt, and snowfall became spring showers, all of which combined to pour more and more water into the mighty Mississippi. But spring rains and rising water levels in the region were nothing new, especially for district engineers who understood the complex nature of the river. By May, it looked as though the river had finally crested and would begin to recede, but the rain just kept coming. Throughout May and June, water levels remained high and by July 1, the district's primary focus became fighting this great flood. This effort, which required personnel to pull together in a singular cause, consumed the district throughout the rest of the summer.

Months before the July 1 opening of the Emergency Operations Center, Water Control had been preparing for the flood fight to come. Emergency Operations, in concert with the Water Control Section, advised locals, provided them with flood fighting supplies, and administered construction contracts. Individuals from water control and EOC worked between 14 and 16 hours a day seven days a week throughout the entire flood fight, and by July 8, these were open 24 hours a day seven days a week.

On July 23, three small sandboils in close proximity were discovered on the Kaskaskia Island Levee at the toe of the 100-foot wide seepage berm. As the day progressed, the three sandboils were becoming larger and larger, carrying more and more

District personnel at the Emergency Operations Center during the 1993 flood

Harold Smith's Corps vehicle found one mile away from levee breech

foundation sands and silts. The levee district's volunteers were vigorously building larger sandbag rings to try to control the three sandboils. Shortly before midnight, the three sandboils merged into a single, large sandboil that flowed uncontrollably, carrying dark gray sand and silt with intermittent belches of foamy and frothy air and water. The levee district volunteers built a larger sandbag ring around the sandboil and uncontrolled seepage flows decreased as the water level in the ring rose. Mark Alvey and Steve O'Connor were called around midnight to assist the Kaskaskia Island Levee District. By the time Alvey and O'Connor arrived on the site, the sandboil had calmed down but was still making dirty water by carrying fine sand and silt. At approximately 9:00 am on July 22, the sandboil suddenly erupted violently, flowing with a two-foot diameter fountain. Alvey, Christopher Coe, and Herb Klein (Levee Commissioner) were trying to raise the sandbag ring to hold more water over the sandboil. Alvey was throwing sandbags into the throat of the sandboil only to have the sandbags thrust back at him. The grass-covered ground surrounding the sandboil started vibrating and slowly rising in front of him. Alvey shouted for the others to stop throwing sandbags and run for high ground. Charlie Dees from Rend Lake observed that a transverse crack had formed across the levee crown as the sandboil appeared to explode from the water pressure that was nearly black in color from the eroded silt. The levee collapsed into the void scoured by the enormous, uncontrolled flows through the sandboil. The levee completely breached by 9:30 am, just less than 24 hours after being discovered as 3 small sandboils. The resulting scour hole was measured to be an average depth of 50 feet with a total volume of 1 million cubic yards of displaced silt and sand deposited on the surrounding farm fields.

On July 24, just two days after floods breached the Kaskaskia Island Levee, Alvey was working with Ken Klaus and Richard Hagan flood fighting at Bois Brule. After Klaus and Hagan returned to their hotel after a 14-hour shift, they received a call in telling them that a sand boil had erupted and required their attention. The two men rushed to the site and began working on the boil, but they soon had to redirect their attention to saving a Corps employee who was plunged into the river after a section of the levee broke. This man was Harold Smith, a long-time district maintenance worker at Rend Lake who was working the night shift and inspecting a sand boil when a section of the levee broke. Smith, who heard the sound of running water, rushed to his truck to back it away from the sandboils. Just as he stepped into his truck, the flood breached a nearby section of the levee. Water quickly rushed in, overturning Smith's truck and thrusting him out of his truck and into the current. Smith was badly injured and fighting for his life, but miraculously, he was still alive. Meanwhile, Klaus and Hagan were rushing to the location to see if they find the lost Corps employee. Thankfully, Hagan was from Bois Brule and used this knowledge to navigate back roads to find Smith. Hagan eventually found Smith clinging to life on the levee and rushed him to the hospital, where he remained for the next four days. Smith's truck was not so lucky, as the district vehicle was not recovered until Easter Sunday 1994, a frightening reminder of just how narrowly Smith had escaped death.

As water levels continued to rise in early July, the district had to close its locks and dams and by July 11, all traffic on the Mississippi above the Ohio River came to a halt. Lock and Dam 25 essentially became an island and flood fighters and supplies had to be taken to the area by boat. At Melvin Price, the concerned crew nervously watched the river rise closer and closer to overtopping the lock walls. Crews continued fighting the flood, coming to and from their 12-hour shifts via johnboat. To make matters worse, crewmembers had to endure 100-degree heat, often working waist-deep in water to try to protect the billion-dollar facility. When water levels finally began to recede, the crew had to rush to put the vital structure back in operation once again, which it did on August 17.

Flood fighting was also intense at the district's levees, as flood fighters had to work vigorously to save the levees while at the same time ensuring the safety of the people in the surrounding area. Sometimes the efforts to save levees were successful, other times not. At Prairie du Rocher, flood fighters won a well-deserved victory. Despite the tenacious and exhausting efforts of flood fighters, the Kaskaskia, Columbia, and Harrisonville levees had all been breached, and flood fighters at Prairie du Rocher feared

Crew at control house of Melvin Price L&D during the 1993 flood

Mark Alvey, far right, and others ringing a sandboil on Kaskaskia Island

their levee was next. District engineers Claude Strauser and George Postal proposed a controlled breach at Stringtown-Ft. Chartres to relieve pressure on the levee and hopefully save it from a more devastating failure. On August 3, the district breached the levee while flood fighters continued to sandbag. In the end, the risky strategy worked, and the flood fighters earned a well-deserved victory.

Another major victory occurred at the Keach Levee, where flood fighters fought to save valuable farmland near the Illinois River. Because the flood occurred in July and August, crops were on the ground and a breach would destroy the harvest, which would have a devastating economic impact for people in the region. However, flood fighters were able to prevent an overflow by using sandbags and a wooden flood fence to raise the height of the levee. As the river continued to rise, the levee was eventually breached. District personnel, National Guardsman and local farmers continued to fight to save the levee, risking their lives in the process. Yet their efforts were ultimately successful, as they were able to brace the levee and repair the breach. These are just a few examples of the courage exhibited by flood fighters during the 1993 flood. While each of them may have different roles as district employees, nevertheless, each joined together, sacrificing their time and in many cases, risking their very lives, all in a cooperative effort to fight the flood and help their fellow citizens.

12

Task Force Guardian and Hurricane Response

It is ironic that of the modern flood fighting duties embraced by the landlocked St. Louis District, the one that earned it significant recognition was in response to a tropical hurricane. Assigned the mission of supporting the Mississippi Valley Division in responding to a hurricane event, the St. Louis District first fulfilled this requirement in the aftermath of Hurricane Katrina. Striking on August 29, 2005, Hurricane Katrina was the most devastating hurricane in history, causing $81 billion in damages, together with Hurricane Rita, which struck less than a month later on September 24 in western Louisiana. Katrina was the third deadliest hurricane, causing more than 1,500 deaths. The storms were both within the top 10 most intense storms on record, and Katrina was one of the largest on record in New Orleans, despite the fact that both were only Category Three on the Saffir/Simpson scale at landfall. Katrina produced the largest storm surge on record throughout much of the impact area (27 feet) and the largest waves ever measured in North America (55 feet). The response to Katrina and Rita was the largest in the Corps, involving more than 6,000 employees and three divisions across a five-state area over more than two years. Another 3,000 employees from other agencies also supported the Corps. Leading the effort in Mississippi and Louisiana was the Mississippi Valley Division, whose response eventually involved all of its districts, including the St. Louis District, which had responsibility for levee rehabilitation. It became the job of the district to oversee construction or rehabilitation of more than 220 miles of levees and floodwalls in a mere nine months, one of the largest construction projects ever attempted by the Corps.[179]

The involvement of the St. Louis District in hurricane response originated in 1998 with the Readiness 2000 program. The Headquarters of the Corps of Engineers (HQUSACE) developed the program to guide division-level response to major disasters using multidiscipline and multidistrict planning and response teams, prescribed mission assignments, advanced contracting

---

[179] Eric S. Blake, Edward N. Rappaport, and Christopher W. Landsea, *The deadliest, Costliest, and Most Intense United States Tropical Cyclones from 1851 to 2006 (and Other Frequently Requested Hurricane Facts)* (Miami: NHC, 2007): 5; Manders, David Tajkowski, and Mike Dace, *Rebuilding Hope: A History of the Response to Hurricanes Katrina and Rita* (Vicksburg: MVD, 2011): v-13; on discrepancies between the Saffir/Simpson Scale and other hurricane factors, see Debi Iacovelli, "The Saffir/Simpson Hurricane Scale: An Interview with Dr. Robert Simpson," Mariners Weather Log 43:1 (April 1999): 10-12.

vehicles, and the 249th Engineer Battalion (Prime Power) for emergency power. After Hurricane Georges passed north of New Orleans later that year, the Mississippi Valley Division started developing a contingency plan based on Readiness 2000 concepts. According to the plan, if the New Orleans District was incapable of functioning, the other districts in the division would assume its mission: Memphis and Vicksburg Districts would handle Federal Emergency Management Agency (FEMA) engineering missions such as debris removal; St. Paul and Rock Island Districts would support ice, water, and housing missions; and St. Louis District would handle civil works missions. Developed and tested over several years, Division Commander Brig. Gen. Robert Crear signed the plan in May 2005, allowing only a single opportunity to train on it in 2005 during Hurricane Dennis prior to Hurricane Katrina in August.[180]

On Thursday, August 25, 2005, Bill Frederick, the National Weather Service employee assigned to the division, started to track the storm, and General Crear prepared to put the plan into action. The division received its first taskers from FEMA on the Saturday before the storm, and Crear pushed these out

Aerial view of New Orleans after Hurricane Katrina

---

[180] William Irwin, "Readiness 2000 tested by storms," *Engineer Update* (Oct. 1998): online; "Mississippi Valley Division Hurricane Contingency Plan (CONPLAN)," May 18, 2005.

to Vicksburg and Memphis districts. The New Orleans District started its evacuation and preparations for the storm. The storm struck the following Monday, and although New Orleans received minimal damage from the storm, the fact that large areas of the city had flooded to 10 feet or more confirmed that there must have been breaches in the levee system surrounding the city. Within days, Corps personnel that remained behind in the city had identified major holes in two of the drainage canals running into Lake Pontchartrain, as well as in the Inner Harbor Navigation Canal (IHNC) and along the Mississippi River-Gulf Outlet. There were also several Mississippi River and hurricane protection levees that received severe damage, with literally dozens of breaches over several miles in Plaquemines Parish near the Gulf of Mexico. Many of the navigation canals and locks in Louisiana were clogged with debris, and the Coast Guard shut down the Mississippi River for several days and limited traffic for part or all of the lower river for two weeks. With 80 percent of the city inundated and most of the 22 pump stations in the city not functioning, by Friday, September 2, Crear called on Rock Island District to assume the unwatering mission as Task Force Unwatering. Its job was to make temporary repairs to the breaches and remove the water through gravity, portable pumps, and restoration of the New Orleans drainage system. He also notified Col. Lewis Setliff of the St. Louis District of his intent to stand up a task force to rebuild the broken levees with a deadline of June 1, 2006, the beginning of the next year's hurricane season.[181]

Corps Emergency Operations personnel on 17th Street in New Orleans

Aerial shot of 17th Street after Hurricane Katrina

---

[181] Damon Manders, Interview with Brig. Gen. Robert Crear, May 29, 2007; James Stark to Crear, ESF#3 Transition/Mission Close Out Plan – Hurricane Katrina (FEMA Louisiana Transitional Recovery Office: ND, MVD); Manders et al., 27-58, 127-128.

Standup of Task Force Guardian

Setliff immediately started organizing teams and planning the response, and on September 14, 2005, received initial funding of $450,000 to start work on damage assessments and surveys. Initial teams moved to division headquarters in Vicksburg, Mississippi, to coordinate collection of aerial photography and other data to determine levee heights before the storms. By September 19, he had established project teams for four geographic areas (Orleans East Bank, New Orleans East, St. Bernard Parish, and Plaquemines Parish), as well as teams for finding borrow pits to acquire levee material and for barge removal to work with the Coast Guard to move barges off levees requiring repair. Delayed by Hurricane Rita, which struck September 24, the advance party from St. Louis arrived in New Orleans on September 26. The remainder of the 73-person task force moved to New Orleans on September 28, and on September 29, the Corps introduced Task Force Guardian to the public. It later brought on additional personnel and contractors to raise the total number to more than 200 task force employees by January 2006. By the end of October, it required additional facilities and rented a floor in the recently repaired Federal Reserve Bank Building in downtown New Orleans on October 26, where it would remain until completion of the mission in June 2006.[182]

Col. Lewis F. Setliff

According to the process established in PL 84-99, Corps district commanders must inform local authorities that they have 30 days to request repair of flood control works. Once it receives a request for rehabilitation, the Corps develops a Project Information Report (PIR) detailing the damages. As with the original project, the benefit-cost ratio for repairs has to exceed 1.0, local authorities have to pay for a percentage of construction, and the Corps can only restore levees to authorized project heights The task force built its PIRs on surveys completed by September 14 using Light Detection and Ranging (LIDAR), which uses lasers bounced off the ground from a plane to quickly

---

[182] David Tajkowski, Interview with Col. Lewis Setliff, May 11, 2007; Commander's Assess., Sept. 14, 19, Oct. 19-29, 2005; Commander's Briefing, Oct. 19-27, 2005 (TF Hope Historical Documentation, Vol. 2-4); SITREP-TF Guardian, Oct. 1-2, 18-22, 2005 (ENGLINK or OH, MVD electronic files); Manders et al., pp. 184-188.

gather elevation data and build a 3-D model. As the Corps Technical Center of Expertise for Photogrammetric Services, the St. Louis District had resident experts in LIDAR and served most Corps districts as well as agencies such as the Environmental Protection Agency, U.S. Fish and Wildlife Service, and other military services. Once it collected data, the task force compared them with data and photographs from before the storm to determine the amount of fill required and develop a cost estimate. It was proceeding with surveys by mid-September. Local levee districts submitted all requests for rehabilitation by early October, and the task force completed PIRs for Orleans East Bank on October 18, New Orleans East on October 19, and St. Bernard and Plaquemines parishes by the end of the month, but it revised them by December and January based on new information. Even as it collected additional information, the task force was proceeding with preparing contracts for the first projects in St. Bernard Parish and other locations.[183]

There were many initial obstacles to proceeding. The biggest issues in these PIRs were how to repair the floodwalls on the 17th Street, London Avenue, and Orleans canals that drained into Lake Pontchartrain; the large number of gaps in the Inner Harbor Navigation Canal and Gulf Intracoastal Waterway; and the

Construction of sheet piling on 17th Street

---

[183] Interview with Setliff; "Corps of Engineers to Restore Pre-Katrina Protection in New Orleans," USACE news release, Sept. 29, 2005; "CEMVS – Center of Expertise for Photogrammetric Mapping," web page (http://mvs-wc.mvs.usace.army.mil/tcx.html, July 18, 2011); Manders et al., pp. 185-200.

Sheet piling construction at canal in New Orleans after Hurricane Katrina

near total devastation of many miles of the New Orleans to Venice and Mississippi River levees in Plaquemines Parish. "The outfall canals were probably the biggest challenge we were faced with that we did not know about going in," Setliff later stated. It would be difficult to make all of the repairs given the two or three-year estimates for completing some of them. The high cost of the repairs – initially $287.7 million, revised to $638.5 million – also posed a problem, as most local government agencies simply lacked the resources to pay 20 percent of repairs as required by law. "Using normal processes during this contingency just would not work, for instance, using a cost share for making the repairs because you had a community with no tax base at all. There was nobody there," Setliff said. On October 12, 2005, Assistant Secretary of the Army for Civil Works John Paul Woodley approved a one-time waiver from cost sharing requirements and made the arrangements with the Office of Management and Budget and Congress. Finally, there were funding issues. Funding for rehabilitation came from two primary sources: Flood Control and Coastal Emergency funds from HQUSACE and operations and maintenance (O&M) funds used primarily to restore Mississippi River levees. By October 9, the task force had awarded 10 contracts worth $86 million; on October 19 it had another $78 million available in FCCE funds, but it was advertising or awarding contracts worth

Repair of levee breach in New Orleans after Hurricane Katrina

$122 million. HQUSACE reprogrammed another $150 million, but by October 28 it was out of money as the Army worked to transfer more funds. By the end of November, it had awarded 36 of 45 expected contracts worth $245 million, but it continued to struggle with just-in-time funding.[184]

Task Force Guardian faced other issues as construction proceeded. One was making sure not to duplicate the errors of the past. By the time the task force arrived in New Orleans, Louisiana State University, the University of California at Berkeley, and the American Society of Civil Engineers (ASCE) had all started investigations into why the floodwalls along the Lake Pontchartrain canals and the IHNC had failed – these works had not only overtopped but shifted several feet causing the largest breaches in the city's defenses. On October 10, 2005, the Corps established the Interagency Performance Evaluation Task Force (IPET), which involved 150 nationally recognized scientists

Flexiboat bridges used as waterbased platforms for closing of canal breaches

---

[184] Setliff quotes from Interview with Setliff; Manders et al., pp. 190-200; Commander's Assessment, Oct. 19-25, Nov. 1-15, 19, 27, 30, 2005; Commander's Briefing, Oct. 21, Dec. 11, 2005 (TF Hope, Vol. 4-6). See also the PIRs dated Oct. 17, 18, and 19, Nov. 30, and Dec. 13, 2005; and Jan. 5 and 20, 2006.

and engineers in both public and private sectors, $26 million in funding, and independent peer review by ASCE and the National Research Council. As it discovered issues impacting rehabilitation, IPET would share information with Task Force Guardian, and task force members sat in on weekly IPET updates. Several of its findings proved crucial. In its January 10, 2006, preliminary report, IPET found that there were likely design flaws and foundation issues that contributed to the floodwall failures, casting doubt on the ability of Guardian to complete the repairs near Lake Pontchartrain by June 1. Instead, it chose to build floodgates at the mouth of the drainage canals that would close during tropical storm events and prevent surge coming in from the lake to protect the canals. This required additional authorization from Congress in February. IPET's interim report published March 10 found that the failure mechanism was I-walls tilting under flood pressure, allowing the crack to fill with water and weaken the structure. I-walls consisted of a single wall sitting on top of sheet piles partially buried in a levee and were thus more unstable but required less real estate. A contributing factor to the failures was weak clay soil foundations under the soil, which had not been detected in soil borings during original construction. Guardian adjusted by driving deeper sheet piles below the clay layer and by installing T-walls shaped like an inverted T, which were more stable than I-walls but took up more space. It stabilized these with H-piles driven at angles to hold the T in place. "Now that we know what to look for, we're out there looking for it," Corps structural research scientist and Information Technology Laboratory Director Reed Mosher said.[185]

Another factor was removing barges in the waterways and often on top of levees. Because they blocked access to some construction sites, the Corps had to remove them prior to proceeding with construction. The Task Force Guardian barge removal team worked with barge owners, the Navy, and the Coast Guard to remove the barges. Initially, it would contact barge owners to remove their property from levees, but where the owner was unknown or unreachable, Corps or Coast Guard contractors would remove it. The team initially identified 51 barges in priority work areas and was in the process of moving 30 of them by October 28, 2005. By the first week of November, the Coast Guard identified another 120 vessels (later expanded to 158). Estimated removal cost was

---

[185] Tajkowski, Interview with Setliff, June 12, 2007; Mark Schliefstein and Bob Marshall, "Canal gates planned before storm season," New Orleans *Times-Picayune* (Wed., Jan. 11, 2006); IPET, *Performance Evaluation Status and Interim Results* (N.P.: IPET, Mar. 10, 2006): I3-I4; Mosher quoted in Marshall, "Omissions revealed in levee design," *Times-Picayune* (Fri., Mar. 17, 2006); Manders et al., pp. 212-227.

$7 million. A contractor had removed 82 of 158 vessels by early February 2006 and had exceeded 110 vessels removed by the end of the month and 150 by the end of March. However, the process slowed by this point, with steady removal of the barges at a rate of about one every day or two until the contractor removed the last vessel on April 16, 2006. This was a major milestone that allowed the task force to step up construction at these sites.[186]

A third obstacle that slowed progress was locating enough fill to rebuild the levees. Initial estimates were two million cubic yards of fill, but this grew to 4.6 million cubic yards by the end of the year with adjustments to the PIRs. Locating and purchasing a sufficient number of borrow pits to obtain soil was a challenge, but the larger challenge was getting soil of appropriate quality. Most of the area around New Orleans was swampland or organic soils, which were unsuitable for building levees. The borrow team conducted tests of numerous sites and worked with Corps real estate personnel to purchase pits as far away as Grammercy and Baton Rouge, Louisiana. The first borrow pit opened on October 24 in Plaquemines Parish, near the Mississippi River levees, but some questioned soil quality there or in St. Bernard Parish. By January 2006, Guardian was importing clay soils from Mississippi to mix with local soil. By March, the Corps had sent more than 36 of an anticipated 51 barges from the borrow pits, which delivered 400,000 cubic yards of soil to St. Bernard Parish and 800,000 cubic yards to Plaquemines Parish. To ensure soil quality, the Corps initially conducted laboratory samples from each load of soil, but the process was lengthy and time-consuming. As the need quickly outstripped laboratory testing of all soils, the Corps adopted a process of on-site inspections with random tests of soil sent to the laboratory.[187]

Meeting the Deadline

Despite the delays caused by funding, barge removal, and locating fill, the task force made significant progress. By February, the task force had placed between 20 percent and 33 percent of required fill, completed 17 of 59 projects by March 21, and was 54 percent complete overall by the end of March.

---

[186] Interview with Setliff, June 12; Commander's Assessment, Oct. 29-Nov. 12, Dec. 13, 2005; Feb. 5, 23, Mar. 28, Apr. 18, 2006; SITREP TF Guardian, Oct. 25, 2005; Commander's Briefing, Feb. 2, 16, 2006 (TFH Vol. 4-10); Manders et al., pp. 207-208, 231-232.

[187] Interview with Setliff, June 12; Commander's Assessment, Oct. 24, 29-Nov. 12, Dec. 13, 2005, Feb. 5, 23, Mar. 28, Apr. 18, 2006; Commander's Briefing, Oct. 3, Dec. 29, 2005, Feb. 2, 16, 2006; SITREP TF Guardian, Oct. 1, 5, Dec. 29, 2005 (TFH Vol. 4-10); John Schwartz, "Too Little Clay, Too Much Sand Is Levee Worry," *NYT* (Sun. Feb. 19, 2006); Manders et al., pp. 209-211, 232-233.

Corps Emergency Operations personnel at New Orleans

As of February 20, the Corps awarded 48 of 52 contracts to local contractors. This required close management of contracts to ensure that funding was available, advertising and awarding contracts according to government standards (including small business awards), and completing 126 contract modifications by early April. It also required coordination with real estate personnel to purchase property, gain rights of way to remove trees or other obstacles, and ensure fair prices to encourage cooperation with the government. Once the Corps awarded the contracts, Setliff closely managed all aspects of the projects through site visits, phone calls, and status updates, including management of personnel assignments, quality control, and material stockpiles. Given the tight schedules and high demand for employees with special skills, it was essential to make sure people were in the right place at the right time to prevent delays. Likewise, while conventional wisdom considered stockpiling on construction projects wasteful, it prevented delays in large projects with tight deadlines. Multifunctional management teams for each construction area helped to maintain the management pressure. "Our philosophy early on was that we wanted to ensure victory back in February, instead of prevent defeat in May. Probably when people look back at this it will be seen as the wave of the future." Certainly, many contractors agreed.[188]

---

[188] Setliff Interview, June 12; Setliff quoted in "Katrina Analysis Has Designers Building Faster and Smarter," *ENR* (Mon., May 1, 2006); Commander's Assessment, Feb. 14, Mar. 7, 21, 28, Apr. 4, 12, May 9, 23, 2006 (TFH Vol. 7-11); Manders et al., pp. 227-239.

By the end of April, a new challenge arose – completing the flood gates at the outfall canals on Lake Pontchartrain. Space was tight near the lake, even after purchasing all available adjacent property. Because of local sewerage agency concerns about the lack of drainage when the gates were shut, the task force included a plan to purchase and install large pumps, although the capacity was less than when open and thus unsatisfactory to local government. The first 10 pumps arrived at the end of April, and the last 34 arrived on May 9, 2006. "We're up against the laws of physics and how many pumps can be built in a certain amount of time," Setliff said. At approximately the same time, contractors installed the 75-ton jackets that would hold the gates at the 17th Street Canal. However, on May 12, Task Force Guardian announced that it would not be able to complete installation of all gates and pumps before June 1. Only the Orleans Avenue Canal gate would be complete. Therefore, to meet the deadline, the task force installed sheet pile across the mouth of the other two canals, leaving enough of a gap in the temporary wall to allow drainage until a tropical storm appeared on the horizon, when contractors could cut off the canals, "just like we did during Hurricane Rita," Setliff added. Most people accepted this as sufficient to meet the deadline, although many still complained about the lack of pumps, which could cause the city to flood if the gates were shut. The Corps continued to work for many months to increase pump capacity and ensure all pumps functioned correctly.[189]

The remaining projects came down to the wire. At the end of April, the task force had completed 22 of 59 contracts and was 73 percent complete overall. On May 22, 2006, with only a week to go, it had completed 38 of 59 contracts and was 92 percent complete overall. This was due in part to the canal gates in Orleans Parish, which would not be complete until after June 1. Six contracts concerned completing the levees, and Setliff focused on these. Suddenly, on May 29, a 400-section of levee at a high school in Buras, Louisiana, in Plaquemines Parish slumped six feet under its own weight. Contractors were in the process of addressing weak soil to raise the levee another two feet when the collapse occurred. It would take another three weeks to repair the section, but at least there was a levee there. On one last section, the task force pushed the contractor all night long, and the project manager called Setliff at 11:50 p.m.

---

[189] Commander's Assessment, Mar. 7, 21, 28, Apr. 12, 18, 25, May 2, 9, 23, 2006 (TFH Vol. 9-11); Setliff quoted in John Schwartz, "Big, Maybe Ugly, but Their Role Heroic," *NYT* (Thurs., Mar. 23, 2006) and Sheila Grissett and Mark Schleifstein, "Gates Won't Be Ready By June 1," *Times-Picayune* (Fri., May 12, 2006); Manders et al., pp. 234-238.

on May 31 to report that the section was complete. Despite the repairs being only at 96 percent overall, mainly due to the closure gates, all of the levees were at authorized height other than the section at Buras. "You can hold the Corps accountable for our work. And I am also very confident that this will perform as it is designed," Setliff said.[190]

After the deadline passed, Task Force Guardian continued in operation until July 1, 2006, when it completed handoff of its responsibilities to other Corps entities. For although the task force met the deadline, it still had contracts to complete, none more important that the closure gates on the Lake Pontchartrain canals. "A lot of work is going to go on beyond that date as we continue to make the system better," Setliff said. With more than $4 billion in new construction authorized in legislation passed since Hurricane Katrina, in January 2006, the Mississippi Valley Division started planning the Hurricane Protection Office (HPO), which stood up from April to June 1. The HPO was a Corps office under division authority to manage the large number of hurricane protection projects, primarily in Orleans, St. Bernard, and Plaquemines parishes. By May, the task force was transferring responsibilities to the New Orleans District, including for removing trees from levees, projects in St. Charles and Jefferson parishes, and its normal civil works responsibilities. Of the 36 active projects on June 1, it transferred 11 to the HPO, 17 to New Orleans District, and the rest it closed out by the end of the month. While it did not complete the closure gates and pumps, it completed levees at Buras, Port Sulphur, and Home Place and closed out numerous small projects, such as repairs to pump stations, back levees, final grading of levees, and addition of safety features at the IHNC. By mid-June, the task force started to transition personnel to the HPO and New Orleans District. All but 15 personnel had vacated the Federal Reserve Bank Building by the end of the month, and another five continued to maintain field offices. These would remain for several weeks closing out contracts.[191]

Task Force Guardian's restoration of the protection of New Orleans by June 1 was, as one news article observed, a "breathless finale that has been called one of this generation's greatest adventures in civil engineering." The task force had overseen removal of 155 barges and other vessels from levees,

---

[190] Setliff Interview, June 12; Commander's Assessment, Apr. 25, May 23, 30, 2006 (TFH Vol. 10-11); Mark Schleifstein, "Levee slumps, repairs to take weeks," *Times-Picayune* (Tues., May 30, 2006); Joe Gyan, "Corps: Storm work is 92% complete," Baton Rouge *Advocate* (Wed. May 24, 2006); Setliff quoted in Brian Williams, "Army: 'You can hold the Corps accountable,'" *MSNBC* transcript (Thurs., June 1, 2006); Manders et al., pp. 238-239.
[191] Setliff quoted in "Katrina Analysis"; Manders et al., pp. 239-244; Commander's Assessment, Jun. 6-Jul. 1, 2006 (TFH Vol. 12).

repaired 195 miles of levees, built 25 miles of new levees and floodwalls, and built three interim gate structures on the outfalls, among numerous other smaller projects. It had managed 59 construction projects worth $557 million, involving 26 contractors (most of them local) and requiring purchase of 894 acres of land worth $63 million. It had moved well over three million cubic yards of earth under a contract worth $47 million. It was an incredible accomplishment for nine months of work. The tight deadline, just-in-time funding, limited materials, and cramped working conditions all worked against success, but Task Force Guardian was able to complete the mission by careful management and by relying on a wealth of civil works experience from St. Louis District, as well as from the New Orleans area and elsewhere. The performance of the task force reflected great credit on the district, which had contributed so much time and effort to help its neighbors from the south.[192]

---

[192] Quote from John Schwartz, "Levees Rebuilt Just In Time, But Doubt Remains," *NYT* (Thurs., May 25, 2006); Task Force Hope Status Report, Sept. 28, 2006 (TFH Vol. 13); Manders et al., pp. 239-244.

Part IV.
Serving the Nation:
The U.S. Army Corps of Engineers and Military Construction

One of the earliest responsibilities of the U.S. Army Corps of Engineers was military construction, and it was for this initially that Congress established the first corps of permanent engineers. Following the War of Independence, Congress had great concerns about enforcement of terms of the Treaty of Paris of 1783, especially given the lack of fortifications along the U.S. frontier. George Washington, Alexander Hamilton, Secretary of War Henry Knox, and French engineer Pierre L'Enfant had all argued eloquently for establishment of a permanent corps of engineers because of the difficulties of drafting experienced engineers to build such protection, and Congress finally acted in 1802. For more than two decades, the primary responsibility of the Corps was construction of fortifications, primarily along the coast. Although after the Civil War the Corps shifted its focus from fortifications to civil works, the military construction mission of the Corps never entirely evaporated, most often being absorbed by combat engineers, many of whom had previously served as civilians in the Corps. There have been periods, nevertheless, of domestic military construction, none as large as during World War II, when military spending in the St. Louis District topped $500 million. The result of that mission was an incredible spurt of activity building military-industrial facilities, some of whom are still in use today.

13

Military Construction and the Industrial Complex

One of the earliest roles of the Army in St. Louis, and the Corps of Engineers nationwide, was building fortifications. When Congress established a permanent Corps of Engineers in 1802, it was first and foremost to improve fortifications throughout the nation to help in enforcement of treaty provisions. The Board of Engineers for Fortifications, led by Brig. Gen. Simon Bernard from 1816 to 1826, helped plan and oversee construction of dozens of coastal and frontier forts. Its work continued under Col. Joseph Totten through the Civil War, bringing considerable innovation to fort-building. At St. Louis, the Corps helped survey the limited number of fortifications left from its colonial era, but other than brief ownership of the Jefferson Barracks after the Civil War and establishment and operation of an engineer depot on that base in the decades that followed, it left most construction to the Quartermaster Corps. This changed in World War II. With the enormous construction requirements of mobilizing for a global conflict, the Army assigned the Corps of Engineers to complete this work. Over four years, the Corps built numerous facilities and helped procure equipment and supplies for contractors supporting the war effort. This had an immediate effect on the economy of the St. Louis area and built up an industrial complex that continued to dominate the economy for decades after the war.

When the U.S. took control of St. Louis, there were already several large Spanish-built fortifications in existence, including the Fort on the Hill on Walnut Street originally constructed in 1780 but greatly expanded in 1793, a stone bastion built off what is now Cherry Street in 1792, a wooden blockhouse overlooking Mill Creek in 1797, and a series of six stone towers erected in 1797 on the edge of town facing south and weSt. Just prior to American occupation, the Spanish noted that the blockhouse and bastion were in good condition, but that the Fort on the Hill and towers were all in various states of disrepair. Another, Fort Don Carlos on the Missouri River, had been abandoned in 1780. The early American government of St. Louis found the fortifications unusable, some because of structural problems and some because of their faulty locations. Over several years, it converted the Fort on the Hill to a jail and courthouse.

By 1806, it had also established a new military installation about five miles away from Don Carlos on the Missouri, which eventually became Fort Belle Fontaine. During the War of 1812, there was a garrison of 200 housed there. To this the Army added a stone battery – Fort Lookout – at Portages des Sioux on the Mississippi River just south of the Missouri. Evidently, however, no federal funds were used in the construction of these installations, for the Department of War kept no record of them nor listed them among fortifications in reports to Congress.[193]

By 1817, soon after Maj. Stephen H. Long arrived to survey and improve fortifications along the Mississippi River, Fort Belle Fontaine was an established military post, housing a rifle regiment led by Capt. Benjamin O'Fallon. After establishing residence at the fort, Long conducted numerous surveys of forts in the area. In 1820, he also conducted a survey of the fortifications in St. Louis. Congress had legislated in 1812 that the government turn over any land not in use to the city. On his recommendation, military commissioner Brig. Gen. Henry Atkinson retained the old ruined stone bastion and a neighboring strip of land, although he authorized removal of the remaining stone in 1824. The city used stone from the other towers as needed to repair streets and buildings until 1860, when the southernmost tower was demolished. In 1820, Atkinson approved expenditures of more than $3,000 on improvements to Fort Belle Fontaine, which until 1824 housed 21 officers and 305 soldiers from the 1st Infantry. By 1826, however, plans were already in the works to move to a new military cantonment a few miles south of St. Louis – the Jefferson Barracks – to provide a greater concentration of regional troops and allow easier response both to the east and weSt. The installation housed the 1st, 3rd, and 6th Infantry regiments or more than 500 personnel under Atkinson, some of whom later deployed in various duties, such as escorting convoys, putting down Native Americans revolts, or in general serving as the western reserve. The base also served as the first infantry school to train personnel serving in the West. At first, soldiers slept in tents, but by 1830 contractors for the Quartermaster Corps were improving the facility and in 1837 completed stone barracks. In 1827, the Army also purchased a 37-acre tract between the barracks and the city to serve as the new St. Louis Arsenal, upon whose opening Fort

---

[193] Primm, pp. 20-23, 28, 40-41, 43, 99-100; Musick, pp. 105-111.

Belle Fontaine closed. It included an arms depot, armory, ammunition manufactures, and several repair shops.[194]

In 1866, Congress authorized transfer of Jefferson Barracks to the Corps of Engineers to serve as the new Engineer Army Depot that supplied Corps projects near St. Louis. It was also the home of Company E of the Engineer Battalion, the primary active duty engineer battalion remaining after the Civil War. Capt. William Ludlow was the first commander of the depot, followed by Capt. P.C. Hains. The Corps purchased the base from the Quartermasters for $20,000 and within two years had completed barracks for officers and enlisted personnel, put up a fence, built several workshops and warehouses, and started storage and repair of engineer equipment. By 1871, however, Congress changed course once again and transferred Company E to join the rest of the battalion at Willet's Point, New York. Instead of maintaining possession of the barracks, the Corps transferred the entire complex to the Ordnance Department. The Corps of Engineers maintained a small contingency to operate the depot as

St. Louis Arsenal, 1905 MHS

---

[194] U.S. Cong., "A Report of the Present Strength of the U.S. Army," H.D. 18 (15th Cong., 1st Sess.); "Fortifications," H.D. 183 (16th Cong., 1st Sess.); *Condition of the Military Establishment, 1823*, H.D. 247 (18th Cong., 1st Sess.): 558; *Report of the Secretary of War, 1826-1866*; NPS, "Jefferson Barracks: The Early Years," *Museum Gazette* (May 1994); Musick, pp. 112-115; Primm, pp. 106-108, 137-8, 150.

a tenant of the facility, but in 1881 the Quartermaster Corps granted a plot of land between the river and the Iron Mountain Railroad to the St. Louis District to maintain the depot near the St. Louis Arsenal. The depot served not only as a storage facility and repair shop, but also as a shipyard and service base for the district. There were numerous attempts to purchase the property from the

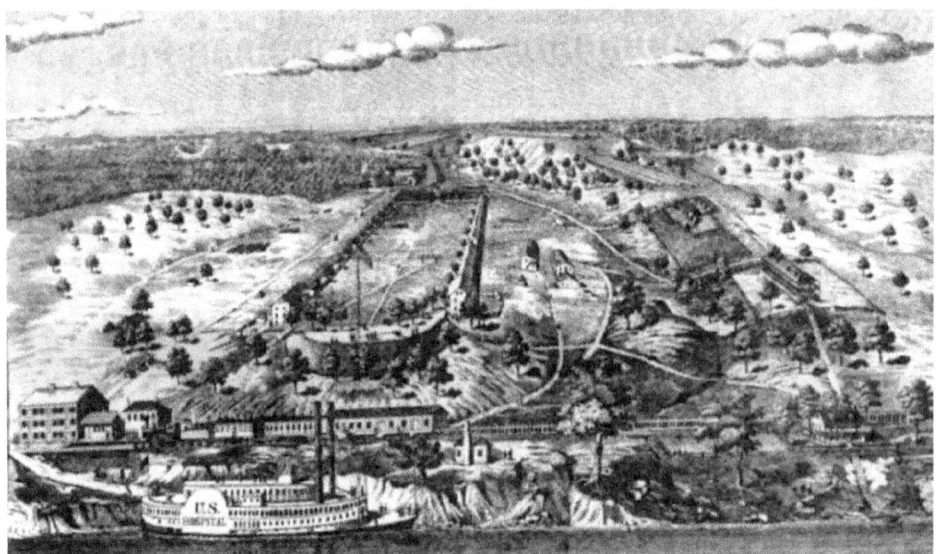

1864 illustration of Jefferson Barracks

Aerial view of Scott Air Force Base

Corps, which the Corps maintained "has proved so valuable to this department and to the government in the past 25 years, that no thought should be entertained of parting with it."[195]

Rebuilt from 1892 to 1900, the Jefferson Barracks remained an active Army training, induction, and demobilization center until after World War I. It continued in use by civilian and veteran groups until 1939, when the Missouri National Guard took command of the barracks. Capable of housing 3,000, it once again became an Army training, induction, and separation center during World War II. The Air Corps, in particular, had expressed interest in the property as early as 1940 and selected the installation as the site of an Air Corps Replacement and Training Center. Prior to World War II, the Quartermasters were responsible for most domestic military construction. With the amount of construction required for mobilization – $10 billion by 1942 – overwhelming the Quartermasters, in 1941 the Army assigned the task to the Corps of Engineers, first for airfields, then all military construction in the U.S. The first project assigned to St. Louis District was construction of the Air Corps Replacement Center, which required upgrade of many facilities at Jefferson Barracks. Following this was the expansion of Scott Field, Illinois, into an Army Air Force Station, which involved demolition of decades-old wooden buildings and reconstruction of everything from runways and hangars to hospitals and barracks. A third Air Corps project involved construction of an airfield for the 124th Observation Squadron at Vichy, Missouri.[196]

By the end of 1941, the district became involved in the first non-Air Corps project – construction of the St. Louis Ordnance Plant, which was responsible primarily for small arms production. The district would oversee design and construction of nine other ordnance and chemical weapons plants in Missouri and Illinois, most of which were designed and built by contracted architect-engineering-construction firms. It also oversaw construction of engineer and medical depots, a military police headquarters, and a factory training school. One of the most unusual projects involved construction of the Alien Enemy Internment Camp at Weingarten, Missouri, near Ste. Genevieve. This was a 160-acre prisoner-of-war (POW) camp with five compounds (four prisoner

---

[195] *Annual Report of the Secretary of War, 1866-1871*; Memo, St. Louis Engineer Office to Chief of Engineers, Aug. 12, 1909 (MVS Archives).
[196] Jefferson Barracks Heritage Foundation, "Chronological History of Jefferson Barracks" (*http://www.jbhf.org/ chronology.html*, Mar. 21, 2011); "Mobilization of the Field (St. Louis District) Organization in World War II" (MVS Archives); Dobney, p. 108; Lenore Fine and Jesse A. Remington, *The Corps of Engineers: Construction in the United States* (Wash.: USACE, 1972): 244-272, 440-476.

St. Louis Ordnance Plant in 2003 (demolished in 2006)

and one guard) and numerous concrete-foundation wooden buildings, including 36-man barracks, two-man officer apartments, canteens, dance halls, guard towers, and fences, notably with hot and cold running water and flush toilets, a luxury for a POW camp. The guard compound housed the 407th, 408th and 410th Military Police. The camp opened on June 22, 1943, with the transfer of 662 Italians from Fort Leonard Wood, Missouri; it received its first German prisoners a week later. By September 1943, it housed 992 officers and 3,515 enlisted soldiers. At its height in June 1945, it housed more than 5,200 prisoners, who were released gradually after the end of the war. Other construction projects followed, eventually totaling more than 20 projects worth an estimated $500 million, which made the St. Louis District's responsibilities one of the largest in the nation. To handle this workload, the district grew from an employment of 777 in April 1941 to a peak of 3,415 in August 1942. This included 32 project managers hired by the district to oversee construction projects – one per project. By 1944, as construction started to decline, many district employees were transferred elsewhere to support more urgent construction requirements – civilians to other districts and many military personnel overseas to serve as combat engineers.[197]

In addition to this construction mission, the district also supported production and procurement missions. The primary production mission involved preparation of landing craft tanks through the installation of ammunition and machinery rigging. Contractors shipped shells from plants on the Illinois and Upper Mississippi rivers, which Corps barge crews assembled at the district shipyard and service base. Altogether, district employees assembled 50 landing craft tanks for shipment downriver to the gulf. Most contractors at the time lacked the amount of equipment needed to complete contracts. Through the Engineer Warehouse and Yards, the district stored and distributed engineer equipment to contractors working throughout its area of operation. This included not only loaning its own equipment for the duration of a contract but also equipment procured from other suppliers. The district procured, inspected, and distributed construction and engineer equipment to contractors in a 10-state area. It administered equipment contracts for suppliers over more than a two-state area. The Upper Mississippi Valley Division office, then in St. Louis, also supported this mission through widespread real estate acquisitions for military construction projects. Although they never left the district, two project managers supported the Manhattan Project developing the first nuclear weapon primarily through the location and procurement of material to support the top secret effort. As construction slowed, much of the equipment found use in other districts for major projects such as construction of the Alaskan Highway. The district performed other procurement duties for military installations within the district, for example providing fire trucks, oxygen tanks, and steel landing mats, as well as procuring, inspecting, packaging, and shipping engineer equipment to overseas location in support of the war effort. The district performed a similar mission during the Korean War from 1950 to 1954 by procuring prefabricated buildings, water purifiers, and electrical generators for use in theater.[198]

In 1940, before American entry into the war, St. Louis had 15 percent unemployment, higher than the national average and higher than the majority of cities roughly the same size. It had suffered greatly during the Great Depression. The growth of the industrial complex in and around St. Louis resulting

---

[197] "Mobilization of the Field Organization"; Dobney, pp. 108-109; David Fiedler, *The Enemy Among Us: POWs in Missouri During World War II* (Columbia, Missouri: U of Missouri P, 2003): 64-66, 180.
[198] "Mobilization of the Field Organization"; Dobney, pp. 108-109, 118-119.

from wartime spending meant first and foremost a sharp increase in employment. Total employment increased from 150,000 in 1941 and reached a peak in 1943 of 600,000. Most of these jobs were in transportation, government, and industry, and there were significant increases in the employment of women and non-whites during this period. By the following year, cutbacks on aircraft production lowered employment to 535,000 and the Bureau of Labor Statistics predicted it would continue to decline. Nevertheless, there can be no doubt that wartime employment helped pull St. Louis out of the high unemployment that it had faced during the Great Depression. Some of this employment declined after the war – ordnance and aircraft product, for example – while industries such as meat packing, leather goods, steel and iron, and machinery stabilized and found other outlets and new markets. Thus, the impact of wartime construction continued for a decade after the war.[199]

Within months of the conclusion of the war, most of the properties operated directly by the Department of War – including Jefferson Barracks – were declared war surplus and sold at auction. Scott Army Air Station became Scott Air Force Base, which managed its own construction. With mobilization of the National Guard during the Korean Conflict, in 1950 Jefferson Barracks became headquarters to all Missouri Army and Air National Guard units in St. Louis. Although the Corps remained involved in military construction, the district did not have any major responsibilities at nearby bases and was only peripherally involved in these missions. Some level of construction occurred in the Korean and later conflicts, but because there was no large-scale war mobilization and construction, the participation of the Corps in later conflicts was primarily through combat engineers. Throughout World War II, the Corps understood that many of the projects which it had laid aside would aid in providing full employment at the end of the war. In 1942, Chief of Engineers Lt. Gen. Eugene Reybold would write that the projects already authorized "provides a backlog of meritorious projects which may be undertaken to cushion the shock of unemployment during the transition period following the present emergency." By 1945, there were more than 650 projects worth $1.7 billion, 150 of them worth $750,000 authorized in 1944. In fact, the Corps had never fully laid aside these projects because "all flood control projects ... are either directly or

---

[199] *Impact of the War on the St. Louis Area: City of St. Louis and St. Louis County, Missouri, Madison and St. Clair Counties, Illinois* (Wash.: DOL, BLS, 1944): 1-19.

indirectly related to national defense." Civil works also formed an important effort during the war.[200]

---

[200] "Chronological History of Jefferson Barracks"; *Annual Report of the Chief of Engineers, 1941*, quotes p. 8; *Annual Report of the Chief of Engineers, 1945*, pp. 6-7.

History of the St. Louis District Office

Prior to 1870, there was no St. Louis District, only project engineers assigned to address issues such as the depth of the St. Louis Harbor or snag removal on the Mississippi or Missouri River. The Corps of Engineers had established an engineer depot at the Jefferson Barracks in 1866, but relocated the last engineer battalion to New York in 1870, transferring the property to the Ordnance Department. With the relocation of the Office of Western River Improvements to St. Louis in 1870 and its abolition and simultaneous establishment of the U.S. Army Engineer Office, St. Louis, in 1872, the district has since maintained a facility in the city.

The first 12 years of its existence, the district office moved no less than three times, from 404 Market Street to 1122 Pine Street, and then to 417 Pine Street. The office was then very small, amounting to only a handful of employees, and most of these smaller buildings no longer exiSt. In 1884, the district moved to the U.S. Custom House, later known as the Old Post Office, on the corner of 8th and Olive streets, where it remained for more than 50 years. Just prior to this time, in 1881 the Army Quartermaster Department granted the district use of a strip of land from the St. Louis Arsenal between the Iron Mountain Railroad and the Mississippi River south of Arsenal Street. This became the Service Base, where the district built numerous shops and warehouses to support projects and maintain floating plant. The depot there replaced the one the district had been operating at the Jefferson Barracks.

Old Post Office Building

Federal Building at 12 Street (now Tucker Blvd.) and Market

In 1935, the district moved to the Federal Building at 12th Street (now Tucker Boulevard) and Market Street, where the U.S. Court House and Customs then lay. This was the location of the district during World War II, although it was from the Service Base that it helped to supply district contractors and armies abroad and build ships for the war effort. During this time, the district greatly expanded in size. It had extended from the Missouri to the Illinois River and up the Missouri to St. Charles in 1928; from the Illinois to Clarksville, Illinois, and up the Missouri to Hermann in 1930; from Clarksville to Clements Station, Missouri, in 1940; and to the lower 80 miles of the Illinois River in 1942.

The office remained at the Old Federal Building until around 1960, when it moved briefly to the Boatman's Bank Building across from the Mercantile Bank Building on Broadway and then to the Frisco Building on 9th and Olive (906 Olive). By this time, with the addition of responsibility for reservoirs being constructed on the Kaskaskia, Big Muddy, Meramec, and Salt rivers, the district was an enormous endeavor. It occupied all of the upper floors of the Frisco Building, the first floor being reserved for local businesses. In the fall of 1970, the office moved to the building (unnamed) at 210 North Tucker, between Olive and Pine. It remained there for 20 years. Finally, on Labor Day 1990, the district moved to the Mart Building, renamed the Robert A. Young Federal Building in 1988, on the corner of Tucker at Spruce (1222 Spruce Street), where it resides today.[201]

210 N. Tucker

Robert A. Young Federal Building

Olive St. (Frisco Building)

---

[201] "The Way I Remember It," *Esprit* (Feb. 2003):12-13; "History of St. Louis Missouri Engineer District, January 1944," manuscript (MVS Archives): 1-6; Memo to Chief of Engineers on Service Base, Aug. 12, 1909 (MVS Archives).

14

War Mobilization on the Mississippi River

While military construction formed a large responsibility during the war, the St. Louis District nonetheless continued its civil engineering function. Even as Europe became engulfed in war in 1939 and 1940, the district was winding up several key projects. The last of the three major locks and dams built in the district – Nos. 26, 25, and 24 – were finally complete in 1940, providing a nine-foot channel in the Mississippi north of the Missouri River. It had developed a plan for bypassing the one spot below the Alton Dam that was consistently below nine feet – the Chain of Rocks. South of the Missouri, the district was 78 percent complete in building permanent regulating works, such as dikes and revetment. Through continuous dredging, it was able to maintain a nine foot channel throughout the year. Ten of the 21 flood control projects Congress had authorized in the 1936 Flood Control Act were complete, and several others were in various stages of completion to bring levees to a standard height of 44 feet. With American entry into the war in December 1941, work on several of these projects took a back seat to the war effort. The proposed Chain of Rocks Canal and Lock, for example, did not get presidential approval until after the war. Nevertheless, the Army realized that, as the primary internal transportation route to the Mid-West, the Mississippi River was critical for the war effort by allowing bulk transportation of war supplies in a protected channel. Continued improvement of the river and protection of adjacent land were necessary, but less and less funding was available for such work the last two years of the war.[202]

Concern for developing and maintaining the Mississippi River and other waterways for national security purposes first arose in the aftermath of the War of 1812. During this conflict, in which the British invaded U.S. soil and burned the capitol, movement of troops and supplies came with great difficulty, harming the war effort. Secretary of War John C. Calhoun submitted his "Report on Roads and Canals" in 1819 as a direct result of these issues. As noted previously, he especially saw the Mississippi River as playing a critical role, as it had during the Battle of New Orleans and in supplying U.S. coastal fortifications. The report in turn led to the first survey of the Mississippi River in 1820 and

---

[202] *Annual Report of the Chief of Engineers, 1940*, p. 1121.

the first authorization of improvements in 1824. The situation had changed, however, by the Civil War. With the South in control of the mouth of the river for much of the war, the federal government and its contractors turned to railroads to transport war supplies, leading to phenomenal growth of the railroads in the decade after the war. Navigation boosters responded by lobbying for a deeper channel to allow improved transportation and also for federal support of the shipping industry. Although Congress authorized a deeper channel, money to complete the projects had not been forthcoming. On the eve of World War I, the project was only 33 percent complete, largely as a result of inconsistent funding. Periodic railroad car shortages and high fares during the war resulting from poor national planning finally convinced industrialists to increasingly use the river and Congress to authorize the development of a federal barge line in 1918 to reduce the strain on the overused railroads. As a result, traffic on the river reached more than 25 million tons. The barge line proved so successful, Congress extended its charter in the Transportation Act of 1920, and it continued to expand and operate through World War II.[203]

Despite the lessons learned from World War I, the transportation infrastructure faced similar problems at the outset of World War II. There had been considerable improvement since 1920. The Corps of Engineers had deepened, straightened, and shortened the channel south of St. Louis while building locks and dams north of it to maintain a nine-foot channel depth. A similar system of locks and dams on the Ohio River, Illinois River, and Gulf Intracoastal Waterway, along with many other rivers and tributaries, created a network of waterways extending 15,000 miles. This was in addition to more than 2,000 miles of federal levees protecting facilities from flooding. Commercial carriers had invested more than $50 million in terminal facilities, which were practically nonexistent prior to World War I. The federal barge line expanded service to the upper river and by 1936 had grown to 21 towboats and 204 barges moving 77.7 million tons of cargo per year, with annual revenues exceeding $6 million. There were 160 regulated commercial carriers operating more than 2,000 barges on the river, making the total number of operators more than 600 and barges more than 5,000. Nevertheless, despite wide availability of barges and lower shipping rates, the long delivery time using barges during the pre-war period, limited waterway access to some installations, and high demand for

---

[203] Calhoun, "Report on Roads and Canals," pp. 1-8; *Annual Report of the Chief of Engineers, 1914*, p. 923; T. Michael Ruddy, "Mobilizing for War: St. Louis and the Middle Mississippi during World War II," [1981] (MVS Archives): 1-4.

rapid delivery from training bases argued for a preference for rail transportation. It typically took 15 days for a tow to make its way downriver, versus four days by train. Many bases and production centers were not located near rivers, and many more lacked terminal facilities needed to load and offload from barges. Some biographers have characterized President Franklin D. Roosevelt's response to the war as reactionary and chaotic despite his reputation for state planning, and his administration did not take any steps to improve the situation until the strain was already evident. By September 1941, increasing pressure on train lines to deliver goods needed by military installations led the Quartermaster Corps to take steps to locate all new installations near waterways and to ensure that they had adequate terminal facilities.[204]

In December 1941, the Secretary of War created the Office of Defense Transportation to coordinate governmental policy on transportation issues. The Inland Waterways Division handled river traffic. One of its first acts in 1942 was to authorize barge lines to tow any available barges to maximize tow usage. By the spring of 1942, oil shortages on the East coast were becoming evident, and pipelines and railroads could supply just over half of the 1.3 million barrels of oil required to meet war demands. Barge traffic, though slower, was cheaper, held more per unit, and could be easily rerouted to meet emerging requirements. In addition, use of inland waterways protected vessels from enemy submarines that were harassing offshore shipping and blockading ports. To enhance barge traffic, the division established a program to convert steel barges designed for dry goods to carry oil while building new wooden barges for dry goods. The Traffic Control Division of the Quartermaster Department put to work idle barges, looked for opportunities to maximize barge use, and sought to reduce rates. By 1943, barges had transported more than 1.7 billion barrels of oil, equivalent to more than seven million tank rail car loads. Barges moved more than 92 million tons of iron, mostly through the Great Lakes. Later in the war, grain for civilian aid programs became more important. Traffic was 65 percent upstream on the Mississippi River during the war versus 90 percent

---

[204] Ruddy, pp. 3-4; "Merchant Marine of the Middle West," pp. 1-3; "Wartime and the River," *Fortune* 26 (Jul. 1942): 69-75, 102-107; Thomas E. Lyons, "Old Man River Mobilizes for War," *Domestic Commerce* 31:8 (Feb. 25, 1943): 3-6; Chester Wardlow, *The Transportation Corps: Responsibilities, Organization, and Operations* (Wash.: Office of Chief of Military History, 1951): 367-369. In Lautenburg's classic and mostly favorable study of the New Deal, Franklin served as a moderator of competing interests, whose programs codified in New Deal legislation often conflicted with his stated desires (84-85). Others, such as David Brody, have argued that "the New Deal was essentially reactive," and that the programs declined with wartime prosperity; management of war assets was in some ways separate from these activities; Brody, "The New Deal and World War II," in John Braeman et al., ed., *The New Deal: The National Level*, Vol. I (Columbus, Oh.: Ohio State UP, 1975): 271.

downstream before it. Within the Army alone, barge shipments increased from 18,000 tons per month in 1941 to 157,000 tons in 1944. For both the Army and Navy, nearly 4,000 ships and submarines built at inland shipyards and floating dry docks moved down the Illinois or Ohio rivers from shipyards in Pennsylvania, Indiana, and Illinois and along the Mississippi, including 2,115 that passed St. Louis. Within the St. Louis District, tonnage passing through the Middle Mississippi increased from 3.4 million in 1941 to 4.4 million in 1944, although the port of St. Louis itself saw only a slight increase until after the war despite an increase in diversity of products carried.[205]

Maintaining a channel in the Middle Mississippi to support this level of traffic fell to the St. Louis District through continuation of construction of permanent works and dredging under the leadership of Col. Roy B. Grower to 1942 and Col. Lawrence B. Feagin to 1946. Overall, the navigation improvement project advanced from 80 to 86 percent complete through 1944. There was a slight decline in permeable dikes (hurdles) installed from 1941 to 1942, but the district was able to main a high level of work during the first two years and even increased the amount of revetment installed. It built 23,000 linear feet of new dikes in 1941, 18,700 in 1942, and 19,800 in 1943, and added 1,800 feet, 2,900 feet, and 5,300 feet of revetment the same years. After 1944, the amount of new construction dropped precipitously to a low of 1,975 feet of dikes and 2,100 feet of revetment. During the same period, the number of dikes and revetment repaired consistently rose, demonstrating the district's growing focus on maintaining the status quo even when new construction was not possible. Dredging, meanwhile, stayed relatively flat at an average of 21.5 miles of channel dredged per year. Flood control also made significant progress during the first two years of the war. The district completed levees at North Alexander in 1942, and East Cape Girardeau, Kaskaskia, and Meredosia Lake and Willow Creek in 1943. Levee projects at Clear Creek, Columbia, Perry County, Wilson and Winkel and Prairie du Pont, and

Col. Lawrence B. Feagin

---

[205] *Big Load Afloat: U.S. Inland Water Transportation Resources* (Wash.: American Waterways Operators, Inc., 1966): 48-50; Ruddy, pp. 4-12; Lyons, pp. 3-6; Wardlow, p. 369; "Wartime and the River," pp. 102-107; Dobney, pp. 107-108.

East St. Louis all progressed to varying degrees. Other projects never got off the ground despite completion of preliminary contracting and real estate work, for example, at Wood River, Ste. Genevieve, Fort Charles, Harrisonville and Ivy Landing, Preston, Grand Tower, and Degognia and Fountain Bluff.[206]

The bigger story and what became the district's primary focus in later years were the severe floods of 1943 and 1944, which threatened to shut down the river and terminal facilities for weeks at a time. The middle river had already faced high water in 1941 and 1942, which left the ground saturated and provided high stages at St. Louis as early as January – it was within inches of flood stage on January 1, 1943 – although stages later declined. When major storms struck the Missouri and Upper Mississippi valleys in early May, stages reached 38.9 feet in St. Louis on May 24, the highest stages since 1844. Another crest followed in June after heavy rains in the Illinois Valley, reaching 34.9 feet on June 26. There were 14 days above flood stage in May and 21 days in June. The following year, after moderate spring rain left the ground saturated once more, three heavy storms struck in April in the Missouri Valley. The gage at St. Louis rose from 31.3 feet in mid-April to 39 feet on April 30, beating the 1943 record by several inches. Another set of storms struck the Upper Mississippi in May, keeping St. Louis above flood stages until May 13 for a total of 23 days. Of the floods, 1943 had a much greater impact. It had been several years since the previous flood, and many refused to evacuate. There were major breaches at the incomplete Perry County Levee and on the Illinois River, but none of the levees completed since 1936 failed. The 1944 Flood was much more severe in this regard, since there were crevasses at several of the complete as well as incomplete levees: Fort Chartres, Harrisonville, Preston, Prairie du Pont, Perry County, Grand Tower, Clear Creek, and Kaskaskia. These flooded over half a million acres, killed 10 people, and caused more than $17 million in damages, which was still less than 1943 because more people and animals evacuated in 1944. They also caused great damages to Corps works. The floods set navigation projects several years, and floodwaters seriously degraded levees at Perry County, Columbia, East St. Louis, Clear Creek, and Kaskaskia.[207]

Congress provided considerable funding for the Corps to respond to the floods. In addition to several hundred thousand dollars left from the Flood Control Act of 1941 for rescue and repair, the St. Louis District received more

---

[206] *Annual Report of the Chief of Engineers, 1941-1945.*
[207] *Ibid.*; "Report on April-May 1944 Flood in the St. Louis Missouri Engineer District," (MVS Archives): 1-14.

Riverfront at Alton, Illinois during 1944 flood

Chester, Illinois during 1944 flood

than $2 million of the $22 million provided by PL 78-138 in 1943 and another $2.2 million of $34 million provided by PL 79-75 in 1944. These appropriations funded a range of flood fighting work, including establishing field offices, managing volunteers and personnel from Scott Army Air Force Station sent to support the mission, supplying personnel, patrolling levees for weaknesses, and bracing weak levees with sandbags, lumber, and fencing. Approximately 80 percent of costs went to protective works to prevent flooding. The district also coordinated with the Red Cross, U.S. Coast Guard, and local agencies to help evacuate personnel, livestock, and farm machinery to higher ground using a fleet of boats, cars, and trucks. After the 1944 Flood, the Corps led efforts not only to repair the levees, but to strengthen them. Total spending on repairs levees within the district, including private levees, was $1.9 million, with an additional $2.5 million spent on levee improvement.[208]

By 1944, the war effort was becoming more intense and drawing more and more resources from the district. With completion of several major projects, the district workforce had dwindled from its peak reached in 1942. Several of the flood control projects were "suspended until after the war," even though new surveys taken after the floods showed that the levees were much further from completion than previous estimates. The floods of 1943 and 1944, as well as high water in 1945, also suspended construction activities for many weeks. Nevertheless, 1944 and 1945 saw authorization of several new projects, to include additional flood protection and the Chain of Rocks Canal. The district conducted preliminary work such as preparation of contracts and purchasing real estate on several of the new projects, including the canal. Between the new projects and destruction of works by the floods, the navigation project was 70 percent complete at the end of 1945.[209]

Throughout the war, the St. Louis District maintained a nine-foot channel. It did so even in the midst of two of the most severe floods St. Louis had ever seen, as well as during severe winter ice floes that prevented work for several weeks during the winter. With the channel maintained by the Corps, the movement of fuel, ammunition, food, materials, machinery, and weapon systems was relatively free throughout the war, which enabled the U.S. to successfully support combat operations abroad. The result was the unfettered growth of shipping on the Mississippi River throughout the war. On the Middle Mississippi alone, there was a 25 percent growth in through-traffic shipping. From

---
[208] "Report on 1944 Flood," pp. 1-14; *Annual Report of the Chief of Engineers, 1943-1945*.
[209] *Annual Report of the Chief of Engineers, 1944-1945*.

Chain of Rocks project cofferdam construction, 1947

1939 to 1945, tonnage passing through St. Louis grew 16 percent to 3.4 million. How much of this was due to the war is debatable since most of this increase occurred before 1941, and shipping from 1941 to 1945 stayed more or less flat. After the war, however, the picture is clear. By 1950, shipping on the Mississippi had grown 36 percent from a wartime peak of 101 million to 138 million tons, while tonnage handled by the port of St. Louis had more than doubled to 4.8 million. With shipping lanes established and industries refocused on commercial endeavors, St. Louis became once again the "Queen of the Mississippi River."[210]

---

[210] Ruddy, pp. 16, 19.

15

Deployments and Combat Engineering

Despite the fact that the Corps of Engineers had responsibilities for civil works, it remained part of the U.S. Army. As such, one of the most important missions of the Corps was supporting the engineering mission of the total army. Sometimes, this mission required Corps personnel to serve overseas, mostly as combat engineers, providing support by building roads, forts, bridges, ports, and basic infrastructure. Corps engineering expertise allowed for the rapid mobility and deployability required for a modern army to function efficiently. Before the twentieth century, the military mission and the civil engineering mission were more connected and often occurred in the same locations. After World War I, the Quartermaster Department was in charge of building Army facilities until November 1940, when the War Department transferred this responsibility to the Corps. Since that day, the Corps has played a vital role supporting domestic military construction. Nevertheless, it also continued to play a role in the military mission, providing essential engineering support to the Army during overseas campaigns in Europe, Asia, and the Middle EaSt. Particularly in the last 20 years, much of this support came from Corps civilians who volunteered for deployment to support the Corps military mission. Until recently, the St. Louis District has not maintained detailed records on who from its civilian ranks served in combat, although many of its military personnel did so, particularly district engineers such as World War II veteran Col. Rudolph E. Smyser, Jr., Korean War veteran Col. Guy E. Jester, and Vietnam War veteran Col. James B. Meanor, Jr.[211]

By December 1941, the Corps was deeply involved in construction activities at home and soon became involved in construction overseas, as the Corps built air bases in the British Atlantic territories and bridges in Italy, France, and Germany. The Corps also assisted the military in beach assaults at Normandy and other landing points, as under heavy fire they destroyed land mines and cleared paths for troops to land. After the war, the Corps played an important role in the rebuilding of Japan. Altogether, the Army sent more than 300,000 engineers overseas in combat roles, many of them drafted from the

---

[211] "Support the Total Army," *Information Bulletin* (Feb. 1983); USACE, *The U.S. Army Corps of Engineers: A History* (Wash., D.C.: Office of History, Headquarters, USACE, 2007); Interview with Meanor; James Towey, Interview with Guy Jester, Aug. 10, 1987 (MVS archives); Dobney, pp. 104-157.

Corps of Engineers' civilian ranks, although the district has kept no record of how many it sent. In some cases, as with Max Lamm, employees received an engineer commission, served for several years in the district supporting military construction and procurement projects, and then deployed to theater as a combat engineer. Others, such as M.F. Carlock, served their entire time as a military officer stateside. A reservist, Carlock was called up, served in St. Louis, Chicago, and New York, and then returned to his civilian job. Most probably he faced a situation similar to James Lawler, who was drafted into the Navy and then eventually received a commission in the Seabees and served in theater. Eventually, most of the officers working in the district transferred to other districts or to theater to serve in combat engineer roles through the remainder of the war.[212]

During the Korean War, the Corps districts and divisions throughout the country shifted their focus to supporting the military effort. The St. Louis District even dispatched the *Dredge Davison* to Korea to assist in the war effort. Army engineers supported troops by building fortifications to stabilize the perimeter and roads that allowed for rapid movement of troops and equipment. They also constructed airfields, ports, and bridges, including the Libby and Teal bridges, which allowed troops movement across rivers. In addition to construction that directly supported the Korean military efforts, engineers constructed water and sanitation systems that the Republic South Korea continued to use after the war ended. During the Cold War, the Corps continued building projects overseas, constructing airbases and early warning facilities at numerous locations. Alaska and Greenland remained important sites because they protected the border with the Soviet Union. Some district personnel supported these efforts through temporary assignments. For example, Carl Barron worked in Alaska in 1955 and 1956 building a 500-man barracks, runways, fuel tanks, and storage areas. Army engineers provided similar support to troops during the Vietnam War, constructing fortifications, ports, and airbases, and one of the most impressive feats of engineering was the construction of 900 miles of paved highway that connected major population centers and aloud for rapid movements.[213]

---

[212] *The U.S. Army Corps of Engineers: A History*; Dobney, pp. 108-109; Rex Van Almsick, Interview with Max Lamm, Mar. 2, 1979; Interview M.F. Carlock, Mar. 19, 1979; Interview with James Lawler, May 15, 1979 (MVS Archives).

[213] *The U.S. Army Corps of Engineers: A History*; William R. Farquhar, Jr. and Henry A. Jeffers, Jr., *Bridging the Imjin: Construction of Libby and Teal Bridges During the Korean War (October 1952- July 1953)* (Fort Belvoir: Office of History, USACE, 1989); Rex Van Almsick, Interview with Carl Barron, May 4, 1979 (MVS Archives).

In the decades that followed these military efforts, the Corps continued to play a key role supporting the Army. When operation Desert Storm commenced in 1990, Chief of Engineers Lt. Gen. Henry Hatch made a call for Corps personnel to volunteer for service in Kuwait so that they could support the war effort. During the campaign, the Corps' Middle East/Africa Projects Office oversaw design, construction, contracting, and real estate services for the Army, and after the war played a critical role rebuilding Kuwait's infrastructure. To carry this mission, approximately 2,000 men and women from the Corps deployed to Kuwait, mostly in the capacity of civilian volunteers, but many also serving as soldiers. Combat engineers from the Corps played an important role in providing engineering and construction support in the combat zone, including building roads, bridges, airfields, bases, and destroying enemy obstacles. Although Corps civilian volunteers played a significant role providing military support, one of their most important functions was providing expertise in contracting, real estate, damage assessment, well drilling, dredging, electrical supply power, and other fields. Early in the war, the delayed flow of engineers and their equipment directly affected the maneuverability of units and their ability to sustain themselves and operate efficiently. Without these brave engineers providing essential support, the safety of tens of thousands of troops and the success of the mission would have been severely compromised.[214]

Ten years after the end of the Gulf War, the U.S. was once again conducting a military campaign in Iraq, and once again, Corps personnel played a vital role supporting this mission. In addition, the Corps personnel have been essential to the War on Terror. To support the Overseas Contingency Mission, the Corps established the Transatlantic Division, which includes the Gulf Region District and North and South Afghanistan districts, and a deployment center that assists Corps

District deployee Joe Kellett in Afghanistan

---

[214] Janet A. McDonnell, *After Desert Storm: The U.S. Army and the Reconstruction of Kuwait* (Wash., D.C.: Department of the Army, 1999): 35-40; McDonnell, *Supporting the Troops: The U.S. Army Corps of Engineers in the Persian Gulf War* (Alexandria: CEHO, 1996): foreword, pp. 1-55; USACE, *The U.S. Army Corps of Engineers: A Brief History* (Fort Belvoir, VA: CEHO, 2007).

civilians deploying to Iraq and Afghanistan. As of 2011, more than 10,000 Corps personnel have deployed to southwest Asia to aid the war effort and rebuilding process. Many of these were Corps civilians who volunteered their services, and others were reservists serving as soldiers. Between 2003 and

Corps-constructed and designed treatment system in Fallujah

2005, Operation Iraqi Freedom overthrew Saddam Hussein's despotic regime, but an equally challenging task was rebuilding the infrastructure of Iraq to provide the stability needed to sustain democracy. In Afghanistan, the Corps undertakes similar projects supporting infrastructure development. These efforts would not be possible without the support of corps personnel whose engineering expertise help make reconstruction efforts possible, as they provide support for thousands of projects, including building hospitals, municipal buildings, water and wastewater treatment facilities, police stations, border forts, roads, airports, seaports and numerous other essentials.[215]

In the St. Louis District, numerous individuals have served in Iraq and Afghanistan since 2002, some as reservists, but most as civilian volunteers. Some of these volunteers have even deployed multiple times. The number of district members deployed to Iraq and Afghanistan at a given time fluctuated with each new deployment and return, with the number usually being between 12 and 14 deployed for anywhere between a few months to a year. Some district volunteers, such as Michael Quinn, who served as an electrical engineer in Afghanistan, were also veterans of Operation Desert Storm and Operation Iraqi Freedom. When asked why he volunteered for deployments, he responded, "there was a need for help, and I wanted to come and contribute to the efforts here." Others, such as Francis Walton, a construction representative in Afghanistan who has been with the district for over 30 years, were deploying for the first time. In fact, Walton enjoyed his efforts so much that quickly requested and received approval for a second six-month deployment.[216]

---

[215] USACE, "FAQ on Gulf Region District and Afghanistan Engineer District," brochure (N.D.).
[216] "USACE Heroes: supporting overseas contingencies," *Esprit* (Aug. 2010); "Deployments in support of OIF/OEF shift from Iraq to Afghanistan," *Esprit* (Fall 2009).

Corps of Engineers completes river bypass in Afghanistan

Corps personnel supervise Afghans constructing drainage trench

While some volunteers used their expertise gained through working for the Corps and applied it to efforts in Afghanistan and Iraq, others, such as Marty Seger, even used skills acquired outside of the Corps. Seger, a crane and towboat operator for the district, worked as a water and wastewater plant supervisor before coming to the district in 1995. An important part of establishing a stable infrastructure in Iraq was providing water and sewage treatment plants, which the Iraqi government had neglected to do. Part of the Corps mission was to provide clean water to the people of Iraq, and Seger played a vital role in the effort, as he was able to use the skills he acquired prior to joining the district to oversee water and wastewater plants in Iraq that provided clean water. Prior to this, Baghdad dumped its sewage into the Tigris river, but the Corps was able to use the wastewater plant it constructed in May 2004 to treat this sewage for the first time in over 15 years, providing nearly 120 million gallons of clean water every day. Corps efforts continued, as volunteers and Iraqis worked together to construct two more plants and restore Baghdad's main water plant, further increasing the city's clean water capacity.[217]

Joe Kellett, the district's Deputy District Engineer for Planning, Programs, and Project Management, shared his primary reason for volunteering: "to make a difference – to change the outcome in Afghanistan." Yet, Kellett went on, making a difference in a war-torn nation was not just about winning military victories, it was about helping develop Afghanistan's infrastructure. This effort required deployees to devote significant time, typically 12-hour shifts seven days a week, overseeing construction and engineering projects. However, Corps efforts were not limited to engineering projects, as continued success required educating native peoples so that they can ultimately achieve self-sufficiency.[218]

These missions were never a direct responsibility of the district. Rather, when the Army and Corps requested help, individual employees volunteered for the duty. Since the end of the Vietnam conflict, all soldiers were volunteers rather than draftees, and many district employees volunteered to serve in the reserves. Others went as civilians under temporary assignment. Some went for the extra money or the adventure, but most went out of a sincere desire to support the troops or to improve conditions in the countries where the U.S. had deployed. Many served in engineering support roles, aiding combat engineers with their duties. Others provided contracting or real estate support. They worked long hours often in very primitive conditions. It was this level of self-sacrifice that defined employment at the district.

District Deployments During the Oklahoma City Bombing and 9-11

After the San Francisco Bay area earthquake of 1989, the federal government recognized the need to improve its response to emergencies. In 1991, the U.S. Army Forces Command responded to this need by formally tasking the Corps with the responsibility of providing structural engineers to participate in the new Urban Search and Rescue Program. In 1992, the pilot training course was held and the formation of the Structures Specialists Cadre was initiated. The training focused on providing the necessary skills to support the FEMA mission and the Urban Search and Rescue Task Force. This support included

---
[217] "Marty Seger Writes from Duty in Iraq," *Esprit* (Apr. 2008).
[218] "Joe Kellett visits from Afghanistan," *Esprit* (Fall 2008).

inspecting and evaluating fully or partially collapsed structures during the search and rescue efforts so that the risk to personnel and victims could be minimized. These specialists were also trained to design shoring systems to stabilize structures so that rescuers could gain safe access to victims. The emergency response system was set up so that search and rescue personnel were available to FEMA to deploy on a mission in a moment's notice (within six hours of a disaster), with the mission that typically lasting between six to 10 days. The first significant test of this system was after the April 19, 1995 Oklahoma City Bombing. Tom Niedernhofer - then as design engineer for the St. Louis District - has previously done work as a structure specialist after the Loma Prieta and Northridge earthquakes in California, Hurricane Andrew in Florida, and the 1993 flood. However, none of this could fully prepare him for the Oklahoma City Bombing. Niedernhofer was one of two structural specialists deployed within just six hours of the disaster. Niedernhofer worked the night shift while the other specialist, and engineer from California, took the day shift. Working 15- to 16-hour shifts, these engineers ensured that the structure was stable enough for rescue crews to begin their efforts. These two specialists remained for eight days, with replacements arriving on the seventh day and a seamless replacement occurring on the eighth. The efforts of these specialists provided protection that helped prevent rescuers from becoming victims themselves.[219]

St. Louis District Structure Specialist Tom Niedernhofer conducting inspection at Oklahoma City bombing site

---

[219] "Belleville man took part in rescue efforts," *Belleville News-Democrat* (April 30, 1995); USACE, "The Urban Search and Rescue Program," Fact Sheet (*www.usace.army.mil/Emergency/Documents/USR2009.pdf*, Sep. 13, 2011); Brian Rentfro, Interview with Tom Niedernhofer, Sep. 19, 2011 (MVS Archives).

Corps structure specialists at World Trade Center

Six years later, that same Tom Niedernhofer was part of a group of five St. Louis District engineers who departed for New York in response to the terrorist attacks of September 11, 2001. These five were part of a group of 15 Corps structures specialists from across the nation who did urban search and rescue work as part of the emergency response to the disaster. Shortly after the attacks, the Corps began mobilizing its emergency response resources, which included deploying its structural specialists. These five engineers – Jeff Stamper, Gary Lee, Vick James, Dave Mueller, and Niedernhofer – received word that that they would be departing from St. Louis on September 13. The five men quickly informed their loved ones that they would be departing on the dangerous mission, boarded the Mississippi Valley Division plane, and set out for Jacksonville, Florida and Wilmington, North Carolina to pick up five additional specialists, with the other five traveling by car. While in route, the engineers tried to get more specific information about their mission, but with no success. They arrived at the Trenton, New Jersey airport and the next morning departed for Camp Kilmer for further instructions. However, even after the engineers received their briefing and equipment, their mission was still

Corps personnel with Chief of Engineers Lt. Gen. Robert Flowers at World Trade Center

not exactly clear, as they would only become keen to it once they arrived in Manhattan. Numerous difficulties impeded their journey, as they encountered road blocks that set them back. Even after they arrived at Caven Point, New Jersey, where they were to cross the Hudson River via ferry, they were delayed further because of the arrival of President George W. Bush at Ground Zero. Because of the delays, the team was not able to cross the Hudson until the morning of the 15th. Niedernhofer was able to get the team FEMA identification cards that would allow them to access Ground Zero, but numerous road blocks made access difficult. The team tried to give assistance inspecting the slurry wall that held back the waters of the Hudson Bay, but city engineers wanted to control those efforts and the structural specialists continued looking for ways to assiSt. That opportunity came on September 17 when some of the team members found the 1010 Command Post, which had search and rescue responsibility for the south central area of the World Trade Center complex, and were able to devote their efforts to search and rescue work at building 4. In the days to come, these engineers were able to help identify falling debris hazards, consult on debris removal, and consult on road pavement settlement that presented hazards to a crane being used in debris removal. Because of the massive resources of New York City, the efforts of the structural specialists were not as essential as was normally the case during such a disaster. Nevertheless, these engineers, alongside New York City fire fighters, policemen, and other brave men and women, contributed their time and risked their own safety in an effort to save lives and protect the safety of others.[220]

---

[220] Rentfro, Interview with Tom Niedernhofer; USACE, "USACE was only Army command with 9-11 missions," *Engineer Update* (Sep. 2011); "Urban Search and Rescue at the World Trade Center: Up Close and Personal," *Esprit* (Oct. 2001).

Service in World War II

Max Lamm started working for the St. Louis District in 1938 in the Levee Section, where he worked diligently conducting levee inspections on the Illinois River and worked on drainage issues until the district became involved in military construction during World War II. He had just started working on the Granite City Engineer Depot, when in 1941, District Engineer Col. Roy Grower approached him about accepting a commission to serve as an officer in the Army Reserves in the Corps of Engineers. Shortly thereafter, Lamm accepted the commission as a second lieutenant and went straight to work for the district.

Construction of Alaska Highway, 1942

At that time, the district had some 32 officers serving as area or project managers – most managers after 1941 were military officers. The area managers were in charge of all projects in a specific area and had several project managers under them. Most were reservists, and some were active duty ordnance officers with an engineering background. Grower worked to have them reassigned to the district, which had one of the heaviest domestic military construction missions in the Corps.

Lamm worked initially as assistant executive officer of the Engineering Warehouse and Yards. He helped to recondition and ship equipment for various projects. A significant amount of this equipment ended up supporting the Alaskan Highway project, one of the largest construction projects in the country. He also stored and shipped surplus material from ordnance factories, and even helped provide supplies to the Manhattan Project. Next, he served as chief of the Inspections Branch, with responsibility over 35 inspectors. These ensured contractors completed jobs correctly and inspected everything from plumbing at facilities to steel landing planks on airfields.

After three months of training at Fort Belvoir in 1944, Lamm finally shipped overseas. Because of his experience at the district at Scott Air Field, he requested work on airfields. Assigned as a platoon leader on the Philippines, he worked building airfields and roads until 1945. Around Thanksgiving, after Japanese surrender, Lamm shipped to Yokahoma, Japan, where he reconditioned a Japanese military academy to house U.S. troops. He shipped for Fort Lewis, Washington, in March 1946.[221]

---

[221] Rex Van Almsick, Interview with Max Lamm, Mar. 3, 1979 (MVS Archives).

Part V.
Conservation and Controversy: The U.S. Army Corps of Engineers and the Environment

By the 1960s, the Corps of Engineers had long been the preeminent engineering organization in the nation. Corps structures provided flood control, hydroelectric power, recreation, water supply, improved navigation, and many other essentials. For engineers on the Mississippi, the most important of these responsibilities was maintaining a safe and dependable navigation channel. However, by the 1960s and 1970s, the more traditional mission of maintaining navigation and providing flood control expanded to include many nontraditional responsibilities. The history of the Corps from the 1960s until the present is essentially the story of how the organization evolved in response to its new responsibilities. The primary catalyst for this change was the National Environmental Policy Act (NEPA). Previously, the St. Louis District's primary concerns were maintaining navigation and providing flood control in a cost-efficient manner. However, NEPA required that the Corps perform all of these traditional functions in an environmentally sensitive manner. In the decades that followed NEPA, the Corps evolved from an organization defined by massive civil works projects into an organization that provided a multitude of nontraditional engineering services, such as curation and archaeological management, recreation, and ordnance removal. Most importantly, during this period the Corps responded positively to its new mission, learning to balance its traditional functions with its new environmental mandate, thereby facilitating economic development while protecting the environment for enjoyment of future generations.

16

Growing Environmental Responsibilities

The post-World War II era saw a growing national concern for the environment that altered the approach, workload, and organization of the St. Louis District. The growing appreciation for maintaining pristine wilderness areas and fighting the government and big business to prevent pollution of natural resources led to the passage of numerous environmental laws and regulations after 1950, with the result that by 1980 the work of the district had changed significantly. This applied to a range of activities, from planning large navigation and flood control construction projects to include multipurpose facilities, to new permitting requirements, to entire new programs to clean up Department of Defense infrastructure. It became, in many respects, a new district with a new focus. While traditional construction activities often initially faced major modifications and delays that frustrated some employees and sponsors, the growth of new activities and programs meant growth in funding and work that would last decades into the future. The navigation and flood control mission continued, but there can be no doubt that, just as flood control defined the decades after 1936, the period after 1970 was the environmental era.

Environmental Planning

In December 1969, Congress passed the National Environmental Policy Act (NEPA) – landmark legislation that had a profound impact on the way the Corps and St. Louis District conducted business. The story of the nation's environmental movement began nearly a century earlier. The nation's desire for environmental protection was largely a response to the rapid growth of industry in the nineteenth and twentieth centuries. As industrialization accelerated, consumption of natural resources increased rapidly. By the end of the nineteenth century, many Americans had become distrustful of big business and wanted to preserve resources and limit impacts on health. One of the most important supporters of this view was President Theodore Roosevelt. An avid outdoorsman and conservationist, he wanted to ensure future generations would be able to enjoy the pristine beauty of the American wilderness. Because unregulated industrial practices and expansion were devastating the environment, leading men such as Roosevelt argued the nation should protect resources from overconsumption and exploitation. Roosevelt's policies resulted in the nation designating more than 230 million acres as national parks and forests and establishing the Forest Service in 1905. Roosevelt based his conservationism on the idea of efficient use of natural resources. However, with the rise of environmentalism, efficient use would evolve into an ideology that the nation must protect nature for its own sake.[222]

In the decades leading up to the 1960s, the nation emerged as a world superpower, and as its prosperity grew, consumption grew along with it. Because of this prosperity, many Americans had leisure time to enjoy nature. This caused many people to develop a greater appreciation of nature and keener awareness of environmental issues. Rising consumption and continued industrialization concerned many people, especially those who had come to appreciate America's wilderness during the prosperity of the post War years. In the climate of 1960s activism, new environmental groups cropped up and older ones became more outspoken. What made the movement unique was its grassroots nature, as many ordinary Americans, such as biology teachers, college students, and members of small communities, became involved, unlike the elitist conservation movements of previous decades. Many modern environmentalists point to Rachel Carson's 1962 book, *Silent Spring*, as the beginning of the movement. *Silent Spring* informed the public about the dangers of pesticides, leading to increased public interest in environmental issues. Over the next few years, environmentalists became much more aggressive in attempts to bring public awareness to environmental issues. For the first time, various environmental groups united their efforts to affect political change. The growing influence of the environmental movement combined with the public's growing concern for environmental issues resulted in Congress passing a series of laws intended to deal with these problems: the Clean Water Acts (1960, 1965, and 1972), the Clean Air Acts (1963 and 1967), the Endangered Species Acts (1964, 1968, 1973, and 1976), and the Water Quality Act (1965), culminating in passage of

---

[222] Benjamin Kline, *First Along the River: A Brief History of the U.S. Environmental Movement* (San Francisco: Acada Books, 1997); Samuel P. Hays, *Conservation and the Gospel of Efficiency: The Progressive Conservation Movement, 1890-1920* (Cambridge: Harvard UP, 1959).

NEPA in 1969. These laws set federally enforceable standards for any project or activity that might have an impact on the environment.[223]

NEPA required all federal agencies to comply with legal mandates "before they make final decisions about Federal actions that could have environmental effects." To oversee this process, the government established the Council on Environmental Quality (CEQ), which ensured agencies followed required processes, advised the president on environmental matters, and supervised implementation of NEPA. NEPA also required agencies to submit an environmental impact statement (EIS) before undertaking projects potentially affecting the environment. In December 1970, President Nixon created the Environmental Protection Agency (EPA) to establish and enforce environmental protection standards, conduct environmental research, and advise the president on environmental policies. Both the CEQ and EPA reviewed each EIS before approving any action. In response to NEPA, the Corps expanded to comply with the new federal requirements. Initially, it revised regulations to include a two-step evaluation process for projects. The first step was a brief environmental study conducted by the district engineer that resulted in an environmental assessment. In the next step, the district engineer determined whether to proceed based on the assessment. If there were any evidence a project might have an environmental impact, the district prepared an EIS. This meant that before any large-scale Corps project could begin, there would have to be a lengthy process of planning, authorization, and review, as well as consideration of any feasible alternatives that might have a less significant environmental impact.[224]

The Clean Water Act of 1977 further increased Corps responsibilities, as Section 404 of the act required the Corps "to protect the aquatic environment by requiring a permit for virtually all physical impacts to our nation's wetlands and water resources." As a result, Corps permitting responsibilities expanded between 1969 and 1975, during which time the Corps received 74,000 permit applications and granted 63,370. The passage of the Endangered Species Act in 1973 also increased Corps environmental planning responsibilities, as it made the protection of endangered plant and animal life a federal responsibility. The

---

[223] Kline, *First Along the River*; Kirkpatrick Sale, *The Green Revolution: The American Environmental Movement, 1962-1992* (NY: Hill and Wang, 1993): 1-45; Hays, *A History of Environmental Politics Since 1945* (Pittsburg: Pittsburg UP, 2000); Philip Shabecoff, *A Fierce Green Fire: The American Environmental Movement* (NY: Hill and Wang, 1993); Richard N. L. Andrews, *Managing the Environment, Managing Ourselves: A History of American Environmental Policy* (New Haven: Yale UP, 1999).

[224] CEQ, *A Citizen's Guide to the NEPA: Having Your Voice Heard* (Wash., D.C.: CEQ, 2007); Jack Lewis, "The Birth of the EPA," *EPA Journal* (Nov. 1985); Andrews, *Managing the Environment*; Carroll Pursell and William Willingham, "Protecting the Nation's Waters: A History of the U.S. Army Corps of Engineers' Regulatory Responsibilities, 1899-1999," manuscript (Feb. 1999): 36-69.

law required the identification of all endangered species and their habitats. Section 7 particularly affected the Corps, as it prohibited any federal action that might have a detrimental impact on endangered species or their habitat. The weight of these new responsibilities fell onto the back of the Corps and, as Richard Andrews writes, showed that "the Corps was subjected to more intense external pressures to implement environmental policy than nearly any other federal agency." These pressures became the catalyst for the organizational changes that occurred in the decades following NEPA.[225]

One response to NEPA was establishment of the Environmental Advisory Board. Chief of Engineers Lt. Gen. Frederick J. Clarke invited six distinguished members of the environmental community to advise him, so he could make changes to allow the Corps to better comply with NEPA. To ensure that districts included environmental considerations in the planning process, the Corps released *Environmental Guidelines for the Corps of Engineers* in December 1970. However, the board was critical of the *Guidelines* because it felt the Corps should require advisory boards at the district level. It also criticized the planning process, insufficient public involvement in projects, and EIS inadequacies. These criticisms came largely because board members desired rapid change, which was difficult due to the decentralized nature of the Corps.

Col. Guy Jester

Another difficulty, described by former District Engineer Col. Guy Jester (1971-1973), was "trying to teach our people how to do an environmental impact statement [and] how to address the environmental problems." Because NEPA provided little guidance on implementation, organizations had to use trial and error to determine the best methods. For example, environmentalists criticized the district's first EIS because it was only eight pages long, compared to the multivolume products of today. However, NEPA offered no precise guidelines for EIS preparation processes, which the Corps developed in response to criticisms and recommendations. NEPA created further challenges because it dramatically increased the

---

[225] *A Citizen's Guide to the NEPA*; Andrews, *Environmental Policy and Administrative Change: Implementation of the National Environmental Policy Act* (Wash., D.C.: Lexington, 1976): 47-91; Andrews, *Managing the Environment*, pp. 39-41; Pursell and Willingham, p. 55.

complexity and time required for project planning. Producing an adequate EIS often required years of studies and compiling data. All these factors exposed the need to improve EIS preparation and planning, but changes would take time, as districts hired new employees and trained old ones to comply with new guidelines. It should be noted that, as an engineering organization, the district's primary concern for more than a century was completing projects in an economically feasible way. It had to reshape this way of thinking abruptly in response to NEPA. As former District Engineer Col. Thorwald Peterson pointed out, "the Corps of Engineers' performance during…the early years of NEPA, [shows] that it was certainly at the forefront of adaptation."[226]

Col. Thorwald Peterson

The real test of NEPA was its implementation at the operating levels of government. For the law to be effective, organizations needed to change their philosophy and implement organizational changes. The evolution of planning and project management revealed how the Corps responded to these requirements. The Environmental Advisory Board suggested to Clarke that the Corps needed a much more intricate planning process. In response, the Corps issued guidelines outlining Corps objectives for project planning, which included an emphasis on public participation in the project planning process. These objectives were exemplified by reorganization at the district level. Districts renamed their units and redefined their roles. To expedite organizational changes, districts expanded their personnel and increased the responsibilities of existing personnel. Historians Daniel Mazmanian and Jeanne Nienaber observed that planning "was seen as the route to [making] better decisions by coming to terms with rapid change, increasing complexity, and new environmental demands." In addition to technical, engineering, and economic factors, planning now included conflict resolution, environmental studies, public relations, and EIS preparation. One way districts addressed

---

[226] Towey, Interview with Jester; Martin Reuss, *Shaping Environmental Awareness: The United States Army Corps of Engineers Environmental Advisory Board, 1970-1980* (Fort Belvoir: CEHO, 1982); Andrews, *Environmental Policy*, pp. 47-91; Ruddy, Interview with Peterson, May 19, 1983 (MVS archives); USACE, *Environmental Statement, Meramec Park Lake* (St. Louis: MVS, Nov. 6, 1970).

these needs was by forming environmental units, such as recreation resource sections, in the Planning Division. Their primary function was EIS preparation, but they also reviewed projects and ensured compliance with NEPA guidelines during the planning process. The fact that the number of environmental personnel in the Corps increased from 75 to 575 between 1969 and 1977 shows the profound impact that NEPA had on the Corps planning process. The planning divisions also had to run public involvement programs and send representatives to public meetings. The goal of environmental planning was to create an "integrated planning process" so districts could address environmental considerations at the beginning of a project. However, because of the backlog of previous projects environmental units needed to address, most were not free to participate at the beginning of the planning process until the late 1970s. By the 1980s, the Corps had dramatically improved its planning process, but still needed to make significant organizational changes to create a planning process that was fast and efficient, as well as sensitive to environmental needs.[227]

The Water Resources Development Act of 1986 was a major catalyst for the Corps to adopt more efficient project planning. The act authorized the Corps to undertake 270 new projects and deauthorized 290 older projects. It also required the Corps to expedite the planning process for all civil works projects. Another catalyst was Chief of Engineers Lt. Gen. Henry J. Hatch's new vision for the strategic planning process. Hatch wanted to improve Corps planning by incorporating strategic planning methods used by corporations. The Corps project management model was inefficient, as it required a project to go through a different manager each time it entered a new phase. Typically, a project had different managers for the planning, engineering, construction, and operations phases. This system was inadequate to meet the demands of planning, so the Corps began using life cycle project management – widely used in the corporate world – to optimize planning. With life cycle project management, a project manager oversaw every aspect of a project through its life cycle. In July 1988, the Corps issued a circular that directed districts to begin implementing project management as part of Initiative-88. For every project, the Corps would appoint a civilian as deputy district engineer, assign a

---

[227] Reuss, *Shaping Environmental Awareness*, pp. 47-91; Mazmanian and Nienaber, *Can Organizations Change?: Environmental Protection, Citizen, Participation, and the Corps of Engineers* (Wash. D.C.: Brookings Inst., 1979): 52; Donita M. Moorhus and Gregory Graves, *The Limits of Vision: A History of the U.S. Army Corps of Engineers, 1988-1992* (Wash. D.C.: USACE, 2000): 1-51; USACE, *Planning Guidance Notebook, ER 1105-2-100* (Wash., D.C.: USACE, 2000), Ch. 2, Sec. 3.

project manager, form a board chaired by the deputy to evaluate projects, and establish a Program Management Office to advise the deputy.[228]

In 1988, former District Engineer Col. Daniel Wilson stated that what made life cycle project management so significant was that it allowed project managers to "cut across organizational lines," i.e., the stovepipe organization in which there was a different manager for each phase of a project. Wilson argued that these changes in philosophy showed that this was not the same "old Corps of Engineers," but a modern organization. The first time the district used these new management techniques was in 1989, when it appointed a life-cycle project manager to oversee the Melvin Price Locks and Dams Project. In 1991, the district changed the Project Management Branch to the Programs and Project Management Division. Planning and project management had always been closely related, and with the new emphasis on life-cycle project management, merging the Planning Division with the Programs and Project Management Division was a logical decision. In 1999 the Planning Division merged with the Programs and Project Management Division to create one "super division", the Planning, Programs, and Project Management Division. Although the Corps certainly would have evolved without NEPA, these environmental responsibilities accelerated the changes that occurred, forever changing the way the Corps did business.[229]

Col. Daniel Wilson

Recreation

In the years after World War II, American prosperity soared, the population expanded, and people had more leisure time to enjoy America's vast natural resources. This caused a surge in the demand for recreation sites, particularly

---

[228] Reuss, *Reshaping National Water Politics: The Emergence of the Water Resources Development Act of 1986* (Fort Belvoir: IWR, 1991), Ch. 4; Moorhus and Graves, pp. 1-6; Alan Atkisson, Interview with Henry J. Hatch, *In Context* 32 (Sum. 1992).

[229] Ruddy interview with Col. Daniel Wilson, July 28, 1988 (MVS archives); Daly and Zoeller Interview with Dace, May 25 and June 10; St. Louis District Organizational Charts (MVS archives); Department of Army, Memorandum for Commander, Mississippi Valley Division, concerning the Implementation Plan for ER 5-1-11, Programs and Project Management (MVS archives).

Aerial of St. Louis in 1950s

closer to large urban areas. However, industrial expansion and prosperity impacted the quantity and quality of recreation resources available because expansion required millions of acres for new subdivisions, highways, industrial sites, airports, and schools. In response to the loss of these resources, Congress established the Outdoor Recreation Resources Review Commission in 1958 to undertake a nationwide study of outdoor recreation. Public Law 85-470 authorized the commission to "determine the outdoor recreation wants and needs of the American people now and what they would be in 1976 and 2000." The law also authorized the commission to "determine what policies and programs should be recommended to ensure that the needs of the present and future are adequately and efficiently met." In 1962, the Commission presented its *Outdoor Recreation for America* report to Congress. The report stated that the increasing demands for recreation meant public agencies needed more money for acquiring and maintaining recreation sites. The report concluded that water was the focal point for recreation and, although plenty of land was available, the government did not "efficiently" meet recreation needs. The commission recommended establishment of a national outdoor recreation policy and development of guidelines for the management of outdoor recreation resources.[230]

The Corps had not initially intended to get into the recreation business, but because the report emphasized water-based activities, the Corps – especially at its numerous reservoirs –came to play an essential role in meeting the nation's recreation needs. The growing importance of recreation for the Corps was evidenced by the 17-fold increase in attendance at its recreation areas between 1953 and 1973. One reason for this increase was the 1944 Flood Control Act, which authorized the Corps to construct, operate and maintain public park and recreational facilities in reservoir areas. In 1962, Congress amended the 1944 act, broadening the Corps' authority to include all water resource projects. Another important piece of legislation contributing to the growth of recreation was the 1965 Federal Water Projects Recreation Act, which required the Corps to give full consideration to recreation opportunities at multi-purpose reservoirs and also defined parameters for cost-sharing with other federal and nonfederal agencies at these sites. Since 1944, the Corps has signed leases with state and local agencies that allow agencies to participate in administration and development of recreation sites. However, those sites under Corps control before the implementation of this cost-sharing principle continued to be operated directly by the Corps.[231]

With the increasing demand for recreation, Corps-built lakes and recreation sites grew exponentially. The first district lake project was Carlyle in Illinois. In response to flooding on the Kaskaskia River, a group of concerned citizens began meeting in 1933 to discuss the possibility of a project at Carlyle. Congress rewarded their efforts in the 1938 Flood Control Act, which approved a major flood control reservoir in the region. However, the outbreak of World War II delayed the project until interest renewed in the 1950s. By 1957, the Corps completed a comprehensive plan for the Kaskaskia

Recreation area at Rend Lake

---

[230] "Outdoor Recreation for America (1962)," in Lary M. Dilsaver, ed., *America's National Park System: The Critical Documents* (Lanham: Rowman and Littlefield Publishers, 1994); Maj. Gen. J.W. Morris, "Recreation Surge" *Water Spectrum* 5:2 (1973).

[231] Increased attendance discussed in Morris, "Recreation Surge"; *Flood Control Act of 1944*, PL 78–534 (78th Cong., 2d Sess., Dec. 22, 1944); *Federal Water Project Recreation Act of 1965* (PL 89-72), as amended; Engineering Regulation 1165-2-400 (August 9, 1980).

Boating at Rend Lake

River Project and the following year Congress authorized the construction of reservoirs at Shelbyville and Carlyle in the Flood Control Act of 1958. Construction on Carlyle Lake was completed in 1967, producing a 26,000 acre reservoir (at normal pool) that was the largest man-made lake in Illinois. While the primary purpose of the lake was flood control, it was a multipurpose reservoir that improved navigation of the Kaskaskia, supplied water to the region, and provided numerous environmental stewardship and recreation opportunities, including camping, picnicking, swimming, boating, fishing, and sailing. The demand for recreation was shown by the increase in visitation, which rose from 929,008 recreation days in 1967 to over 4 million by the 1990s. In 2000, the Kaskaskia Navigation Project was combined with the Carlyle Lake Project. When the Kaskaskia project was authorized in 1962, the original purpose was aiding commercial navigation through construction of a lock and dam that would allow for the creation of a 9-foot navigation channel. However, project benefits were not limited to navigation, as the area offers numerous recreational opportunities. Approximately 5,000 recreational crafts lock through Kaskaskia each year and the project also includes four major public boat ramps and a popular marina at New Athens. In addition, the project has provided the opportunity for development of numerous recreational opportunities for local communities, such as the city of Evansville.[232]

The district used what it learned at Carlyle during construction of Rend and Shelbyville lakes. Construction of Shelbyville Lake was completed in 1970 and Rend Lake was completed just two years later. Like other district reservoirs, Shelbyville and Rend were multi-purpose facilities, with recreation being just one of their purposes. Recreation demands increased significantly at Shelbyville, growing from approximately 1.2 million in 1970 to just over 3 million by 2001. The district used what it learned during the development of the Illinois reservoirs and applied it to those in Missouri: Mark Twain and Wappapello. The construction of Mark Twain Lake and Clarence Cannon Dam had been considered long before Congress approved it with the Flood Control Act of 1962. Since the 1930s, a reservoir had been discussed as a means of flood control, but it was not until 1983 that the project was completed. In addition to supplying flood control, hydroelectric power, and 4.5 million gallons of clean water, the project has offered numerous recreation opportunities, such as camping, fishing, hunting, boating and hiking. Moreover, because the district was able to apply what it had learned during construction at the Illinois lakes, it was able to develop an area that included the diversity of recreational opportunities and facilities required at a modern site. Wappapello, which was constructed between 1938 and 1941, was originally part of the Memphis District but was transferred to St. Louis in the early 1980s. The primary function of the reservoir was to minimize flooding in the St. Francis Basin, but the lake also offered opportunities for recreational development and environmental stewardship. After the transfer, the St. Louis District consolidated facilities for efficiency and brought the recreation areas up to current standards. The Corps developed and

Mark Twain Lake visitor center

---

[232] USACE, *Master Plan, DM No. 10, Carlyle Lake, Illinois* (St. Louis: MVS, 1997); "Carlyle Lake/Kaskaskia Navigation Project," *Esprit* (June 2001). It should be noted that visitation figures between 1967 and 1991 are based on the same method of measurement, however, in 1992 the Corps adopted the Visitor Estimation Reporting System (VERS), meaning that those figures after 1991 cannot be accurately compared to earlier figures. In some cases, because of the new standardized system of measurement, visitor numbers declined while actual visitation decreased.

Carlyle Lake at sunrise

altered recreation facilities in response to the evolving and diverse use patterns of visitors. This development included modernization of facilities, expanded forms of recreation opportunities, and easy access for disabled persons. Additional opportunities are offered by concessionaries that provide dining, cabins, and boat rental and by local organizations partner with Wappapello to offer visitors numerous family-oriented special events. Visitation at the lake fluctuated between 1.1 and 2.1 million visitors from 1963 to 1982 and has remained around 2 million since 1983. The Corps has outgranted lands to the Missouri Department of Natural Resources (MDNR) for operation of Lake Wappapello State Park and to the Missouri Department of Conservation (MDC) for fish and wildlife management. In addition, the district promotes habitat improvement and maintains a refuge on project lands.[233]

The Corps had constructed the majority of its reservoirs in the 1960s and 1970s. Since this time, visitor needs and expectations have changed dramatically, requiring the Corps to respond by modernizing areas to meet current recreation demands. Modernization included upgraded sanitary facilities and toilets (flush toilets replace pit toilets), as well additions such as laundry

---

[233] "Carlyle Lake," *Esprit* (Jan. 1996); USACE, *Master Plan, DM No. 10, Carlyle Lake, Illinois* (St. Louis: MVS, 1997); USACE, *Master Plan, DM No. 9, Clarence Cannon Dam and Mark Twain Lake* (St. Louis: MVS, 2004); Visitation data after 1992 based on VERS. Morris, "Recreation Surge"; "Celebrate the Lakes," *Esprit*, special lakes issues (June 2001).

Corps hunter safety course

buildings and shower areas. The district also began building new and improving old access roads to areas, paving walking areas and parking lots, adding picnic areas, constructing swimming areas, and modernizing campsites by adding electricity and longer pads for recreational vehicles use. In addition, the district improved areas to make them accessible for the disabled and also to provide a greater diversity of non-water-based recreational opportunities such as hiking trails, improved campgrounds, playgrounds, visitor centers, picnic areas, hunting areas, historic and educational sites. By 1999, the Corps recognized the need for modernization of its facilities nationwide, so it established a Recreation Facilities Standards Task Force to develop a commonly applied set of recreation facility design standards and levels of service for the modernization of Corps recreation areas. This lead to the Recreation Area Modernization Program (RAMP), which included guidelines and standards for modernization at areas. In 2005, Shelbyville Lake was one of six lakes that the Corps chose to receive funds for modernization.[234]

The district's recreational improvements were not limited to reservoirs. It also modified navigation pools to provide public access. Thousands of visitors used each year used the slack-water pools created by the nine-foot channel project to fish, swim, boat, and sightsee. Recognizing the need for recreation

---

[234] USACE, *Master Plan, DM 7B, Lake Shelbyville, Illinois* (St. Louis: MVS, 2004).

opportunities near St. Louis, the district evaluated recreational activities in the region and found that many of the top activities were not water-based, such as walking, pleasure driving, picnicking, observing wildlife, bicycling, and running. In response to demands for these activities, the district developed the Rivers Project Master Plan in 2001. The goal of the project was to provide recreational, environmental stewardship, and environmental education opportunities while balancing these goals with economic development. Numerous recreation opportunities existed along the Mississippi, Illinois, and Kaskaskia rivers. Because commercial and private interests used the waterways, and because of the fragile balance between human activities and protecting the environment, it was essential to develop projects in a way that balanced commercial, environmental, and recreational needs. To meet this challenge, the district began evaluating Corps-managed public lands and the opportunities for development. The district also evaluated user demands to determine which activities it should focus on developing. Overall, the most popular activities were boat-fishing, sightseeing, recreational boating, and bank-fishing, representing 75-percent of total activities. However, studies revealed a significant demand for activities such as camping, picnicking, swimming, hiking, and bicycling, which were especially prevalent in the St. Louis metropolitan area, as people desired increased opportunities near riverfronts. To

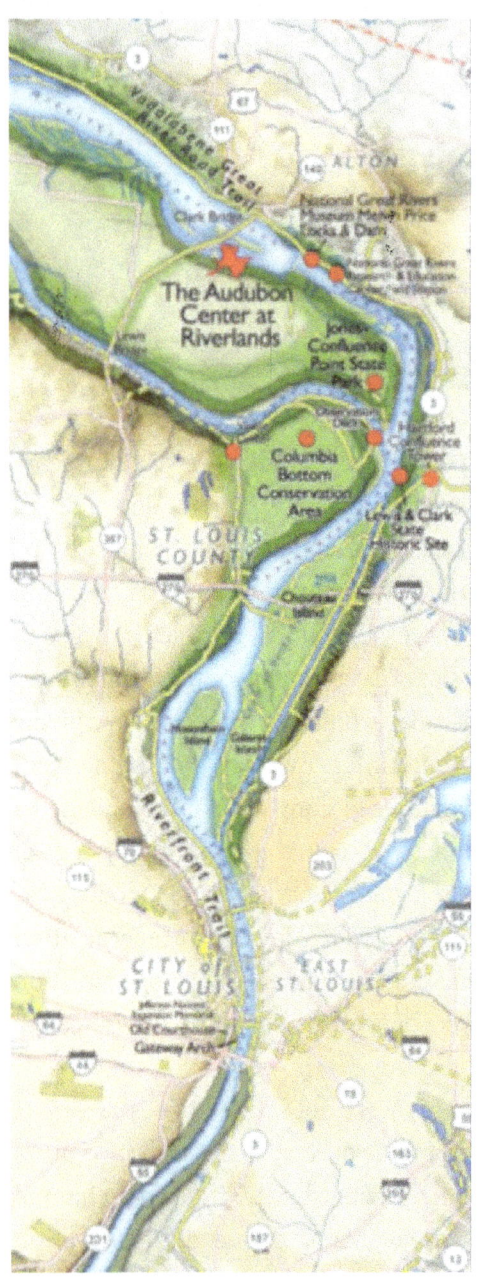

Map of Riverlands

address these needs, the district improved recreation opportunities in much the same way it did at reservoirs – modernizing facilities, developing sites to address the need for additional activities, and creating safer and more accessible sites. As of 2011, there were 28 Rivers Project areas in the district's navigation pools, offering numerous recreational opportunities while providing the convenience of modern amenities.[235]

With the increasing number of Corps reservoirs, the need for improved water safety at these areas became apparent. In 1971, there were nearly 500 water-related fatalities at Corps lakes and the average number of fatalities remained around 300 throughout the decade. In the mid-1970s, the Chief of Engineers, recognizing that the Corps needed to intensify its water safety efforts, issued a directive to this effect. These efforts helped to reduce fatalities to around 200 annually by the mid-1980s. In 1986, the Corps began its National Water Safety Program, which centralized water safety efforts across districts nationwide in order to ensure that the quality of program was consistent Corps-wide. The program's aim was to identify life-threatening concerns associated with water-based recreation and increase public awareness of safe practices through various forms of educational media. During its first 25 years, the program has seen the number of reported water-related fatalities at Corps-managed areas decline to nearly half the average of the 1970s and early 1980s. In 1994, headquarters formed the National Water Safety Products Advisory Committee to provide field-level input on water safety products and development. The committee also provided information on the efficacy of the program at the level of individual recreation areas at the district level. This grassroots-level information helped to facilitate site-specific improvements to water safety. The St. Louis District oversees recreational safety at its more than 300,000 acres, which include five reservoirs, five navigational projects, 80 miles on the Illinois River, 36 miles on the Kaskaskia, and 300 miles on the Mississippi. These areas attract approximately 17 million visits per year, over 60 percent of which participate in water-based activities. The Corps began keeping statistics on water-related fatalities in 1998 and has used the data collected as a means to measure the efficacy of its water safety efforts. The data revealed that drowning was responsible for 86 percent of deaths, with boating and swimming being responsible for 89 percent of these deaths. The St. Louis District responded to these figures by launching educational campaigns at target groups, one being

---

[235] USACE, *Rivers Project Master Plan* (St. Louis: MVS, 2001).

children in grades K-7 and the other being teenagers and adults. The statistics collected were used to determine the focal points of the education program, which were swimming and boater safety. The district has used public service announcements, newsletters, commercials, outreach programs, poster contests, billboards, internet, safety courses, printed materials, and various other sources of media to carry out its campaign. At individual areas, personnel were trained in safety procedures, signs were posted, and rescue equipment made available to optimize efficacy. The objective of these efforts was to decrease fatalities by 50 percent by the end of 2009, with 2007 being the base year. To meet this objective, the district must have only 6 in FY08 and 4 in FY09. In 2008, the district had just one fatality and two in 2009.[236]

In addition to the improving recreation opportunities in navigation pools and at reservoirs, the district used these areas for environmental improvements. At Mark Twain, Shelbyville, Wappapello, and Carlyle lakes, the district, in cooperation with other responsible agencies, seeks to maintain steady pool elevations which enhance the quality of spawning. The district also used water level fluctuations at its navigation pools on the Mississippi to improve vegetative growth and optimize habitat conditions. It also enhanced fish and wildlife protection by providing environmental demonstration areas that various species used as habitat. These areas were especially important for waterfowl, which use wetlands for sustenance while making their migrations. Enhanced areas included the Riverlands Environmental Demonstration Area near Melvin Price Locks and Dam and fish and wildlife management areas at district reservoirs. Resource managers oversaw these areas to ensure the maximization of wildlife conservation while providing recreational opportunities that were compatible with protecting the environment. These sites also provided numerous educational opportunities, as visitors could observe species in a natural habitat and learn the importance of balancing human activities and the environment.[237]

---

[236] USACE, "Water Safety Program Summary" (*www.corpslakes.usace.army.mil/employees/watersafety/pback.cfm*, Dec. 29, 2011); USACE, St. Louis District Boating and Water Safety Strategic Campaign Plan (St. Louis: MVS, 2008); USACE, Corps of Engineers Public Water Related Fatalities FY97-FY10 (*www.corpslakes.usace.army.mil/employees/watersafety/pdfs/COE_Water-related_Fatalities_FY98-10%20Division%20Summary.pdf*, Dec. 29, 2011).

[237] "State parks and wildlife management areas," *Esprit* (Ap. 1996); "Wildlife management area," *Esprit* (Jan. 1996); "Waterfowl management," *Esprit* (Mar. 1996); "Sustaining the Mississippi River," *Esprit* (Oct. 1995).

John F. Marzec

John F. Marzec dedicated his career in service to the Corps, the St. Louis District and to the public. During his service as Chief of the Natural Resource Management Branch (1976 to 1997), he provided direction not only for the district, but for national programs, helping to shape an entire generation of biologists, foresters, rangers and land use planners. His innovative leadership helped to establish a framework for how project operations are done today, as he demanded a balanced program that emphasized all program elements including flood control, recreation, natural resources, water supply and navigation.

Marzec's leadership style was ahead of its time, as practices now commonplace were championed by him decades before they became mainstream. He required cross-training between the district and field, established work details at HQUSACE, promoted staff visits to other projects and encouraged field staff to regularly share successes and failures. John served as a mentor and role model for many who have become leaders in the District, including Dennis Fenske, Beth Pitrolo, Andrea Murdock (Lewis), Dennis Foss, Gary Stilts, Dave Berti, Jim Lynch, Bob Wilkins, Stan Ebersohl, Jim Hill, Andrew Jefferson and others. His efforts were instrumental in creating the professional project management organizations that exist in the district today.

Marzec was also a leader in using public involvement in the planning process. He recognized the need for public input in solving difficult problems, so in 1985 he kicked off the Traditional Access Plan, which facilitated use of full public involvement. He also used public consensus building in the Shoreline Management Plan at Lake Shelbyville.

John was also instrumental in utilizing contracting as a method of increasing the purchasing power and freeing hired labor for more critical tasks. He established a staffing structure that was responsive and efficient in the use of new technologies and business methods. He worked tirelessly to empower Operations Managers to create an effective organizational structure. John understood that without funding, nothing could be done; so he worked throughout his career to develop an adequate O&M base funding level.

Near the end of his career, he became the first Operations Project Manager for the Rivers Project Office. In addition, he restructured and consolidated the Mississippi River Lock and Dams and River resource management functions into one Operational Project.

Archaeological Collections Management

In 1906, Congress passed the Antiquities Act, the first in a series of laws and regulations emphasizing the importance of preserving the nation's cultural and archaeological resources. These laws required the curation of materials removed from federal lands, including the more than 25 million acres owned or leased by the Department of Defense. This DoD land contains more than 32,000 known archaeological sites, nearly 8,000 of which can be or are listed on the National Register of Historic Places.

After World War II ended, the over 6 million returning soldiers needed to return to work. However, many of their positions had been filled in their absence, so one challenge the nation faced was creating new jobs for the returning soldiers. One way to create jobs was to undertake a number of infrastructure and civil works projects, many of which involved the Corps. At some project locations, the Corps uncovered cultural resources that required archaeological excavation. After recovering the cultural resources (i.e. material remains), the Corps sent the collections (the artifacts and the records associated with the investigations) to repositories located throughout the country. The problem that the Corps and other federal agencies faced was curation of the collections

Dr. Michael "Sonny" Trimble awarded Decoration for Exceptional Civilian Service

removed from the sites, as no long-term national management plan existed and the collections were spread out at various repositories across the country as late as the 1980s. Even if such a plan existed, many federal agencies lacked the funds and expertise needed to efficiently manage these collections. In response to this need, the Corps issued a regulation providing a general policy and guidance concerning the curation of cultural resources. "However," as Dr. Michael "Sonny" Trimble, chief of the St. Louis District's Curation and Archives Analysis Branch, indicated, "the curation guidelines and standards applicable in 1984 [were] very general and often vague."[238]

During the previous 30 years, the district had undertaken more than 92 collection-generating projects. It stored these collections at 10 repositories scattered throughout Missouri and Illinois. The problem for those managing the collections was that "the numerous laws establishing federal ownership of archaeological materials did not provide agencies or repositories with clear guidelines for provision of financial support necessary for long-term curation." In August 1987, the Department of the Interior published a proposed curation rule that would establish curation guidelines for federal agencies to follow. When codified in 1991, the new regulation established

> *definitions, standards, procedures, and guidelines to be followed by Federal agencies to preserve collections of prehistoric and historic material remains, and associated records, that are recovered in conjunction with Federal projects and programs under certain Federal statutes. (36 CFR Part 79:1)*

Before facility   **After collections facility**

---

[238] USACE, *Saving the Past from the Future: Archaeological Curation in the St. Louis District* (St. Louis: MVS, 1991): 1-15, 30, 89, quote on 9; USACE, "Chapter 6: Environmental Engineering," Unpublished manuscript (MVS archives); Department of the Interior, "Department of Defense: Archaeological Collections Management" (*www.doi.gov/pam/dodarc.html*, Feb. 17, 2011).

Shortly before the Department of the Interior published its proposed rule, Terry Norris, the district archaeologist at the time, hired Dr. Michael "Sonny" Trimble for a four-year term to provide additional technical assistance on some standard Corps archaeological work. Trimble began reading over draft federal curation regulation and congressional records and soon discovered the proposed legislation for the Native American Graves Protection and Repatriation Act (NAGPRA) and the new federal curation guidelines (36 CFR Part 79). He quickly realized the dramatic impact that these new regulations would have on archaeology because federal agencies simply did not have the requisite people for conducting the kind of work required by this legislation. In addition, since Trimble had a background in museum management, a field that few archaeologists specialized in, he could apply this expertise to the new federal curation requirements. Moreover, he knew that the Corps had enormous archaeological collections, second only to the Smithsonian amongst Federal government collections. Trimble soon realized that the requirements of this new legislation, given the size of the Corps' archaeological collections, presented a unique opportunity for him to essentially start a business within the Corps inventorying and overseeing the proper curation of these collections. Understanding that all federal agencies would have to adhere to these new guidelines and would not have the capacity or expertise to handle the workload, Trimble went to district archaeologist Terry Norris to discuss the possibility of the district doing this work and providing its expertise to other districts and agencies. Trimble saw this work as a challenge that gave him the freedom to develop innovate ways to approach archaeological collections management. In order to find out the extent of the efforts required to assess and inventory collections across the country, he began with the district's collections. The time and effort required far exceeded anything that Trimble had expected. One reason it was so challenging was that much of the archaeological materials had been sent away to various specialists across the country for analysis. Trimble had to track down these materials and request that it be returned to the district. Over the next year, Trimble wrote up his findings and published them in a volume that became the template for how people composed their reports in the future. Once Trimble had figured out how to do inventory at a district level, he could apply that same knowledge at the national level.

After conducting numerous investigations to assess its collections, the district determined that they were deteriorating and the facilities housing the collections were inadequate for providing proper long-term care. The district responded to these findings with a number of corrective actions. It coalesced all of its collections into two repositories and developed cooperative agreements with these facilities for the proper care of collections. The district also developed a set of archaeological collections standards to ensure uniform curation of all collections. To raise public awareness about the importance of protecting the nation's cultural resources, the district initiated a series of public lectures and exhibits. The district had quickly become a leader in the field of collections management and soon began advising other federal agencies on the proper methods of archaeological collections management. To carry out this mission, the district assembled a team of archaeologists, anthropologists, museum studies specialists, collections managers, biologists, and archivists. These professionals, under the director of Trimble, provided the district with a team of skilled experts who could meet the challenges of large-scale archaeological collections management.[239]

In December 1994, Director of Civil Works Maj. Gen. Stan Genega established the Mandatory Center of Expertise for Archaeological Curation and Collections Management in the St. Louis District. He chose the district because its Curation and Archives Analysis Branch had played a key role in assessing, advising, and improving curations management in other districts. The Corps established the center to "ensure USACE compliance with the curation and/or data requirements mandated by Public Law 101-601, Native American Graves Protection and Repatriation Act (NAGPRA)" (ER 1110-3-109) and to oversee curation management in other Corps districts and federal agencies as well as to "assist Headquarters, Divisions, and Districts in carrying out the curation requirements of the Corps civil works program." Between 1998 and 2000, the center conducted assessments at 165 repositories across the nation that were curating Corps collections. The center used assessments to help facilities comply with the federal curation regulation and educate Corps cultural resources staff nationwide on the proper methods of curation and collections management. It provided technical assistance to agencies including the Navy, Marines, and Air Force, as well as the Bureau of Land Management, Bureau of Indian Affairs, and U.S. Fish and Wildlife Service.[240]

---

[239] "Environmental Engineering," pp. 7-11, *Saving the Past from the Future:*, quote on p. 8; "DoD: Archaeological Collections Management."
[240] DoD: Archaeological Collections Management"; "Environmental Engineering," pp. 7-11; "MCX-CMAC History" (*www.mvs.usace.army.mil/engr/curation/MCXHistoryTxt.html*, Feb.17, 2011).

The center also is charged with ensuring the Corps complies with the requirements of NAGPRA. Passed in 1990, the law requires federal agencies to inventory human remains and associated funerary objects of Native Americans and provide federally recognized Native American tribes, Native Hawaiians, and Alaskan Natives with an inventory of the collection. Upon request, agencies must repatriate collections to those federally recognized tribes, Native Hawaiians, and Alaskan Natives that have been determined to be culturally affiliated with the human remains and objects. To ensure compliance with the new law, the center used its own staff and contractors throughout the U.S. to collect data on skeletal remains and artifacts. Personnel from the center provided assistance in the drafting of compliance documents and identification of the cultural affiliation of the human remains. In recognition of the center's achievements in archaeological curation, it received the Vice President's Hammer Award in 1999 recognizing significant contributions in support of reinventing government principles.[241]

In addition to the center's role in providing technical assistance to other federal agencies, it participated in a number of other important projects and programs, including locating and mapping historic shipwrecks, aiding the U.S. Army Central Identification Laboratory in Hawaii (now the Joint POW/MIA Account Command) in the recovery of missing military personnel, and providing technical assistance to the General Services Administration (GSA) after it discovered a mass grave of former slaves in New York City. The historical shipwrecks project grew out of the need for documentation of shipwreck locations on the Middle Mississippi. During the nineteenth and early twentieth century, steamboats dominated the river. However, because of the hazards involved in navigating the Mississippi and its tributaries, a large number of these boats sank. Historians had long been familiar with the history of inland navigation during this period, but they lacked information about the precise nature and location of shipwrecks buried in siltation by a meandering river. The historical shipwrecks project produced a report listing and mapping the location of nearly 700 vessels that had sank in this small section of the rivers during the nineteenth and early twentieth century. This data has helped historians

---

[241] *Native American Graves Protection and Repatriation Act*, PL 101-601 (101st Cong., 2nd Sess.); USACE, "Champion of Your Heartland's Water Resources" District Brochure (St. Louis: MVS, 2001); "Mandatory Center of Expertise for the Curation and Management of Archaeological Collections," *Esprit* (Dec. 1995); "Native American Graves Protection and Repatriation Act," *Esprit* (Dec. 1995); "District Gets Hammer Award," *Esprit* (Feb. 1999).

deepen their understanding of inland navigation during the "Golden Age of the Steamboat."[242]

In the mid-to-late 1990s, the Central Identification Laboratory in Hawaii asked for the center's assistance in searching for, excavating, and recovering missing military personnel lost in Southeast Asia during the Vietnam War. Archaeologists from the center participated in nearly 130 recovery excavations and identified at least 31 military personnel. Another example of the center's growing reputation was the GSA's request that it provide technical assistance in the analysis and reburial of the remains of a mass grave of 400 former African and African American slaves discovered in New York City in 1991. The GSA sought a suitable curation facility for the artifacts and advice on how to manage its collections, so it contacted Trimble and asked for his assistance on the project. The center agreed to provide technical assistance, especially during the challenging re-interment phase of the project. With the center's help, the GSA was able to successfully analyze, inventory, and re-intern the remains.[243]

Undoubtedly, the highest-profile project the center undertook was its excavation and analysis of mass gravesites in Iraq. In 2004, after the capture of

Mass grave site in Iraq

---
[242] USACE, "Historical Shipwrecks on the Middle Mississippi and Lower Illinois Rivers" (St. Louis: MVS, 2004).
[243] "Mandatory Center of Expertise," *Esprit*; "St. Louis and New York U.S. Army Corps of Engineers Districts partner on one of the greatest archaeological discoveries of our time," *Esprit* (Nov. 2003).

Saddam Hussein, the Department of Justice's Regime Crimes Liaison Office asked Trimble to assemble a team of experts, including forensic experts and archaeologists, to recover evidence of genocide in prosecuting Hussein's regime. The Iraqi Mass Graves Team estimated that more than 400 mass graves dotted the countryside. Through professional excavations of X mass grave sites; analysis of all human remains, clothing, and other material remains; careful review of more than 90,000 images; and meticulous attention to the maintenance of the chain of custody for all these materials, the team was able to document what happened to these Iraqi men, women, and children. During Trimble's 4.5 hours of testimony at Saddam Hussein's trial, he was able to provide palpable evidence of the guilt of Hussein and other former Baath Party officials, ultimately leading to their conviction. However, what began as a mission to prove genocide turned into something much more for the Iraqi Mass Graves Team: the repatriation of the remains. Trimble indicated that his personal goal was to return the bodies "to their families so that they may have closure, so that they may rebury them with honor, reverence, and love." The team accomplished this goal when it returned the remains wrapped in cloth to the Kurdish people. The Kurds buried these remains in a national cemetery that honors the memory of those whose lives were lost.[244]

Trimble and the center's staff continue to provide support to the Corps in their main mission areas—NAGPRA and archaeological curation—and to other federal and state agencies as requested.

---

[244] "Setting the Record Straight" *Esprit* (Jan. 2007); "Proof Positive" *Esprit* (Fall 2005); Donna Miles, "Forensics Team Gives Voice to Saddam's Fallen, Shows U.S. Values," *Armed Forces Press Service* (Apr. 2008); Kristi Mayo, "Digital-Image Management at Mass Gravesites," *Evidence Technology Magazine* (May-June 2008); "Dr. Michael 'Sonny' Trimble: Giving voices to Iraq's murdered peoples" *Esprit* (Nov. 2006).

Veterans Curation Project

After spending time in Iraq uncovering mass Iraqi gravesites and giving testimony against Saddam Hussein's regime, Michael "Sonny" Trimble returned home concerned for the fate of many of the wounded veterans coming home from Iraq and Afghanistan. Trimble had an additional concern: overseeing the proper documentation - as required by the National Historic Preservation Act - of the more than 47,000 boxes of archaeological materials collected from excavations at Corps project sites since the 1950s. In an effort to address these dual concerns, he conceived the idea to employ wounded veterans and give them on-the-job training processing archaeological collections. In the summer of 2009, this conception became a reality, as the Corps funded $3.5 million to the project, which the St. Louis district's Center of Expertise used to design and manage the project's implementation. By October 20, 2009, the project had opened its first center in Augusta, Georgia. In 2010, the Corps opened two additional facilities in Washington, D.C. and St. Louis, Missouri. Every six months, each facility hires 10 veterans, whom it trains in curation skills that these veterans can use to acquire jobs. At the end of six months, a new group of veterans is employed and trained. For some of these veterans, making the transition back to civilian life can be difficult, as attested by Walter Sinnott, a Purple Heart recipient who suffers from Post Traumatic Stress Syndrome. Sinnott explains that his work on the project provided him with more than just a paycheck or job skills; it provided him with the opportunity to sit "down with people and interact...with them on a normal level," which helped immensely in dealing with the difficulties of making the transition back to civilian life. He is just one of many veterans making this difficult transition who have benefitted from the project.

Veterans receiving curation training

Permitting

As early as 1880, District Engineer Maj. Oswald H. Ernst complained that erosion of banks due to cultivation, logging, and clearing to reduce snags had impacted navigation. Congress initially addressed this problem in 1881 when it established a standard navigational channel, but river industries threatened the health of the river in other ways. Because loggers used water to transport timber, logs clogged the river, mills cut canals to transport logs, and saw mills discharged sawdust directly into the river. Other industries altered the river, cut trees for fuel, or discharged pollutants. While the Corps was responsible for regulating certain activities as early as 1890, it was not until passage of the 1899 Rivers and Harbors Act that Congress defined Corps regulatory responsibilities. Section 10 made it illegal to obstruct or alter navigable waters without first acquiring a permit from the Corps. The Refuse Act (Section 13) prohibited dumping refuse "other than that flowing from streets and sewers and passing therefrom in a liquid state." Over time, Congress expanded these limitations to timber, oil, and other pollutants, although the primary emphasis was impact to navigation. The Fish and Wildlife Coordination Act of 1934 authorized the secretaries of Agriculture and Commerce to advise federal agencies to protect wildlife, and its 1958 amendments enabled agencies to request permit denial, although their advice was not compulsory.[245]

Other laws expanded permitting in the decades that followed. The Supreme Court case *Zabel v. Tabb*, in which a Florida developer sued the Corps because it denied a permit to dredge Boca Ciega Bay, strengthened Corps regulatory responsibilities to include non-navigation factors. After a 1969 fire on the Cuyahoga River in Cleveland, Ohio, revealed the level of pollution on the nation's waterways, Congress passed the Federal Water Pollution Control Act Amendments of 1972. Its goal was "to restore and maintain the chemical, physical, and biological integrity of the nation's waterways." Disputes over whether the expanded permits applied to non-navigable waterways such as wetlands led to the 1975 Supreme Court case *Natural Resources Defense Council v. Calloway*, which interpreted Section 404 to include wetlands. Congress passed amendments to the 1972 Act, leading to what is now known as the Clean Water

---

[245] Dobney, pp. 1-63; Hays, *Conservation*, pp. 27-48; Pursell and Willingham, pp. 1-35; O'Brien et al., pp. 17-20; *Annual Report, 1880*, p. 1369; *Rivers and Harbors Act of 1899; Regulatory Program of the U.S. Army Corps of Engineers*, 33 CFR Part 320, General Regulatory Policies, p. 1; USACE, *Regulatory Program: Applicant Information*, EP 1145-2-2, May 1985, p. 2; USACE, "Water Resources Policies and Authorities," *Digest of Water Resources Policies and Authorities*, EP 1165-2-1 (Wash., D.C.: 1999) Ch. 21.

Act of 1977, which extended Corps regulatory responsibilities to wetlands. The amendments gave the Environmental Protection Agency (EPA) and the Corps authority to implement Section 404 of the Clean Water Act, and also gave the Corps authority "to issue permits, after notice and opportunity for public hearings for the discharge of dredged or fill material into the navigable waters at specific disposal sites.[246] Problems over the precise interpretation of Section 404 persisted into the 1980s, particularly the definition of "navigable." Section 404's qualification "waters of the United States" did little to alleviate ambiguities, as the Corps interpreted this broadly. However, opponents of this interpretation maintained that Corps regulatory responsibilities should apply strictly to traditional navigable waters. In 1985, the Supreme Court decided in *U.S. vs. Riverside Bayview Homes, Inc.* that the Clean Water Act covered wetlands adjacent to navigable waters. This ruling significantly broadened the scope of Corps jurisdiction and made it possible to develop comprehensive guidelines for wetlands protection. In 1986, the Corps introduced the "Migratory Bird Rule," which clarified extending its jurisdiction to waters that provide habitat for migratory birds. Also in 1986, the Corps published the Final Rule for Regulatory Programs of the Corps of Engineers at 33 CFR Parts 320 through 330. This rule has been amended over time to now include Parts 331 and 332. In 1987, with its regulatory jurisdiction more clearly defined, the Corps issued the *Wetland Delineation Manual*, the purpose of which was "to provide guidelines and methods to determine whether an area is a wetland." The manual defined wetlands as "those areas that are inundated or saturated by surface or ground water at a frequency and duration sufficient to support, and that under normal circumstances do support, a prevalence of vegetation typically adapted for life in saturated soil conditions." Several attempts were made in 1989 and 1991 to modify the 1987 manual, but on August 27, 1991, the use of the 1987 manual became mandatory for making official wetland delineations. The Corps is currently developing Regional Supplements to the 1987 manual to account for regional variations in plants, soils, and hydrology. In August 1993, the Corps and the EPA published their final wetlands regulations, which tightened up

---

[246] *Zabel v. Tabb*, 430 F. 2D 199 (5th Cir. 1970); *Regulatory Program: Tribal Consultation and Coordination*, p. 1; Pursell and Willingham, pp. 32-35; *Applicant Information*, p. 2; "Water Resources Policies and Authorities," Ch. 2; *Solid Waste Agency of Northern Cook County, Petitioner v. U.S. Army Corps of Engineers* 99-1178, 531U.S. 159 (S.C. 2001); Clean Water Act, P.L. 92-500 (92nd Cong., 2nd Sess.): Sec. 101(a), 404, USACE, "Wetlands and Waterways Regulation and Permitting," (MVS Archives); "Regulatory: The Regulatory Program," *Esprit* (Nov. 2005); *The Clean Water Act Jurisdictional Handbook* (Wash., D.C.: Environ. Law Inst., 2007): 1-9; Garrett Power, "The Fox in the Chicken Coop: The Regulatory Responsibilities of the U.S. Army Corps of Engineers," *Virginia Law Review* 63 (May 1977): 504-558.

loopholes in the previous regulations and ensured that anyone who excavates material from wetlands must obtain a permit.[247]

From the late 1970s through 1990s the Corps faced the challenges of adapting its traditional regulatory responsibilities to include wetlands protection. These challenges bogged down the permitting process, which took more than 120 days for some individual permit applications. One reason the process took so long was the increased number of permit applications that resulted from the Clean Water Act of 1977. To compound this problem, manpower shortages made it difficult to process the increasing number of applications in a timely manner. By 1988, the total number of annual permit applications had increased to around 70,000, and by 1997, that number had increased to around 100,000. Of these applications, the Corps denied less than one percent. Another reason was the growing complexity of the permitting process and the lack of a precise definition for wetlands, as no such definition existed before the release of the *Wetlands Delineation Manual* in 1987. To improve the permitting process, the regulatory program simplified regulatory guidelines, producing a more efficient

Spunky Bottoms wetland restoration

---

[247] USACE, *Corps of Engineers Wetlands Delineation Manual*, (Wash., D.C.: HQUSACE, 1987): 9; USACE, *Recognizing Wetlands* (Wash., D.C.: HQUSACE, 1998); *The Clean Water Jurisdictional Handbook*, pp. 11-13; Danny McClendon, "Sand and Gravel mining in Missouri Streams," *Esprit* (Nov. 1995).

and timely permit process. According to a 1984 report, *Wetlands: Their Use and Regulation*, in 1980 approximately one-third of all issued permits took longer than 120 days to process, but by 1983 the average processing time was about 70 days. Section 404 of the Clean Water Act required that federal agencies make every effort to process permits within 90 days, so the Corps had already improved its average processing time for all permits within the minimum. However, the Corps continued to try to improve processing times for permits by setting a goal of 60 days for all permits. The Corps set 120 days as its goal for processing the more difficult individual permits. Because these permits represented actions that would have a far greater environmental impact, the process was far more complex and was often delayed by factors outside Corps control. In the 1990s, the Corps continued to improve the efficiency of its permitting process, with 90 percent of all decisions coming in less than 60 days. In 1994, the average decision time for individual permits was 115 days, and by 1997, the Corps made a decision in less than 120 days for 79 percent of individual permits.[248]

After 2000, the Corps regulatory program faced new challenges regarding the definition of "navigable waters." In the 2001 case *Solid Waste Agency of Northern Cook County vs. the U.S. Army Corps of Engineers*, the Supreme Court ruled that Congress had not intended for the Clean Water Act to include isolated waters not adjacent to navigable waters. This interpretation narrowed the scope of the Corps regulatory responsibilities to where it was before the "Migratory Bird Rule." In 2006, the meaning of "waters of the United States" was the subject of debate in *Rapanos vs. United States*. The main issue was whether the "waters of the United States" included isolated waters that extended into non-navigable tributaries connecting navigable waters. Based on the decision, the Corps and EPA developed the "significant nexus" test to determine if a wetland is within the scope of the Clean Water Act. Essentially, a nexus is a link that must exist between navigable and non-navigable water for it to fall under the scope of the Clean Water Act. Once again, the definition of "navigable waters" and "waters of the United States" had changed, and once again the Corps had to reevaluate its wetlands responsibilities.[249]

---

[248] *Wetlands Delineation Manual*; U.S. Cong., *Wetlands: Their Use and Regulation* (Wash., D. C.: GPO 1984): 1-28, quote on 11; Pursell and Willingham, pp. 83, 130, 155.
[249] *The Clean Water Act Jurisdictional Handbook*, pp. 11-22; *Solid Waste Agency v. USACE*; Memo, CWA Jurisdiction Following the U.S. Supreme Court Decision in *Rapanos v. United States*, June 5, 2007 (MVS archives); U.S. Cong., 'The Supreme Court Addresses Corps of Engineers Jurisdiction over "Isolated Waters": The SWANCC Decision' (Wash., D.C.: CRS, 2001).

District wetland restoration area

One method of meeting Section 404 requirements was the mitigation of adverse effects on the environment by restoring, creating, enhancing, and preserving wetlands. The concept of mitigation banks, in which restoration of wetlands at specific sites offsets harmful activities, evolved in the early 1980s. By 1988, the H.W. Bush administration set "no net loss of wetlands" as its goal. In February 1990, the Corps and EPA issued a memorandum supporting mitigation banking. The goal of permitting was not the prevention of wetlands development, but its regulation, which the Corps accomplished by protecting the environment while

Example of a stream mitigation bank

allowing development. Mitigation banking helped the Corps achieve this dual function. To better understand mitigation banking, the Corps tasked the Institute for Water Resources to conduct a study of existing banks. The 1992 report outlined the pros and cons of mitigation banking, noting that the concept was still somewhat controversial. In 1995, the Corps and several other federal agencies, including the EPA and Fish and Wildlife Service, issued policy guidance on mitigation banks, after which the Corps used mitigation banks as a means not only to "compensate for aquatic resource losses," but to provide "developers [with] an efficient method to practically and economically mitigate for small wetland impacts." Even so, mitigation banks were not an instant success, nor were they intended to be, as it would take time to develop their effective use. The main criticism of mitigation banking was that there was no accurate data on their efficacy. However, the fact that wetland loss decreased significantly after the 1970s showed the success of mitigation and regulation. The number of acres lost annually during the 1970s and 1980s was 290,000, but by 1995, that number dropped to 117,000 acres lost annually. Yet, because of the controversial nature of permitting and mitigation, the Corps still received criticism, highlighting the inherent challenges of simultaneously permitting development with wetlands protection. While environmentalists complained that not enough was being done to protect wetlands, others complained that Corps efforts intruded too much on the rights of private property owners.[250]

The St. Louis District launched a new initiative to meet these challenges when it started the first stream mitigation bank in the nation. The mitigation bank program not only compensated for the loss of wetlands, but also for losses in other aquatic resources, such as streams. Mitigation for streams, however, proved far more difficult because new streams could not be created to compensate for the loss of impacted streams. In 2000, the district addressed this problem by creating the Fox Creek Stream Mitigation Bank, which took a stream in a deteriorated state and improved it to compensate for stream impacts. Other Corps districts soon adopted this innovative approach and began using stream mitigation banks and in-lieu fee programs as a means to offset wetlands losses and allow the Corps to reach the its goal of no net loss of wetlands.[251]

---

[250] Pursell and Willingham, pp. 95-96, 113-115, 157, 160; GAO, *Wetlands Overview: Problems With Acreage Data Persist* (Wash., D.C.: GPO 1998): 9.
[251] Craig Litteken, "St. Louis District Stream Mitigation Banks," *Aquatic Resources News* (Summer 2003); Phil Brown, "District starts first stream mitigation bank in the nation," *Esprit* (May 2000).

In 2001, the National Academy of Sciences issued a report on the Corps' use of mitigation. The report contained two major criticisms: 1) the compliance monitoring program was inconsistent and 2) many Corps mitigation projects had been unsuccessful. In response to these criticisms, the Corps issued Regulatory Guidance Letter 01-01, which provided Corps regulatory programs with guidance on how to improve mitigation. Although the guidance letter contained some innovative ideas, some environmental groups took issue with it. To address these issues, the Corps met with these groups and in 2002 released Regulatory Guidance Letter 02-02, which addressed many of their concerns. One issue was that there was no consistent policy among districts, and most district policies were not consistent with national policies. The Corps addressed this issue by developing a standard template for developing district guidelines, and by 2004 all districts had mitigation guidelines that provided greater standardization and consistency. Another innovation was the development of the Mitigation Rule. Issued on April 10, 2008, the final Mitigation Rule required "equivalent standards for all forms of mitigation, and objective of sustainable and accountable mitigation, and strongly encourages a watershed approach." The Mitigation Rule also established a preference to use mitigation banks, followed by in-lieu fee mitigation, and then permittee-responsible mitigation, all based on a watershed approach. This rule also addressed the criticisms made in the 2005 GAO Report on Wetlands Protection, which determined that the Corps did "not have an effective oversight approach to ensure that compensatory mitigation is occurring. While the Corps made significant strides in improving permitting, balancing the economic development of wetlands while protecting wetlands remains one of the more difficult challenges facing the Corps.[252]

Ordnance Removal and FUSRAP

In the early 1970s, the town of Times Beach, Missouri, decided to spray unpaved roads with oil. This seemed a simple and practical solution for its dust problem. However, after many people in the town became ill in the late 1970s, the EPA took soil samples to determine the source of the problem. The results were shocking: the soil contained large amounts of dioxin, a powerful carcinogen. After the Meramec Basin flooded in 1982, fearful that flooding could spread

---

[252] USACE, *Regulatory Program 2002-2008 Report* (Wash., D.C.: GPO 2008) pp. 5, 19-23; GAO, *Wetlands Protection* (Wash., D.C.: GPO, 2005), quote in "Highlights."

Times Beach in December 1982

the toxins, the EPA asked the St. Louis District to do a flood control study at Times Beach. The district was already quite familiar with the Meramec Basin region, making it a perfect fit to assist the EPA at Time Beach. Because of the nature of the work, the district gained valuable experience working with hazardous, toxic, and radioactive waste (HTRW). The EPA also asked the district if it could provide aerial photographs of the region. The district did so quickly and at a cost $20,000 less than other bids. The EPA rewarded the district's efforts by providing additional surveying and mapping work. This experience in HTRW cleanup and removal provided an opportunity for future work assisting the Huntsville Division, the technical center of expertise on HTRW, in its investigation of potential sites. In 1984, the district contacted Huntsville about preparing preliminary assessments for potentially contaminated sites based on the work for EPA. Impressed by the district's experience, Huntsville hired it to do HTRW work, which it did from 1984 to 1991.[253]

By 1990, the district's HTRW work was beginning to decline, but the experience the district gained made it a perfect fit to assist Huntsville Division with the Defense Environmental Restoration Program (DERP). The Corps

---

[253] "Environmental Engineering" (MVS archives); "Around the nation: Times Beach, Mo., Board Moves to Seal Off Town," *NYT* (Apr. 27, 1983); "Joint Federal/State Action Taken to Relocate Times Beach Residents" EPA Press Release (Feb. 22, 1983); Daly and Zoeller interview with Dace; Ruddy interview with Dace; Ruddy interview with Beech, Jul. 11, 1985 (MVS archives); Interview with Col. James Craig, Sep. 2, 1992 (MVS archives).

had designated Huntsville the Mandatory Center of Expertise in charge of DERP. The program originated with the 1980 Comprehensive Environmental Response, Compensation, and Liability Act (CERCLA), which required cleanup of environmentally harmful wastes. In 1983, Congress approved establishment of an Environmental Restoration Defense Account, a fund for cleanup at active and former Department of Defense (DoD) sites. Between World War I and the 1960s, the military tested or used munitions, ordnance, and other hazardous materials at many installations. Over time, the DoD closed, transferred, or sold many of these sites, disposing of hazardous materials using best practices of the time. As development occurred around these former military sites, the possible dangers and need for cleanup became apparent. The Army assigned the Corps responsibility for cleanup in 1984. In 1986, Congress amended CERCLA, establishing DERP to clean up contamination at formerly used defense sites (FUDS). After the Corps named Huntsville the center of expertise for DERP, the division had a heavy task assessing and inventorying more than 10,000 former defense sites potentially containing contamination. In November 1991, Mike Dace, future chief of the Ordnance and Technical Services Branch, contacted Huntsville about assisting with the program. The St. Louis District had assisted the division on HTRW work, and at division request, district personnel met with division leaders. By the spring of 1992 Huntsville asked the district to prepare a project management plan describing how it could use Archive Search Reports (ASRs) to aid in cleanup at former defense sites. Impressed by the district's plan, the division awarded it a $4 million contract to begin inventorying, evaluating, and preparing ASRs.[254]

The first task was putting together a team to develop an inventory of chemical warfare sites. Initially, what would become the Ordnance and Technical Services Branch consisted of only four engineers and a secretary. The district had to quickly hire historians, archivists, and munitions and safety specialists to research, assess, and inventory sites and compile ASRs. It borrowed project managers and assistants from other branches and divisions to assist on the project. By summer

Mike Dace

---

[254] "Environmental Engineering"; Daly and Zoeller interview with Dace; "The District's newest mission Ordnance and Explosive Waste," *Esprit* (Dec. 1992).

1993, the branch was starting to take shape. It completed and sent its master inventory to Huntsville for comparison with the existing list. After completing this task, the district began preparing ASRs, prioritizing them by risk. Historians, archivists, safety and munitions specialists, project managers, and engineers worked together compiling the reports. Archivists and historians visited archives, libraries, local historical societies, and military history centers and interviewed locals, people associated with the site, and anyone else who could provide valuable information. They evaluated historic maps and photographs and compared them to modern ones to determine the location of hazards. After gathering and evaluating this information, a project manager oversaw compilation of ASRs containing a site's history, its present state, and its use of ordnance, explosives, and other hazardous materials. The Corps then used the data to perform cleanup at the site. Since the program began, the Corps inventoried more than 10,000 properties, with cleanup planned or ongoing at more than 3,000 properties. Because some properties required more than one cleanup project, the total number of projects is around 5,000 and growing. As of 2007, program expenditures were nearly $4 billion with an estimated $18.7 billion required for completion. As of 2011, the district had completed more than 3,000 ASRs, each taking anywhere from a few months to more than a year to complete. The district took responsibility for preparing these reports at a time when job growth within the district was slow. However, the program provided the district with a needed boost by creating millions of dollars worth of new work preparing search reports. Moreover, its experience

500 lb toxic chemical bomb found at Attu Island

Project Manager Rady Curtis conducting research at NARRA

District ordnance and explosives safety specialist Randy Fraser performing site inspection

in dealing with HTRW paved the way for additional work, as the Corps gave the district responsibility of cleaning up five contaminated sites under the Formerly Utilized Site Remedial Action Program (FUSRAP).[255]

During the early 1940s, the government began work on the Manhattan Project to create the first atomic bomb. The Army created the Manhattan Engineering District to carry out this mission, which included working with highly radioactive substances. In 1946, Congress passed the Atomic Energy Act, which established the Atomic Energy Commission to carry out the mission of the new law. This mission included researching peaceful ways to use atomic energy. Some of this research took place at sites within the St. Louis District. The Mallinckrodt Chemical Plant in downtown St. Louis extracted uranium and radium from ore. From 1946 to 1957, the Manhattan Energy District used a site near Lambert Airport to store the radioactive byproducts of this process. In 1966, a private company purchased the airport site and transferred radioactive materials to Hazelwood Interim Storage Site on Latty Avenue, later selling them to another company, which shipped them to Colorado. As a result of all this movement and also of natural processes, these and adjacent sites were contaminated with radioactive material. Although the actual levels of radioactivity are low enough that they do not pose an immediate threat, the radioactivity will remain in the soil for thousands of years without proper cleanup.[256]

In 1974, the Department of Energy started FUSRAP to clean up sites such as the ones in and around St. Louis. The Department of Energy continued to oversee the program until October 1997, when the Energy and Water Development Appropriations Act transferred responsibility for the program to the Corps. This transfer had an especially profound impact on the St. Louis District, as its five FUSRAP sites contained approximately half the total volume of the $500 million program. These sites were the Madison Site in Illinois, St. Louis Downtown Site, St. Louis Airport Site, Vicinity Properties, and the Hazelwood Interim Storage Site. The cleanup process began with the collection and review of information on the site. The district then conducted a remedial investigation/feasibility study to determine the type of contamination, its location, and cleanup alternatives. In addition, the district informed the public about the project's progress and encouraged public participation throughout. The

---

[255] Ibid.; USACE, "Champion of Your Heartland's Water Resources" Brochure (MVS: 2001); "District looks for chemical warfare weapons," *Esprit* (Jan. 2004); USACE, "DERP-FUDS fact sheet," (Wash., D.C.: USACE, 2000).
[256] "Environmental Engineering"; "What is FUSRAP?" Web site (*www.mvs.usace.army.mil/eng-con/expertise/fusrap.html*, Mar. 22, 2011).

district then chose an alternative and presented it in a Proposed Plan, which it sent out for public comment and review. After reviewing comments, the district developed a Remedial Design describing the cleanup plan in detail. Lastly, the district began Remedial Action or cleanup. After cleanup was complete, subsequent five-year reviews collect information on the efficacy of cleanup to ensure that FUSRAP objectives have been met. Since undertaking responsibility for its five sites, the district successfully proposed and implemented remedies at these locations, with the success of each cleanup being subject to a five-year review.[257]

By 1986, the environmental era that started with the passage of NEPA in 1969, was firmly entrenched in the Corps. Not only had responsibilities for the environment grown in project planning, the St. Louis District had assumed or developed new programs for recreation, archaeological research, permitting, and ordnance removal. These new responsibilities required more employees and funding, so that more than more of the district's budget was related to environmental programs. This was due, in part, to a decline in spending on traditional construction activities as the district had to reevaluate flood control and navigation projects in light of environmental regulation. Two projects in particular came to a near standstill because of environmental protests. Yet the growth in other areas more than made up for this lag in construction projects, while the district started to adapt even non-environmental programs to make them more ecologically friendly.

---

[257] Ibid.; "Building a virtual team: FUSRAP's experience" (May 1999).

17

The Meramec Dam Controversy

As the St. Louis District entered the environmental era, it faced numerous setbacks to ongoing construction projects. Some, such as the Kaskaskia River Lock and Dam, were more or less complete, and only received criticism and modification after the fact. Some studies did not go forward at all. One of these was the Meramec Dam and Reservoir. Planning for the dam had been ongoing since the Great Depression, but from the outset, a large number of citizens questioned the value of the project. Despite opposition, the project finally reached a construction phase when Congress passed the National Environmental Policy Act (NEPA), requiring the district to obtain input from other agencies and the public. The result was a cessation of work while the district sought to reconcile the positions of agencies to determine the best plan to address flooding in the region. Yet unlike other projects that eventually proceeded once this process was complete, public outcry against the dam and ineffective defense of the project eventually led to its cancellation. The controversy lasted more than a decade, creating long-lasting suspicion of the Corps even as the district sought to find a workable solution that met all requirements.

Meramec River near Sullivan, Missouri

The Meramec River Basin extends for 100 miles, stretching southwest across eight Missouri counties and draining 4,000 square miles. Located within this basin are the Meramec River and several tributaries, including the Bourbeuse and Big rivers. Beginning as a small stream near Salem, Missouri, the river flows 220 miles across the basin until it empties into the Mississippi River in Arnold, Missouri. As the basin stretches southwest, the terrain becomes rugged and the population sparse. In 1960, around half the basin's population of 212,000 lived in this rugged region, and the other half lived near St. Louis. Those settled near St. Louis benefitted from a growing economy, while the sparsely populated southwestern region fell into economic decline, in part due to migration near St. Louis. As the St. Louis suburbs grew and more people settled in the Meramec floodplain, the risk of flood damage dramatically increased. The 1915 flood, which left more than 2,000 people homeless and twelve dead in Valley Park, Missouri, shows how devastating a rising Meramec could be. The population growth that occurred in the region in the decades that followed exponentially increased the destructive potential of floods.[258]

The primary catalyst for studying flood control in the Meramec Basin was the Rivers and Harbors Act of 1925 and House Document No. 308, which directed the Corps to conduct surveys and submit reports on the potential for multipurpose use of 200 waterways, including the Meramec. The St. Louis District Engineer submitted the 308 report on the Meramec in April 1929. This study, which was the first comprehensive, multipurpose study of the Meramec, concluded that "the best practicable coordinated plan of improvement on the Meramec Basin is for a single earth dam at mile 63.4 in the Meramec River... designed primarily for bankfull local flood control...and so far as practicable, for Mississippi flood control." However, the report recommended that "no detailed survey or project study be made...at this time..." because the benefits of the project would not be "commensurate with the cost."[259]

---

[258] Edward L. Ullman, Ronald R. Boyce, and Donald J. Volk, *The Meramec Basin Water and Economic Development, Report of the Meramec Basin Research Project, Vol. I: Summary and a Program of Water Resource Development Proposals* (Wash. UP, 1962), pp.13-20; Arnold, pp. 11-38.
[259] Dobney, pp. 78-84; Camillo and Pearcy, pp. 57-65; Anfinson, *River We Have Wrought*, pp. 152-153, (Aug. 23, 1915); "Remembering the Great Mississippi Flood of 1927," *Esprit* (Mar. 2002); Red Cross, *The Mississippi Valley Flood Disaster of 1927: Official Report of Flood Operations* (Wash.: Red Cross, 1927); *Report on the Meramec River*, HD 686 (71st Cong., 3rd Sess.): 1.

Origins of the Project

The recommendations of the 308 report seemed to doom any hope for developing the basin in the near future. However, the Great Depression became the catalyst for development. President Franklin D. Roosevelt's New Deal policies expanded the role of the federal government and increased spending, thus renewing interest in public works. To garner support for a lake on the Meramec, approximately 50 citizens from St. Louis formed the Lake Meramec Association in 1933. Its recommendation was that the Public Works Administration undertake the project "at the expense and under the direction of the Federal Government." The organization urged the project "for the purpose of providing water recreational facilities for the people of the nearby city of St. Louis." While the primary goal of developing the basin remained flood control, this increasing interest in recreation was a portent of things to come.[260]

In June 1938, the Senate authorized the Corps to study three potential flood control dams, one of which was on the Meramec. The primary purpose of these dams was flood control in the lower Meramec Basin, with flood control on the Mississippi River playing a secondary role. Over the next few years, the district continued to study the basin to form a comprehensive flood plan. Simultaneously, the district attempted to coordinate these efforts with various state and federal agencies. In 1942, the National Resources Planning Board created the Meramec Cooperative Investigation Field Committee to coordinate efforts and produce a cooperative report on the basin. W.W. Horner was named consulting engineer and coordinator for the field committee, which began meeting in June 1943. Each agency in the investigation completed an independent report and sent it to the other members for review, included as appendices to the cooperative's final report. While the other agencies were conducting their investigations, the Corps was conducting its own study. By 1945, the agencies' investigations were nearly complete and the field committee began work on a full report. After completion of several additional studies and revisions,

Valley Park flood, 1945

---

[260] Memo, B.M. Harloe to Division Office, UMVD, Feb. 7, 1934 (MVS archives).

the committee published its report in August 1949. However, the report was not without controversy.[261]

The Meramec Dam project had opposition as early 1938 when Congress first authorized it. Some opposition came from people who feared losing land, others because of possible wildlife impacts, and others because of fears that a large lake would alienate small watercraft owners. But early opposition was not strong and fell more into the category of concern. That began to change between 1945 and 1950 as new concerns emerged. The opposition leader was a Catholic priest named George Hildner, chairman of the Meramec Basin Resources Committee, which actively opposed a dam on the river. In September 1945, Hildner summarized the concerns of the opposition succinctly: "If these things [dams] are a benefit to us, we want them, and if not, we don't want them." The problem for opponents was that they simply did not believe benefits of a dam outweighed its possible negative impacts. For example, some Franklin County farmers complained that these "dams will destroy more good bottomland above the dam than would be protected from flooding below the dam." Some people were concerned that the project focused too much on national interests and not enough on the interests of those living in the basin. Others feared the potential environmental impact. Still others wanted development, but argued that the Corps should explore alternatives to a large reservoir. However, because Congress already authorized the Corps to build the reservoirs, the cooperative investigation felt that it had no choice but to recommend the dams.[262]

In response to opposition, the Chief of Engineers recommended "expenditures on this project be held to the absolute minimum until it is clear that there is no organized opposition to the improvements proposed." Although Congress approved the project, it still had to run the gauntlet of public opinion before it could advance any further. The district scheduled four public hearings to gauge support for the project. In his opening address at the first of these in December 1949, District Engineer Col. Rudolph Smyser articulated that the basic purpose was to inform the public and allow them to express their opinions on the proposed project. The meetings revealed that opposition to the project was loosely

---

[261] U.S. Cong., *Flood Control Act of 1936; Flood Control Act of 1938*, PL 75-761 (June 28, 1938); MVS, *A Meramec Chronology of the Corps of Engineers and Missouri's Meramec Basin, 1880 to 1983*, (MVS archives): 3; "Three Flood Control Dams Near City in Bill," *Post-Dispatch* (June 13, 1938); Memo, P.S. Reinecke, dams in the Meramec River Basin, Aug. 4, 1938 (MVS Archives); *Summary Report of the Meramec Cooperative Investigation Filed Committee* (MVS archives); Memo to Col. Kittrell, Meramec River Basin—Outline of Investigation, Apr. 19, 1949 (MVS archives).

[262] "Minutes of Meeting, Union Chamber of Comm., Union, Mo., Sept. 10, 1945 (MVS archives); Resolutions—32nd Annual Meeting of Franklin Cty. Framer's Association, Union, Mo., Nov. 12, 1949; *Summary Report*, Sec. II, p. 6.

MERAMEC RIVER BASIN
PRINCIPAL FEATURES UNDER STUDY

Original plan for development of Meramec Basin that included multiple reservoirs

organized yet effective. Of those who spoke, 33 supported the project, and 76 opposed it. Only 1,496 people signed the petition supporting the project, while 2,978 signed the petition opposing it. To summarize its position, the Meramec Basin Resources Committee published a pamphlet, *A Shameless Sham*, which preached "preservation not ruination" and offered an alternative flood control plan. Besides the opposition's call to protect the rural culture of the basin and conserve the environment, its most damning criticism was that the project was not economically feasible. Horner and the cooperative investigation came to the same conclusion, estimating that "the annual charges for carrying all these flood abatement measures would be about three times the flood damages eliminated." In contrast, the Corps estimated that the project would generate more than $11 million in revenue annually. However, dam opponents had already planted the seed of doubt in the public's mind, so when Missouri Gov. Forrest Smith came out in opposition to the project in late December 1949, he essentially sealed its fate.[263]

One reason why the project failed was that people simply did not believe it would be economically beneficial. The primary objective of the project was flood control, yet the economic benefits from flood control amounted to only 19 percent. This meant the Corps had to consider benefits other than flood control to justify a large reservoir. The most important non-flood control benefit was recreation; however, because the primary concern was flood control and navigation, recreation was a tertiary concern that the Corps could not use as the sole basis to justify a project. This began to change in the 1950s and 1960s. As the economy soared, an affluent society desired recreation resources for enjoying its newfound wealth and leisure time. In response to the nation's needs, Corps responsibilities evolved to include multipurpose water resource planning, an important part of which was recreation. Because of its proximity to St. Louis, the Meramec Basin offered great potential to meet recreation needs. Moreover, because of economic stagnation in many rural areas of the basin, recreational development offered economic benefits that could revitalize these rural communities. Recreation needs combined with flood control would stir up interest in a Meramec reservoir once again.[264]

The growing interest in recreation coincided with other important developments in the basin, namely, a severe drought between 1952 and 1957 and a flood in June and July 1957 that caused an estimated $3.9 million in damages. The Corps estimated that the three dams would have prevented $3 million of these damages. The drought and subsequent flood, when combined with the economic needs of the region, led some communities to form local committees to discuss the basin's needs. The most influential of these was the Meramec Basin Corporation. Formed in June 1958, the corporation's objective was to develop an overall plan, secure an objective research study, and undertake an information campaign to bring public awareness to the advantages of developing the

---

[263] OCE to Division Engineer, UMVD, Public Hearings on the Meramec Basin Reservoirs, Dec. 23,1947; Meramec Public Hearings, Opening Address by Col. Smyser, Dec. 13, 1949; Meramec Basin Resources Committee, *"A Shameless Sham": The Army Engineer "Plan" for the Meramec Basin*, 1950; "Cooperative Studies," Draft, Oct. 3, 1947, p. 11 (MVS archives).
[264] Forrest Smith, "Statement on Meramec Basin Reservoirs", Dec. 21, 1949 (MVS archives); Ullman, *The Meramec Basin Water and Economic Development, Report of the Meramec Basin Research Project, Vol. I: Summary and a Program of Water Resource Development Proposals*, (Wash. UP, 1962): 34-40.

basin. Hopes for a project received a boost when Missouri Gov. James Blair stated in a December 17, 1958 letter that he hoped the Corps would "proceed with the restudy as soon as funds were available." As the Corps waited for Congress to appropriate funds and approve a restudy, the corporation sponsored independent research by Edward Ullman of Washington University. This 1962 study focused primarily on economic development of the basin. It supported building reservoirs in the region, but this support was linked to economic and recreational benefits. The study reported that in the years following World War II, attendance at Corps reservoirs was growing at a rate of about 28 percent annually. Thus, the need for recreation was considerable and would continue to grow. To meet these needs, the study suggested that a large reservoir be built as close to St. Louis as possible. Because this study coincided with the district's study, the district used some Ullman report findings in its own study. However, the approach of the Ullman study was much narrower than the district's study. The district's mandate was to study multipurpose planning as a fundamental goal for the development of the basin, which meant it had to consider flood control, recreation, and economic benefits to evaluate the feasibility of a reservoir.[265]

In April 1960, Congress authorized the district to undertake a new, comprehensive study of the basin, funded starting the following fiscal year. To gain a sense of public opinion, the district held new public hearings, the first of which was in St. Clair, Missouri, in April 1961. Reactions at the meetings varied, but District Engineer Col. Alfred J. D'Arezzo stated that a "vast majority" of people were open to a restudy and a new project. In addition to public hearings, the Corps released an information bulletin in September 1962 outlining the history of the previous project in the basin, the planning procedures for any future project, and the primary aims of this project. Public support for the project was strong initially; however, organized opposition would soon emerge in the form of the Meramec Rivers Association. At a public hearing held

Col. Alfred J. D'Arezzo

---

[265] Status Report on the Meramec Basin Flood Control Project; *The Meramec River Basin: An Information Bulletin*, (St. Louis: MVS, 1962); Excerpt, "The Meramec Basin Blues" *St. Louis Magazine* (N.D.); Meramec Basin Reservoirs Missouri: Digest of Preliminary Information (MVS, 1959): 9 (MVS archives); Ullman, p. 35.

Valley Park during 1961 Meramec flood

in St. Clair on December 18, 1963, the district revealed its plan for developing the basin. Most of those who spoke supported the district's plan, with only 11 of the 53 speakers expressing opposition. The next day, the *Globe-Democrat* headline read: "Cannon Goes All-Out for Meramec Basin Plan." The support of Rep. Clarence Cannon of Missouri was crucial for advancing the project, as he was the head of the powerful House Appropriations Committee. With the support of both Cannon and the public, the Meramec plan looked as though it would finally become a reality.[266]

On January 30, 1964, the district submitted *The Meramec River, Missouri Comprehensive Basin Study* to the Lower Mississippi Valley Division. The study recommended a series of reservoirs primarily for the purposes of flood control and navigation. The largest of these reservoirs was located at the Meramec Park Lake site, which offered the highest cost-to-benefit ratio (1:1.9) of the five sites studied. The district projected the Meramec Park site to produce more than $3.8 million in annual benefits, making it twice as beneficial as the

---

[266] "Meramec Park Lake Chronology of Events Leading to Present Status" (May 3, 1972), p. 2; *Meramec Chronology*, p. 19; *Meramec River Basin Information Bulletin*, D'Arezzo comments in excerpt, *Globe-Democrat*, April 9, 1961; "Group will Oppose Meramec River Plan," *Globe-Democrat* (April 10, 1963); Remarks by Col. James B. Meanor, Public Hearing, St. Clair, Mo., Dec. 18, 1963; Record of Public Hearing, Dec. 18,1963 (MVS archives); "Cannon Goes All-Out for Meramec Basin Plan," *Globe-Democrat* (Dec. 19, 1963).

Map of proposed Meramec reservoir

next closest sites at Pine Ford and Union, which were each projected to produce around $1.8 million in annual benefits. The Meramec Park site simply fit best with the Corps mandate to follow a multipurpose approach in considering various factors other than flood control and navigation when making a determination about the best site for a reservoir. The division engineer submitted the study to the Chief of Engineers on June 15, 1965. The Chief of Engineers agreed with the study's recommendations and sent his report to Congress, where it was printed as House Document 525, 89th Congress, 2nd Session. On November 7, 1966, Congress authorized the Meramec River Basin project by including it in the Flood Control Act of 1966. The act authorized the construction of three reservoirs and 19 angler use sites; the Meramec Park and Union reservoirs, which were already authorized under the Flood Control Act of 1938, were included in the plan. The plan divided the project into hierarchical phases, with the most important projects being part of the first phase. The most important site was Meramec Park Lake, so the district worked toward its completion first.[267]

In June 1967, the district completed preconstruction planning for the Meramec Park site and started acquiring real estate. The district spent more than $2.2 million acquiring 8,841 of the 40,800 acres needed for the project. The district planned to use 22,100 acres specifically for meeting recreation needs. Most of the controversy in these early years of the project centered on land acquisition. In 1968, the district released a pamphlet on policies and procedures for land acquisition. This pamphlet was intended to educate the public and assuage any fears concerning the purchase of land. Naturally, some citizens complained that they would have to sell their lands, and others complained about land speculation, but overall these complaints were minimal. In 1972, the Civil Works Appropriations Act provided $3 million for construction. Just as construction was set to begin, opponents of the project emerged.[268]

Growth of Opposition

The most profound effect of the construction delay was that it allowed opposition groups an opportunity to mobilize. These efforts received a further boost in 1969 with passage of NEPA, which required the Corps to prepare and submit an Environmental Impact Statement (EIS) for certain projects, including the Meramec Park Lake project. The law changed the scope of Corps planning, as the Corps would now have to justify projects environmentally as well as economically. In other words, the district could not justify the project solely on the basis of its cost-to-benefit. The district completed the EIS in November 1970 and filed it with the Council on Environmental Quality in February 1971. The EIS stated the district chose the site because "the Meramec Park Lake area receives relatively heavy use as compared to other portions of the Basin." It went on to point out, "In the absence of this project this portion of the Meramec Basin will continue to develop in a disorganized manner. Ultimately, this uncontrolled development will destroy the highly desirable natural qualities of the area, and eliminate a severely needed source of recreation for the St. Louis area." According to the EIS, some of the region would be lost to inundation, but these areas would be "replaced by other desirable qualities of considerably

---
[267] USACE, Notice of Comprehensive Basin Study of Meramec River, Missouri (LMVD, 1964), "Meramec Park Lake Chronology," pp. 3-5; U.S. Cong., *Brief Report on Meramec River, Missouri Basin Plan* H.D. 525 (89th Cong., 2nd Sess.).
[268] "The Meramec Project: A Progress Report" (MVS archives); "Meramec Park Lake Chronology."

greater public use potential." It concluded that there would be no significant impact on the environment. Any alternatives would be either ineffective within the context of multipurpose development or cost prohibitive. Excluding appendices, which included the recommendations of various state, federal, and local agencies, the statement was eight pages long, which was minuscule compared to the multivolume statements that the Corps would later produce. However, the district believed that many of these concerns had already been addressed in the Comprehensive Basin Plan and the Ullman study.[269]

Those opposed to the project were quick to criticize the EIS. The first group to challenge it was the Coalition for the Environment. In late April 1971 the coalition, which represented 50 affiliated groups, issued a statement claiming that the EIS contained "undocumented assertions, conflicting statements and significant omissions." Mark Paddock, chairman of the coalition's Open Space and Land Use Committee, sent a letter to the Council on Environmental Quality suggesting that the Corps consider alternatives to a large reservoir. The letter proposed creating an "Environmental Conservancy District" that he claimed "would provide for the continued natural character of this beautiful valley and would provide even greater recreational opportunities" However, the district's primary charge was to build a multipurpose structure for flood control. The other justifications for the project, such as recreation, water supply, and economic benefits, were important, but they were secondary considerations that made the project possible from a cost-to-benefit standpoint. The district essentially expressed this same view when

Anti-dam pamphlet by Don Rimbauch

---

[269] USACE, *EIS, Meramec Park Lake* (St. Louis: MVS, 1970); Ruddy, pp. 67-71.

it responded to June 24, 1971 letter from Paddock. In this letter, Paddock was sympathetic because requirements of NEPA were new, but he argued that this did "not relieve the Corps of the responsibility to prepare an Environmental Impact Statement which meets all the requirements of the National Environmental Policy Act." He went on to question the district's claims concerning the flood control and water quality benefits of the project, and he rejected the claim that the benefits would offset environmental impacts. The district's response was that the benefits would more than offset the loss of land and effects on the environment. While 5,900 acres of pastureland would be inundated by the project, this loss would be "more than balanced by the benefits attributable to reduction of flood damages on the 21,280 acres of crop and pasturelands below the reservoir." The district also noted that it had discussed alternatives in the Comprehensive Basin Study and concluded that these alternatives were not effective. These conclusions were backed by the findings of the independent Washington University Study, which also suggested a large reservoir was the best means to address the needs of the basin. The district simply included factors such as flood control when making its determination, leading it to conclude the Meramec Park site was best from a multipurpose perspective.[270]

On November 30, 1971, the new district engineer, Col. Guy Jester, requested a meeting with the coalition and Meramec Basin Association (the Sierra Club declined this invitation) to discuss plans for development of the basin and to hear their opinions concerning preparation of a supplemental EIS. At the December 9, 1971 meeting, Jester informed those present that he approved an in-depth review of the Comprehensive Basin Study to identify areas requiring additional environmental impact information. The district also filed a supplemental EIS with the Council for Environmental Quality. Jester also suggested the establishment of an advisory committee, and those present at the meeting concurred. The day after the meeting, the district sent an invitation to the participating organizations requesting that each appoint two persons to serve on the committee. On February 3, 1972, the district once again urged the Sierra Club to participate in the committee's work, but for a second time it declined to do so.[271]

---

[270] "Environmentalists: 'No' To Meramec Lake Project," *Globe-Democrat* (April 27, 1971); "Meramec Park Lake project assailed by environmental group" *Globe-Democrat* (June 26, 1971); Letter, Mark Paddock to Col. Carroll LeTellier, June 24, 1971; Reply in letter from Coalition for Environment, June 24, 1971, (MVS archives).
[271] Litigation Report, *Sierra Club et. al. v. Robert F. Froehlke, et. al.*, Dec. 26, 1973, Sec. 8 (MVS Archives).

Over the upcoming months, the district continued its in-depth review and inventory of the Meramec Basin, with the supplemental study set for completion in October 1972. However, on September 25, 1972, shortly before the district was due to submit its supplemental EIS, the Sierra Club, Ozark Chapter, filed a lawsuit against the Corps. In the months to come, the Sierra Club and the Ozark Chapter's outspoken director, Jerry Sugerman, would become the leaders of those opposed to the project. The Sierra Club alleged, among other things, that the district had not complied with the requirements of NEPA because of the insufficiency of the Meramec EIS. In July 1973, the U.S. District judge refused to grant an injunction to stop construction on the project and gave the district until October 1, 1973 to revise the EIS. The district filed its revised supplemental Final Environmental Impact Statement with the Council on Environmental Quality on September 27, 1973. The final EIS came to the same conclusions as the first, but included extensive data and background research – four volumes and several hundred pages. On December 26, 1973, the Sierra Club responded by refiling an amended suit alleging the revised EIS did not consider the entire Meramec Basin but instead focused only on the site of the reservoir. It also alleged that the district's claims concerning the benefits

Aerial shot showing location of proposed reservoir

of the project were inaccurate and that a nonstructural solution would be a more desirable alternative. The case was set for trial in November 1974.[272]

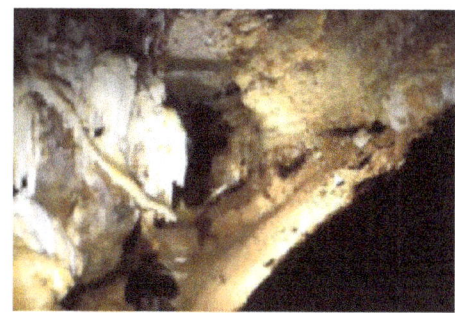

One of the many caves found in the Meramec Basin

In the months leading up to the trial, two new issues emerged to complicate the Meramec project: the Indiana Bat and the Onondaga Cave. The Indiana Bat became an issue because the 1973 Endangered Species Act required federal agencies to consider the possible effects of a project on endangered species. When the Sierra Club found out that the reservoir might affect a large number of these bats, on September 20, 1974 it amended its suit to include these claims. The other issue emerged when Lester Dill, owner of the Onondaga Cave, alleged the reservoir would inundate several caves in the region, including the one he owned. On June 21, 1974, Dill filed a suit to block construction of the reservoir. Although these suits were intended to halt construction, Congress appropriated $4.6 million for the

Aerial showing the site of Meramec Dam during early construction phase

---

[272] *Meramec Chronology*, pp. 49-50; "The Meramec Dam Plan" Mar. 1974 (MVS archives,); Ruddy, p. 75; Litigation Report, *Sierra Club et. al. v. Robert F. Froehlke*.

project in June 1974 and construction on the Meramec access road and visitor center began shortly thereafter.²⁷³

Indiana Bat

The opening testimony of the Sierra Club trial began on November 26, 1974. The issue of the Indiana Bat played only a minor role in the trial, as the district judge concluded that construction of the reservoir had not "shown any indication of harassing or endangering the Indiana Bat." On the other two issues – the cost-to-benefit ratio and nonstructural alternatives – the court ruled that the district had adequately disclosed the necessary environmental information on alternatives, and the project's cost-to-benefit ratio of 1 to 1.9 was in fact accurate. On March 19, 1975, Judge Kenneth Wangelin ruled in favor of the Corps. In response to the ruling, the St. Louis *Globe-Democrat* contained an editorial conveying optimism that the project may finally be able to move forward, as "one of the last serious challenges to completion of the project has been eliminated." However, the project still had to overcome the obstacles of the Lester Dill suit and an appeal by the Sierra Club to the U.S. Court of Appeals.²⁷⁴

On April 7, 1975, just 19 days after the district court ruled for the Corps, the Sierra Club filed its appeal of the decision. Its allegations were mostly the same as in the previous case; however, the suit gave more attention to the Indiana Bat and alleged violation of the Endangered Species Act. The bat issue was essentially a non-factor in the previous trial because the plaintiffs added it just weeks before the trial, and the Sierra Club's claims were unsubstantiated. However, the plaintiffs claimed that even though the reservoir would not inundate the caves the bats live in, construction could disrupt hibernation cycle and cause them to die. In addition, they claimed that the entire region served as a fragile ecosystem for the bat. Because of these possible impacts, the Sierra Club wanted the district to halt construction pending more accurate studies. The court accepted the appeal on September 10, 1975, and required the Corps to provide a report on possible effects of the reservoir on the bat. The district had

---

[273] *Sierra Club v. Froehlke*, Cause No. 72C584(3), (U.S. Dist. Ct., East. Dist. of Mo.); *Meramec Chronology*, pp. 51-52; News clipping, *Globe-Democrat* (June 5, 1974) (MVS Archives).
[274] *Sierra Club v .Froehlke*; Editorial in *Globe-Democrat* (Mar. 21, 1975).

already planned a study, which was set to begin in July 1975, in cooperation with the Missouri Department of Conservation and the U.S. Fish and Wildlife Service. On April 23, 1976, the Court of Appeals upheld Judge Wangelin's decision and ruled in favor of the Corps, thus eliminating one of the two legal actions against the project.[275]

The other legal challenge remaining was the Lester Dill suit. Dill had been negotiating with the Corps over the sale of his lands, but he soon grew frustrated with negotiations and filed suit to prevent the construction of the reservoir. Don Rimbach, an amateur geologist and cave enthusiast, sided with Dill and began to speak out publically against the reservoir. Because a number of caves dotted the region, Rimbach argued, construction on the project should be halted because these caves were important natural resources needing protection. He also argued that in addition to being important natural resources, these caves presented a possible safety hazard to the reservoir and should thus be studied thoroughly before the district begins construction. However, in May 1976, largely in response to the Corps' legal victory over the Sierra Club, Dill dropped his suit. While the Corps won two major victories over dam opponents, it nonetheless began to lose in the court of public opinion.[276]

The Fight for Public Opinion

Rimbach's arguments concerning the safety of the dam and the Sierra Club's allegations that the project would have a significant environmental impact may not have convinced the courts, but they had brought public attention to the issues. Often, opponents encouraged opposition by presenting information out of context. For example, the opposition claimed - based on information that was taken out of context from the EIS– that the reservoir would flood 12,600 acres and protect only 11,800. The facts were that the reservoir would protect 11,800 acres from flooding and provide partial protection for 28,760 acres in the portion of the Meramec Valley between the proposed dam and the confluence of the Meramec and Bourbeuse Rivers, but the opposition had already planted the seed of doubt in the public's mind. To compound the problem, the Teton Dam collapsed in June 1976, providing an opportunity to argue that the Meramec project should be halted. Although the Teton Dam was not a

---

[275] *Sierra Club v. Froehlke*, Brief of Appellants, No. 75-1252 (8th Cir., 1975).
[276] Ruddy, pp. 75-76; James Gamble and Don Rimbach, "Should the Meramec River be dammed or should it be left alone: For the dam and Against the dam," *The Midwest Motorist* (Feb. 1976); Litigation Report, *Lester Dill v. James R. Schlesinger*, Civil 74-246 C (2) (EaSt. Mo. DiSt. 1974).

Corps project, opponents were able to use the disaster as propaganda to bring public support to their side. The problem for the Corps was that it could not publically debate these issues with the opposition, as former District Engineer Col. Guy Jester observed, "the Corps itself doesn't push a project; it is the people who want the project who have to push it." The district could promote the project by releasing information to the public, but it could not actively promote it. From the Corps' point-of-view, its information campaign, which was based on technical information and facts, was not as effective as the emotional rhetoric of project opponents. Moreover, those groups that did support the project, namely the Meramec Basin Corporation, were simply not as effective at illuminating the fallacies of the opposition's arguments or evoking a positive response from the public to ensure that the project would reach completion.[277]

After its defeat in the courts, the Sierra Club turned to a new strategy to stop the project. This included proposing an alternative plan for developing the basin, which it published as the "Meramec Heritage Riverway" plan in June 1976. The plan was the brainchild of Sugerman, who argued that it would cost only $69 million, whereas the Corps project would cost $115 million. The plan offered a nonstructural solution to address the basin's flood control and recreation needs. The plan proposed using land already purchased for the project to develop flood control and recreation while preserving the Meramec in its natural, free flowing state. It listed additional water skiing, reservoir fishing, and minor flood control reductions as the only advantages of the Corps project, but it ignored additional advantages of the dam such as water supply and economic benefits. Moreover, the 52-page report contained little, if any, substantive analysis, especially when compared to the Corps multivolume study that had already addressed those criticisms that the alternative plan did make. The Sierra Club even asked Congress "to authorize and fund a full federal review of the alternative plan by the appropriate Federal agency" and "declare a moratorium on further project development."[278]

---

[277] For information on the acreage that would have be protected from flooding, see USACE, Final *EIS, Meramec Park Lake* (St. Louis: MVS, 1973), Section One-29; Martin Towey, Interview with Col. Leon McKinney (Aug. 11, 1987); Towey, Interview with Jester; Interview with Dace; Ruddy interview with Jester (June 7, 1983) (MVS Archives). These interviews shed light on Corps perspective of the propaganda campaign and the role of public opinion in the determining the fate of the project. An overview of the public debate between the Meramec Basin Corporation and Rimbach can be found in *The Midwest Motorist* (Feb. 1976); however, much of the public's information and misinformation is in newspaper articles (e.g. *Post-Dispatch* and *Globe-Democrat*), which served as a public platform for the project's opponents and proponents.
[278] "Alternative plan to Meramec Dam outlined by Sierra Club," *The Cuba Free Press* (June 10, 1976); Jerry M. Sugerman, "Report on the Meramec Heritage Riverway, and Other Alternatives To the Meramec Park Reservoir Project," (Sierra Club, 1977) (MVS Archives).

The alternative plan included rhetoric claiming superiority over the Corps plan, but provided little factual evidence. The Corps considered the acquisition of land as a nonstructural alternative, but as of 1975, it would have cost $158 million and not $69 million as the Sierra Club claimed. Thus, the alternative plan was not more cost efficient than the Corps project. In addition, the alternative plan would not provide the same economic, recreation, and flood control benefits. It claimed that there were ample recreation resources in the basin already, such as canoeing, hiking, and river fishing, even though studies had shown that such recreation activities were not as popular as activities on large lakes. Furthermore, a large reservoir would not eliminate opportunities for canoeing, hiking, and river fishing, as many such opportunities would still exist on much of the upper Meramec and its tributaries. The Sierra Club's proposals in the alternative plan and its criticisms of the Corps were essentially the same as those previously addressed in the courtroom. The district responded that it had already "thoroughly and professionally analyzed" similar alternatives "during the analysis of the Meramec Basin Plan, both prior to authorization and subsequent to authorization to the project." Thus, there was no need to consider the Sierra Club's plan. Taking all of this into consideration, the alternative plan seemed to be nothing more than yet another means to stop construction once the other Sierra Club strategies had failed.[279]

While the Sierra Club's plan may not have been a viable alternative, it did increase skepticism of the project and brought public awareness to the possibility of a nonstructural solution. The alternative plan was also a rallying point for opposition to the Corps plan, especially among politicians. Having been defeated in the courts, the Sierra Club turned to the political arena to stop the project. Candidates voiced their opinions on the project. One of the most outspoken dam opponents was John Danforth, who was running for the U.S. Senate and was a supporter of the alternative plan. Danforth opposed the project because it was "not worth the price tag or the irreparable ecological damage." He claimed "the accuracy and validity of the Corps' flood control cost-benefit analysis is subject to serious question." He outlined his views on the Meramec Dam in a position paper released in April 1976, which echoed many of the same themes the Sierra Club expressed. This should come as no surprise considering

---

[279] *Sierra Club v Froehlke, Cause No. 72C584(3);* "Meramec Basin Projects Fact Sheet, price levels as of October 1976" (MVS archives); Response to RCGA request on "Alternative Plan to Meramec Dam Outlined by Sierra Club" (Jul. 14, 1976); "Canoeing on the Meramec and the Impacts on Canoeing Caused by the Project" (Apr. 2, 1977) (MVS Archives); Ruddy, 79-80.

Sugerman had served on Danforth's staff. Besides Danforth, congressional candidate Richard Gephardt and gubernatorial candidate Joseph Teasdale both publically opposed the project. Even presidential candidate Jimmy Carter opposed the dam, comparing it to one he vetoed while governor of Georgia. Supporters of the project included Missouri Gov. Kit Bond, congressional candidate Robert Young, and Reps. Richard Ichord and William Burlison. Other politicians, such as Sen. Thomas Eagleton remained neutral and asked for a referendum to gauge the public's opinion on the project.[280]

Thomas Eagleton

The most significant impact of the 1976 election was that it brought increased public interest to the issues. Much of this attention was inaccurate and misleading, such as the claims of the alternative plan or that the Meramec would be another Teton. Both opponents and proponents voiced opinions on the matter in the *Post-Dispatch* and the *Globe-Democrat*, but these often reflected more about the attitudes of the editors than they did about the public's opinion. Numerous polls showed public support both for and against the project. For example, the St. Louis Engineers Club favored the project by a vote of 375 to 257, but the Automobile Club of Missouri poll showed that 1,301 of 1,500 opposed the project. While these polls were far from scientific and revealed little of the true nature of overall public opinion, they did show the trend toward using a referendum to determine the fate of the project. Some politicians

John Danforth

even favored a referendum. Bond asked for a vote on the project in eastern Missouri; Eagleton refused to give his opinion until a referendum was taken. The day after Bond expressed his desire for a referendum in the *Globe-Democrat*,

---

[280] Danforth comments in excerpt, *Post-Dispatch* (Apr. 22, 1976); Danforth, "The Meramec Dam: Position paper 1" (Apr. 22, 1976) (MVS Archives); Interview with Dace; "Jimmy Carter campaigning in St. Louis," *Post-Dispatch* (Mar. 24, 1976); most candidates' views are in *Post-Dispatch* and *Globe-Democrat* from Mar. to Sept. 1976. The *Globe-Democrat* offers more proponent view; the *Post-Dispatch* includes mostly the opposing views.

the *Post-Dispatch* headline read: "Sierra Club Wants State-Wide Dam Vote." Even though it would be another two years, the fate of the project was tending toward a referendum.[281]

When the election results came in, Teasdale, Danforth, and Carter all won their respective races. The election of dam opponents in key races signaled the beginning of the end for the project. Of those elected, Danforth was the most outspoken critic of the project. He went so far as to bring in Sugerman to be a member of his staff and help him oppose the project. Some politicians, such as Eagleton and Teasdale, recommended that project funds be halted pending the outcome of a referendum. Eagleton, who was originally a proponent of the dam, was highly criticized for his equivocating views, as he seemed content to follow the whim of public opinion rather than take a definite stance. The *Post-Dispatch* reported that eight of 12 members of the Missouri congressional delegation favored delaying the project. Others, such as Ichord, warned against taking such as stand, as it would create difficulty for Missouri to obtain federal funds for future projects. However, even Ichord agreed to conduct a poll of the residents of the three counties of the project area, but he resisted a statewide or 13 county referendum.[282]

Let the Voters Decide

The December 26, 1975, *Post-Dispatch* headline read: "Spending for Meramec Dam may be halted until vote." This proved prophetic in light of President Carter's February 21, 1977, message to Congress, in which he included the Meramec project as one of 19 water projects on his "hit list." This list included projects Carter wanted eliminated because they were what he considered "pork barrel" projects that inflated the federal budget. Carter believed that, if possible, the Meramec River should be kept in its free flowing state. President Gerald Ford's budget for fiscal year 1978 included $10 million for Meramec construction, but Carter wanted the project reevaluated to determine if it would remain in the federal budget. Because the project was on the hit list, the district had to

---

[281] "Meramec Opponents Cite Teton Dam Break," *Post-Dispatch* (June 8, 1976); Polls in Post-Dispatch (Jul. 11 and 27, 1976); *Globe-Democrat* article excerpt on referendum (Sept 13, 1976); "Sierra Club Wants State-Wide Dam Vote," *Post-Dispatch* (Sept. 14, 1976).
[282] Excerpts, *Post-Dispatch* (Dec. 19, 1976); *Post-Dispatch* (Feb. 6, 1977); *Globe-Democrat*, (Jan. 8, 9, and 18, 1977); *Post-Dispatch* (Jan. 9, 1977); *Globe-Democrat* (Jan. 13, 1977) (MVS Archives).

submit an evaluation to the Office of the Chief of Engineers, who would submit it to the president no later than April 15, 1977.[283]

As part of the project review process, the district held another public meeting. This meeting, the so-called "Meramec Shoot-out," was scheduled for March 26 in Sullivan, Missouri. In the weeks leading up to it, even many who supported the project recommended halting funding until its fate was clear. Lower Mississippi Valley Division Engineer Maj. Gen. Frank Koisch recommended to Congress that appropriations for the project should stop for the time being, as there was "no sense in spending money on a project that is about to be shut down." Even Ichord, a staunch supporter of the project, agreed that "there is no reason to spend vast sums…until its future is decided." When the meeting finally took place, it showed a mixture of support and opposition to the project. Estimated attendance was more than 2,000. Of the approximately 100 people who spoke at the meeting, 60 opposed the dam, and 40 supported it. The next day's *Post-Dispatch* and *Globe-Democrat* headlines read: "Cheers, Boos at Meramec Dam Hearing" and "Marathon Dam Hearing Claims no Clear

Col. Leon McKinney

Victor," revealing the inconclusive nature of the meeting. The opinions voiced by both sides expressed mostly the same issues that were prevalent throughout the project and, just as before, there was no clear consensus. Some dam opponents called for McKinney to be fired, accusing him of conducting the meeting improperly by giving false information and being biased against dam opponents. Transcriptions of the meeting revealed that these allegations were false, and supporters of the dam sent numerous letters to Washington praising McKinney's conduct and implored officials in Washington to not allow these accusations to mislead them. The contrasting tone in the letters reveals how heated and personal the debate had become. Although there was no clear consensus against the dam, in spite of the fact that the Corps' review revealed that the project's cost-to-benefit ratio was 1 to 1.5, Carter decided to delete

---

[283] *Public Works for Water and Power Development and Energy Research Appropriation Bill, 1978: Hearings Before a Subcommittee on Appropriations, House*, 95th Cong., 1st Sess., Pt. 9 (Wash.: GPO, 1977): 86-87, 203-206; Excerpts, *Post-Dispatch* (Dec. 23, 1976); *Globe-Democrat* (Jan. 17, 1977); Letter to LMVD, Review of Corps Projects, Mar. 1, 1977 (MVS Archives).

funding for the project for 1978. Carter's unwavering opposition should come as no surprise, as he had stated while campaigning for the presidency that "We ought to get the Army Corps of Engineers out of the dam-building business." For Carter and many opponents of the dam, environmental concerns took precedence over the economic benefits.[284]

After Carter eliminated appropriations for the Meramec project, he began pushing for deauthorization. His administration also began pressuring Corps Headquarters and the Lower Mississippi Valley Division to ensure that the St. Louis District would not discuss the project publically. When the White House began issuing news releases supporting the Sierra Club's misleading information, it told McKinney that the district should not publically contradict this information. From McKinney's point-of-view, he was a public servant who was being asked to at the very least withhold important information from the public, and in some cases even lie publically about the project's benefits. When McKinney refused to comply, he was threatened with reassignment. In light of such pressure, a referendum was beginning to look more and more like one of the last hopes for the project.[285]

With the possibility of a referendum seeming more likely, a debate ensued over the extent of such a vote. Dam supporters argued that it was essentially a regional issue and should be limited to those counties directly affected by the project. In contrast, opponents argued for a wider vote that would include counties outside the boundaries of the proposed reservoir. Some even argued for a statewide vote. In January 1978, the Missouri Senate committee distributed a bill for a non-binding advisory vote on the project. The state senate passed the bill and Governor Teasdale signed it in April. The August 8 vote would include 12 counties and St. Louis. For proponents, a strong showing of support at the polls could pressure Washington to include appropriations for the project for the upcoming fiscal year. In fact, the House Appropriations Committee had already approved $12 million for construction contingent on the outcome of the "non-binding" referendum. Even Danforth, a staunch opponent of the

---

[284] USACE, "Public Information Brochure" (St. Louis: MVS, Mar. 1977); USACE, Project Review, Meramec Park Lake (St. Louis: MVS, Mar. 8, 1977); News Release, "Army Engineers Announce Schedule of Public Meeting on 19 Water Resource Projects," Mar. 24, 1977 (MVS archives); Excerpts, *Post-Dispatch* (Mar. 27, 1977); *Globe-Democrat* (Mar. 28, 1977); Excepts, *Post-Dispatch* (Apr. 17, 1977); "Exultant Carter Has Harsh Words for Meramec Dam in Visit Here," *Post-Dispatch* (Mar. 24, 1976); Carter quote from "When a Campaign Vow Crashes Into a Pork Barrel," *Washington Post* (Apr. 1, 1977); "Digest of Public Meeting on Meramec Park Lake at Sullivan" (St. Louis: MVS, Mar. 26, 1977) (MVS Archives). Of more than 30 letters, only a few make accusations against McKinney. Letters from Duane Woltjen, Sierra Club Ozark Chapter spokesman, to Carter and Lt. Gen. John Morris were the most vehement and accused McKinney and dam supporters of incompetence and misrepresentation of the facts.
[285] Towey interview with McKinney provides a discussion of the pressures on the district from Washington.

project, stated that he would reconsider his opposition if a referendum showed statewide approval. Others, such as Eagleton, promised to support the project if a regional referendum showed support. However, both sides came to agree that a referendum was necessary to determine the fate of the dam. Over the next four months, both opponents and proponents campaigned vigorously for fate of the project.[286]

The Meramec Basin Association led the campaign for those who supported the dam, while the Sierra Club led the campaign of the opposition. Much of this campaigning took place in local newspapers, but it also included flyers, information bulletins, and public speakers. In one case, Wehrenberg Theaters aired a short anti-dam film, narrated by Marlin Perkins of the TV show, "Wild Kingdom," before its feature presentations. Various groups released polls claiming to reveal the public's opinion on the project. These polls ranged from statewide, to basin-wide, to only the three counties affected by the reservoir. In April, Ichord released the results of a three-county poll he had taken, which showed strong support in the counties directly affected – 62 percent in Washington, Franklin, and Crawford. Other polls showed much weaker support both statewide and in urban regions.[287]

A severe blow for dam supporters occurred when the Director of Civil Works Maj. Gen. Charles McGinnis recommended to the Senate Subcommittee on Public Works that Congress delete funding for five projects, including the Meramec. He stated that, as part of the executive branch, he must present the president's views. In other words, if the White House was against the project, it was not McGinnis' role to contradict its policy. Much like McGinnis, the district was in a similarly difficult position, as it could not speak publically about the project unless responding to questions, and even then, district personnel had to be careful about how they responded. Thus, the fate of the project was ultimately in the hands of its proponents, and their public support campaign was not as effective as their opponents' campaign. While project supporters argued that the effects on the environment would be minimal when compared to the economic benefits, opponents were nevertheless able to exploit anxieties about the environment. Ironically, the whole dam discussion had started because of

---

[286] Excerpts, *Post-Dispatch* (Jan. 18, 1978); *Post-Dispatch* (Jan. 28, 1978); "House Clears Meramec Dam Referendum," *Post-Dispatch* (Apr. 4, 1978) (MVS Archives).
[287] While not debated exclusively in local papers, positions on the referendum can be found in the *Post-Dispatch* and *Globe-Democrat*. "Head of Theaters Showing Anti-Dam Film Target of Suit," *Globe-Democrat* (Jul. 26, 1978).

the need for flood control, yet flood control became an auxiliary consideration for many, both opponents and proponents.[288]

The election results revealed just how effectively dam opponents turned public support against the dam – 64 percent voted against it. Most opposing the dam came from counties not directly affected by it. In St. Louis and St. Charles counties, the results were overwhelmingly against the dam, with 214,677 of the 325,488 opposed. However, two of three counties impacted by the dam, Washington and Crawford, voted in favor of it, while Franklin County voters split the vote almost evenly, with 51 percent opposed. Dam proponents argued that the scope of the referendum was unfair, as voters in regions unaffected by the dam determined the fate of a project impacting only three counties. In other words, urban opposition to the dam offset the support for the dam that existed in the regions that would benefit most from a reservoir. The Senate quickly withdrew the $12 million earmarked for the project, and the debate quickly shifted to deauthorization and how to dispose of the land acquired for the project.[289]

Continued Controversy

The referendum essentially sealed the fate of the dam. However, it did not end the controversy surrounding the project. This controversy manifested itself in the form of heated political debates about the provisions of the deauthorization bill. More specifically, the debates concerned guidelines for disposal of the 28,000 acres acquired for the project as well as how to address the still prevalent issues of flood control and water supply. In July 1981, Rep. Wendell Bailey of Missouri introduced a deauthorization bill that included provisions for a year-long study to determine how to dispose of the land. In addition, his bill included possibility of a smaller dam in the future. Danforth and Eagleton objected to such a plan, in large part because it left open the option for a future dam. In contrast, their bill included provisions for selling back the land at what the former landowners originally paid for it or the current market price, whichever was less. The proposed bill also included provisions for distributing 5,122 acres to Missouri for use as state parks and recreation areas.

---

[288] McGinnis' statements in excerpt, *Globe-Democrat* (June 30, 1978) (MVS Archives). Interviews with Dace and McKinney (Aug. 11, 1987) reveal the district's perspective on the referendum and the Carter administration's positions on the dam. They also discuss how the district was hamstrung in its efforts to support the dam. McKinney described proponent efforts a "no-sided" campaign in comparison with the campaign of opponents.
[289] Referendum results in excerpts, Aug. 9, 1978 editions of *Globe-Democrat* and *Post-Dispatch*; Article in excerpts, *Globe-Democrat* (Aug. 11, 1978) (MVS Archives).

Over the next few months, the deauthorization debate would enter a stalemate, as neither side was willing to compromise.[290]

Around the time that debates over deauthorization were occurring, water supply emerged as an important determinant for future plans in the basin. To assess these needs, the Institute of River Studies at the University of Missouri-Rolla conducted a study of the water supply needs of the basin. The findings revealed that while streamflow was more than enough to meet anticipated needs in most years, shortages could still occur in severe drought years. However, these years were infrequent. The study revealed that water supply could be an issue in the future, and thus the district believed that "the public interest would be best served by planning for contingency supplies, to allow for uncertainties in predicting future events." From the district's perspective, it was trying to anticipate future problems with water supply and address them in any future plans for the basin. However, dam opponents saw this as just another ploy to keep the Meramec project alive. Even after the deauthorization of the project, the issue of water supply would continue to be prevalent in debates about plans for the basin.[291]

In addition to debates over water supply and deauthorization, there was still the glaring problem of flood control. Because of the controversy surrounding the project, people often lost sight of the fact that the most important function of the reservoir was flood control. If a large reservoir was not a viable solution for flood control, then alternative means needed to be explored. In an attempt to address this problem, the Missouri Department of Natural Resources, Upper Mississippi River Basin Commission, and U.S. Water Resources Council agreed on the need for a special study of flood plain management. In June 1981, the group released its findings in *Out of Harm's Way*. The report recommended that the state or federal government purchase lands in the river's flood plain, as well as zoning lands to prevent development in regions susceptible to flooding. The study also recommended other non-structural solutions for flooding, such as controls on quarrying and dredging operations, better flood preparation, bank stabilization, and building levees in areas especially prone to flood damages, such as Valley Park. In light of the public's growing aversion to large

---

[290] "Bailey Introduces Bill To Deauthorize Dam," *Rolla Daily News* (Jul. 17, 1981).
[291] "Water Supply is issue in Meramec projects," *Globe-Democrat* (Oct. 16, 1981); Institute of River Studies, *Meramec River Basin Water Supply Study*, (St. Louis: University of Missouri-Rolla, 1979); USACE, *Meramec River Basin Water Supply Study* (St. Louis: MVS, 1979).

reservoirs, the nonstructural methods of flood control suggested by this study would become more and more prevalent in future planning for the region.²⁹²

In July 1981, nearly two years after the referendum, legislators were still debating deauthorization. Standing in the middle of these debates was Rep. Robert Young. Before making a decision to commit to either plan, Young met with District Engineer Col. Robert Dacey, Meramec Project Coordinator Michael Dace, and former District Engineer Guy Jester in June 1981. From the district's perspective, it was just responding to Young's request and supplying neutral facts, not biased conclusions. From Young's perspective, he simply wanted the district to bring him up to date on the situation so he would know the facts before making a decision. However, from the perspective of dam opponents, such as Eagleton, it seemed as though the district was lobbying and trying to revitalize interest in the project. Eagleton called the meeting a "flagrant intervention in the political process" and accused the district of "pumping up" Young to oppose a dead project. Eagleton met with Chief of Engineers Lt. Gen. Joseph K. Bratton to voice his complaints. However, Bratton told Eagleton that the district engineer has a responsibility to respond to such requests, and thus he was not at fault. After the meeting, Eagleton stated that he was satisfied and would make no further comment.²⁹³

Col. Robert Dacey

After the controversy from this meeting settled, the two sides were able to compromise on a deauthorization bill. A major issue for Eagleton and Danforth was that Bailey's plan included provisions for a future study of a smaller scale project. In return for Bailey dropping this provision, Danforth and Eagleton agreed to a provision to sell land at its current market value. Young drafted the bill, which became Public Law 97-128. President Ronald Regan signed it into law in December 1981. The deauthorization bill included a provision that

---

²⁹² Missouri Department of Natural Resources, Upper Mississippi River Basin Commission, *Out of Harm's Way: Lower Meramec Valley Flood Damage Reduction Study, Summary Report* (St. Louis: MVS, June 1981).
²⁹³ Interview with Dace; "Young denies being influenced on dam project," *Globe-Democrat* (Aug. 1, 1981); "Army Corps Accused Of Politicking," *Post-Dispatch* (Aug. 2, 1981); "Corps Head Appeases Eagleton About Briefing Young On Dam," *Post-Dispatch* (Aug. 6, 1981).

gave the state between 3,382 and 5,122 acres of Meramec project lands. It also included a provision for a $20 million fund for non-reservoir flood control efforts on the lower Meramec, as well as provisions for a water supply study. Former landowners would have one year to buy back their lands at market price. After this year, the district would dispose of whatever lands remained by public auction. Because the General Services Administration was normally charged with land disposal, this responsibility would be a unique challenge for the district in the years to come.[294]

Before the district could dispose of land, it had to wait for the Missouri legislature to decide on the 5,122 acres offered to the state as part of the deauthorization bill. Controversy arose over these acres, as some argued the Corps should return this land to its previous owners. In addition, there was debate over how to finance and maintain the land. In April 1982, the Missouri legislature accepted 5,122 acres, offering some land at auction and the remaining land as state parks. The bill provided for a 600-foot strip along each side of the river to be protected from development. On October 18, 1983, District Engineer Col. Gary Beech officially deeded this land to the state of Missouri. The remaining task for the Corps was disposing of more than 20,000 acres. The first step was to offer these lands to former owners. The district sent letters containing offers to more than 500 former landowners, who had one year to respond. Because the market value of the lands fluctuated, some former landowners expressed anger over the resale values. Others wanted the courts to decide the issue. In the end, former owners purchased only 2,400 acres, leaving approximately 18,000 acres for the district to sell at three public auctions. These

Col. Gary Beech

---

[294] "Compromise reached on Meramec Park Lake," Macon *Chronicle* (Nov. 25, 1981); "Meramec compromise," Boonville *Daily News* (Dec. 3, 1981); "Congressman Wendell Bailey Reports On Meramec Deauthorization," Willow Springs *News* (Dec. 10, 1981); U.S. Cong., *Act to deauthorize several projects within the jurisdiction of the Army Corps of Engineers*, PL 97-128 (97th Cong., 1st Sess.) "Congress Passes Bill to Kill Meramec Dam," *Post-Dispatch* (Dec. 17, 1981); "Reagan's Pen Kills Meramec Dam Project," *Post-Dispatch* (Dec. 30, 1981).

took place between June 1987 and June 1988, producing approximately $7.4 million.[295]

In retrospect, there was no single factor that prevented completion of the Meramec Dam. Instead, the project ran a gauntlet of challenges that eventually culminated in its deauthorization in 1981. When support for the project was at its apex, funds were limited due to the nation's involvement in Vietnam. When funds for construction became available, Congress had passed NEPA, forever changing the way the Corps and other agencies evaluated its projects. When the project began in the 1960s, its economic benefits were sufficient to justify its construction. Even though the project remained beneficial from an economic perspective, by the 1970s economic benefits alone were not enough to justify the project. Even if the project's economic gains offset the environmental impact of the project, the fact remains that the proponents of the dam simply did do an effective enough job informing the public about the positives of the project. Instead, the public chose to follow the rousing rhetoric of dam opponents, who were far more effective at getting their opinions heard, and more importantly, believed. In December 1982, a flood devastated the basin, causing approximately $150 million in damages. Dam proponents argued that the reservoir would have significantly reduced flood damages, while opponents still claimed otherwise. Nonetheless, the flood highlighted the fact that some solution to the problem was still necessary. Proponents tried to use this as an opportunity to stir up renewed interest in a reservoir, but opponents soon ended any such hopes. In a sense, the Corps' role was essentially unchanged, as it still had to find solutions for the Meramec Basin. In another, the Corps would never be the same, as its methods for addressing problems such as those that existed in the Meramec Basin would have to evolve in response to NEPA and the public's growing desire to protect the nation's natural resources.[296]

---

[295] "Governor Bond signs Meramec lands bill," Sullivan *Tri-county News*, (Apr. 29, 1982); "Army Corps preparing to unload dam project land," *Globe-Democrat* (Oct. 4, 1983); "Meramec land bill said all right," Crawford *Mirror* (May 6, 1982); Memo, Meramec Park Lake Disposal Project, Oct. 17, 1983 (MVS archives). "Meramec Lands Offered At Prices 50% Below and Above Purchase Prices," *Independent-Journal* (Dec. 15, 1983); "Landowners Of Meramec Dam Project Land Met To Discuss Problems of Repurchase," Sullivan *Independent News* (Dec. 21, 1983); "Corps Needs to Be More Flexible On Dam Land Prices," *Rolla Daily News* (Jan. 27, 1984); "Corps of Engineers To Auction Property from Meramec Dam," *Post-Dispatch* (June 25, 1987); "Landowners decide on suit to bring down land prices," *Tri-County News* (Feb. 1, 1984); *Auction After-Action Report* (St. Louis: MVS, 1988).

[296] "Thousands Flee Rampaging Rivers," *Globe-Democrat* (Dec. 6, 1982); Editorial in *Globe-Democrat* (Dec. 12, 1983); Interview with Dace.

Carter "Hit List"

When the 1976 presidential election race began, few people outside of Georgia had ever heard of the little known governor of that state. Yet Jimmy Carter's message, which promised to cut back government spending and eliminate what he called "pork barrel" projects, spoke to many voters who had become disillusioned with Washington. For Carter, pork barrel projects were unnecessary, highly expensive, and represented some of the worst examples of government waste. While governor of Georgia, Carter halted one such project by vetoing a proposed dam on the Flint River. Carter felt that his action had not only removed an expensive and unnecessary project, but had also protected the environment by keeping the river free-flowing. While on presidential the campaign trail, Carter vowed that he "would get the Army Corps of Engineers out of the dam-building business." In my opinion, he added, "we have built enough dams in this country and [he] will be extremely reluctant as president to build anymore." So, it came as no surprise that when the Carter campaign visited St. Louis in March 1976, he voiced opposition to the Meramec Dam. Proponents and opponents alike knew that his election would likely doom the dam.

When the election results came in, Carter had won by a narrow margin. This victory was a crushing blow for the future of large civil works projects like the Meramec Dam. The administration quickly began compiling a preliminary list of projects already under construction that should be halted. Eventually, the administration reduced this list - which became known as the Carter "hit list" - to 19 projects, one of which was the Meramec Dam. When the administration released the list, many legislators were furious, as they had devoted a great deal of time and effort to see these projects come to fruition. After further review, the administration agreed to reduce the number of projects on the "hit list" to nine; however, the Meramec remained. From the beginning of his campaign, Carter was indifferent to the economic, flood control, and recreational benefits of the dam. He had already determined that this was a pork barrel project and that protecting the environment and keeping the river in a free-flowing state took precedence over any of the aforementioned benefits that might accrue. In other words, Carter was determined to halt the project. The administration soon began pressuring Corps headquarters, which in turn led to pressure on the St. Louis district. Faced by opposition from without and within, the fate of the project was determined long before the outcome of the "non-binding" referendum that would prove the *coup d'état* for the Meramec Dam.

Flint River in Georgia just downstream of proposed Corps dam site

18

Replacement of the Alton Dam

Among the major Corps projects delayed by the National Environmental Policy Act (NEPA) and other environmental regulation, perhaps the most important was the replacement of Lock and Dam No. 26 at Alton, Illinois. As noted previously, with the passage of the Rivers and Harbors Act of 1930, Congress increased the channel depth to nine feet, which the Corps maintained through a series of locks and dams on the Upper Mississippi that created slack-water navigation pools. By the 1940s, this nine-foot channel project had successfully turned the Upper Mississippi System into an intra-continental highway, leading to explosive growth in the number of vessels navigating the river and in the size of the tows carrying valuable coal, petroleum, grain, and other essential goods to and from markets. These tows, which had carried maximum payloads of approximately 5,000 tons prior to the nine-foot project, could now carry a maximum of 50,000 tons, facilitating the rapid growth of the nation's economy. Although commercial navigation grew throughout the entire Upper Mississippi due to the new nine-foot channel, certain locales experienced especially rapid growth. One was the Alton Dam. Yet by only the 1950s, it was obvious that the facility had structural issues requiring significant repair, and that the size of the lock was prohibitive for processing the growing level of traffic. By the following decade, the St. Louis District began planning for replacement of the lock, but new environmental requirements delayed and altered the plans, demonstrating again how the environmental movement greatly impacted navigation in the district.[297]

Although the Alton dam employed the best-known engineering principles of the time, there were a number of unforeseen engineering issues with the structure that became manifest in the years following its completion. For one, the structure's foundation was not stable, as the vertical piles that anchored it were driven into sand that rested atop overlying bedrock. Because of scouring and filling during construction, foundation materials under much of the dam were much weaker than when initially tested. The weak foundation caused the structure to shift, with lock walls moving as much as 10 inches and dam piers

---

[297] O'Brien, pp. 11-20; "The Mississippi River Navigation System and Locks and Dam 26," Feb. 1976 (MVS Archives); DuWayne A. Koch, "Tomorrow's Waterways," *Water Spectrum* N.D. (MVS Archives).

moving in excess of two inches downstream. This produced problems such as cracking, joint separation, underseepage, and voids that developed around the piles. In addition, scouring just below the dam caused a 300-foot-long and 10-foot deep hole to develop. One scuba diver investigating the structured said that the piles were so exposed that it was like walking through a forest. To ensure that the structure remained stable, the Corps performed numerous costly repairs. For example, in 1964 the Corps expended $186,000 on repairs, and just six months into 1968, the Corps had expended another $276,000. These repairs would have to continue in the years to come just to maintain the structure, and far more costly expenditures were required for long-term solutions to these structural problems.[298]

View of Lock and Dam 26 in 1938

In addition to structural deficiencies, the growth of navigation on the upper Mississippi system and especially at Alton made it apparent that the dam's locking capacity was inadequate to meet future demands. There are two primary reasons for this inadequacy. First, the structure was located between the confluence of the Illinois River, 15 miles upstream, and the Missouri River, eight miles downstream. The traffic from these two rivers combined with Mississippi traffic, causing the Alton site to be particularly congested. For example, in 1938, the dam's first year of operation, 1.4 million tons locked through the dam, but by the 1950s, 20 million tons moved through the locks annually. This annual

---

[298] Arthur Johnson, "St. Louis District Begins Design of Alton Locks," ASCE Annual Meeting, Oct. 18-22, 1971(MVS Archives); Dobney, p. 151; David Chenoweth, "Trials at Alton," *Water Spectrum* (Wint. 1977-78); "Mississippi River Navigation System"; A detailed assessment of the state of old Lock and Dam No. 26 can be found in *Report on Replacement, Lock and Dam No. 26, Mississippi River, Alton, Illinois* (St. Louis: MVS, 1968).

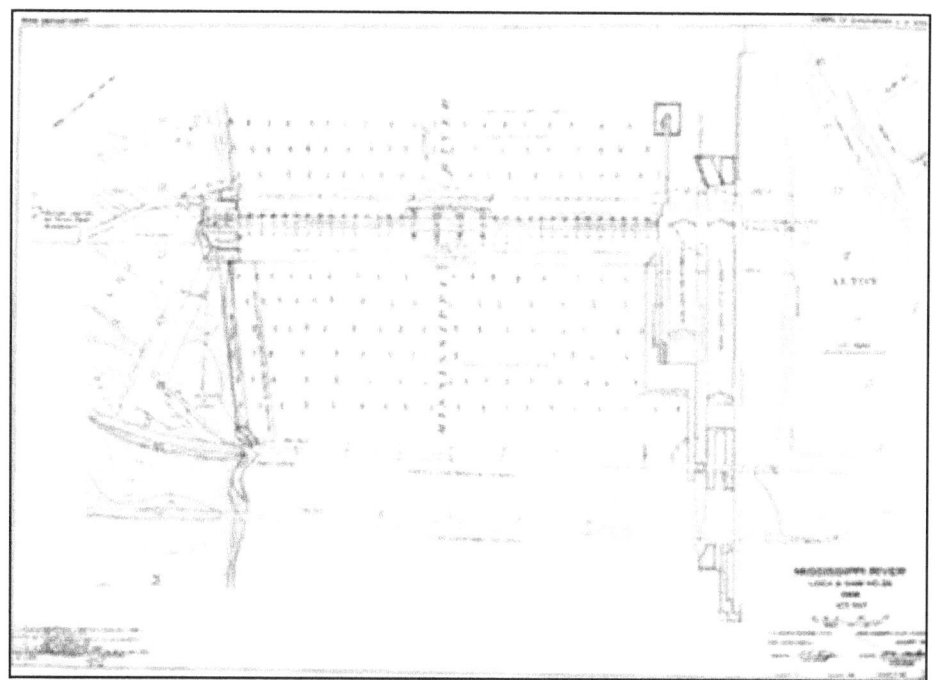

Lock and Dam 26 site map, 1934

tonnage had increased to 40 million by 1967. This dramatic increase exposed the second major inadequacy of the Alton Dam—its 600-foot and 350-foot locks simply were not capable of meeting the demands created by the growth of navigation because they required longer tows to split for multiple lockages. The Corps estimated

First vessel through L&D 26

that the practical capacity of the locks was 41.5 million tons, which would be reached in 1968. The problem was already beginning to manifest itself in the form of delays, as waiting tows congested the site and created a transportation "bottleneck." Barge companies complained that they were losing $1.2 million annually because of congestion delays at the dam. Moreover, repairs to the structure caused further delays when the Corps closed the main lock for 29 days in February 1968 to recondition the lower gates. During these repairs, around 900 tows experienced delays ranging from several hours to seven days.

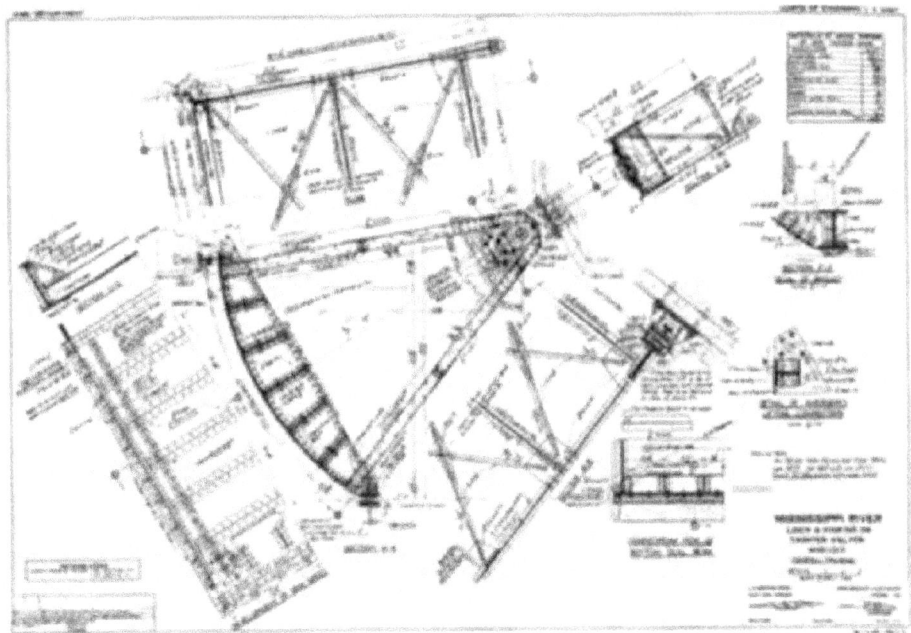

Tainter valves of main gate, Lock and Dam 26, 1933

Because traffic continued to increase, delays would become even worse in the future.[299]

Repair or Replacement?

As early as the 1950s, the Corps recognized the need to address inadequacies of the dam. By September 1956, the Office of the Chief of Engineers approved the initiation of an authorization report for rehabilitation. The Corps charged engineering firm Tibbetts-Abbett-McCarthy-Stratton with the study. The Corps released the report on this study in June 1957, and shortly thereafter the district held a public hearing to discuss a rehabilitation and expansion project. However, the rehabilitation plan would take several years to materialize, and by the time it did, the focus was beginning to shift away from rehabilitation and toward replacement. In August 1964, the district released a major study on

Crack in auxiliary lock wall

---

[299] *Report on Replacement*, pp. 1-21.

the replacement of Alton Dam. This report incorporated many of the findings of the 1957 study, both of which recommended construction of a 110-foot by 1200-foot lock to accommodate increasing traffic. By June 1965, the Board of Engineers for Rivers and Harbors approved the plan, prompting a new public hearing to discuss the project. Held in St. Louis on February 15, 1966, the meeting showed that overall support for a larger lock was strong, especially among navigation interests. However, the Office of the Chief of Engineers questioned the advisability of replacing the existing lock and instead recommended construction of a new dam. To make a determination about which plan of action was best – replacement or rehabilitation – representatives from the district, Board of Engineers for Rivers and Harbors, Office of the Chief of Engineers, and Lower Mississippi Valley Division held a conference in August 1966 and concluded that a more detailed study was needed to make a determination.[300]

Closeup of crack in lock wall

Aerial of old Lock and Dam 26

---

[300] *Locks and Dam No. 26 (Replacement)*, "Chronological Events Prior to Project Document" and "Investigations."

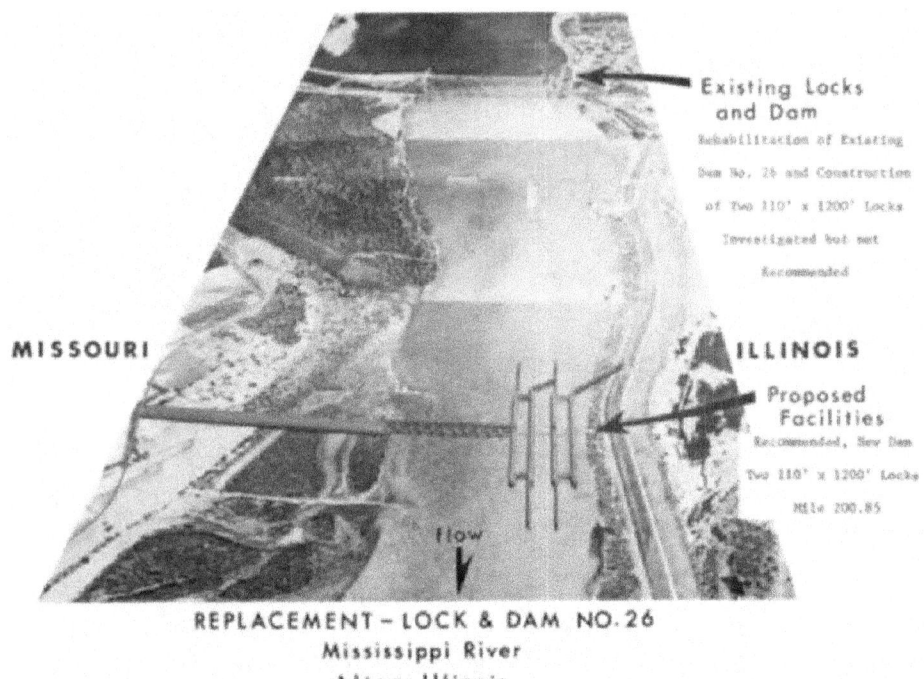

Map of existing structure and proposed replacement location

Over the next two years, the district held additional conferences and conducted further studies on the best plan of action. These studies and discussions centered on navigation, lockage time and delays, the structural integrity of the existing facility, and the costs and benefits of both repair and replacement. By May 1968, the study was nearing completion, and the district held a public meeting in Alton to reveal its plans. Various state and local agencies attended the meeting, as well as concerned citizens and representatives from commercial interest groups. Once again, overall support for the project was strong, especially with waterway interests. These interests unanimously approved the project because they saw it as a solution to costly delays that drove up shipping costs, which increased prices for consumers. In addition, there appeared to be little environmental opposition, as the U.S. Fish and Wildlife Service acknowledged that the project "will have relatively minor adverse effects."[301]

Shortly after the public hearing, the district submitted its report to the division office, Board of Engineers for Rivers and Harbors, and Office of the Chief of Engineers for approval. The Secretary of the Army, Stanley Resor, approved

---

[301] *Report on Replacement*, Ex. A, letter, U.S. Fish and Wildlife Service to Col. Edwin Decker, Jun. 14, 1968; Arthur Johnson, "St. Louis District Begins Design of Alton Locks"; MVS, "Statement of Findings Locks and Dam No. 26 (Replacement), Upper Mississippi River Basin, Mississippi River, Alton Illinois," 1974 (MVS Archives).

TABLE 1

NUMBER OF CRAFT AND LOCKAGES

Year	Passenger	Towboats	Barges	Pleasure	Total	Lockages Total
1958	6	5,804	24,286	1,699	31,795	7,627
1959	2	6,305	25,069	1,963	33,339	8,248
1960	3	6,176	25,180	2,366	33,725	8,205
1961	5	6,555	25,948	2,111	34,619	8,510
1962	6	6,926	29,169	1,944	38,045	9,172
1963	9	6,941	30,498	1,989	39,437	9,138
1964	32	7,561	34,915	2,239	44,747	10,109
1965	46	8,550	36,750	1,889	47,235	10,439
1966	18	8,048	39,452	2,131	49,649	11,209
1967	35	8,355	41,621	1,935	51,946	11,304

it in July 1969 and used his authority under the 1909 River and Harbor Act to authorize it – Section 6 of the act gave the secretary authority to approve a project if "its entire reconstruction is absolutely essential to its efficient and economical maintenance and operation." Such modifications to a structure "shall be considered and approved by the Board of Engineers for Rivers and Harbors and be recommended by the Chief of Engineers before the work of reconstruction is commenced." The Secretary had already used this authority to expand facilities on the Ohio River without specific congressional approval and now he was using this same authority once again. He sent his request to the Chairman of the Senate Appropriations Committee, which approved funds for fiscal year 1970.[302]

The report the Secretary approved discussed three specific factors leading to the conclusion that the Corps should build a new dam. First, as discussed above, the structure had deteriorated and needed extensive repairs to ensure its safety and functionality. Although the Corps did not know when it would fail, it was necessary to be proactive to protect navigation. If a major failure occurred, the effects would be economically devastating. At the least, the Corps needed to perform extensive repairs on the existing dam, and the district determined

---

[302] *Locks and Dam No. 26 (Replacement)*; U.S. Cong., *River and Harbor Act of 1909*, P.L. 60-317 (60th Cong., 1st Sess.); "Mississippi River Navigation System."

that this was not an option for several reasons. The cost of rehabilitation would be nearly the same as the cost of replacing the existing structure, an estimated $214 million for rehabilitation versus $203 million for replacement. The existing structure would approach its 50-year lifespan when the district completed repairs. Pile driving adjacent to the structure could weaken the foundation and cause the structure to "walk" downstream. Finally, even if repaired, engineering principles used during the construction of the old dam were not up to the standards of modern engineering.[303]

The second factor the report discussed was the impediment to waterborne commerce that the existing structure presented. Its locks simply were not capable of meeting future commercial demands. Thus, whether the district built a new structure or rehabilitated the old one, the locks would have to be expanded. However, expanding the locks and performing repairs would require a shutdown of river traffic while the district performed the improvements. An interruption of river commerce could have a devastating impact on the economy, as shippers would have to move goods by more expensive modes, such as railroads, leading to increased costs for consumers. This relates to the final justification for the project: its cost-benefits savings. Based on 1968 tonnage, a new structure would produce approximately $10 million in annual benefits from savings on transportation costs. Moreover, annual benefits would grow with the increase in annual tonnage. The report estimated that annual tonnage at the site would increase from 46 million to 174 million tons between 1970 and 2030. Based on this projected growth, the report estimated maximum annual benefits could reach as high as $31 million. Much of the projected savings would benefit shipping industries, but groups such as farmers and electric companies would benefit as well. These two industries provided consumers with essential good. For example, approximately 25 percent of the total grain produced in the Midwest passed through the locks annually. Electric companies relied on coal to supply power, much of which was shipped by barge. One utility estimated that without waterborne commerce, electrical rates for consumers would increase by 19 percent. Because of the breadth of the Mississippi navigation system and the nation's reliance on the system for essential goods and services, the Alton dam was more than just a local issue; it was a national

---

[303] *Report on Replacement*, sec. IV, V and VI.

issue that could have a dramatic impact on the future economic growth and energy needs of not only the Midwest, but the entire nation.[304]

Considering the disadvantages of rehabilitation, the Corps decided on replacement. The district considered four possible sites before determining that a site two miles downstream was the best choice. The site had several advantages over the existing site and other sites considered. The location allowed a straight, two-mile approach to the locks. One problem with the existing structure was that the nearby shoreline jutted out into the river, causing approaching tows to take an indirect approach to the lock. The straight approach would allow safer and more efficient locking. In addition, building at this location would allow the existing dam to remain operational during construction, preventing a costly hiatus for shipping. Moreover, the location would enhance Alton's waterfront, improve operation of barge-loading facilities, and provide various recreational opportunities. Construction difficulties would be minimal, and the structure leveraged current design criteria, making it adequate for

Aerial view of old L&D 26 just before beginning construction of Melvin Price Locks and Dam

---

[304] Ibid.; Dobney, p. 151; "Fact, Fiction on Alton dam replacement," Response by American Waterways Operators to *Reader's Digest* (MVS Archives).

meeting all loading conditions. The proposed structure included two 100-foot by 1,200-foot locks. Rather than being side-by-side, these would be separated by two tainter gates, allowing for more efficient locking. The sill depth at the new locks would be 18-feet deep, providing more clearance space for nine-foot draft tows and allowing more efficient navigation of locks during periods when ice accumulates on the bottom of tows. The dam would also consist of nine 110-foot by 42-foot tainter gates. In addition, the foundation of the new locks and dam would be on battered steel H-piles driven into bedrock at an angle to form a web-like foundation, which was far more stable than wooden friction piles driven into sand.[305]

The preconstruction planning phase began when Congress allocated funds for the project in May 1970. The district's initial estimates were that the project would take 11 years to complete, with construction set to begin in 1974. Preconstruction planning included various studies on both the existing and replacement structure. Because it would be at least 11 years before the new dam was complete, the district had to maintain and increase the capacity of the Alton dam. To increase its capacity, the district explored means such as switchboats and mooring facilities. However, most investigations and studies during this phase concerned the replacement structure. The district conducted a study on the appropriate lock sizes, concluding that two 1,200-foot locks were necessary. The district oversaw numerous other investigations as well – alternate studies, model studies, field surveys, hydraulic analyses, and pile driving and load tests to determine foundation characteristics and feasibility of using H-piles. During the planning and design stages, the Corps and other reviewing offices held several conferences to discuss and review ideas developed during these various studies. In addition, the Waterways Experiment Station conducted various model tests, passing its findings and recommendations along to the district for consideration during the dam's design. Besides studies on the structure itself, the district also performed studies on the best means of cofferdam construction and possible recreation opportunities provided by the project. The district incorporated these findings into its design memoranda, the first of which, on hydrology, the Corps approved on July 29, 1971. Soon thereafter, the Corps approved the general design memorandum, moving the project swiftly

---

[305] *Report on Replacement*, Sec. V; further discussion of the state of the facility can be found in Richard C. Armstrong, "Replacement—Locks and Dam No. 26: Plans Considered," Proceedings of the ASCE, in *Journal of the Waterways and Harbors Division* (Feb. 1970): 49-63; "Statement of Findings"; Johnson, "St. Louis District Begins Design"; O'Brien, p. 132.

toward construction. With the studies completed, the district made relatively few changes to the original plan. Most notably, the size and number of tainter gates changed and the overall cost increased from $203 million to $358 million, mostly because of inflation. The district, division, Waterways Experiment Station, and Office of the Chief of Engineers agreed to the revisions and the project's cost estimates at a series of conferences held in August and September 1972.[306]

The district planned to carry out a three-stage construction sequence on the replacement structure. During the first stage, after completion of cofferdam, the contractor would build 6.5 gate bays. During the second stage, the contractor would construct the half gate bay of the dam and the river lock. During the final stage, the contractor would complete the land lock and two gate bays in the separation between the two locks. On August 6, 1974, shortly before construction on the first stage cofferdam was set to begin, a controversy ensued, as 21 railroads, the Izaak Walton League, and the Sierra Club issued a temporary restraining order against opening bids for construction on the first stage cofferdam.[307]

Environmental Objections

On January 1, 1970, President Richard Nixon signed NEPA into law, forever changing that the Corps and other federal agencies would do business. The immediate effect of the law was the requirement to file an environmental impact statement (EIS) for any project that would have an impact on the environment. Concurrent with the other studies and reports for the replacement of the Alton dam, the district quickly set to work on an EIS for the project. The Corps filed the draft EIS with the Council on Environmental Quality on March 15, 1974. The district received approximately 40 letters from various groups and federal, state, and local agencies revealing a mixture of support and opposition. Those who supported the project saw it as an opportunity to increase navigational capacity of the river and promote economic growth

---

[306] *Locks and Dam No. 26 (Replacement)*, Sections 2, 9, 10, 13, 17, 19, and 21; Johnson, "St. Louis District Begins Design"; Minutes of Meeting, Review Conference on Locks and Dam No. 26 (Replacement), Board of Consultants and Government Representatives, WES, Jul. 31-Aug. 2, 1972 (St. Louis: MVS); a chronological listing and summary of meetings between 1970 and 1971 are in USACE, *Locks and Dam No. 26 (Replacement) Conference, 18-19 November 1971* (St. Louis: MVS, 1971). For a more detailed discussion of these conferences, including those from 1972-1973, see "Civil Works Project Files, L & D No. 26—Conferences" (MVS Archives); The increase in the estimated cost of the project was due to inflation and the cost of repairing the existing facility concurrently.

[307] *Locks and Dam No. 26 (Replacement)*, Sec. I; *Izaak Walton League of America, Et Al. v. John O. Marsh*, 655 F.2d 346 (D.C. Cir. 1981).

in the region. Letters opposing the project came mostly from environmental and conservation groups who feared that the project would have a detrimental impact on the environment. Much of this concern related to fears that the project was part of a plan to expand the capacity of the entire upper Mississippi. These letters did not outright oppose the project, but urged the Corps to halt the project until after further studies. Moreover, they argued that if it was a part of a 12-foot channel project, it required a system-wide EIS to meet NEPA requirements. Other letters questioning the project came from groups and agencies who felt that the cost-benefit figures were inadequate and that the district should consider other means of transporting goods. Finally, some letters expressed the opinion that the district should pursue rehabilitation rather than replacement because it was more cost-efficient.[308]

The district reviewed these comments and included them in the final EIS, which it filed with the Council on Environmental Quality on July 2, 1974. The statement concluded that environmental impacts would be minimal. The only adverse impacts that the statement cited were inundation of 600 acres, potential impacts to habitats along the river due to industrial growth, and possible bank erosion and sedimentation because of increased traffic. However, these impacts were considered minor, especially considering the economic benefits that would occur because of increased waterborne commerce. The statement considered alternatives to the project, but concluded that all of them were inadequate to meet the demands of growing waterborne commerce. One possible alternative was rehabilitation, but the cost was the around the same as replacement and required either the construction of a temporary lock or a halt to through navigation for one to three years, which would have a detrimental economic impact. Once economic losses were included, rehabilitation hardly seemed a viable alternative.[309]

Some concerned groups were not convinced about Corps intentions, and on August 6, 1974, just a month after the district filed its final EIS and a day before bidding on the first stage cofferdam was to begin, 21 railroads, the Izaak Walton League, and the Sierra Club filed suits in district court seeking an injunction to stop construction. The court granted a temporary injunction and on September 6 issued a preliminary injunction on further activity on the project. The

---
[308] USACE, *Final Environmental Statement, Locks and Dam No. 26 (Replacement), Upper Mississippi River Basin, Mississippi River, Alton Illinois* (St. Louis: MVS, 1974), see App. H for letters received and Sec.9, pp. 183-273, for Corps responses.
[309] Ibid., see also Sec.5 and 6 on adverse environmental impacts and alternatives.

Confluence of the Mississippi and Ohio rivers

court then combined these suits. The trial was set to begin on March 3, 1975. However, the Secretary of the Army was able to convince the court to delay the trial while the Corps awaited clarification on the exact extent of the secretary's authority.[310]

There were many reasons why the plaintiffs filed suit. The railroads opposed the project primarily because they claimed federally financed maintenance of the river system represented an unfair subsidy to the barge industry, although it was not the only mode of transportation that received federal subsidies. From the Corps' perspective, it was simply responding to its congressional mandate to maintain efficient navigation for waterborne commerce. Unfortunately, this mandate placed the Corps between two rival industries. The controversy over Lock and Dam No. 26 was essentially "a very classic meeting ground between two old adversaries, the railroads and the barge industry," District Engineer Col. Thorwald Peterson pointed out. "In effect, the St. Louis District was caught in the middle. Lock and Dam No. 26 was where the battle was fought, but the real issue was user fees." The user fee issue was the other reason why railroads opposed the project, as they wanted the barge industry to cover the cost of maintenance. However, it was not the responsibility of the Corps to

---

[310] *Izaak Walton League v. Marsh*; Leon E. McKinney, William R. Sutton, and Jean-Yves Perez, "Locks and Dam No. 26, Rehabilitation Versus Replacement," *TME* (Mar.-Apr., 1980).

decide the issue of user fees but of Congress. To the railroads, this mandate seemed favoritism for the barge industry. One railroad representative charged the Corps with "promoting its own construction self-interest and the interest of a narrow band of shippers." Barge representatives retorted that "the project was essential to the economic well-being of the St. Louis area." Another reason for railroad opposition was that they claimed increasing the capacity of the locks would lead to an increase in the capacity of the river, which would cause profits to plummet. While it may seem on the surface that declining railroad profits should not be a federal concern, these companies received federal aid to prevent them from declaring bankruptcy. If the Corps project had an adverse affect on the industry, this would inhibit railroads from repaying federal loans. Railroads also claimed that thousands of jobs would be lost if increased river commerce caused their profits to decline.[311]

Environmentalists had their own though often related reasons for opposing the project. For example, environmentalists also feared that increased lock capacity would lead to an increased capacity on the entire upper river. They argued that the plan was nothing more than a clever ruse to create a 12-foot channel based on the idea that increasing the lock's capacity would lead to a shifting transportation bottleneck that would move up the river, thus creating the need for increased capacity at each locale. They feared that this increased capacity would have a devastating impact on riverine ecology. They cited as further proof the proposed 18-foot sill depth. Because the larger sill depth can accommodate tows with a 12-foot draft, the logical implication, at least for the environmentalists, was that it *would* necessarily lead to a 12-foot channel. The plaintiffs also argued that the Corps did not have specific congressional approval for the project. The authority that the Corps cited was Section 6 of the 1909 River and Harbors Act, which gave the Secretary of the Army authority to approve projects deemed necessary to maintain efficient navigation of the Upper Mississippi. Because the proposed structure was part of the nine-foot channel, the secretary and Corps believed they were simply carrying out their congressional mandate. The Corps had already used this same authority to expand and improve facilities on the Ohio River. However, the plaintiffs argued that because the increased lock capacity would "necessarily"

---

[311] Ruddy, Interview with Peterson; *Izaak Walton League v. Marsh*; "Corps Promotes Dam, Rail Spokesman Says," *Post-Dispatch* (Sept. 12, 1975); CBO, *Alton Locks and Dam: A Review of the Evidence*, Staff Working Paper (Wash., D.C.: CBO, 1976); "The Mississippi River, Locks and Dam 26: Issues and Answers," *Post-Dispatch* (Feb. 22, 1976), provides an excellent overview of the arguments of all sides of the issue.

lead to a multi-billion dollar 12-foot channel, it required specific congressional authority. Moreover, because impacts would be system-wide, approval needed to be part of a system-wide policy. These criticisms led environmentalists to claim the project's EIS was inadequate because it was too localized and did not consider alternatives, arguing that a system-wide EIS was necessary to comply with NEPA.[312]

After reviewing the evidence, U.S. District Court Judge Charles Richey issued a temporary injunction ordering the project to be delayed "until the defendants obtain the consent of Congress and cured the defects of the environmental impact statement." Richey, who interestingly enough had worked for the Corps during World War II, went on to state that "the decision to expand the capacity of this part of the Upper Mississippi River Navigation System from 46 to 190 million or more tons is, in essence, the decision to expand the capacity of the entire system." Thus, either the Corps must submit an EIS that takes into account the system-wide impacts of a 12-foot channel, or it must modify the project.[313]

The St. Louis District responded swiftly by beginning preparation of a draft supplement EIS that would take into account the system-wide rather than regional effects of increased navigation. Meanwhile, the district began preparing a Formulation Evaluation Report on the project to present an updated analysis of traffic projections, alternatives considered, and system constraints. The major issues surrounding the project fall into three specific but often interrelated categories: engineering debates, impacts on the railroads, and environmental impacts. The district's responses to all of these criticisms referred to the 1968 report on the existing structure. To support the report's recommendations, the district cited numerous engineering conferences and studies analyzing the project subsequent to the report. These studies concluded that the old lock and dam had deteriorated to the point that a major rehabilitation was the only solution. However, as the district had already pointed out, rehabilitation would cost almost the same as the proposed replacement. Thus, the district had chosen to replace rather than rehabilitate.[314]

---

[312] *Izaak Walton League v. Marsh*; Interview with Peterson; CBO, pp. 4-9; "Conflict Snarls Midwest Waterways Expansion," *Washington Post* (Jul. 7, 1975).
[313] "Corps Promotes Dam, Rail Spokesman Says," *Post-Dispatch*; "Conflict Snarls Expansion."
[314] USACE, *Draft Supplement Environmental Statement, Locks and Dam No. 26 (Replacement), Vol. I, Upper Mississippi River Basin, Mississippi River, Alton, Illinois* (St. Louis: MVS, 1975); USACE, *Design Memorandum No. 11, Formulation Evaluation Report, Locks and Dam No. 26 (Replacement)*, Vol. I (St. Louis: MVS, 1975).

Although consensus about the deteriorated state of the dam was nearly unanimous, there was no consensus about the best solution. Because of the district's cost estimates, based on the need for significant cofferdams and a temporary lock to allow continued navigation, it concluded that replacement was the best option. The cost of the temporary lock and the cofferdams would be approximately $200 million, thus driving up the cost of rehabilitation. The district also explored extensive grouting as a means to repair the structure, which was very expensive. In addition, pile driving during rehabilitation would result in vibrations that could further weaken the structure. Lastly, rehabilitation would be the equivalent of what Jester described as a "chrome-coated Model T." In other words, the Corps should not make massive expenditures on an outdated structure if it could construct a superior one for the same cost. However, others believed that the district had overestimated the cost of rehabilitation, that costly cofferdams and a temporary lock were not necessary, and that the Corps could repair the locks individually, using non-vibrationless techniques, without closing the river to commerce.[315]

The district responded to opponents by arguing that it had already explored all possible alternatives, concluding that replacement downstream was the best solution. While cheaper alternatives 'seemed viable on first glance, analysis revealed that there were serious engineering deficiencies in them and that correcting these deficiencies would dramatically increase the cost of rehabilitation. The debate concerning the best engineering solution for Lock and Dam No. 26 continued to be controversial, with each side believing its plan to be the best solution. From the Corps' perspective, no other group had invested more time, effort, and engineering expertise into evaluating the solutions to the problems at No. 26. However, in an effort to assuage those who were critical of the Corps' rehabilitation tests, in May 1977 the Corps entered into an agreement with the U.S. Department of Transportation (DOT), which had been critical of the plan, to conduct an 18-month testing program to resolve the uncertainties associated with rehabilitation plans. The study was set for completion in December 1978.[316]

The other issue surrounding the project was the impact of increasing the river's capacity. For the railroads, this impact was on the economy; for

---
[315] "Locks and Dam 26: Issues and Answers"; "Playing the Waiting Game with Locks and Dam 26," brochure (National Committee on Locks and Dam 26, N.D.) (MVS Archives); McKinney, Sutton, and Perez, "Rehabilitation Versus Replacement"; CBO, *Alton Locks and Dam*; USACE, *Locks and Dam No. 26 (Replacement), Supplement No. 2 to Design Memorandum No. 2, General Design Memorandum* (St. Louis: MVS, 1979).
[316] Ibid.

environmentalists the impact was on riverine ecology. Both groups based their claims on the 18-foot sill depth, a shifting bottleneck, and previous studies on a 12-foot channel. The Corps responded by pointing out that recent engineering studies supported using an 18-foot sill depth for ships with a nine-foot draft, which were 17 percent more efficient than a 14-foot sill. Since optimum sill depth in a 12-foot channel was between 21 and 25-feet, the Corps argued the sill depth did not reveal plans for a 12-foot channel. Concerning claims that greater locking capacity would lead to a shifting bottleneck, the Corps pointed out that No. 26 was located at a heavy traffic location that required greater capacity. Rather than a shifting bottleneck, ships delayed at No. 26 would move more quickly upriver to locks and dams that have more than enough capacity to meet these demands. The Corps also responded to accusations that its previous feasibility studies for a 12-foot channel revealed its intentions, noting that this study was merely one of numerous such studies that the Corps often undertakes to decide the feasibility of possible projects. This study concluded that the project was economically unfeasible and that the Corps would need specific congressional approval to proceed.[317]

In the months following the injunction, the district continued preparing a supplement EIS as well as a Formulation Evaluation Report to reevaluate to economic impacts of the project. The draft took into account the impact of the project on the entire upper river system as well as alternative modes of transportation as a viable alternative to replacing the dam. It reached the same conclusions as the first EIS – two 1,200-foot locks were necessary, and increased capacity would have minimal environmental impact. The district filed the draft supplement, the final EIS, and the Formulation Evaluation Report with the Council on Environmental Quality in June 1975. To offer the public an opportunity to review the project, the district scheduled two St. Louis public meetings for July and September 1975. In addition, it scheduled two public meetings in LaCrosse, Wisconsin, and St. Paul, Minnesota, in December 1975. Approximately 200 people, 32 of whom gave statements, attended the first meeting on July 21. Overall, the meeting revealed strong support for the project. However, many people requested additional time to review the EIS and Formulation Evaluation Report and a subsequent meeting to discuss the contents of these documents further. Another meeting took place on September 11 and 12, 1975. Approximately 300 people attended the meeting, 49 of whom made oral

---

[317] "Eighteen-foot Sill Depth Decision Made Based on Nine-foot Channel," and "Waterways Vs. Railroads," *Post-Dispatch* (Feb. 22, 1976); *Final EIS*.

statements. Once again, overall support for the project was strong, with 32 of the 49 speakers favoring it. Like previous discussions of the project, those who favored it felt that the increased capacity was necessary for economic growth, but those who opposed felt that it threatened the railroads and would have a negative environmental impact. The same was true of the letters sent by those reviewing the documents, as they revealed overall support for the project, with the exception of environmental and conservation groups, and the railroads.[318]

In August 1975, the Corps asked the Board of Engineers for Rivers and Harbors to review the project. By February 1976, the board had completed its review, recommending the replacement of two 1,200-foot locks project with a single 1,200-foot lock project that included provisions for a second lock in the future. The district agreed with the Board's recommendation, and planning was soon underway on a single 1,200-foot lock with an annual capacity of 86 million tons. In March, the Corps sent a draft recommendation to concerned governors and agencies for comment. In addition, the district began preparing a revised draft supplement EIS and a new draft EIS, both of which it filed with the Council on Environmental Quality on March 19. The single 1,200-foot lock proposal had a number of advantages, but the most important was that it would eliminate the primary reason for railroad and environmental opposition – the dramatic increase of the river's capacity. If the project would not dramatically increase the river's capacity, there was no need for system-wide analysis of environmental and economic impacts. The Secretary of the Army also withdrew his approval for the two-lock proposal under authority of Section 6 of the 1909 River and Harbor Act, eliminating the other reason why the court had granted the injunction on construction – lack of specific congressional approval. In July 1976, the Chief of Engineers forwarded his report to the Secretary of the Army recommending a single 1,200-foot lock with an estimated cost of $391 million. On August 24, the Secretary sent the report, along with comments, recommendations, and all other relevant studies, to Congress for review and approval. In addition, the Corps provided Congress with a Supplemental Economic Data Report that included updated and revised data on the project's cost-benefit analyses. The same day, the Corps also filed its new Final EIS with the Council on Environmental Quality. Congress began

---

[318] *Design Memorandum No. 11,*; *Draft Supplement EIS*; *Supplement No. 2 to DM No. 2*; Upper Mississippi River Basin Commission, *Replacement of Locks and Dam 26, Proceedings of Public Information Meetings* (Minn.: UMRBC, 1975).

discussing, debating, and listening to statements on the proposed project, but it would take another two years for Congress to make a decision.[319]

New Studies and Authorization

In the two years leading up to congressional authorization of the project, opponents and proponents articulated their arguments to Congress, and various groups undertook new studies analyzing the project. One outspoken agency was the DOT. It had already undertaken a review of the two-lock proposal, the findings of which it included in its September 1975 Advisory Report. This study questioned Corps economic analysis of the two-lock proposal, but concluded that a single 1,200-foot lock was necessary before the end of the century to meet future traffic demands. In addition, because it would take between eight and 11 years to complete the project, the DOT recommended that construction should begin within five years. The question was not whether the district should construct a 1,200-foot lock, but whether it should be a replacement or a rehabilitation project. Such engineering analysis was the subject of great controversy, as various proposals claimed to be able to rehabilitate the old structure for less than the Corps estimated. Concerning the effects of increased lock capacity on the railroads, the DOT concluded that a single 1,200-foot lock would not have a significant impact, but a two to three year comprehensive study was necessary to more precisely determine these effects.[320]

In a May 2, 1977 statement before the Senate Subcommittee on Water Resources, Secretary of Transportation Brock Adams suggested that further studies were necessary to determine the best course of action. This suggestion resulted in an 18-month joint study with the Corps that aimed at ending the controversy over replacement versus rehabilitation. The study was approved and scheduled for completion in December 1978. However, replacement proponents complained that numerous studies had already been conducted and new studies would cost the taxpayers, drive up the project's cost through inflation, and further delay it. Because cofferdams were a major contributor to the high cost of rehabilitation, the study explored the feasibility of doing repairs without them. In addition, it analyzed the structure's foundation to determine

---

[319] *Supplement No. 2 to DM No. 2*, Sec. I; Michael Isikoff, "Logjam breaking up at Alton locks and dam," *Illinois Issues* (Jan. 1979); McKinney, Sutton, and Perez, "Rehabilitation Versus Replacement"; *Izaak Walton League v. Marsh*.

[320] "Statement of Robert H. Binder, Ass. Sec. for Policy, Plans and International Affairs, DOT, before the Subcom. on Water Resources of the Sen. Pub. Works Com., concerning the replacement of Alton Locks and Dam," Probability of Failure folder (MVS Archives).

just how weak it was and to determine the best method of strengthening the soil characteristics. The most effective way to strengthen the soil was through chemical grouting, but such methods were very expensive, driving up the cost of rehabilitation to the point that it would cost nearly the same as replacement. Once again, Corps studies revealed that replacement was the best option.[321]

Another controversial study was the Cushing study, so-called because its principal consultant was Jerome J. Cushing, a civil engineer who had previously worked for the Harza Engineering Company, which provided an independent cost estimate for Lock and Dam No. 26. The Illinois DOT hired Cushing to serve as a consultant on its plan for constructing a new lock and rehabilitating the existing structure. The IDOT report, completed in March 1976, suggested the dam could be rehabilitated for approximately $46 million, a fraction of what the Corps estimated. The report also claimed its plan would take less time to complete and included plans for a second lock constructed without delaying waterborne commerce. In response to this study and other similar ones, the National Committee on Lock and Dam 26 hired Sverdrup and Parcel, a respected engineering firm, to review the studies. The firm's review was critical of the Cushing study's cost estimates and proposed engineering methods. The firm argued that once these engineering deficiencies and cost estimates were corrected, rehabilitation would cost nearly the same as replacement. With such conflicting opinions on the matter, determining the best option for Lock and Dam No. 26 was becoming an increasingly difficult task.[322]

During the spring and summer of 1977, the appropriate House and Senate committees held hearings on the merits of the project. While Congress debated the economic, environmental, and engineering issues associated with the proposal, another controversial issue emerged – user fees. In May 1977, Judge Richey lifted the temporary injunction because the Secretary of War had withdrawn Section 6 approval because the proposed facility would now contain only one 1200-foot lock, thus nullifying arguments about the effects of increased

---

[321] "Statement of Brock Adams, Sec. of Trans., before the Subcom. on Water Resources of the Sen. Com. on the Env. and Pub. Works, concerning Alton Locks and Dam authorization legislation and navigation user charges," Probability of Failure folder (MVS Archives); "Playing the Waiting Game with Locks and Dam 26," brochure (National Committee on Locks and Dam 26, N.D.) (MVS Archives); Isikoff, "Logjam breaking up"; The findings of the DOT and Corps study are discussed in McKinney, Sutton, and Perez, "Rehabilitation Versus Replacement," and in *Supplement No. 2 to Design Memorandum No. 2*, Sec. 2 and 6-03.

[322] Cushing, *Maintenance of Locks and Dam 26 (Alton, Illinois), Executive Summary*, 1976; "Playing the Waiting Game with Locks and Dam 26," brochure (National Committee on Locks and Dam 26, 1979); Questions for Deposition of Jerome Cushing, in deposition documents (MVS Archives). It should be noted that the Western Railroads Association, which was vehemently opposed to the project, previously employed Cushing as a consultant. Also, a group composed largely of supporters of the barge industry hired the engineering firm to analyze the various studies , the point being that these competing special interest groups often muddled the best engineering solution, and the Corps was often caught in the middle of these debates.

traffic. The issue over user fees was now the major impediment to congressional authorization of the project. Once Congress resolved this issue, it could approve the project and construction could begin. Railroads in the region had long argued that the barge industry had an unfair advantage because the federal government financed maintenance and improvements on the Upper Mississippi River System. Supporters of the barge industry argued that in the past the railroads had received huge federal land grants allowing them to expand at the expense of river transportation. Ultimately, politicians would decide the user fees issue on the floor of Congress. On June 22, 1977, Senator Pete Domenici of New Mexico agreed to sponsor a bill that would authorize the replacement project in exchange for a fuel-tax user fee. The debate now shifted to just how much the fee should be. Rail supporters wanted the tax to be high, forcing the barge industry to pay for all improvements to the river. Environmental groups also called for a high tax, with some wanting a fee of 63 cents per gallon on diesel. After intense lobbying and negotiations, Congress set the tax at 10 cents per gallon. The compromise resulted in Congress passing the Inland Waterways Revenue Act on October 21, 1978. In addition to authorizing construction of a single-lock replacement for Lock and Dam No. 26, the law had three other important provisions. First, it established a savings account that would cover approximately half the cost of the replacement project as well as providing funding for future projects. Second, the law charged the Upper Mississippi River Basin Commission to "prepare a comprehensive master plan for the management of the Upper Mississippi River System." Last, it provided for construction of a second lock, of a size to be determined, pending the findings of the study. With the law passed and the project approved, Congress appropriated funds for construction starting in October 1979.[323]

Although the project now had congressional approval, this was no guarantee that it would come to fruition. There was still the legal battle, as the plaintiffs filed an amended suit in response to recent events. The five-day trial commenced on September 10, 1979. The plaintiffs' allegations were essentially the same as they had been in 1974. However, they did add the charge that the

---

[323] *Izaak Walton League of America, Et Al. and Atchison, Topeka, and Santa Fe Railway Company, et al. v. Clifford R. Alexander, et al.* Civil Action No. 74-1190 (D.C. Cir. 1979); For an overview for the background and debate surrounding user fees, see Isikoff, "Logjam breaking up"; Todd Shallat, "Colossus Above St. Louis: Remaking the Mississippi at Melvin Price Locks and Dam," *Illinois Heritage* (Jul.-Aug., 2005); Tom Littlewood, "Clash of transportation interests basis of conflict at Alton locks and dam," *Illinois Issues* (Apr. 1977); "It's the Missouri Pacific vs. the Bargemen, and the prize is the coal and grain of the Great American Heartland," *St. Louis Magazine* (Sept. 1979). For the Corps' perspective on user fees, see Interview with Peterson and Michael Ruddy, Interview with Daniel Flippen, Sept. 3, 1984 (MVS Archives).

post-authorization decision to undertake the project ignored certain procedures and provided inadequate economic and environmental data. The Corps responded that Congress had made the decision with its specific approval. The court concurred, but ruled that the Corps should have held a post-authorization public meeting on the single-lock project. Concerning compliance with NEPA, the plaintiffs contended that the Corps did not consider three current proposals in the final EIS of 1976 and did not consider several other alternatives, including rehabilitation, investment in alternative transportation modes, and more efficient methods of congestion control. In addition, the plaintiffs held to their previous arguments, accusing the Corps of not adequately considering the environmental impacts of the increased traffic through the facility. Finally, they alleged that the Corps relied on "secret" data that prevented an adequate review of its records.[324]

After five days of testimony and rebuttal, Judge Richey ruled the Corps was guilty of violating its own regulations by not holding a post-authorization public meeting. However, he ruled in favor of the defendants on all other charges. He found that the administrative record was complete and that no "secret" data inhibited analysis of the EIS. He also ruled that the EIS adequately considered alternatives and that no system-wide EIS was necessary because the structure's capacity would not necessarily lead to a 12-foot channel project. Because NEPA required the Corps to study only impacts related to physical impacts, the court decided that if the EIS showed the project had no significant physical impacts, it had no significant environmental impacts. This meant that a more comprehensive, system-wide study would be superfluous, because NEPA only requires analysis of likely impacts and not all possible impacts. In light of the outcome of the trial, the environmental arguments against the project seemed to hold little weight. And some, such as Colonel Peterson, argued that the environmental issue was never significant because "the environment simply was not that affected. But the environment was used as a basis to marshal political support and to make the case in the courts against the replacement project." The plaintiffs appealed the decision, and the case came before the appellate court in January 1981. After reviewing the evidence, Judge Shelly Wright upheld the district court's ruling. The crux of the appellant's argument remained its

---

[324] A discussion of the legal disputes leading up to the October 1979 trial and the deposition and trial summary can be found in *Izaak Walton League and Railways v. Alexander*, in the MVS Archives. A summary of the preceding case as well as its appeal can be found in *Izaak Walton League v. Marsh*; Interview with Peterson.

contention that the Corps had violated NEPA and refused to reveal the methodology it used to determine the cost-benefit ratio of the project, but the judge quickly dismissed these claims as being without merit because not only had the Corps disclosed this methodology, it had actually helped appellants to "adapt the Corps' computer programs for use on appellants' computer system." She added that the "appellants have failed successfully to attack the Corps' conclusion that the physical impact of the project would be minor." She went on to say that although the appellants were able to produce two biological experts that supported these claims, "they were unable to identify any other experts who supported their claims." With the district court's ruling upheld, the Corps could now focus its attention on completing construction on the first phase of the project.[325]

Construction Proceeds

Construction on the first stage of the project began late in 1979. Completed in November 1980, the first contract for this stage was for revetment on the Illinois side to protect against the flow restrictions caused by the cofferdam. The next task was construction of the first stage cofferdam. The district's

Construction stages at Lock and Dam 26R

---
[325] Ibid.

Stage one construction

design memorandum called for a 25-acre cofferdam extending 1,000 feet, the largest ever constructed on the Mississippi. Once cofferdam construction was complete in December 1981, the dewatering process began, as contractors pumped approximately 100 million gallons of water a day from the site so that excavation could begin. Flooding did occur during excavation in the spring of 1982, but posed little threat, as the cofferdam was still relatively undeveloped at that time. By December 1982, excavation was complete, and pile driving and concrete work commenced, as crews began work driving the nearly 4,800 battered and vertical H-piles into the foundation material. These piles were

Second stage construction

Second stage cofferdam during October 1986 flood

the foundation on which the crews would construct the six-and-a-half tainter gate bays, representing the bulk of the superstructure.[326]

Although the Corps overcame the legal challenges to the project, other challenges arose that threatened to halt construction, namely inclement weather, which resulted in the loss of more than 97 workdays after construction began. In addition, scouring caused by rapid flows threatened the cofferdam with underseepage. Thankfully, the district possessed the foresight to address underseepage in its design memorandum, which included using a large rock beam upstream of the cofferdam to deflect flows.

Flooding of second stage cofferdam, 9 October 1986

Second stage construction of main lock, November 1987

Grouting around the structure also helped to address underseepage. The most severe threat to construction was that the river would overtop the cofferdam, causing a catastrophic failure. December 1982 posed the greatest threat, as the worst December flood on record caused the river to rise to within two feet of overtopping the cofferdam. As torrential rains continued to pour down and water levels continued to rise, the St. Louis District took the initiative to prevent a failure, and on December 3 issued orders to partially flood the cofferdam. This action delayed pile driving for nearly a month, but stabilized the structure. However, a reason for optimism soon emerged, as water levels began to drop, fostering hope that the project might narrowly escape a catastrophe. Maurice Risken, project manager for the first phase contract, expressed optimism when he stated that the crews had "suffered the worst the river can give us and we came through just fine." Flooding in the spring of 1983 also posed a threat, but thankfully the worst threats passed. The remaining construction of

---

[326] USACE, "Riverlands Area, Melvin Price Locks and Dam," (St. Louis: MVS, N.D.) (MVS Archives); "Navigation lock design becomes research project," *ENR* (Aug. 6, 1987); "Dewatering the Mississippi," *ENR* (Dec. 9, 1982); "Navigation lock design becomes research project," *ENR* (Aug. 6, 1987); USACE, "Opening the Waterways" Decommissioning Ceremony Invitation Packet (St. Louis: MVS 1990); USACE, "Salute to the River, Opening the Waterways, the Dedication of Melvin Price Locks and Dam," (St. Louis: MVS, 1994); "Army mud shoes beat Ol' Miss," *ENR* (Dec. 16, 1982).

stage one continued on schedule, reaching completion in February 1985. Stage two proceeded rather smoothly when compared to the challenges of the first stage. Crews completed the construction, dewatering, and excavation of the second stage cofferdam in January 1986. With the cofferdam completed, work began on the two-and-a-half gate bays and the main lock.[327]

During the construction stages of the project, Congress passed Public Law 97-118 in December 1981, officially designating the facility "Melvin Price Locks and Dam." This name would take effect immediately upon the termination of Price's term of service to the Congress. Price, a 21-term representative and staunch supporter of the project, passed away on April 22, 1988, upon which Congress named Lock and Dam No. 26 in his honor. In February 1990, the first lock on the structure became operational. That same year, the district tore down old Lock and Dam No.26, a structure that had played such a vital role on the river for a half century, officially replacing it with Melvin Price Lock and Dam.[328]

Corps projections for navigation growth proved accurate, as 80 million tons moved through the 86 million-ton lock in its first year of operation. In addition, construction of a second lock was underway, a project wrought with its own challenges and controversies. As described above, a second lock was part

Third stage construction of auxiliary lock

---
[327] Ibid.
[328] "Salute to the River."

of the original replacement plan. However, the controversy over the effects of the increase in navigation required the Corps to delay plans pending the results of further studies. The law that authorized the first lock – the Inland Waterways Revenue Act – included provisions for a second lock; however, approval of this lock was contingent on the outcome of a study on its environmental and economic impacts. Section 101 authorized the Upper Mississippi River Basin Commission to direct this study and use its findings to prepare a comprehensive master plan for the management of the Upper Mississippi River System. In addition to the commission, eleven other state and federal agencies participated in the study. The study would evaluate the various impacts of increased navigation resulting from a second lock and assess the system-wide rather than regional impacts of an increase in navigation. The study should determine whether a second lock was needed, and if so, what the optimum size of the lock should be. Shortly after Congress passed the law authorizing the master plan in October of 1978, the three-year study began.[329]

Last blast of old Lock and Dam 26

---

[329] Information on the annual tonnage at Mel Price Locks and Dam can be found at "Melvin Price Locks and Dam, Alton, Illinois," Web Page (*www.mvs.usace.army.mil/navigation1/melvin%20lock.html*, May 23, 2011); Upper Mississippi River Basin Commission, *Comprehensive Master Plan for the Management of the Upper Mississippi River System* (Minneapolis: UMRBC, 1982), Ch. 1; USACE, *Draft Environmental Impact Statement, Second Lock at Locks and Dam No. 26 (Replacement), Mississippi River, Alton, Illinois and Missouri* (St. Louis: MVS, 1986), Sec. 3. The first chapter provides an overview of the master plan and its history, objectives, and approach with a more detailed discussion of the study's analysis in the subsequent chapters. Documents pertaining to public review and the agency comments are in the second volume of the master plan.

On January 1, 1981, the commission completed its preliminary plan and submitted it to the public and the appropriate federal, state, and local agencies for comment and review. The plan identified the economic, environmental, and recreational needs of the river system, set objectives for meeting these needs, and recommended guidelines for meeting these objectives. Related to these studies was the impact of increased navigation, more specifically, the impact of a second lock. The study collected and analyzed data pertaining to the impacts of a second lock on other forms of transportation such as railroads, the economic benefits a second lock would have for the nation, and the environmental impacts of increased navigation. The study also investigated means to avoid or minimize these impacts. The district then discussed contents of the study in a series of public meetings held in the spring of 1981. In addition, a series of formal public meetings took place during November 1981, providing each affected state an opportunity to present formal responses to the study and afforded the commission an opportunity to alter to the study based on these comments and recommendations. On December 14, 1981, the commission approved the final report and sent the master plan to Congress for approval. However, approval of the second lock would take another three years.[330]

The master plan's conclusions and recommendations favored construction of a 600-foot lock. In addition, it recommended the project not be subject to NEPA. Concerning the system-wide environmental effects of the increase in the river's capacity, the study concluded these would be minimal. However, it recommended establishment of 10-year habitat rehabilitation, enhancement, and resource monitoring programs, discussed below. After nearly three years of debate, Congress passed the Supplemental Appropriations Act in August 1985. The law authorized construction of a 600-foot lock at Melvin Price and approved appropriations for the master plan's environmental management recommendations. In November 1986, Congress passed additional authorizing legislation in the Water Resources Development Act of 1986. Section 1103 authorized construction of the second lock and implementation of an environmental management program for the Upper Mississippi. One recommendation that Congress did not include was exemption from NEPA – the district would have to prepare an EIS for the second lock. Preparation of a draft EIS began soon after Congress passed authorizing legislation. The district completed its draft EIS and filed it with the Council on Environmental Quality in September

---

[330] *Comprehensive Master Plan*, Ch. 1; *Draft EIS, Second Lock*, Sec.3.

1986. Because the master plan had already studied the impacts of the second lock, the district used it as its primary reference document. Preparation of the draft EIS posed several challenges. One was that there were resource data gaps in the master plan that placed limitations on the study's understanding of the environmental consequences of increased navigation. The district addressed this problem by disclosing these data gaps. The Fish and Wildlife Service was also critical of limiting the scope of the draft EIS to impacts on the main stem of the Mississippi and Illinois Rivers and not tributaries. The master plan did not include such studies, so no data existed for the impact on tributaries. Lastly, an issue arose during the public hearings because engineering and design plans were proceeding before environmental management work had begun. To address this issue, the district coordinated its construction and design efforts with environmental management efforts so that both would take place concurrently.[331]

Once the district submitted the draft EIS, a controversy arose over mitigation. "The initial draft Environmental Impact Statement that we put out was pretty well rejected by all the ... agencies as being inadequate and incomplete because we did not identify levels of mitigation," stated then District Engineer Col. Daniel Wilson. In response to these criticisms, the district included all of them in a supplemental draft EIS filed in November 1987. After the supplemental draft EIS was returned with comments and suggestions, the district incorporated into the final draft EIS. However, the district still needed to define the level of mitigation that needed to occur, which was difficult to assess. Moreover, because data gaps existed, no accurate determination could be made without further studies. The district recommended undertaking a plan of study, which began in 1988, to address these issues and determine the proper level of mitigation. However, the Fish and Wildlife Service responded by creating a panel to prepare reports on the proper levels of mitigation, eventually arguing for an annual mitigation of around $29 to $78 million just for the second lock. Many viewed such costly proposals as excessive, especially considering the second lock did not increase the total capacity of Melvin Price Lock and Dam, but provided redundancy in case the main lock closed for a time. Environmentalists did not view the second lock in this way, but as a means for the Corps to increase river capacity. These unresolved issues and the possibility of a delay in

---

[331] *Draft EIS, Second Lock*, Sec. 1-Summary; Ruddy, Interview with Wilson.

the construction of the second lock hovered over the project when the district filed its final EIS in 1988.[332]

Construction on the third and final stage of the project was set to begin, and delays that prevented inclusion of the second lock in stage three construction would be costly. Once stage three was complete without the second lock, it would be far more expensive to go back and add the second lock later. However, the Corps and environmental groups worked together to solve the disagreement over the proper level of mitigation, finally decided at an August 26, 1988, interagency meeting with representatives from the Corps, including St. Louis District Engineer Col. James Corbin, and environmental groups, including the Izaak Walton League and the Fish and Wildlife Service. Those present made several agreements pertaining to the plan of study, eliminating the major impediment to construction of the second lock – mitigation. In February 1989, the district released the plan of study. Just over three years later, the $970 million structure with a capacity of approximately 142 million tons, was finally complete.[333]

The Environmental Management Program

In addition to studying the effects of a second lock, the Upper Mississippi River Basin Commission also undertook an environmental study of system, the results of which became part of the master plan's recommendations for the establishment of an environmental management program. This aspect of the master plan would become the major catalyst for establishment of the Corps' Environmental Management Program. However, interest in a program of environmental management on the river goes back even further than the master plan. In 1976, Congress passed a Water Resources Development Act, Section 117 of which included provisions for the Corps to "investigate and study, in cooperation with interested States and Federal Agencies, through the Upper Mississippi River Basin Commission the development of a river system management plan." The responsibility for carrying out these investigations, known as the Great River Resource Management (GRRM) study, fell on three Corps districts – St. Paul, Rock Island, and St. Louis – each of which represented a Great River Environmental Action Team. Each district's team was responsible

---
[332] Quote and discussion of mitigation can be found in Interview with Wilson; Interview with Flippen; *Final EIS, Second Lock*, Sec. 1.3; USACE, *Plan of Study, Navigation Effects of the Second Locks, Melvin Price Locks and Dam* (St Louis: MVS, 1991).
[333] *Plan of Study*; "Salute to the River."

for undertaking management studies within its section of the Upper Mississippi. St. Paul and Rock Island completed their studies in September and December 1980, respectively, and two years later, the St. Louis District completed its study. Each district submitted recommendations outlining ways to improve environmental management to the Board of Engineers for Rivers and Harbors. After reviewing these studies, the board made its recommendations to Congress. Although the GRRM study was a significant first step toward initiating an environmental management program, it was not a terminal study. In other words, it highlighted the fact that the only way to fully address the upper river's long-term environmental needs was to conduct additional studies. The long-term impact of the GRRM study was that many of its findings were included in the master plan (discussed below). However, the immediate impact of the GRRM studies was that their findings were incorporated into the Corps' maintenance program on the Upper Mississippi River, resulting in the environmental enhancement of operation and maintenance, dredging, and disposal activities for little additional cost.[334]

While the GRRM studies were ongoing, the Upper Mississippi River Basin Commission was initiating its own study, the findings and recommendations of which became part of the master plan. The authorization of the master plan came from the Waterways Revenue Act that authorized the construction of the replacement for Lock and Dam No. 26. Although the focus of this study was the impact of a second lock on the river system, its scope was not limited to this purpose, as it was also charged with studying the environmental needs of the river system and developing a program for environmental management and habitat rehabilitation and enhancement. Both the GRRM and master plan studies focused on the need for environmental management, but the GRRM study focused only on the Upper Mississippi, while the master plan focused on the entire upper river system. The completed master plan included recommendations for an initial 10-year environmental management program that would include a habitat rehabilitation and enhancement program, and a long-term resources monitoring program with a computerized inventory and analysis system. In response to these recommendations, Congress passed the Water Resources Development Act of 1986, also known as the "Upper Mississippi

---

[334] A discussion of the GRRM Study and its relationship to the master plan can be found in the following sources: *Comprehensive Master Plan*, Chapter 1; USACE, *Final EIS, Second Lock at Locks and Dam No. 26 (Replacement), Mississippi River, Alton, Illinois and Missouri*, Foreword; U.S. Cong. *Water Resources Development Act of 1976*, PL 94-587 (94th Cong., 2nd Sess.): Sec. 117.

River Management Act," which declared the Upper Mississippi System to be a nationally significant ecosystem and officially authorized the establishment of the Environmental Management Program (EMP).[335]

While the statutory basis for the EMP comes from Section 1103 of the 1986 Water Resources Development Act, the program received initial authorization in the 1985 Supplemental Appropriations Act. During this "early action" phase of the EMP, Congress appropriated $2.5 million for the newly established program and articulated the basic framework for the EMP. The subsequent authorization in the 1986 act outlined in detail the EMP's programmatic elements. The Corps responded by issuing a general plan to guide implementation. The guidelines included programs for habitat rehabilitation and enhancement, long-term resource monitoring, and computerized inventory and analysis of these resources, all of which were included in the master plan's recommendations. In addition, much like the GRRM study that preceded it, three Corps districts – St. Paul, Rock Island, and St. Louis – would manage the program. Congress also recognized the need for continual monitoring and reevaluation to adapt it in response to the changing needs of the ecosystem. Thus, when the authorization expired, the Corps and other cooperating agencies could offer recommendations that allowed the program to evolve each time Congress renewed authorization. Although the Corps holds overall program management responsibility, it is an overall multi-participant program in which a number of agencies, including the Corps, the U.S. Geological Survey, the Environmental Protection Agency, the Fish and Wildlife Service, and five states – Missouri, Illinois, Minnesota, Iowa, and Wisconsin – cooperate to improve, enhance, and manage the ecology of the entire Upper Mississippi River System.[336]

Between the 1985 and 2003, Congress allocated just over $247 million for the EMP. Congress assigned the largest proportion of these funds to Habitat Rehabilitation and Enhancement Projects (HREP). Between 1985 and 2003, Congress allocated $145 million for habitat projects; and in 2009 alone, Congress allocated $23 million for such projects. As of 2010, Congress had allocated just over $241 million for habitat projects out of the nearly $391 million in total EMP funds. However, these funds meant little if the programs they supported did not affect the necessary environmental impacts. The primary

---

[335] *Comprehensive Master Plan*, Chapter 1; *Final EIS, Second Lock*, Foreword; USACE, *Rock Island, Report to Congress, An Evaluation of the Upper Mississippi River System Environmental Management Program* (Rock Island: MVR, 1997), Ch. 1.
[336] *Rock Island, Report to Congress*, Exec. Sum. and Ch. 1.

responsibility for ensuring program efficacy and policy implementation fell on the Corps, particularly habitat projects, for which the Corps was the lead agency. This HREP effort included the planning, design, construction, and monitoring of projects that enhance or rehabilitate fish and wildlife habitats. The positive impacts of HREP can be seen in the various habitat projects that each participating district successfully completed. As of 2010, the EMP has completed 53 HREPs, improving fish and wildlife habitat on approximately 95,100 acres. An additional 34 pending projects are in various stages of design, and, once completed, these will produce around 80,000 additional acres of habitat.[337]

The St. Louis District implemented numerous HERPs on its stretch of the Mississippi, which begins just below Lock and Dam 22 at Saverton, Missouri and continues until the confluence of the Mississippi and Ohio Rivers. In addition, the district implemented habitat projects on the first 80 miles of the Illinois River and the lower 35 miles of the Kaskaskia River. Each of these projects took into account the unique circumstances of a particular area and then employed a variety of techniques used in various combinations to rehabilitate and enhance the environment. These techniques included dredging selected backwaters and side channels to restore aquatic habitat, constructing dikes and beams to prevent heavy silt loads from entering habitat areas, and building islands to decrease wind-generated disturbances, thus reducing turbidity and creating habitat for small aquatic plants and animals. By 2000, the district was receiving $3 million annually for habitat projects, with a great potential for continued program growth. As of 2000, the district had used these funds to complete seven projects, including HREP areas at Pharrs Island and Swan Lake, totaling more than $27 million worth of environmental improvements. Completed in 1992, Pharrs Island was the second HREP project that the Corps undertook. The area consisted of a 605-acre complex of four islands of bottomland hardwood timber and backwater and interior wetland habitats. Silt deposits had reduced the productivity of this once rich wetland by filling in portions of the backwaters, which provided habitat for various species, including migrating waterfowl and wintering bald eagles. To address this issue, the district constructed a dike to protect the remaining wetland habitat from

---

[337] Ibid; USACE, *Upper Mississippi River Restoration Environmental Management Program, 2010 Report to Congress* (Rock Island: MVR, 2010), Exec. Sum.

the influx of sediments and create a slackwater habitat for fish to spawn and mature.[338]

As of 2011, the district had completed eight HERPs and had another 16 awaiting approval, in planning, or under construction. Of completed projects, one of the most ambitious was Swan Lake, approved in 1993 and complete in 2001. The lake extended eight miles along the Illinois River, providing an important backwater habitat for spawning, rearing, and wintering fish, as well as migratory birds. However, sedimentation, erosion, and fluctuating water levels had reduced the size of this important habitat. Without addressing the problem, sedimentation would reduce the surface area of the lake by 30 percent within 50 years. The district addressed this problem using dredging, dikes, levees, water control and fish passage structures, and hillside sediment control basins, completed at a cost of $15 million. Through their efforts, the district reduced sedimentation and ensured continued existence of a lake that provides 2,900 acres of the vital wetland habitat. However, reducing sedimentation and its buildup in the lake is an ongoing challenge, one that would remain unmet were it not for EMP and district efforts.[339]

In addition to HREP, the EMP conducts a Long Term Resource Monitoring Program that allows the Corps to use environmental monitoring, research, and modeling with data management to better manage the river and implement habitat rehabilitation and enhancement projects more efficiently. One advantage of monitoring resources is that the EMP can analyze the data collected and use it to document system-wide ecological trends and investigate specific resource problems, such as the impacts of navigation on the environment, as well as numerous other problems affecting riverine ecology, such as sedimentation, water level fluctuation, and lack of aquatic vegetation.[340]

These are only a few examples of EMP projects that led to the enhancement and restoration of over 95,000 acres of vital habitat as of 2010. Numerous projects are either under construction or planned for future construction. In response to the overwhelming success of the program, as detailed in the 1997 report to Congress evaluating the EMP, Congress reauthorized the project in

---

[338] "Corps environmental work gets a boost through UMRS-EMP," *Esprit* (Jan. 2000); USACE, "Swan Lake," brochure (Rock Island: MVR, N.D.); USACE, "Pharrs Island," brochure (Rock Island: MVR, N.D.); "The District and the Environment and the Planning Connection, Environmental Management," *Esprit* (Sept. 1995).
[339] USACE, "Upper Mississippi River System Environmental Management Program Post-construction Performance Evaluation Report 2010 for Swan Lake Habitat Rehabilitation and Enhancement Project," (MVS: St. Louis, 2010), 2-26.
[340] *Upper Mississippi River Restoration EMP*, Exec. Sum.

Environmental demonstration area at Riverlands

the 1999 Water Resources Development Act. The law also required that the Corps submit a report to Congress every six years, outlining the achievements of the program, future plans, and changes needed to ensure the continuing success of the program. Part of what has made the program so successful has been its flexibly, as its continues to evolve to meet both present and future environmental needs. The irony of the program is that although it is the most successful program of environmental rehabilitation and enhancement in the nation's history, the program itself was the result of the replacement of the Alton dam, a project so vehemently opposed by environmental groups because they feared the detrimental impacts the replacement structure would have on the environment. Such fears proved illusory, but only because of the significant and ongoing efforts to develop environmental programs. Through cooperation with other agencies, the district was able to develop similar programs that went past mitigation of the lock and dam to address environmental planning for the river as a whole.[341]

---

[341] Ibid.

National Great Rivers Museum

On October 15, 2003, seven years after initial funding for the project began, approximately 300 people gathered to celebrate the opening of the National Great Rivers Museum at Melvin Price Locks and Dam. The $5.2 million, 12,000 square foot museum is considered the "crown jewel" of the Corps 11 regional visitor centers across the nation. The museum was possible because a number of federal, state, and private agencies came together in a cooperative effort to achieve a singular goal: telling the story of the Mississippi River. The two primary groups overseeing the project were the Corps and the non-profit Meeting of the Rivers Foundation, both of which saw the museum as an opportunity to educate the public on the economic, industrial, environmental, cultural and recreational significance of the river. While much of the public is aware that the Mississippi plays a significant role in their lives, few people truly understand just how vital a role the river played in the history of the nation and how far-stretching the impact of the river has been and continues to be on their lives. In order to educate the public on the extent of the river's impact, the museum uses numerous educational resources and exhibits that tell visitors the multi-faceted history of the river from a variety of perspectives. In addition, the museum educates visitors on the role the Corps has played and continues to play on the history of the river, thus providing a history not only what the Corps has done for the river, but why the Corps has done it. Exhibits have included a larger scale model of a meandering river outside the museum and a micro-model complete with river engineering structures, both of which have helped visitors to better understand how the river works and the role the Corps river engineering structures have played in shaping the river. The museum also offers over 20 interactive exhibits, including the Steer the Barge, which allows visitors to steer a tow stimulator, and a miniature water- management model in which visitors can attempt to control water levels by adjusting the flow through a series of miniature dams. If visitors want to see how the real thing works, they can take a tour of Melvin Price Locks and Dam, which shows visitors how the structure works and explains what a vital role it has played in creating and maintaining a pool essential for commercial navigation. In addition to educating visitors about the navigational and cultural history of the river, the museum offers numerous exhibits and educational opportunities for both children and adults who want to better understand the environmental importance of the river and the fragile ecological balance that exists between humans and the numerous species of fish, plants, and wildlife that live in and around the river.

View inside the National Great Rivers Museum

19

Environmental River Engineering

In June 1972, a diverse group that included biologists from state and federal conservation agencies, as well as river engineers from the St. Louis District, set forth on the first ever Mississippi coordination trip to discuss the present and future environmental health of the Mississippi River. This annual coordination trip has since become a tradition in the St. Louis District, with literally dozens of citizens representing a diversity of interests making the trip. The journey begins in St. Louis, Missouri, and continues for two days as an eclectic mix of engineers, biologists, towboat captains, and government representatives journey down the river on a trip that Claude Strauser describes as nothing short of "magical." No one could understand this magical event better than Strauser, a long-time district river engineer who fathered the trip, witnessing its evolution from a small gathering of engineers and biologists to an entirely new branch of engineering called "environmental river engineering." However, relations between these diverse groups were not always so amicable. When the event first began in the early 1970s, few could agree about what constituted a healthy river. For engineers, it meant maintaining a safe and dependable navigation channel, as mandated by Congress; for environmentalists, a healthy river was one that was rich in biological and habitat diversity, and any effort to improve

Mississippi coordination trip

the river should start with improving its biological health. The passage of the National Environmental Protection Act (NEPA) forced these two seemingly incompatible groups – river engineers and biologists – to come together to coordinate and discuss how the goals of maintaining navigation and protecting the environment could somehow co-exist. The story of this evolving relationship and the engineering evolution that occurred because of it is the story of environmental river engineering.[342]

Environmental river engineers look to Col. James Simpson, district engineer from 1873 to 1880, as one of the most important sources of their engineering philosophy. Although Simpson himself did not have environmental goals in mind when he wrote that any "permanent improvement must of necessity be designed and executed in entire harmony with the natural laws of the river," modern river engineers applied this philosophy to the plethora of challenges they faced after the passage of NEPA. When Simpson arrived in St. Louis, the Mississippi had nearly doubled in width, as the once narrow and deep natural state of the river had given way to wide and shallow state that impeded commercial navigation. In 1881, Congress authorized the Corps to maintain a dependable eight-foot navigation channel on the Middle Mississippi, thus beginning a century-long effort to reverse the effects of human activity along the Mississippi by deepening the river. For the stretch of river above St. Louis, the Corps accomplished this through a series of locks and dams and by dredging. Below St. Louis there were the challenges of the open river. Erosion, sedimentation, meandering channels, and dangerous river bends all presented unique challenges for the river engineer. To combat these problems, engineers designed dikes, revetments, and various other river training structures. Although considered permanent, these structures were only temporary solutions, and regular dredging was still necessary. If engineers were to develop permanent solutions, they would need to act as Simpson had suggested, using the natural laws of the river to improve the channel. By the late 1960s, the Corps had successfully returned the river to something very close to its original physical dimensions. But shortly thereafter Congress passed NEPA, and the Corps would soon have to reevaluate the improvements that had helped it to achieve this goal. From that day forward, it was no longer enough for the Corps to merely maintain a safe and dependable navigation channel; it had to maintain it in an environmentally sensitive manner. Engineers would have to

---

[342] "Middle Mississippi Coordination Trip," *Esprit* (Aug. 2000); Daly and Zoeller Interview with Strauser.

take Simpson's philosophy and apply it to an entirely new set of challenges that required them to use the natural laws of the river to improve both navigation and the environment.[343]

The First Coordination Meeting

In 1970, shortly after the passage of NEPA, the Missouri Department of Conservation contacted the district regarding the environmental impacts of its numerous river engineering structures. Engineers knew quite well the navigational advantages of these structures, but they knew very little about their environmental impacts. So biologists and engineers began evaluating these impacts and discovered that the issues affecting the environment were very similar to those affecting navigation: erosion and sedimentation. From a navigational perspective, eroding banklines meant a wider river that was shallower and not as conducive for navigation. Erosion also led to increased sedimentation, thus clogging the navigation channel and requiring costly dredging to remove. In addition to sedimentation and erosion, the river channel often tried to take shortcuts, especially around sharp river bends, by eroding the bank and trying to carve out a new channel. To correct this, the Corps constructed revetments that stabilized the bankline. Although this effort saved the main channel and prevented a new one from developing, it created dangerous currents that were perilous to navigate. Moreover, it caused sediment to accumulate on the inner bank, thus narrowing the channel around river bends and forcing the current downward where it scoured out an excessively deep and narrow navigation channel.[344]

For biologists, erosion and sedimentation were just as harmful as they were for engineers, but for different reasons. One problem was that erosion increased the amount of sediment in the river. Each year the Mississippi carried hundreds of millions of tons of sediment deposited in the Gulf of Mexico or in the river itself. River engineers tried to control where and how much sediment accumulated by designing and building structures that altered the river's flow. Before the passage of NEPA, Congress mandated that the Corps maintain a safe and dependable navigation channel, so engineers designed structures in accordance with this charge. Although such a design criterion enhanced the

---

[343] USACE, *Environmental River Engineering on the Mississippi* (St. Louis: MVS, 1995).
[344] *Environmental River Engineering*; USACE, "Bendway Weirs," brochure (MVS, 1993); "River Engineering," Web Page (*www.mvs.usace.army mil/arec/basics.html*, June 30, 2011).

navigability of the river, it did little to enhance the environment. Because these structures directed quicker flows into the main channel, sediments accumulated in slow moving, shallow areas, converting aquatic habitats into terrestrial ones. Sedimentation, for biologists, was precisely this process of converting habitats, a process that they viewed as detrimental because it led to a homogeneous rather than diverse riverine ecology. A homogeneous river ecology is less healthy than a diverse ecology because it does not provide enough habitats for species to thrive. For example, small fish need shallow areas with vegetation for protection from predators. Without such protection, they have less chance of maturing, and the river has less diversity. Environmentalists believed that, although river engineers had designed structures that returned the river to its natural dimensions, they had done so in a way that did not increase the river's ecological diversity. The challenge for river engineers was designing and modifying navigational structures to enhance the environment while carrying out the congressional mandate of maintaining the navigability of the Mississippi.[345]

NEPA was essentially the opening page in a new chapter of the Corps' history, but the precise nature of this new chapter was undetermined, as a number of inherent difficulties accompanied the new law. One problem was that the law was vague. "Nobody really knew how to implement it," Strauser pointed out. It said "you will coordinate and consult," but it gave no precise instructions as to how organizations were to carry out this mandate. In the St. Louis District, the task of coordinating and consulting with various conservation agencies fell on the shoulders of the young Strauser. With this task in hand, Strauser sought the advice of Jack Niemi, then chief of Project Management. He asked Niemi what the law meant by "coordinate and consult," and Niemi, just as puzzled by the requirements as other agencies under the umbrella of NEPA, replied that he did not think that there was anyone who really knew exactly what this meant, "but your job is to try to figure out what these fellows want, understand what they want, and try to develop some sort of dialogue." By "these fellows," Niemi meant state and federal agencies, such as the Missouri and Illinois Departments of Conservation and the U.S. Fish and Wildlife Service, with whom the district would soon schedule a coordination and consultation meeting.[346]

---

[345] *Environmental River Engineering*; Jack Niemi and Claude Strauser, "Environmental River Engineering," *PIANC Bulletin* No. 73 (1991).
[346] Daly and Zoeller interview with Strauser; "St. Louis District Chronology" (MVS Archives); "Using the river's magic," *Southeast Missourian* (June 21, 2007); Video interview with Claude Strauser on annual Environmental Coordination Trip on the Mississippi River (*www.semissourian.com/gallery/1855/*, Jun. 30, 2011); "Environmental River Engineering," *Esprit* (Sept. 1996); "Middle Mississippi Coordination Trip."

This initial meeting was far from congenial, as both sides simply talked at one another rather than actually communicating. As a result, each representative would speak his mind and defend his own organization without regard for the opinions of others. This rather adversarial relationship did not facilitate the cooperation necessary to affect permanent and positive environmental changes on the river. Another major impediment to constructive communication was that both sides were involved in "either/or" discussions. Engineers must "either" protect the navigational and economic interests of the river "or" the environmental interests, but both goals seemed mutually incompatible. The first step away from mere talking and toward discussion required both engineers and environmentalists to recognize that they were both ultimately working toward the same goal – improving the river. In an effort to overcome the communication barrier between engineers and environmentalists, the district organized a coordination trip on the Middle Mississippi. The district held the first trip, comprising six state and federal officials, in June 1972. This coordination trip served two functions. First, it broke down the communication gap that existed between the various representatives, allowing them to come together in a more informal setting better suited for amicable communication. The other advantage of the trip was that it allowed a unique opportunity for officials from environmental agencies to play an active role in the process of improving the river. Rather than relying on second hand knowledge and observing from a distance, officials coordinating with the district could now experience the impacts of their suggestions first hand. Once officials began playing a more active role in improving the river, they began to recognize that their goals were not so disparate after all. However, the positive relationship that would eventually develop as a result of the this cooperative effort would take several more years to materialize.[347]

The initial impact of these early coordination trips was that biologists from the participating agencies were able to work with engineers to develop a set of objectives for improving the navigational and environmental well-being of the river. Engineers understood their general objective of maintaining navigation in an environmentally sensitive manner, but it was not yet clear how they could accomplish this. So, the district adopted a team approach, allowing biologists to explain environmental problems and engineers to develop structural solutions to these problems. The primary environmental problem that biologists wanted

---

[347] Ibid.

the district to address was the lack of habitat diversity on the river. Biologists explained that a healthy riverine ecology must have a balance of the four primary habitats: fast water, slow/quiet water, wetted edge, and terrestrial. Once engineers were aware of this environmental objective, they began working to develop engineering solutions that promoted diversity without compromising navigation. This objective initiated the design and construction of numerous experimental structures, the first of which was a notched dike that engineers completed shortly before the first annual Mississippi coordination trip in June 1972. This trip set the precedent for how engineers and biologists would coordinate and consult in the decades to come. Typically, they looked at particularly troubled areas of the river and discussed a five-year plan for improving these areas, laying out in detail the planned improvements. In this way, the program would evolve to meet the dynamic river's ever changing needs in the decades to come, with engineers eventually designing and implementing more than 200 modifications that significantly improved the ecological health of the river without sacrificing navigational needs.[348]

Environmental River Engineering Experiments

Besides facilitating better communication and setting a precedent for future meetings, this first trip allowed biologists to actually observe with their own eyes the impacts of a structure that they themselves had suggested. This structure was a notched dike, which biologists suggested as a possible beneficial modification in 1971. Fishery biologists were particularly concerned with the accumulation of sediment in dike fields. This sediment converted aquatic habitats to terrestrial, decreasing the biological diversity of the river. Biologists hoped that by placing notches in dikes, water could move through the dike fields, thereby reducing sedimentation and the conversion of habitat. The district experimented with this modification at a dike field just below Ste. Genevieve, Missouri. Although it did not work as hypothesized, it produced results that were more beneficial than expected. Rather than merely preventing accumulation of sediment and creating a flow path, it allowed development of all four primary habitats. A further benefit was that it allowed biologists and conservation agencies to see that district engineers took them seriously. This was an important step toward breaking down the communication barrier and

---

[348] "Environmental River Engineering"; Daly and Zoeller interview with Strauser; "Using the river's magic," *Southeast Missourian*; Video interview with Strauser; "Middle Mississippi Coordination Trip."

showing biologists that engineers were working hard to improve the riverine ecology.[349]

Notched dikes on the Mississippi River

Notched dikes

---

[349] *Environmental River Engineering*; Niemi and Strauser, "Environmental River Engineering"; Daly and Zoeller Interview with Strauser; "St. Louis District Chronology"; "Environmental River Engineering."

To assess the engineering efficacy of the notched dikes, the district contracted the University of Missouri-Rolla's Institute of River Studies to collect engineering data on the structures. The Missouri Department of Conservation collected the environmental data on the structures. The data from both studies showed that the biological diversity in the notched dike fields tested was greater than at traditional dike fields. In addition, this increased diversity did not diminish the navigability of the river. The UM-Rolla study concluded that "the goal of providing habitat diversity around navigation structures…while at the same time preserving an acceptable navigation channel has been achieved in this study area." The results of these studies proved that the goals of engineers and biologists were not incompatible.[350]

The initial notched dike structure was the first of numerous modified designs that engineers implemented on the river. These structures were the product of years of experimentation, modification, and analysis by the district in cooperation with the Missouri and Illinois Departments of Conservation and the Fish and Wildlife Service. To reach the optimum design criteria, engineers and biologists worked together experimenting with and evaluating a variety of notch sizes, shapes, and locations. As a result, these designs constantly evolved along with the environmental river engineering program itself. The only way for engineers at the time to determine the most effective modification was to conduct field tests on the river itself, so while later engineers would have the advantage of using micro-models, engineers during this early stage often had to use the river itself as their test model. Typically, engineers would design a modification, implement it on the river, and then compare its impacts to the data collected from traditional structures. Biologists would then evaluate the structural modification to determine if it effectively created diversity of habitats. To make matters even more complex, the dynamics of the river required engineers to constantly modify structures in different ways to meet the unique challenges that each section of the river presented. Thus, one type of notched dike modification might work at one location, but another location might require a completely different modification. Considering the multitude of challenges facing environmental river engineers at the time, they needed a great deal of freedom to test experimental modifications on the river itself, and thankfully, as Strauser points out, the district gave engineers "tremendous amount of latitude" to do just that.[351]

---
[350] Niemi and Strauser, "Environmental River Engineering"; Daly and Zoeller Interview with Strauser.
[351] *Environmental River Engineering*; Niemi and Strauser, "Environmental River Engineering."

Soon after, the district began experimenting with other nontraditional structures, such as stepped-up dikes, chevron dikes, and off-bankline revetment. Engineers designed stepped-up dike fields so that each dike rose like a staircase, increasing two feet over the previous one. This innovation used the river's energy to reduce the amount of sediment deposited in the field by pushing sediment out of the areas around the submerged dikes. As the river rose, a higher dike received the impact of the river's energy and removed the accumulated sediment from around the lower dike. This process continued as the river rose until the energy of flow cleared out the excess sediment from the entire dike field. As a result of reduced sedimentation, these fields contained a greater diversity of habitats. When needed, river engineers further modified these structures by adding notches to the stepped-up dikes, creating even greater habitat diversity. Chevron dikes it adopted as a method of improving navigation by scouring the channel from the center of the channel. In addition to reducing sedimentation, the chevron dikes created small islands between the dikes, sometimes aided by dredge material deposition, which served as valuable wildlife habitats. Moreover, the rocks in the dikes provided important habitat for various microorganisms that many fish depend on for food. The overall impact of these structures was to provide for all four primary habitats, thus facilitating greater ecological diversity.[352]

Chevron dikes

Construction of chevron dike

Environmental modifications to revetment were another important innovation. Engineers used revetment to stabilize banks that were susceptible to erosion. Typically, engineers did this by covering banks below the waterline with protective mattresses, removing vegetation grading the bank above the

---

[352] Niemi and Strauser, "Environmental River Engineering"; *Environmental River Engineering*; "River Engineering," Web Page (*www.mvs.usace.army.mil/arec/basics.html*, June 30, 2011); "Arches in the river aid navigation."

Off-bankline revetments

waterline to produce the desired slope, and then covering the bank with rock or concrete. Traditional revetment used rocks of a uniform size and distributed them in a uniform way. However, biologists felt that this uniformity did not provide the necessary diversity of habitats, so environmental river engineers began designing revetment to include greater variation that provided a greater diversity of habitats. A further innovation that created even greater habitat diversity was off-bankline revetment. Conservationists opposed revetment because it required removal of trees and vegetation. However, the alternative –

Dike using various sizes of rocks allowing for a greater diversity of habitats

leaving the riverbank in a natural state – led to erosion. Off-bankline revetment provided a solution that allowed vegetation to remain along the banklines while protecting banks from erosion. It did this by placing rock just off the bank, creating a side channel between the bank and the revetment. These innovations protected banks from erosion in a way that improved habitat diversity. An early 1980s study led by the Missouri Department of Conservation compared large-stone to smaller-stone revetment and natural riverbanks. The study concluded that at the four sites evaluated, larger stone accounted for 52 percent of the total weight of fish caught, while the smaller stone accounted for 21 percent. The two natural banks accounted for just 15 percent and 12 percent of the total weight respectively. Thus, the district's modifications created habitats that provided even greater species diversity than at natural banklines.[353]

The district introduced numerous other innovative modifications to the Middle Mississippi, such as notched closure structures and hard points. Because the Corps mandate was to maintain the navigation channel, river engineers blocked flows into side channels to ensure the river's energy flowed into the main channel. This redirected flow reduced sedimentation in the main channel, but it caused side channels to clog with sediment, thus converting aquatic habitats to a terrestrial ones. To address this problem, the district developed notched closure structures. These structures contained notches that dip below the water, allowing flow to continue through the side channel. Because flow continued through the side channel, a diversity of habitats flourished. In addition, these structures allowed enough of the river's energy to be directed into the main channel to maintain navigation. Hard point structures, which river engineers introduced to deepen side channels, created scour holes

Notched closure structure

---

[353] Ibid; "River Engineering," Web page.

that provided important deep-water habitats that were essential for many fish species. The implementation of notched closures and hard points resulted in side channels becoming one of the most important areas on the river, providing all four primary habitats to many important aquatic species.[354]

One development that had enormous navigational and environmental benefits was the bendway weir. Developed initially to widen river bends, as discussed previously, these angled underwater rock weirs had greatly reduced sedimentation in bends, widened the river, and eliminated dangerous flanking movements by tows traveling through the bends. However, the environmental benefits of the weirs were equally profound. The Corps conducted hydroacoustic surveys of the fish populations at bendways between 1992 and 1995, which showed that the population density is approximately twice as high as the population at bends without weirs. A 1996 survey conducted by the UM-Rolla's Institute of River Studies yielded even more impressive results, showing that fish populations at the three bends it tested were an average of 13 times higher than at the one bend studied that did not have weirs. The reason the weirs were so environmentally successful was that they created all four primary habitats by widening the channel. In addition to the benefits for aquatic species, the sand bar on the inner portion of the bend provided an important habitat for the endangered Least Tern.[355]

One challenge for the environmental river engineering program was developing methods to accurately test experimental modifications in a practical, timely, and cost efficient manner. Engineers essentially had two options: test experimental structures using the river itself as a model, or use large-scale models, such as those at WES, but both options had inherent flaws. The cost and time required to conduct field experiments made this option impractical for assessing and meeting the numerous needs of the river. Engineers had to design and construct modifications, wait for the river's reaction to the modifications, and then evaluate the impacts and make modifications as needed. Despite these challenges, environmental river engineers in the district had used this method rather successfully throughout the 1970s and 1980s. The other option

---

[354] *Environmental River Engineering*; "River Engineering," Web page.
[355] "Hydroacoustic fish sampling of bendway weirs," *Esprit* (Sept. 1996); *Bendway Weirs on the Mississippi River*, pp. 38-49; Institute of River Studies, University of Missouri-Rolla, *Fish Populations in Bendway Weir Fields, Results of the November 1996 Hydroacoustic Surveys Performed on the Middle Mississippi River* (St. Louis: MVS, 1997); T.M. Keevin, G.L. Hempen, R.D. Davinroy, R.J. Rapp, M.D. Petersen, and D.P. Herzog, 2002 "The use of high explosives to conduct a fisheries survey at a bendway weir field on the Middle Mississippi River," *Proceedings of the Twenty-Eighth Annual Conference on Explosives and Blasting Technique, Las Vegas, Nevada, Feb. 10-13, 2002* (Cleveland: International Society of Explosives Engineers, 2002): 381-391.

for engineers was to use large-scale models at the Waterways Experiment Station (WES). Although these models made a profound impact on engineering designs, they were often impractical for smaller projects because some models were as large as a football field, expensive to operate, and time consuming, with some experiments taking months to complete. Even though both options had shortcomings, the complexities of moving water and sediment flow required engineers to rely on them. Unfortunately, there were no simple rules or set of equations that engineers could use to analyze sediment flows or see how they impacted wildlife, so they had to conduct real-life experiments to assess each case individually. These tiresome techniques led many engineers to hypothesize about possible solutions to the problem[356]

As discussed previously, in 1993, Rob Davinroy tested a concept for micro-models that were smaller and less expensive and time-consuming to operate than large physical models at WES or experiments in the river itself. In response to this revolutionary technology, the St. Louis District immediately began developing plans to use it extensively to address many of the river's environmental problems. Through the work of the Applied River Engineering Center, micro-modeling had a profound impact on environmental river engineering and the relationship between biologists and engineers. In the past, one of the reasons a communication gap existed between engineers and biologists was that they spoke different languages. When combined with the evolved relationship between biologists and engineers facilitated by the annual coordination trips, micro-models allowed both sides to experience the changes on the river and watch it improve over time. Engineers no longer had to rely on complex technical reports to communicate their analysis of the river. Instead, representatives from conservation agencies used the model to explain what changes needed to occur on the river, and then the engineers actually showed the impacts to the biologists. Because both sides were able to cooperate and communicate, a team mentality developed that allowed positive relationships and even friendships to develop. These congenial relationships were the result of a transition that began in the 1970s. When both sides first began talking, their conversations were always in the form of "either/or". In these debates

---

[356] Robert Davinroy, *Physical Sediment Modeling of the Mississippi River on a Micro Scale* (Master's thesis, University of Missouri-Rolla, 1994): 4-13 on physical models on the Mississippi and 14-49 on a discussion of the inherent problems with physical models and analyzing sediment transportation; also USACE, *St. Louis District, Environmental Documentation* (St. Louis: MVS, 2006): Ch. 7, for further discussion of the engineering difficulties involved in analyzing sediment transportation on the Mississippi; "Managing sedimentation using micro modeling," Esprit (Sept. 1996); Robert Davinroy, "River Replication," *Civil Engineering* (July 1999).

there was always a winner and a loser because protecting the environment and maintaining navigation seemed to be two incompatible goals. However, over the years these debates evolved into discussions in which "and" replaced "either/or", thus allowing both sides to come to the realization that the simultaneous environmental and navigational health of the river was possible.[357]

The Applied River Engineering Center quickly proved its success. Micromodels allowed engineers to try nontraditional and experimental alternatives that would otherwise be too impractical to attempt. Because of their speed and cost efficiency, engineers could experiment with alternatives that allowed them to develop the optimum design. For example, biologists were worried about a side channel of the Mississippi known as Santa Fe Chute. This was an important habitat for aquatic life, but because of sedimentation, it was in danger of becoming terrestrial. Engineers and biologists used micro-modeling to develop

Strauser receiving the Presidential Award for Design Excellence from President Bill Clinton

---

[357] Daly and Zoeller Interview with Strauser; Davinroy, "River Replication."

a solution to this problem. They found that installation of nine alternating dikes would restore habitat diversity to the channel. This area now provides a rich diversity of habitats that are essential for a healthy riverine ecosystem. This technology also allowed the district to develop a solution to sedimentation problems at Bolter's Bar, eliminating the need for dredging while at the same time allowing water to continue to flow into the biologically important side channels.[358]

Early in his career, Strauser was having a discussion with fellow river engineer Jimmy Graham, who was on the verge of retirement just as Strauser's career was beginning. However, before ending his career, he passed along to Strauser one final piece of advice for the district's future river engineers: to leave the river a better place than it was when they found it. For the next four decades, the environmental river engineers of the St. Louis District pursued this objective with gusto. And just like Graham and the district's other engineers, they pass this objective on to future engineers who will continue to work in response to the constantly evolving needs of a dynamic river, working always to leave it better than they found it. While these engineers will come and go, their story will continue because of the mark each of them leaves on the river.[359]

---

[358] *Environmental River Engineering*; "Managing sedimentation using micro modeling," *Esprit* (Sept. 1996); Davinroy, "River Replication"; David Gordon, "A Remedy for the Chronic Dredging Problem," *Engineer: Professional Bulletin for the Army Corps of Engineers* (Oct.-Dec. 2004).
[359] Daly and Zoeller Interview with Strauser.

Woody Structures

In the summer of 2009, the Westvaco Corporation, which owned a paper mill in Wickliffe, Kentucky, donated a number of logs to the St. Louis District for use in creating habitat diversity on the Mississippi River. The company could not process the logs, which would ordinarily be used for paper, because they contained metal from nails. However, rather than see the logs destroyed, the district contacted the company and asked for permission to use the logs to create environmental structures in the Mississippi River. Westvaco donated the logs and under the authority of the Avoid and Minimize Program, the district placed 15 wood structures consisting of logs bundled together in two locations along the main channel border of the Mississippi River. The log bundles formed a single large wood pile that aquatic species could use as a habitat in the main channel border. After the success of the initial bundles, the district placed numerous additional woody structures were in the river, all of which provided areas of cover, reproduction and forage for fish species, as well as allowing for the accumulation of organic debris that is an essential food source for aquatic insects.

Logs being bundled for use as woody structures

Woody structure being lowered into river

Woody structure behind dike

20

Environmental Pool Management

In 1994, the Corps began experimenting with the way it managed its navigation pools. These experiments would lead to an entirely new water control management program, changing the way the Corps had managed the Mississippi since the late 1920s. The catalyst for this new program was an ongoing discussion between biologists from conservation agencies and engineers from the St. Louis District about the management of water levels in the navigation pools. Prior to efforts to maintain a navigable channel on the Mississippi, the river remained in a natural state in which water levels fluctuated, allowing aquatic macrophytes (vegetation) to grow during low-water periods, usually during summer months. During high-water periods, inundation of vegetated regions provided important habitat for various aquatic species as well as migratory waterfowl, which used this vegetation as an important food source. These natural fluctuations and the habitat diversity they promoted were an essential part of the ecological health of the Mississippi River. The nine-foot channel project had altered the river's natural state, disrupting the normal ebb and flow of the river. Finding a solution to this problem would require a cooperative effort between engineers, biologists, and conservation agencies, as well as a willingness to experiment. However, as with many of the environmental challenges the Corps faced, it would have to determine how it could meet these challenges without compromising navigation.[360]

As of 1994, the Corps had essentially used the same methods of water level management for nearly 70 years. This system consisted of using a series of slack water pools to control the river's natural ebb and flow, preventing water levels from dropping so low that safe navigation was impeded. This system was an overwhelming success from a navigational perspective, but it also had environmental shortcomings. For biologists, although the nine-foot channel project allowed the river to be navigable year-round and provided benefits such as large pools to serve as spawning grounds, it did so at the expense of the natural ebb and flow of the river. Without these fluctuations, there were no low-water periods for wetland vegetation to grow. To assess the importance of vegetation,

---

[360] USACE, *Environmental Pool Management* (St. Louis: MVS, 1998); "River Gamblin'," L.A. *Times* (Mar. 27, 1997); USACE, *2004 Report to Congress, Upper Mississippi River System Environmental Management Program* (Rock Island, Ill.: MVR, 2004): 15.

the Upper Mississippi River Committee conducted a study, *Fishes Interactions with Aquatic Microphytes*, analyzing just how much fish actually depended on these habitats. The study concluded that more than half the fish species on the Upper Mississippi use this vegetation as a food source, a place to lay eggs, and a place for larval fish to hide from predators and mature. As the essential nature of these habitats became ever more apparent, the Corps and biologists continued to work toward developing a solution to the problem.[361]

In addition to affecting aquatic species in the Upper and Middle Mississippi, the absence of vegetation had a dramatic impact on the waterfowl population. Migrating waterfowl followed the Upper Mississippi during their annual migrations, spending a good deal of time feeding in vegetated areas. These birds, and especially females carrying eggs, relied on the vegetation and the insects found in the vegetation as a high-protein food source that provided them with the energy necessary to complete their journey. Without the necessary abundance of this food source, many birds were not able to complete these migrations, thus leading to a decline in various waterfowl species. By the 1980s, the population of waterfowl throughout North America had declined so dramatically that a number of private and governmental agencies from the U.S., Canada, and Mexico formed a joint venture called the North American Waterfowl Management Plan to address the problem. The group recognized the Upper Mississippi River as one of 34 waterfowl habitat areas that were a major concern, due in large part to the shrinking number of macrophyte communities.[362]

The natural ebb and flow of the river and the growth of aquatic vegetation it promoted also had an impact on the water quality and aquatic life on the river and the Gulf of Mexico. This is because vegetation filters out many of the impurities contained in water by absorbing them and using them as nutrients. For example, macrophytes absorb ammonium nitrate, nitrate, nitrate nitrogen, and phosphorus. As the soil dries, nitrogen is released safely into the atmosphere rather than entering the river. The filtering of these impurities was especially important on the Mississippi because studies had shown that the

---

[361] *Environmental Pool Management*; Interview with Strauser; Daly and Zoeller interview with Busse; D. Busse, K. Dalrymple, and C. N. Strauser, "Environmental Pool Management," in Upper Mississippi River Conservation Committee, *Proceedings of the Fifty-First Annual Meeting of the Upper Mississippi River Conservation Committee* (Rock Island: MVR, 1995); Upper Mississippi River Conservation Committee, *Fishes interaction with aquatic macrophytes with special reference to the Upper Mississippi River System* (Rock Island, 1988).

[362] *Environmental Pool Management*; North American Waterfowl Management Plan, Plan Committee, *North American Waterfowl Management Plan, A Strategy for Cooperation* (May 1986) and *1994 Update to the North American Waterfowl Management Plan: Expanding the Commitment* (1994).

river contained high levels of nitrogen from urban and agricultural sources. Much of this nitrogen entered the Gulf of Mexico, fertilizing algae and causing huge algal blooms to develop. The algae eventually died, absorbing oxygen as they decomposed. The absorption of oxygen created a hypoxic – low oxygen – zone that could not sustain most aquatic species. One solution to this problem was dropping the water levels for an extended period of time to allow soil to dry and vegetation to grow; however, before 1994, the Corps did not use this method because of its possible negative impacts on navigation.[363]

Experiments in Water Level Management

The St. Louis District uses a water level management method called hinge-point control. This method involves determining where in the navigation pool the hinge-point is — where the waterline from the flat pool intersects the waterline during drawdown. As the river's flow increases, water control managers open the dam gates and the waterline in the pool tilts on the hinge-point, raising the waterline upstream and lowering it downstream. The waterline teeters on this hinge-point, creating a pool with a waterline that declines at an angle as it moves downstream. When the dam's gates closed, the pool's waterline flattened, rising downstream and lowering upstream.

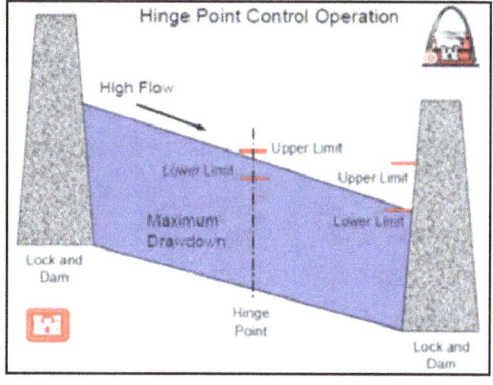

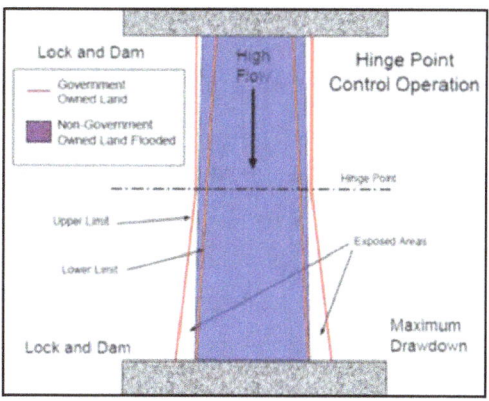

The key to this whole process was ensuring that the waterline never dropped below the hinge-point, which negatively impacted navigation. Because of the unknown variables presented by a dynamic river, the Corps typically worked in the middle of the hinge-point range to allow slightly

---
[363] *Environmental Pool Management*; "River Gamblin'," *L.A. Times*.

more depth. Although this method was extremely successful for maintaining navigation, the level and length of drawdown did not allow sufficient growth of vegetation. Typically, the drawdown was between 0.5 and 1.5 feet for no longer than 20 days. While the Corps allowed greater duration and level of drawdown when possible, its responsibility to protect navigation limited opportunities. Moreover, neither environmentalists nor engineers knew how long or how much drawdown vegetation needed for optimum results. Some environmentalists wanted drawdown for months at a time, which would halt commercial navigation for the entire summer. Other biologists merely asked the Corps to study drawdown to determine if it could balance navigational and environmental goals simultaneously. In 1994, at the annual Mississippi Coordination Trip, biologists and engineers discussed a solution that initiated what became known as environmental pool management.[364]

The focus of the 1994 coordination trip was water level management. Representatives from the Missouri and Illinois Departments of Conservation and U.S. Fish and Wildlife Service discussed pool management schedules with Corps representatives, requesting that the Corps conduct a study on extended drawdowns at Pool 25. In response to the request, Corps representatives asked biologists for a detailed write-up of their proposed water management study. That same evening, Missouri biologist Ken Dalrymple drew up his proposed plan and presented it to Claude Strauser, then Chief of Potamology, and Dave Busse, a senior member of water control management. Dalrymple requested the Corps institute a study to evaluate the feasibility of his plan. Busse's response was quick and to the point: "No." He stated "It was unnecessary to study the proposal. Let's just do it." After engineers and Missouri Department of Conservation representatives determined the exact parameters of the experiment, Busse called Joan Stemler in Water Control and advised her to develop a general plan and simply stated "implement the plan." After these instructions, Stemler

Dave Busse

---

[364] *Environmental Pool Management*; Interview with Strauser; USACE, *Water level Management Opportunities for Ecosystem Restoration on the Upper Mississippi River and Illinois Waterway* (Vicksburg: MVD, 2004); *Rivers Project Master Plan*, Sec. 4; USACE, "NESP Information Paper, Dam Point Control" (St. Louis: MVS, N.D.).

devised and issued the set of pool instructions and initiated environmental pool management. In a single day, the St. Louis District had implemented a new water management schedule, changing how the Corps conducted water control management for 70 years. However, numerous challenges remained for the infant program.[365]

The parameters of this first experiment were to drawdown the pool for a minimum of 0.5 foot for at least 30 days between May 1 and July 31, the optimum period for growth and seed production. In addition, the district raised the pool no faster than 0.1 foot a day, facilitating even greater vegetation growth. Lastly, the district ensured that these parameters did not interfere with the safety and dependability of the navigation channel. Because the Corps had never tried this type of water management plan, biologists and engineers were unsure just how successful the experiment would be. Fortunately, the district was able to coordinate its efforts with other agencies, such as the Missouri Department of Conservation, to ensure its success. One of the greatest challenges of the experiment fell on the shoulders of water control managers, who had to manipulate pools to within an inch to achieve optimum results. After drawdown, water managers slowly raised the river at a minuscule rate of around an inch a day. To make this challenge even more difficult, water control managers had to constantly monitor the hydraulic situation upstream, always being aware of minute changes in the river that could have an impact on how they should manage water levels. Although challenging, the district was able to successfully implement the experimental plan at Pool 25 without any negative impacts on navigation or any additional cost to taxpayers.[366]

While district personnel carefully monitored the hydraulic situation, a natural resources management committee formed so that it could monitor vegetative responses. The committee used natural resources managers to work in the field, monitoring the experiment and collecting data. These resource managers also corresponded with water control managers to optimize the efficacy of drawdown. They then collected and analyzed data from the experiment, presenting their findings to the district so that it could determine the success of the experiment. When the first experiment ended in the summer of 1994, biologists and district personnel were amazed at just how successful it had been. The drawdown allowed approximately 2,000 acres of vegetation to grow, with

---

[365] Interview with Strauser; Interview with Busse; *Environmental Pool Management*; "River Gamblin'," *LA Times*.
[366] *Environmental Pool Management*; "River Gamblin'," *LA Times*.

plants growing between two and three feet in the dewatered area. In addition, seed production was excellent, providing a large number of waterfowl with sustenance during their migration that fall. Most importantly, the district and the committee determined that the project should continue so that they could conduct more extensive research.[367]

Although the 1994 experiment was a great success, the district needed additional quantitative data to make a more definitive judgment about the success of drawdown. So the district and Natural Resources Management Committee agreed to conduct experiments in 1995 and 1996 as long as discharge remained in a range that would not negatively impact navigation. The Missouri Department of Conservation and the Environmental Management Technical Center monitored vegetative response during the experiment, which was far more extensive and the data far more detailed than in the previous experiment. From mid-June through July, the district held water levels from one to three-feet lower than maximum regulated levels at Pools 24, 25, and 26. The district and resource managers also monitored Pool 22 during the experiment, using it as a base of comparison for the test pools. In addition, the district collected aerial infrared photographs of the sites, using these to analyze vegetative response, especially near waterlines. The district and biologists conducted 20 surveys of vegetative response at eight locations in 1995 and six in 1996. Their analysis revealed that plants typically grew seven to 10 inches during the 30-day drawdown period, but grew even faster as water levels began to slowly rise. Near the waterline at sites where drawdown occurred, total acreage of vegetative growth was between 255 and 880 acres. For comparison, surveyors found just 51 acres of vegetation at Pool 22. In addition to the positive vegetative response, biologists concluded that the drawdown had no negative impact on fish, invertebrates, or any other aquatic species. The success of these experiments and the

Growth of vegetation after pool drawdown

---

[367] Joseph H. Wlosinski et al., *Response of vegetation and fish during an experimental drawdown in three pools, Upper Mississippi River* (USGS, Aug. 2000); *Water Level Management Opportunities*.

quantitative data they yielded provided the district with the impetus to continue experimenting with environmental pool management.[368]

Creating a vegetative response that facilitated a healthy riverine ecology was not as simple as drawing down pools at a fixed level and time. The Corps and biologists had to respond to the changing ecological needs of the riverine ecology in determining the optimum parameters in a given year. The key to the program was carefully monitoring vegetative and wildlife responses. Longer duration drawdowns produced a vegetative response detrimental to certain fish species. Between 1999 and 2002, Southern Illinois University conducted a detailed study at Pool 25 that quantified the response of vegetation, fish, waterfowl, macroinvertebrates, and zooplankton to drawdown. It collected data on drawdowns of varying duration and levels. The greatest drawdown occurred in 1999, when levels remained at two feet below full for 54 days and induced the greatest

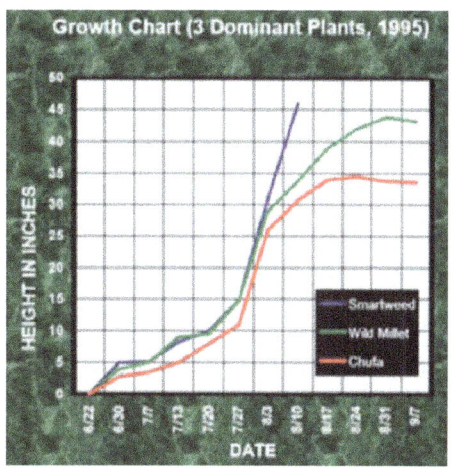

Monitoring of vegetation growth at pool resulting from drawdown

---

[368] *Response during an experimental drawdown*; Wlosinski et al., "Vegetation Response to a Water Level Experiment," Web page (*www.usgs.gov/reports_publications/psrs/psr_1997_07.html*, July 26, 2011).

vegetative response. Minimal drawdown occurred in 2000, producing little vegetative response, and moderate drawdown occurred in 2001, producing moderate response. The study concluded that the variations produced differences in abundance and composition of vegetation, which impacted aquatic life. For example, longer drawdowns earlier in the year produced greater vegetative response, but moderate drawdowns later in the summer produced less vegetation but more desirable habitats for fish. However, these variations did not affect seed biomass available for waterfowl, so water control managers could manipulate pools to optimize fish and macroinvertebrate diversity. Fish response was dramatic, as biologists collected more than 34,000 fish representing 23 species. During 2000 when drawdown was minimal and vegetation sparse, fish were sparse because emergent vegetation provided habitat for small fish and were an important food source. The most prevalent use of emergent vegetation was as a nursery habitat for young fish. The study concluded by recommending continued environmental pool management to produce beneficial conditions for waterfowl and fish. It also showed that optimum pool management did not necessarily mean lengthy drawdowns, but rather drawdowns that responded to the specific ecological needs of a particular pool.[369]

Vegetative growth at backwater area impacted by environmental pool management

Expansion of Environmental Pool Management

In response to the positive assessments of environmental pool management, other districts began experimenting with pool drawdowns as well. In 2001 and 2002, St. Paul District implemented environmental pool management at Pool 8. The district began drawing down water levels beginning on June 30, 2001, and continued with drawdown until mid-September. The district

---

[369] James E. Garvey et al., *Responses of Fishes, Waterbirds, Invertebrates, Vegetation, and Water Quality to Environmental Pool Management: Mississippi River Pool 25*, (Carbondale, Ill.: Southern Illinois University, 2003); USACE, *Water Level Management Opportunities*.

implemented drawdown again in 2002. The results were similar to those in the St. Louis District, as vegetative and fish response was strong. Moreover, the number of waterfowl surveyed in Pool 8 was nearly double the number of those surveyed at Pool 7, which did not implement drawdown. In 2005 and 2006, the St. Paul district experimented with drawdown once again with similar positive results. The district also determined that these drawdowns did not have a negative impact on navigation. Just as in the St. Louis District, St. Paul continued experimenting with drawdowns to determine optimum length, intensity, and time of the year to implement this water control method. Moreover, just as in St. Louis, St. Paul was using environmental pool management to change the way it had managed water control for the previous 70 years.[370]

In recognition for environmental pool management, the district was the recipient of numerous awards, including the National Performance Review Board's Hammer Award and the Chief of Engineers Design and Environmental Awards Program's Honor Award. Much like environmental river engineering, environmental pool management was possible because conservationists and district personnel were able to bridge the communication gap that once existed between the two sides, initiating a dialogue that facilitated environmental change. Because implementation of environmental pool management required no additional cost and presented no impediments to navigation, the only real barrier to implementing the program was a willingness to experiment with nontraditional means of water control management. Ironically, one of the most important environmental innovations the district implemented occurred because environmentalists and engineers met on a barge one summer day to have a friendly discussion about how to improve the river, none of which would have been possible two decades earlier. The St. Louis District had worked since 1970 to improve its environmental record. By 2000, it had made the transition to considering environmental impacts equally with others. The environmental pool management program, as with environmental river engineering, was the best example of cooperation across multiple agencies to achieve national environmental goals.[371]

---

[370] *Upper Mississippi River Pool 8 Drawdown Results* (Water Level Management Task Force, 2007).
[371] USACE, "Champion of Your Heartland's Water Resources" (St. Louis: MVS, Sept. 2001).

Riverlands Environmental Demonstration Area

Map of Riverlands EDA

Vegetative growth at navigation pool

Bird watching at Riverlands EDA

One of the district's significant environmental enhancement projects was the Riverlands Environmental Demonstration Area. Riverlands, a restoration area near the Missouri side of Melvin Price Locks and Dam, opened in June 1998. This area consisted of 1,200 acres of prairie-marsh wetland reserve that served as important habitat for various fish, waterfowl, and native plant species. The area was especially important for migratory birds that used the reserve annually. In addition, the area was open to the public for educational services for visitors who wanted to observe native and migrating wildfowl and other wildlife species. It allows visitors to observe species in a setting that very closely resembles the natural state of the region before the impacts of human settlement. In 2006, the district renamed it the Riverlands Migratory Bird Sanctuary in response to the Audubon Society designating it an important bird area. The bird sanctuary encompasses 3,700 acres that include the 1,200 acres of restored wetlands and prairie, as well as backwater areas at Ellis, Teal, and Heron Ponds, all of which provide excellent habitats for fish, waterfowl, and other wildlife.[372]

---

[372] USACE, *Rivers Project Master Plan* (St. Louis: MVS, 2001), Sec. 8; "Riverlands Migratory Bird Sanctuary," Web page (*www.mvs.usace.army.mil/Rivers/RMBS.html*, July 26, 2011); "EDA dedicated," *Esprit* (July 1998).

Conclusion

As the city of St. Louis grew in the first half of the nineteenth century, river transportation grew with it. However, before the improvements of the Corps, the river was treacherous to navigate or even impossible to navigate during certain times of the year. Creating and maintain the navigability of the Mississippi River was essential for the growth and prosperity of not only St. Louis, but the entire Mississippi River Basin. Moreover, these improvements facilitated westward expansion and the growth of the nation as a whole. The district's earliest efforts towards achieving this goal included the removal of snags, dredging, and the removal of sandbars to maintain the St. Louis Harbor. During the second half of the eighteenth century, these efforts evolved to include permanent improvements to contract the river and maintain its navigability. No district engineer embodied this philosophy of permanent improvements more than Col. James H. Simpson. His vision was to harness the natural energy of the river and use it to do the work of contracting and deepening the navigation channel. This philosophy would become even more prevalent in the twentieth century, especially with the rise of the environmental movement and the passage of NEPA.

By the early twentieth century, Corps efforts to maintain a navigable channel came to include the construction of a series of locks and dams that would make the river navigable year-round through the creation of a nine-foot channel. During this time, flood control also became a major responsibility of the district, as it began construction of a series of floodwalls and multi-purpose reservoirs that could be used for flood control, recreation, water supply, and hydroelectric power. By the second half of the twentieth century, the district had successfully contracted the river and deepened the channel so as return it to something resembling its state prior to development along the river. However, the improvements to the river came at a cost to the environment. The modern history of the district is one in which it evolved in response to the challenges of simultaneously maintaining and regulating navigation, protecting again flooding, and protecting the environment. The district has and continues to strive to achieve balance between these responsibilities, creating a river that is navigable and simultaneously ecologically healthy. While the era of massive civil works projects may have passed, the district continues to be at the forefront of Corps districts through innovations such as Environmental River Engineering, Environmental Pool Management, Hydraulic Sediment Response Modeling and Integrated River Management. Just as it is the responsibility of river engineers to leave the river in a better state than what they found it, so too is it the responsibility of all district personnel to leave the district in a better state than what they found it. This pursuit will no doubt continue into the twenty-first century, inspiring future engineers towards innovations far from ordinary.

Appendix A

St. Louis District Commanders

Office of Western River Improvements

John Bruce, 1824-1825
Maj. Samuel Babcock, 1825-1826
Henry M. Shreve, 1826-1841
John W. Russell, 1842-1843
Maj. Stephen H. Long, 1843-1854
Col. J.E. Johnson, 1854-1855
Col. Stephen H. Long, 1855-1861
Col. John N. Macomb, 1866-1870
Lt. Col. William F. Raynolds, 1870-1872

Engineer Office, St. Louis

Lt. Col. William F. Raynolds, 1872-1873
Col. James H. Simpson, 1873-1880
Maj. Oswald H. Ernst, 1880-1886
Maj. Alexander M. Miller, 1886-1893
Maj. Charles J. Allen, 1893-1896
Lt. Chester Harding, 1896
Maj. Thomas H. Handbury, 1896-1899
Maj. Edward Burr, 1899-1901
Maj. Thomas L. Casey, Jr., 1901-1906
Col. Clinton B. Sears, 1906-1908
Capt. Gustave R. Lukesh, 1908
Col. William H. Bixby, 1908-1910, 1917
Lt. Clarence H. Knight, 1909, 1910
Lt. Col. Charles L. Potter, 1910-1912
Col. Curtis M. Townsend, 1912-1915
Maj. Wildurr Willing, 1915-1917, 1919-1920
Lt. Col. Clarke S. Smith, 1917

William S. Mitchell, 1917-1919
Maj. Dewitt C. Jones, 1920-1922
Maj. Lunsford Oliver, 1922-1924
Maj. John C. Gotwals, 1924-1930
Capt. Sylvester E. Nortner, 1930
Maj. William A. Snow, 1930-1933
Maj. Bartley M. Harloe, 1933-1935
Lt. Col. Paul S. Rienecke, 1935-1940
Col. Roy W. Grower, 1940-1942
Col. Lawrence B. Feagin, 1942-1946
Col. Rudolph E. Smyser, Jr. 1946-1949
Col. Beverly C. Snow, 1949-1951
Col. Fred E. Ressegieu, 1951-1954
Col. George E. White, Jr., 1954-1957
Col. Charles B. Schweizer, 1957-1960
Col. Alfred J. D'Arezzo, 1960-1963
Col. James B. Meanor, Jr. 1963-1966
Col. Edwin R. Decker, 1966-1970
Col. Carroll N. LeTellier, 1970-1971
Col. Guy E. Jester, 1971-1973
Col. Thorwald R. Peterson, 1973-1976
Col. Leon McKinney, 1976-1979
Col. Robert J. Dacey, 1979-1982
Col. Gary D. Beech, 1982-1985
Col. Daniel M. Wilson, 1985-1988
Col. James E. Corbin, 1988-1991
Col. James D. Craig, 1991-1994
Col. Thomas C. Suermann, 1994-1996
Col. Thomas J. Hodgini, 1996-1999
Col. Michael R. Morrow, 1999-2002
Col. C. Kevin Williams, 2002-2005
Col. Lewis F. Setliff, 2005-2008
Col. Thomas E. O'Hara, 2008-2011
Col. Christopher G. Hall, 2011-

Appendix B

St. Louis District Chronology

1802	Congress authorized creation of the modern U.S. Army Corps of Engineers.
1803	St. Louis and the Louisiana Territory became part of the U.S.
1804	Capts. Meriwether Lewis and William Clark left St. Charles to explore the Missouri River.
1819	Maj. Stephen H. Long started Missouri River Expedition on the steamboat *Western Engineer*.
1824	Congress passed the first act giving the Corps the responsibility for and appropriating $75,000 to improve navigation on the Ohio and Mississippi Rivers. Corps of Engineers establishes the position of Superintendent of Western River Improvement.
1826	Congress passed the Rivers and Harbors Act of 1826, the first rivers and harbors legislation to combine authorization for both surveys and projects. Henry M. Shreve hired as Superintendent of Western River Improvements, introduced snag removing vessel design.
1835	Joseph N. Nicollet began exploration and mapping of Northwest.
1837	Lt. Robert E. Lee arrived in St. Louis to restore and protect the harbor. Lee constructed a dike from Illinois to Bloody Island, diverting the current to the Missouri side of the island and into a sandbar in the harbor.
1842	Col. Stephen H. Long becomes Superintendent of Western River Improvement.
1844	During the Mississippi River Flood this year, the river crested on June 27 at an estimated height of 41.32 feet on the present St. Louis gage, long considered the flood of record at St. Louis.
1861	Publication of A. A. Humphreys and Henry L. Abbot's *Report Upon the Physics and Hydraulics of the Mississippi River*, one of the most thorough analyses of the Mississippi River ever completed. The St. Louis gage was established on the Mississippi River.
1865	The American Civil War ended. River commerce on the Middle Mississippi declined as wartime conditions assured the rapid ascendancy of the railroad over the steamboat.
1866	Corps of Engineers established depot and assumed control of Jefferson Barracks until 1871.

1867	Construction of the Eads Bridge at St. Louis begun by civil engineer James B. Eads.
1870	The Office of Western River Improvements transferred from Cincinnati to St. Louis and charged with surveying the St. Louis and Alton Harbors, and the banks opposite the Missouri River.
1872	St. Louis Engineer Office established. The Rivers and Harbors Act of 1872 provided $100,000 for improvement of the Mississippi River between the mouths of the Missouri and Meramec Rivers to guarantee a regularized channel through the St. Louis Harbor sufficiently deep enough to accommodate the large amount of river traffic docking in the harbor.
1873	Col. James H. Simpson became District Engineer from 1 January 1873 through 30 March 1880. The district's boundary extended from the mouth of the Missouri River on south to Cairo, Ill.
1875	In the 1875 Annual Report to the Chief of Engineers, Simpson instituted a policy of permanent river improvement structures.
1879	Act of Congress 28 June 1879 created the Mississippi River Commission (MRC). The first meeting is held in Washington, D.C., on 19 August.
1881	Congress established an eight-foot project depth for the Mississippi River from St. Louis to Ohio River and six-foot depth from St. Louis to the Missouri River. Maj. Oswald Ernst experimented with jet dredge.
1884	Congress placed the St. Louis District under the MRC, but returned it to the oversight of the Office of the Chief of Engineers in 1886.
1888	Rivers and Harbors Act set expenditures on snag removal at a maximum of $100,000 annually. St. Louis District establishes Service Base south of St. Louis.
1890	The Rivers and Harbors Act of 1890, revised in 1892, gave the Corps jurisdiction and authority over the protection of navigable waters from pollution or obstructions.
1894	Maj. Charles J. Allen experimented with portable jetties and vessel-mounted jet dredges.
1896	Congress authorized the construction of dredges "with the view of ultimately obtaining and maintaining a navigation channel from Cairo, down, not less than 250 feet in width and nine feet in depth."
1899	The Rivers and Harbors Act of 1899 compiled all laws for protection of navigable waters. Section 10 gave the Corps the authority to regulate activities that might lead to potential obstructions to navigation.

1902	Congress created the Board of Engineers for Rivers and Harbors to approve or reject river development projects.
1903	The Flood of 1903, while reaching only 38 feet on the St. Louis gage, devastated the rich agricultural areas, towns, industries, and land transportation systems. The few small private levees could not withstand the flood. More 20,000 refugees were forced from their homes during the flood.
1905	The Rivers and Harbors Act of 1905 stipulated that dredging be the primary means of maintaining a navigation channel on the Middle Mississippi River. While the Act allowed hurdle work and revetments as auxiliary aids to improve the channel, the primary emphasis was on temporary improvements. The Mitchell Report first recommended federal flood control works on the Middle Mississippi.
1907	The Rivers and Harbors Act of 1907 authorized a 6-foot channel on the Upper Mississippi River using open river regulation.
1908	The Western Division was established with headquarters in St. Louis, and district offices at St. Paul, Kansas City, St. Louis, Memphis, and Vicksburg. The Western Division had jurisdiction over specific work on the Mississippi River from its headwaters to Baton Rouge.
1910	The Rivers and Harbors Act of 1910 adopted a return to permanent improvement structures over dredging as the primary means of establishing a navigation channel.
1917	Devastating floods on the Lower Mississippi River in 1912, 1913 and 1916 led Congress to pass the first Federal Flood Control Act (Ransdell-Humphreys Act), which authorized federal contributions of 50 percent for flood control projects.
1918	Northern MRC District established in St. Louis. The Federal Control Act created a federal barge line between St. Louis and New Orleans. From 1917 to 1920, the value of river commerce increased from $15 million to $31 million.
1923	The Flood Control Act of 1923 makes the construction of levees for flood control on the Mississippi River between the mouth of the Ohio River and the Rock Island as the responsibility of the MRC.
1925	The Rivers and Harbors Act of 1925 directed the Corps and the Federal Power Commission to jointly survey and submit reports on all navigable streams indicating what multi-purpose water resource development possibilities existed for navigation, hydropower, flood control, and irrigation.

1927	The Rivers and Harbors Act of 1927 authorized surveys in House Document 308. The resulting "308 Reports" embodied the first systematic efforts at comprehensive basin development planning.
	The Flood of 1927 devastated the Mississippi valley from Grafton to New Orleans. The high water caused 17 breaks in the main levee line and 209 crevasses on the tributaries of the Mississippi River. The river crested on the St. Louis gage at 36.1 feet and remained above flood stage from April 13 to May 1.
1928	Congress passed the Flood Control Act of 1928, which committed the federal government to a definite program of flood control, authorized the Mississippi River & Tributaries Project (MR&T). The MRC abolished the Northern District, transferred work to the Rock Island and St. Louis Districts, and extended the boundary of the St. Louis District from the Missouri River to the Illinois River.
1929	The Corps of Engineers abolished the Western Division and established the Lower Mississippi Valley Division (LMVD) and the Upper Mississippi Valley Division (UMVD), including the St. Louis District. The MRC relocated its headquarters from St. Louis to Vicksburg.
1930	Congress passed The Rivers and Harbors Act of 1930 authorizing the 9-Foot Channel Project on the Upper Mississippi River. The final survey report, issued in 1931, called for the construction of 24 new locks and dams and the incorporation of three existing structures into the project.
1931	The USGS took over measuring discharge velocity on the St. Louis gage.
1933	The northern boundary of the St. Louis District was extended to just south of Saverton, making the District responsible for 300 miles of the Mississippi River.
1934	Construction began on Lock & Dam No. 26
1935	Congress passed the Emergency Relief Appropriation Act, which provided funds to the Works Progress Administration. Construction began on Lock & Dam No. 25.
1936	The Flood Control Act of 1936 authorized 300 flood control projects nationwide. Of these, 48 were reservoirs, including Wappapello Lake in the Memphis District. In the St. Louis district, the Act authorized building or enlarging existing levees at East Cape Girardeau, North Alexander, Clear Creek, Preston, Degonia & Fountain Bluff, Perry County, Fort Chartres & Ivy Landing, Harrisonville, Columbia, E. St. Louis, Prairie DuPont, Chouteau, Nameoki and Venice. Construction began on Lock & Dam No. 24.

1938	Flood Control Act of 1938 authorized construction of Carlyle Lake and the Joanna Reservoir (now Mark Twain Lake), and additional projects at Miller Pond, Grand Tower, Kaskaskia Island, Wood River, and Stringtown (deauthorized by PL 99-622 in 1986). Construction of Lock & Dam No. 26 completed. Memphis District began construction of Wappapello Lake.
1939	For the first time in 50 years, the St. Louis District reported that it had performed no snagging operations. Lock & Dam No. 25 completed.
1940	St. Louis gage reached its lowest level in recorded history at −6.2 feet on January 16 and remained below zero for 181 continuous days from 5 September 1939 to 3 March 1940. Lock & Dam No. 24 completed.
1941	Memphis District completed Wappapello Lake. St. Louis District began military construction in support of World War II.
1943	The Flood of 1943 hit the Middle Mississippi River. From St. Louis to Cairo, the river reached the highest stages experienced since the 1844. On May 24, the river crested at 38.88 feet on the St. Louis gage.
1944	The 1944 Flood Control Act formalized Corps participation in the development of recreation facilities at reservoirs, authorizing multi-purpose projects.
1945	Congress authorized the construction of the Chain of Rocks Canal and Locks 27.
1949	Construction of the Chain of Rocks Canal and Locks 27 began.
1950	The Flood Control Act of 1950 authorized the Cape Girardeau Flood Protection Project.
1953	Chain of Rocks Canal and Locks 27 completed. The federal government sold the Federal Barge Line to private investors.
1954	The Corps abolished the Upper Mississippi Valley Division and transferred the St. Louis District to the Lower Mississippi Valley Division.
1955	Congress authorized the construction of the St. Louis Flood Protection Project.
1956	Construction began on the Cape Girardeau Flood Protection Project.
1958	The Flood Control Act of 1958 reauthorized Carlyle Lake along with a reservoir at Shelbyville. The Act also authorized Dam 27. Construction of Carlyle Lake began in November.

1959	Construction of Dam 27 began. Construction of the St. Louis Flood Protection Project began.
1962	The Flood Control Act of 1962 reauthorized the Joanna Reservoir along with Rend Lake. The Rivers and Harbors Act of 1962 authorized the Kaskaskia Lock & Dam.
1963	Construction of Lake Shelbyville began.
1964	Drought conditions caused the St. Louis gage to remain below 0.0 for 100 consecutive days from November 1963 to March 1964. The St. Louis area experienced an accumulated precipitation deficit of 42 inches from 1952 to 1964. On 26 January 1963 the river dropped to −5.8 feet and on 1 January 1964 it reached −5.6 feet. Dam 27 completed. Cape Girardeau Flood Protection Project completed.
1965	The St. Louis District completed Comprehensive Basin Summary Report for the Meramec Basin Project, which called for 13 reservoirs, five local flood protection projects, and 21 angler-use sites. Construction of Rend Lake began. Joanna Reservoir renamed the Clarence Cannon Dam and Reservoir.
1967	Carlyle Lake completed.
1969	Congress passed the National Environmental Policy Act (NEPA), which established preparation of the environmental impact statement (EIS) as an integral element of the Corps' pre-authorization process on all projects and permit-granting activities. The Secretary of the Army directs the St. Louis District to plan and design the replacement of Lock & Dam No. 26. The original plan called for a new dam and two new 1,200-foot locks to be constructed 2 miles downstream from the existing structure.
1970	The St. Louis District submitted the EIS for the Meramec Park Lake Project. Lake Shelbyville and Rend Lake completed. The St. Louis District established the first Environmental River Engineering Program in the nation to implement the Environmental River Engineering Project on the Middle Mississippi River.
1971	Construction of Clarence Cannon Dam and Reservoir began.
1972	The River Engineering Unit completed the first ever notched-dike structure. The district held the first ever Mississippi River coordination trip. The Corps of Engineers completed the Upper Mississippi River Comprehensive Basin Study, which found a 12-foot navigation channel on the Upper Mississippi not economically feasible. Congress passed the Federal Water Pollution Control Act (FWPCA), which created guidelines affecting standards for EIS. Later amendments established Section 404 permits. Claiming the district was in

	violation of NEPA, the Sierra Club filed a lawsuit against the Corps to stop construction of the Meramec Dam.
1973	The Mississippi River on the St. Louis gage experienced the then highest levels in recorded history when it reached 43.3 feet. Despite the fact that the river remained above flood stage for a then record-setting 77 consecutive days, Corps flood control measures prevented more damages than occurred for the first time. Congress passes the Endangered Species Act, which required federal agencies to consider the possible effects of a project on endangered species.
1974	Environmental groups and the railroad industry filed suits to stop the construction of the Lock & Dam No. 26 Replacement. The St. Louis Flood Protection Project and the Kaskaskia Lock & Dam were completed.
1976	The Formulation Evaluation Report and a Draft Supplemental EIS for the Lock & Dam 26 Replacement Project recommended construction of a single 1,200 foot lock and a new dam, but recommended that additional studies be completed prior to authorization of a second lock.
1977	Congress passes 1977 Clean Water Act, Section 404 of which greatly increases the Corps permitting responsibilities.
1978	The Missouri State legislature approved referendum on the Meramec Park Lake Project, resulting in a lopsided victory by opponents. Congress passed the Inland Waterways Act (PL 95-502), which authorized construction of a new dam and lock as the Lock & Dam 26 Replacement Project and required completion of a master plan for the entire Upper Mississippi River Basin before consideration of a second lock.
1979	Construction begins on Lock and Dam 26 Replacement.
1981	Public Law 97-128 deauthorized the Meramec Dam. As a part of PL 97-128, Congress also designated the Clarence Cannon Dam and Reservoir as Clarence Cannon Dam and Mark Twain Lake. Congress designates the Lock & Dam 26 Replacement as the Melvin Price Lock and Dam.
1982	Wappapello Lake is transferred from the Memphis District to the St. Louis District.
1984	Clarence Cannon Dam and Mark Twain Lake completed.
1986	Congress passed PL 99-662, the Water Resources Development Act of 1986 (WRDA 86). It authorized construction of a 600-foot auxiliary lock at the Melvin Price Locks and Dam and established the

	Upper Mississippi River System Environmental Management Plan (EMP).
1989	Drought conditions prompt St. Louis gate to reach −5.2 feet. During 1988-1989, 44 daily low stage records were established at St. Louis and 128 daily low stage records at Cape Girardeau. District begins construction of first ever Bendway Weir field.
1990	Lock & Dam No. 26 was decommissioned and demolished. Full operation of Melvin Price commenced.
1992	The St. Louis District established the Avoid and Minimize Program to reduce environmental impacts of increased navigation traffic due to second lock at the Melvin Price Locks and Dams. District Ordnance and Technical Services Branch is established to prepare Archive Search Reports for Huntsville Division.
1993	The Flood of 1993 surpassed all previous floods in the United States. On August 1 the Mississippi River set a high water mark on the St. Louis gage at 49.58 feet and reached an all-time high in terms of flow at 1,070,000 cfs. The river remained above flood stage for a new-record 80 consecutive days and for a new-record 148 days during the calendar year
1994	The St. Louis District implemented the first ever Environmental Pool Management Plan. The district established the Applied River Engineering Center (AREC), which used Micro Modeling to solve a variety of sedimentation related issues. Melvin Price Auxiliary Lock completed. Director of Civil Works Maj. Gen. Stan Genega established the Mandatory Center of Expertise for Archaeological Curation and Collections Management in the St. Louis District.
1997	The Lower Mississippi Valley Division was abolished with the establishment of the Mississippi Valley Division.
2001	District develops the Rivers Project Master Plan to provide recreational, environmental stewardship, and environmental education opportunities.

Appendix C

Notable Engineers in the St. Louis District

James B. Eads

James B. Eads was a self-educated civil engineer whose early career was marked by the invention of the diving bell and his partnership in a steamboat salvaging firm. His engineering reputation grew to the highest level as a result of the construction of the bridge that bears his name. His reputation was enhanced further by his successful attempt to open the mouth of the Mississippi River to oceangoing vessels through a system of jetties designed to narrow and deepen the South Pass. In 1876, Eads testified before Congress that the same principle he used at the South Pass could be extended upstream to deepen the channel and improve navigation the length of the lower Mississippi River, and this proposal ultimately was a factor in the creation of the MRC in 1879, of which Eads was a member. Eads advocated a "levees-only" plan to close all outlets and line the river with a system of levees located directly on the banks of the river to increase the volume of flow and deepen the channel, as his jetty system had done at the South Pass. After the MRC Committee on Outlets and Levees did not recommend the closure the Atchafalaya River as an outlet, Eads resigned from the MRC.

Henry Flad

Flad came to the United States from Germany during the German Republican Revolution of 1848. He eventually settled near St. Louis and found employment as a railroad engineer. During the American civil war, he enlisted in the Union army as a private and eventually rose to the rank of colonel. After the war, Flad earned international respect as a civil engineer when, as an assistant engineer to the world-renown James B. Eads, he helped to construct the famous, steel-arched Eads Bridge across the Mississippi River. Flad was the designing force behind many of the boldest and awe-inspiring features of the bridge. Flad became a member of the MRC in 1890. As chairman of the MRC Committee on Dredges and Dredging, Flad authored a favorable report on dredging as a temporary expedient for relieving low water shoaling. At his recommendation, the MRC authorized the construction of an experimental dredge, the *Alpha*. Flad personally supervised the construction of the *Alpha*, which quickly proved the value of dredging and convinced the Commission to construct more dredges. Flad, in turn, pioneered the design and construction of the MRC dredging fleet and its attending plant. Flad's efforts ultimately lead to a fundamental shift in MRC policy, whereby dredging served as permanent compliment to contraction works for improving low water navigation.

John Ockerson

After graduating from the University of Illinois, Ockerson became employed as an assistant engineer in the Great Lakes survey and served as a federal inspector of the Eads jetty surveys in 1876. Ockerson's 45-year affiliation with the MRC dated back to its creation in 1879; first as an assistant engineer and, from 1898-1924, as a member. As an assistant engineer, he guided the Commission's surveys and physical examinations of the river from its headwaters to the Gulf of Mexico, and the surveys and maps he produced were so exceptionally complete and accurate that they were in great demand worldwide. He was a long-time member of several standing committees, including the Committee on Dredges and Dredging, the Committee on Outlets and Levees, and the Committee on the Separation of the Red and Mississippi Rivers, and was instrumental in shaping the direction of MRC policy. The MRC often anointed the tall, dignified, and eloquent Ockerson as the Commission's point man in articulating MRC policy to Congress, his peers in the engineering community, and the people of the Mississippi Valley.

Charles D. Lamb

He began his career in the district in 1882, serving in the capacity of assistant engineer until his death in 1923. He served as superintendent of the engineer boatyard during most of his career. During the early part of his career, he was in charge of construction of the longitudinal dike opposite Alton, Illinois, one of the first river-regulating works built in the district. In 1888 he made a preliminary examination and survey of the Kaskaskia River.

Gaston G. Crane

He was a member of the St. Louis District from 1883 to 1930, serving in various capacities during that time, such as overseer and supervisor of construction and master of the dredge. He possessed and intimate knowledge of all branches of field work in the district and ensured that this work was completed in an economical manner. The towboat Crane is named in honor of his service to the district.

William S. Mitchell

Mitchell was employed continuously with the Corps from 1878 to 1931, retiring at the age of 74. In 1904 he became the principal civilian engineer. During World War I he was appointed district engineer, the first civilian to hold the position. He also directed the survey and report on a system of drainage with levees from the American Bottoms, which was the later basis for the East Side Levee District. He designed a fleet of four towboats and 19 large, steel barges. He also designed numerous hydraulic dredges which were essential for maintaining the navigability of the river.

William M. Penniman

Penniman was employed in the district from 1891 until his death in 1934. During this time he served in many different capacities, including timekeeper, transitman, Master of Dredge, junior engineer, assistant engineer, engineer, senior engineer, and principal engineer. He was principal civilian assistant to the St. Louis District from January 6, 1923 until his death.

James E. Kennedy

Kennedy worked for the district from 1892 until 1938, during which time he served in various capacities on river regulating works and dredging operations, as well as overseer, Master of Dredge, construction superintendent, and senior superintendent. In 1923, he became an office superintendent, providing guidance and counsel on all river activities in the district. In his later years, he focused his efforts primarily on dredging. His knowledge of the river and its history were unequalled in the district during his long career.

Edward C. Constance

Constance was a member of the district from 1904 to 1943, with the exception of a six-year period in which he worked in the Kansas City District. He served in various capacities for the district, including river construction and supervisor of a large construction party. He designed numerous river construction jobs, new floating plants, and modifications to older plants. He also designed equipment for the district, including repair and upkeep of all district plants. He prepared specifications and contracts for floating plant as well as river construction. He was also in charge of the engineer depot shops and general supply and repair organization of the district.

John C. Debolt

Debolt was employed in the district from 1924 until his death in 1954. He began his career with the Corps as a surveyman and in 1927 became an inspector in charge of large construction jobs, including piling dikes and bank protection. He later worked in the district office on plans and specifications and on examination and survey reports for navigation and flood control structures. He also served as Assistant Chief of Operations, Construction Division, and as head of the River Regulating Works Maintenance Section. He was the recipient of the Meritorious Civilian Award in 1944 for his service to the government.

Marshall Gray

Gray worked for the Corps from 1923 until his retirement in 1965. He served as principal draftsman in the Louisville District from 1923 to 1930. From 1930 to 1954, he worked in the Upper Mississippi Valley Division office in St. Louis, serving as engineer in charge of all drafting work in connection with preparation of plans for locks and dams on the Mississippi River. He transferred to the St. Louis District in 1954. He worked as information officer for the district, devoting long hours and tireless effort to informing the public about Corps plans and programs. In 1963, he received the Meritorious Civilian Service Award for his efforts to facilitate cordial relations between the Corps and the media and public.

Walter F. Lawlor

Lawlor began his civilian career with the Corps in November 1931 and continued his service to the district until his retirement in 1969. His initial assignment was inspector on Illinois River levee construction. He eventually had complete responsibility for the design and supervision of construction on all levees in the district. In 1946 he was named Chief of the Engineering Division, a position he held until his retirement. Lawlor was a decisive leader with keen judgment and an ability for directing a broad field of engineering, while also possessing exceptional knowledge of details pertaining to specific projects. In 1968 he was awarded the Meritorious Civilian Service Award for his outstanding executive leadership in engineering.

Lowell C. Oheim

Oheim began his career with the district in 1927, a career which continued until his retirement in 1970. He began as a Boatman and advanced to the position of Surveyman, Inspector, Engineer Aide, Engineer of the Lock and Dam Branch and, lastly, Chief of Construction and Operations Division, a position he held from 1958 until his retirement. He demonstrated superb ability in his management of the Construction-Operations Division and also in his advice and knowledge of river operations. During his tenure as Chief of Construction-Operations the district shifted from construction of levees to construction of complex flood protection projects, pump stations, and flood control reservoirs. In 1966 he received the Meritorious Service Award for his efforts and was also named St. Louis Federal Civil Service Employee of the year in 1965.

John W. Gurley

Gurley began his career with the district in 1934 as a sub-surveyman and retired in 1972 as Chief of the Operations Division. His technical abilities contributed heavily to the Mississippi River system being the corridor of navigation it is today. He established the framework for Lake Management which became the model for the Corps.

Alfons J. Tiefenbrun

Tiefenbrun began his career with the Corps in 1931 and continued service until his retirement in 1972. His initial assignment was hydraulic computations and studies. He was promoted to assistant chief of Hydraulics, a position he held until he was deployed for service in World War II. After reaching the rank of Colonel at the end of his service in 1946, he returned to the district in the Reports Branch of the Engineering Division. His efforts in the district resulted in the authorization of much of the work on the Illinois, Salt, Kaskaskia, Big Muddy, and Meramec rivers. His also played a prominent role in the initial authorization of the replacement for Locks and Dam No. 26.

Otto K. Steffens

Steffens worked for the Corps for 36 years, half of which was spent in service to the St. Louis District (1967-1984), during which time he was Resident Engineer for the St. Louis Flood Protection Resident Office. In 1970, he became the Resident Engineer for the construction of Clarence Cannon Dam and Reservoir and served in that capacity until his retirement.

Homer L. Duff

Duff's career with the district began in 1938 and continued until his retirement in 1986. He served with remarkable distinction as Comptroller, Supervisory Civil Engineer, Civil Engineer, and Hydraulics Engineer. All of his service was in the district except for his duty with the U.S. Navy Seabees between 1943 and 1945. His efforts as the LMVD representative contributed greatly to the legislative action that resulted in the creation of the Corps Revolving Fund appropriation.

Jack R. Niemi

Mr. Niemi began his long career with the district in 1962. He served as Chief of the Engineering Division from 1973 to 1989 and as Deputy District Engineer for Project Management from 1989 until his retirement in 1993. Niemi was the recipient of numerous awards during his career, including the Presidential Award for Design Excellence, the Meritorious Civilian Service Award, a Professional Recognition Award from the American Society of Civil Engineers, and the Department of the Army Achievement Award. He also received the Engineer of the Year Award from the St. Louis Chapter of the National Association of Professional Engineers and was honored as Engineer of the Year of the Lower Mississippi Valley Division.

Emmett Hahn

Hahn's 35-year career with the district began in 1964 and continued until his retirement in 1999. During this time he worked in the Planning and Engineering divisions and eventually became Chief of the district's Readiness Branch. The 1993 flood focused national attention on Hahn and he became one of the most quoted people in America during the event. At the time of his retirement, he was recognized as an expert in flood damage reduction and emergency operations.

Thomas J. Mudd

Mudd began working for the district as a Structural Engineer in 1961. In 1968 he was promoted to the position of Supervisory Civil Engineer and assigned the role of leading the design effort for the Melvin Price Locks and Dam Project. Mudd left the district in 1987 to work at the Ohio River Division and later at the Waterways Experiment Station until his retirement in 1995. He will always be remembered in the district as "Mr. Mel Price" as the innovations he pioneered in the design and construction of the structure are a testament to his excellence as a structural engineer.

Claude Norman Strauser

Strauser began his career in 1969 as a Junior Engineer Trainee for the district. He quickly realized his desire to work as a river engineer on the Mississippi, so he chose the River Stabilization Branch, of which he eventually became chief, as his permanent assignment. The River Stabilization Branch became part of the Hydrologic and Hydraulic Branch and Strauser became chief of the branch in 1999 and continued as such until his retirement in 2005. Strauser is considered the father of a new type of river engineering known as Environmental River Engineering. He was one of the Corps leaders in terms of balancing the traditional function of maintaining navigation with the environmental mission of the Corps that arose after the passage of NEPA. Strauser played an essential role in working to create a waterway that serves as a highway for water commerce while at the same time remaining environmentally healthy.

Mike Dace

Dace began his career with the Corps in 1969 as Design Engineer in the Design Branch, where he remained until 1976. In 1976 he became a member of Project Management and became project manager for the proposed Meramec Park Lake project. In addition to the Meramec project, which was deauthorized in 1981, Dace worked as a project manager on numerous other projects during his tenure, including an eight-month stint as Chief of the Project Management Division in 2006. Dace began working on a flood control study for the district at Times Beach, Mo. in 1982. During the study, the district gained experience with hazardous, toxic, and radioactive waste and with aerial photography. The district used this experience to obtain future work preparing preliminary assessments for the DERP-FUDS program. Dace played the essential role in obtaining this DERP-FUDS work for the district, the result of which was the establishment of the Ordnance and Technical Services Branch, of which Dace would serve as Chief until his retirement in 2006.

Bibliography

Secondary sources

Abbot, Henry. "The Physics of the Mississippi River." *Van Nostrand's Engineering Magazine* 20:130 (Jan. 1879): 1-6.

Afinson, John O. *The River We Have Wrought: A History of the Upper Mississippi.* Minneapolis: University of Minnesota Press, 2003.

_____. "The Secret History of the Mississippi's Earliest Locks and Dams," *Minnesota History* (Summer 1995): 254-267.

Andrews, Richard N. L. *Environmental Policy and Administrative Change: Implementation of the National Environmental Policy Act.* Washington D.C.: Lexington Books, 1976.

_____. *Managing the Environment, Managing Ourselves: A History of American Environmental Policy.* New Haven: Yale University Press, 1999.

Armstrong, Richard C. "Replacement—Locks and Dam No. 26: Plans Considered." *Journal of the Waterways and Harbors Division* (Feb. 1970): 49-63.

Arnold, Joseph L. *The Evolution of the 1936 Flood Control Act.* Fort Belvoir: Corps of Engineers History Office, 1988.

Barry, John. *Rising Tide: The Great Mississippi Flood of 1927 and How it Changed America.* New York: Simon and Schuster, 1997.

Bogue, Margaret B. "The Swamp Land Act and Wet Land Utilization in Illinois, 1850-1890." *Agricultural History* 25:4 (Oct. 1951): 169-180.

Bond, James W. *The East St. Louis, Illinois, Waterfront: Historical Background.* St. Louis: National Park Service Division of History, 1969.

Braeman, John et al., ed. *The New Deal: The National Level.* Vol. I. Columbus, Oh.: Ohio State University Press, 1975.

Bray, Martha Coleman. *Joseph Nicollet and His Map.* Philadelphia: American Philosophical Society, 1980.

Brooks, Robert R. "Robert E. Lee – Civil Engineer." *Civil Engineering* 10:3 (Mar. 1940): 167-169.

Busse, D., Dalrymple, K., and Strauser, C. N. "Environmental Pool Management." Upper Mississippi River Conservation Committee. *Proceedings of the Fifty-First Annual Meeting of the Upper Mississippi River Conservation Committee.* Rock Island: Rock Island District (MVR), 1995.

Camillo, Charles A. and Pearcy, Matthew T. *Upon Their Shoulders, A history of the Mississippi River Commission from its inception through the advent of the modern Mississippi River and Tributaries Project.* Vicksburg, MS: Mississippi River Commission, 2004.

Cooper, Christopher and Block, Robert. *Disaster: Hurricane Katrina and the Failure of Homeland Security*. New York: Times Books, 2006.

Cullum, George E. *Biographical Register of the Officers and Graduates of the United States Military Academy at West Point, New York, since its establishment in 1802*. Vol. II-IV. New York: USMA. (*http://penelope. uchicago.edu/ Thayer/E/ Gazetteer/Places/America/United_States/Army/USMA/Cullums_Register/*, Jan. 19, 2011).

Daniel, Pete. *Deep'n As It Come: The 1927 Mississippi River Flood*. Fayetteville, Ark.: University of Arkansas Press, 1996.

Davinroy, Robert. *Physical Sediment Modeling of the Mississippi River on a Micro Scale*. Master's thesis, University of Missouri-Rolla, 1994.

_____. "Bendway Weirs, A New Structural Solution to Navigation Problems Experienced on the Mississippi River." *PIANC Bulletin*. 69 (1990).

_____. "River Replication." *Civil Engineering*. (July 1999).

Dieckmann, R.J. and Dyhouse, G.R. "Changing history at St. Louis—adjusting historic flows for frequency analysis." First Federal Inter-Agency Hydrologic Modeling Conference, April 20–22, 1998. Las Vegas: IAHMC, 1998: 4-31 – 4-36.

Dilsaver, Lary M. Ed. *America's National Park System: The Critical Documents*. Lanham: Rowman and Littlefield Publishers, 1994.

Dobney, Frederick J. *River Engineers on the Middle Mississippi: A History of the St. Louis District, U.S. Army Corps of Engineers*. St. Louis: Mississippi Valley Division, St. Louis District, 1978.

Dorsey, Florence. *Road to the Sea: The Story of James B. Eads and the Mississippi River*. New York: Rinehart, 1949.

Dyhouse, Gary. "Effects of Federal Levees and Reservoirs on 1993 Flood Stages in St. Louis." *Transportation Research Record* 1483 (1995): 11-17.

Farquhar, William R., Jr. and Jeffers, Henry A., Jr. *Bridging the Imjin: Construction of Libby and Teal Bridges During the Korean War (October 1952- July 1953)*. Fort Belvoir: Corps of Engineers Office of History, 1989.

Fiedler, David. *The Enemy Among Us: POWs in Missouri During World War II*. Columbia, Missouri: University of Missouri Press, 2003.

Fine, Lenore and Remington, Jesse A. *The Corps of Engineers: Construction in the United States*. Washington D.C.: U.S. Army Corps of Engineers, 1972.

Frank, Arthur D. *The Development of the Federal Program of Flood Control on the Mississippi River*. New York: AMS, 1968.

Fremling, Calvin R. *Immortal River: the Upper Mississippi in Ancient and Modern Times*. Madison: University of Wisconsin Press, 2005.

Giraud, Marcel. *History of French Louisiana*. Vol. 1. Baton Rouge: Louisiana State University Press, 1953.

Gladfelter, Herbert S. *Fifty-Five Years of Dredges and Dredging on the Mississippi River in the Memphis District*, Vol. 1, Pt. A. Memphis: U.S. Army Corps of Engineers, 1952.

Goetzmann, William H. *Army Exploration in the American West, 1803-1863*. New Haven, Yale University Press, 1959.

The Great Flood of 1993: Causes, Impacts, and Responses. ed. Stanley A. Changnon. Boulder: Westview Press, 1996.

Hays, Samuel P. *Conservation and the Gospel of Efficiency: The Progressive Conservation Movement, 1890-1920*. Cambridge, Mass.: Harvard University Press, 1959.

_____. *A History of Environmental Politics Since 1945*. Pittsburg: Pittsburg University Press, 2000.

Hill, Forest G. *Roads, Rails, and Waterways: The Army Engineers and Early Transportation*. Norman: University of Oklahoma Press, 1957.

History of the Board of Engineers for Rivers and Harbors. Fort Belvoir, Va.: Corps of Engineers History Office, 1980.

Hollon, W. Eugene. *The Lost Pathfinder: Zebulon Montgomery Pike*. Norman: University of Oklahoma Press, 1949.

Iacovelli, Debi. "The Saffir/Simpson Hurricane Scale: An Interview with Dr. Robert Simpson." *Mariners Weather Log* 43:1 (April 1999): 10-12.

Johnson, Leland R. *The Falls City Engineers: A History of the Louisville District, U.S. Army Corps of Engineers*. Wash.: Corps of Engineers History Office, 1974.

_____. *The Ohio River Division, U.S. Army Corps of Engineers: The History of a Central Command*. Cincinnati: Ohio River Division, 1992.

Kemper, James. *Rebellious River*. Boston: Bruce Humphreys, 1949.

Keevin, T.M. et al. "The use of high explosives to conduct a fisheries survey at a bendway weir field on the Middle Mississippi River." *Proceedings of the Twenty-Eighth Annual Conference on Explosives and Blasting Technique, Las Vegas, Nevada, Feb. 10-13, 2002*. Cleveland: International Society of Explosives Engineers, 2002.

Kline, Benjamin. *First Along the River: A Brief History of the U.S. Environmental Movement*. San Francisco: Acada Books, 1997.

Lavender, David. *The Way to the Western Sea: Lewis and Clark Across the Continent*. New York: Harper and Rowe, 1988.

Leopold, Luna B. and Maddock, Jr., Thomas. *The Flood Control Controversy: Big Dams, Little Dams, and Land Management*. New York: Ronald Press, 1954.

Leuchtenburg, William E. *Franklin D. Roosevelt and the New Deal, 1932-1940*. New York: Harper and Row, 1963.

Lewis, Jack. "The Birth of the EPA." *EPA Journal* (November 1985).

McCall, Edith. *Conquering the Rivers: Henry Miller Shreve and the Navigation of America's Inland Waterways*. Baton Rouge: Louisiana State University Press, 1984.

McDonnell, Janet A. *After Desert Storm: The U.S. Army and the Reconstruction of Kuwait*. Washington, D.C.: Department of the Army, 1999.

_____. *Supporting the Troops: The U.S. Army Corps of Engineers in the Persian Gulf War*. Alexandria: Corps of Engineers Office of History, 1996.

McKinney, Leon E.; Sutton, William R.; and Perez, Jean-Yves. "Locks and Dam No. 26, Rehabilitation Versus Replacement," *The Military Engineer* (March-April, 1980).

Manders, Damon; Tajkowski, David; and Dace, Michael. *Rebuilding Hope: A History of the Response to Hurricanes Katrina and Rita*. Vicksburg: Mississippi Valley Division, 2011.

Mayo, Kristi. "Digital-Image Management at Mass Gravesites." *Evidence Technology Magazine*. (May-June 2008).

Mazmanian, Daniel; and Nienaber, Jeanne. *Can Organizations Change?: Environmental Protection, Citizen, Participation, and the Corps of Engineers*. Washington D.C.: The Brookings Institute, 1979.

Merritt, Raymond H. *The Corps, the Environment, and the Upper Mississippi River Basin*. Washington, D.C.: Historical Division, Office of the Chief of Engineers, 1984.

Moorhus, Donita M., and Graves, Gregory. *The Limits of Vision: A History of the U.S. Army Corps of Engineers, 1988-1992*. Washington D.C.: U.S. Army Corps of Engineers Quadrennial History, April 2000: 1-51.

Musick, James B. *St. Louis as a Fortified Town*. St. Louis: R.F. Miller, 1941.

Niemi, Jack and Strauser, Claude. "Environmental River Engineering." *PIANC Bulletin*. 73 (1991).

Nichols, Roger L. and Halley, Patrick L. *Stephen Long and American Frontier Exploration*. Newark: University of Delaware Press, 1980.

O'Brien, William P. et al. *Gateways to Commerce: The U.S. Army Corps of Engineers' 9-Foot Channel Project on the Upper Mississippi River*. Denver: National Park Service, 1992.

Ockerson, John A. "Dredges and Dredging on the Mississippi River." *ASCE Transactions* 40 (1898): 215-348.

Peterson, Elmer. *Big Dam Foolishness: The Problem of Modern Flood Control and Water Storage*. NY: Devin-Adair, 1954.

Petersen, William J. *Steamboating on the Upper Mississippi*. Iowa City: State Historical Society of Iowa, 1968.

Pinter, N.; Thomas, R.; and Wlosinski, J.H. "Assessing flood hazard on dynamic rivers." *Transactions of the American Geophysical Union*. 82:31 (2001): 333-339.

Prelini, Charles. *Dredges and Dredging*. New York: D. Van Nostrand Co.: 1911.

Primm, James N. *Lion of the Valley: St. Louis, Missouri*. Boulder, Col.: Pruett, 1981.

Reuss, Martin. "Andrew A. Humphreys and the Development of Hydraulic Engineering: Politics and Technology in the Army Corps of Engineers, 1850-1950." *Technology and Culture* 26 (Jan. 1985): 1-33.

_____. *Reshaping National Water Politics: The Emergence of the Water Resources Development Act of 1986*. Fort Belvoir, Va.: Institute for Water Resources, 1991.

_____. *Shaping Environmental Awareness: The United States Army Corps of Engineers Environmental Advisory Board, 1970-1980*. Fort Belvoir: Corps of Engineers History Office, 1982.

Ruddy, T. Michael. *Damning the Dam: The St. Louis District Corps of Engineers and the controversy over the Meramec Basin Project from its inception to its deauthorization*. St. Louis: St. Louis District, 1992.

Sale, Kirkpatrick. *The Green Revolution: The American Environmental Movement, 1962-1992*. New York: Hill and Wang, 1993.

Schubert, Frank N. *Vanguard of Expansion: Army Engineers in the Trans-Mississippi West, 1819-1879*. Washington, D.C.: Historical Division, Office of the Chief of Engineers, 1980.

Shabecoff, Philip. *A Fierce Green Fire: The American Environmental Movement*. New York: Hill and Wang, 1993.

Shallat, Todd. "Colossus Above St. Louis: Remaking the Mississippi at Melvin Price Locks and Dam." *Illinois Heritage* (July-August, 2005).

_____. *Structures in the Stream: Water, Science, and the Rise of the U.S. Army Corps of Engineers*. Austin: University of Texas Press, 1994.

Snyder, Frank and Guss, Brian. *The District: A History of the Philadelphia District, U.S. Army Corps of Engineers, 1866-1971*. Philadelphia: U.S. Army Corps of Engineers, 1974.

Townsend, C. McDonald. *The Hydraulic Principles Governing River and Harbor Construction*. New York: MacMillan, 1922.

Tuttle, James R. "Overview of Hydrometeorology Subbasin Flow Contributions and Water Levels, Mississippi River Drought '88'." *American Public Works Association*. (Vicksburg: Lower Mississippi Valley Division, 1988): 1-12.

U.S. Army Corps of Engineers. *The U.S. Army Corps of Engineers: A Brief History*. Fort Belvoir, VA: Corps of Engineers History Office, 2007.

_____. *The U.S. Army Corps of Engineers: A History*. Washington, D.C.: Corps of Engineers History Office, 2007.

Wardlow, Chester. *The Transportation Corps: Responsibilities, Organization, and Operations*. Wash.: Office of Chief of Military History, 1951.

"William Arthur Snow." *ASCE Annual Report* (Jun. 10, 1941): 333-341.

Wilson, Joan. *Herbert Hoover: Forgotten Progressive*. Boston: Little, Brown, 1975.

Primary Sources

Archival material

"Affidavit of Donald C. Sweeney." *http://www.mvr.usace.army.mil/PublicAffairsOffice/NavStudy/Sweeney Affidavit.htm*, June 29, 2011.

Brochure. "Applied River Engineering Center." St. Louis: St. Louis District (MVS), 1997. MVS Archives.

Brochure. "Bendway Weirs." St. Louis: MVS, 1993. MVS Archives.

Brochure. "Blueprint for Action." Rock Island: MVR, N.D. MVS Archives.

Brochure. "Carlyle Lake, Illinois." St. Louis: MVS, 1996. MVS Archives.

Brochure. "Champion of Your Heartland's Water Resources." St. Louis: MVS, 2001. MVS Archives.

Brochure. "Clarence Cannon Dam and Mark Twain Lake." St. Louis: MVS, 2007. MVS Archives.

Brochure. "Environmental Management Program: Restoring and Monitoring on the Upper Mississippi River System." Rock Island: MVR, N.D. MVS Archives.

Brochure. "FAQ on Gulf Region District and Afghanistan Engineer District." USACE, N.D. MVS Archives.

Brochure. "Locks and Dam 26: Bottleneck on the Mississippi." American Waterways Operators, N.D. MVS Archives.

Brochure. "Mel Price Locks and Dam." St. Louis: MVS, 2005. MVS Archives.

Brochure. "Micro Modeling." St. Louis: Applied River Engineering Center, 2000. MVS Archives.

Brochure. "Playing the Waiting Game with Locks and Dam 26." National Committee on Locks and Dam 26, N.D. MVS Archives.

Brochure. "Public Information Brochure." St. Louis: MVS, Mar. 1977.

Brochure. "Swan Lake." Rock Island: MVR, N.D. MVS Archives.

"Canoeing on the Meramec and the Impacts on Canoeing Caused by the Project." St. Louis: MVS, Apr. 2, 1977. MVS Archives.

"Civil Works Project Files, L & D No. 26—Conferences." St. Louis: MVS, N.D. MVS Archives.

Commander's Assessments, Sept. 14, 2005-Jul. 1, 2006. Task Force Hope Historical Documentation Vol. 2-12.

Commander's Briefing, Oct. 3, 2005-Feb. 16, 2006. TF Hope Historical Documentation, Vol. 2-7.

Danforth, Sen. John. "The Meramec Dam: Position paper 1." Apr. 22, 1976. MVS Archives.

"Digest of Public Meeting on Meramec Park Lake at Sullivan." St. Louis: MVS, Mar. 26, 1977. MVS Archives.

"Fact, Fiction on Alton dam replacement." Response by American Waterways Operators to *Reader's Digest*. MVS Archives.

Fact Sheet. "Building a virtual team: FUSRAP's experience." May 1999. MVS Archives.

Fact Sheet. "Cape Girardeau (Floodwall), Missouri." *www.mvs.usace.army.mil/pm/cape-floodwall/index.html*, Mar. 31, 2011.

Fact Sheet. "DERP-FUDS fact sheet." Washington, D.C.: HQUSACE, 2000.

Fact Sheet. "East St. Louis and Vicinity, Illinois." *www.mvs.usace.army.mil/pm/esl-vicinity/index.html*, Apr. 6, 2011.

Fact Sheet. "Kaskaskia River." St. Louis: MVS, 1964. MVS Archives.

Fact Sheet. "Meramec Basin Projects Fact Sheet." MVS Archives.

Fact Sheet. "Upper Mississippi River System Navigation and Ecosystem Sustainability Program, Jan. 1, 2011." *http://www2.mvr.usace.army.mil/projects/dsp_factsheet.cfm?ProjID=F5C2680A-9D38-8690-BF35D7AB9AA74F7C*, June 29, 2011.

Fact Sheet. "Wappapello." *http://www.mvs.usace.army.mil/wappapello/wap-facts.htm*, Apr. 26, 2011.

Flannery, Toni. "How Young Robert E. Lee Helped Save the St. Louis Waterfront." News Clipping. MVS Archives.

Information Paper. Kaskaskia River Watershed Based Pilot Project for FY 2014. N.D. MVS Archives.

Information Paper. Kaskaskia Watershed Association, Inc. N.D. MVD.

Lowe, Gary P. "Alton to Gale Organized Levee Districts, Illinois and Missouri (Continuing, Deficiency Corrections) Letter Report." Presentation. Jul. 15, 2010. MVS Archives.

"A Meramec Chronology of the Corps of Engineers and Missouri's Meramec Basin, 1880 to 1983." N.D. MVS Archives.

"The Meramec Dam Plan." St. Louis: MVS, Mar. 1974. MVS Archives.

"Meramec Park Lake Chronology of Events Leading to Present Status." May 3, 1972. MVS Archives.

"The Meramec Project: A Progress Report." N.D. MVS archives.

Minutes of Meeting, Review Conference on Locks and Dam No. 26 (Replacement), Board of Consultants and Government Representatives, Waterways Experiment Station. July 31-August 2, 1972. St. Louis: MVS. MVS Archives.

Minutes of Meeting, Union Chamber of Commerce, Union, MO. Sept. 10, 1945. MVS Archives.

"The Mississippi River Navigation System and Locks and Dam 26." St. Louis: MVS, Feb. 1976. MVS Archives.

"Mississippi Valley Division Hurricane Contingency Plan (CONPLAN)," May 18, 2005. Task Force Hope Electronic Archives.

News Clippings. St. Louis *Globe-Democrat* and *Post-Dispatch*. MVS Archives.

News Release. "Army Engineers Announce Schedule of Public Meeting on 19 Water Resource Projects." Mar. 24, 1977. MVS Archives.

News Release. "Corps of Engineers to Restore Pre-Katrina Protection in New Orleans." Sept. 29, 2005. Task Force Hope Historical Documentation, Vol. 2.

News Release. "Joint Federal/State Action Taken to Relocate Times Beach Residents." Washington, D.C.: EPA, February 22, 1983.

News Release. "US Army Corps Responds to Navigation Study Critics." Wed. Feb. 28, 2001. *http://www.mvr. usace.army.mil/PublicAffairs Office/InternetNews/ TopStory/CorpsResponds.htm*, June 29, 2011.

News Release. "U.S. Census Bureau Delivers Missouri's 2010 Census Population Totals, Including First Look at Race and Hispanic Origin Data for Legislative Redistricting." Feb. 24, 2011. (*http://2010.census.gov /news/releases/operations/cb11-cn49.html*, May 31, 2011.

"NESP Information Paper, Dam Point Control." St. Louis: MVS, N.D.

"Notice of Comprehensive Basin Study of Meramec River, Missouri." Vicksburg: LMVD, 1964. MVS Archives.

"Opening the Waterways." Decommissioning Ceremony Invitation Packet. St. Louis: MVS Archives, 1990.

Pamphlet. "Historical Shipwrecks on the Middle Mississippi and Lower Illinois Rivers." St. Louis: MVS, 2004.

Pamphlet. Meramec Basin Resources Committee. *"A Shameless Sham": The Army Engineer "Plan" for the Meramec Basin*. 1950. MVS Archives.

Pamphlet. "One Hundred Years on the Mississippi River." Memphis: Memphis District, 1967.

"Proposal to Raise East Side Levees." News Clipping. June 28, 1935. MVS Archives.

Record of Public Hearing. Dec. 18, 1963. MVS Archives.

"Resolutions—32nd Annual Meeting of Franklin County Framer's Association, Union, Mo." Nov. 12, 1949. MVS Archives.

Response to RCGA request on "Alternative Plan to Meramec Dam Outlined by Sierra Club" (Jul. 14, 1976).

"Salute to the River, Opening the Waterways, the Dedication of Melvin Price Locks and Dam." St. Louis: MVS, 1994.

SITREP-TF Guardian, Oct. 1-25, Dec. 29, 2005. ENGLINK or Task Force Hope Electronic Archives.

Smith, Forrest. "Statement on Meramec Basin Reservoirs." Dec. 21, 1949. MVS Archives.

Statement. Brock Adams, Secretary of Transportation. Subcommittee on Water Resources, Senate Committee on the Environment and Public Works. Alton Locks and Dam authorization legislation and navigation user charges. May 2, 1977. MVS Archives.

Statement. Col. James B. Meanor. Public Hearing, St. Clair, Mo. Dec. 18, 1963. MVS Archives.

Statement. Col. Rudolph E. Smyser. Meramec Public Hearings. Dec. 13, 1949. MVS Archives.

Statement. Robert H. Binder, Assistant Secretary for Policy, Plans and International Affairs, Department of Transportation. Subcommittee on Water Resources, Senate Public Works Committee. Replacement of Alton Locks and Dam. June 17, 1976. MVS Archives.

"Status Report on the Meramec Basin Flood Control Project." N.D. MVS Archives.

Stemler, Joan and Jackie Taylor. "The Kaskaskia Flood of 2002: A Case Study on Cooperation and Conflicting Project Purposes." St. Louis: MVS, 2002.

St. Louis District Chronology. MVS Archives.

St. Louis District Organization Charts, 1958-1978. MVS Archives.

"St. Louis Eleven-mile flood protection: Project Moves Ahead." Presentation. St. Louis: MVS, 1966. MVS Archives.

Task Force Hope Status Report, Sept. 28, 2006. Task Force Hope Historical Documentation, Vol. 2.

U.S. Army Corps of Engineers. *Auction After-Action Report*. St. Louis: MVS, 1988. MVS Archives.

Web page. "Applied River Engineering Center." *www.mvs.usace.army.mil/eng-con/ expertise/arec and www.mvs.usace.army.mil/arec /riverengineering_data. html*, May 26, 2010.

Web page. "CEMVS – Center of Expertise for Photogrammetric Mapping." *http:// mvs-wc.mvs.usace.army.mil /tcx.html*, July 18, 2011.

Web page. "Chronological History of Jefferson Barracks." Jefferson Barracks Heritage Foundation. *http://www.jbhf.org/ chronology.html*, Mar. 21, 2011.

Web page. "Department of Defense: Archaeological Collections Management." *www. doi.gov/pam/dodarc.html*, Feb. 17, 2011.

Web page. "Electric Co-ops in Missouri." *www.amec.org/coops.html*, May 10, 2011.

Web page. "MCX-CMAC History." *www.mvs.usace.army.mil/engr/curation/MCX-HistoryTxt.html*, Feb.17, 2011.

Web page. "Melvin Price Locks and Dam, Alton, Illinois." *www.mvs.usace.army.mil/ navigation1/melvin%20lock.html*, May 23, 2011.

Web page. "River Engineering." *www.mvs.usace.army mil/arec/basics.html*, June 30, 2011.

Web page. "Riverlands Migratory Bird Sanctuary." *www.mvs.usace.army.mil/Rivers/ RMBS.html*, July 26, 2011.

Web page. "The Upper Mississippi River System Environmental Management Program, UMRS-EMP." *www.mvs.usace.army.mil/pm/WelcomePage.htm*, June 8, 2011.

Web page. "The Urban Search and Rescue Program." Fact Sheet. *www.usace.army.mil/Emergency/Documents/USR2009.pdf*, September 13, 2011.

Web page. "What is FUSRAP?" *www.mvs.usace.army.mil/eng-con/expertise/fusrap.html*, March 22, 2011.

Web page. Wlosinski et al., "Vegetation Response to a Water Level Experiment." *www.usgs.gov/reports_publications/psrs/psr_1997_07.html*, July 26, 2011.

Congressional documents

U.S. Congress. *Annual Report of the Chief of Engineers, 1866-2008*. 39th – 110th Congress.

_____. *Annual Report of the Secretary of War, 1824-1857*. 18th – 35th Congress.

_____. "Application of Arkansas that Capt. Henry M. Shreve May Be Allowed to Enter Six Sections of Land in the Raft of the Red River for Reclaiming the Same." H.D. 1347. 24th Cong., 1st Sess.

_____. *Brief Report on Meramec River, Missouri Basin Plan*. H.D. 525. 89th Cong., 2nd Sess.

_____. "Captain Henry M. Shreve, Jan. 4, 1848." H.R. 30. 30th Cong., 1st Sess.

_____. "Communication, of the 12th instant, from Mr. James B. Eads, a member of the Mississippi River Commission." H.D. 10, Pt. 2. 47th Cong. 1st Sess.

_____. *Comprehensive Report on Reservoirs in Mississippi River Basin*. H.D. 259. 74th Cong., 1st Sess.

_____. *Condition of the Military Establishment, 1824*. H.D. 262. 18th Cong., 2nd Sess.

_____. *Control of Floods in the Alluvial Valley of the Lower Mississippi River*. Vol. 1. H.D. 798. 71st Cong., 3rd Sess.

_____. *Congressional Record*. House. 70th Cong., 1st Sess., Pt. 1 (Dec. 1927).

_____. *Condition of the Military Establishment, 1823*. H.D. 247. 18th Cong., 1st Sess.

_____. "Compensation to Persons Engaged in the Several Exploring Expeditions under Captain Pike." H.D. 259. 10th Cong., 2nd Sess.

_____. *Flood Control in the Mississippi Valley*. H.D. 90. 70th Cong., 1st Sess.

_____. "Fortifications." H.D. 183. 16th Cong., 1st Sess.

_____. *Harbor and Approaches to St. Louis*. H.D. 772. 59th Cong., 1st Sess.

_____. "Harbor at St. Louis." H.R. 14. 23rd Cong., 2nd Sess.

_____. "Harbor of St. Louis." H.D. 298. 25th Cong., 2nd Sess.

_____. *Harbor of St. Louis*. H.R. 203. 28th Cong., 1st Sess.

_____. "Henry M. Shreve, Mar. 3, 1836." H.R. 383. 24th Cong., 1st Sess.

_____. "Henry M. Shreve, Jun. 7, 1844." H.R. 538. 28th Cong., 1st Sess.

_____. "Henry M. Shreve—Navigation on the Ohio River." H.D. 74. 21st Cong., 2nd Sess.

_____. "Henry M. Shreve – Snag Boat." H.R. 272. 27th Cong., 3rd Sess.

_____. House Committee on Flood Control, *House Flood Control Hearings*. Vol. 5. 70th Cong., 1st Sess.

_____. "Improvement of Red River." H.D. 123. 24th Cong., 1st Sess.

_____. "Inland Water Transportation: Hearings on the subject of Inland Water Transportation." Dec. 13, 1918. 65th Cong., 1st Sess.

_____. *Kaskaskia River, Illinois*. H.D. 232. 85th Cong., 1st Sess.

_____. *Kaskaskia River, Illinois*. S.D. 44. 87th Cong., 1st Sess.

_____. *Kaskaskia River Levees, Illinois*. H.D. 351. 88th Cong., 2nd Sess.

_____. "Letter from the Sec. of War transmitting copies of the Reports of H.M. Shreve and R. Delafield on the improvement of navigation on the Mississippi and Ohio rivers." H.D. 9. 21st Cong., 2nd Sess.

_____. "Letter from Henry M. Shreve to the Hon. C.A. Wickliffe on the Subject of Navigation on the Mississippi River." H.D. 11. 20th Cong., 1st Sess.

_____. *Letter from the Secretary of War Transmitting A Report on Improvement of the Red River*. S.D. 64. 27th Cong., 1st Sess.

_____. "Memorial of E.T. Langham and A.W. McDonald." H.D. 278. 24th Cong., 1st Sess.

_____. "Memorial of the Legislature of Missouri." H.D. 21. 23rd Cong., 1st Sess.

_____. "Memorial of a Number of Citizens of St. Louis, Missouri." S.D. 185. 28th Cong., 1st Sess.

_____. *Mississippi River at Cape Girardeau, Mo*. H.D. 204. 81st Cong., 1st Sess.

_____. *Mississippi River at St. Louis, Mo*. S.D. 57. 84th Cong., 1st Sess.

_____. *Mississippi River between Coon Rapids Dam and Mouth of Ohio River*. H.D. 669. 76th Cong., 3rd Sess.

_____. *Mississippi River between Mouth of Missouri River and Minneapolis, Minnesota (Interim Report)*. H.D. 290. 71st Cong., 2nd Sess.

_____. *Mississippi River between Ohio River and Mouth of Missouri River*. H.D. 231. 76th Cong., 1st Sess.

_____. *Mississippi River between St. Louis, Mo., and Lock and Dam No. 26*. S.D. 7. 85th Cong., 1st Sess.

_____. *Mississippi River from Cape Girardeau, Mo., to Rock Island, Ill.* H.D. 628. 63rd Cong., 2nd Sess.

_____. *Mississippi River, Urban Areas at Alton, Ill.* H.D. 397. 83rd Cong., 2nd Sess.

_____. "Missouri-National Road." H.D. 140. 24th Cong., 1st Sess.

_____. *National Defense and National Foundries.* H.R. 206. 26th Cong., 1st Sess.

_____. "Ohio and Mississippi River." H.R. 337. 21st Cong., 1st Sess.

_____. *Operations of the Topographical Bureau during the year 1839.* S.D. 58. 26th Cong., 1st Sess.

_____. "Pre-Emption to the Sand Bar, in Front of St. Louis." H.D. 197. 24th Cong., 1st Sess.

_____. *Public Works for Water and Power Development and Energy Research Appropriation Bill, 1978: Hearings Before a Subcommittee on Appropriations, House of Representatives.* 95th Cong. 1st Sess. Pt. 9. Washington, D.C.: GPO, 1977.

_____. "Relative to the Title to the Island Opposite St. Louis." H.D. 1539. 24th Cong., 1st Sess.

_____. *Rend Lake Reservoir, Illinois.* H.D. 541. 87th Cong., 2nd Sess.

_____. *Report by a Special Board of Engineers on Survey of Mississippi River from St. Louis, Mo., to its Mouth.* H.D. 50. 61st Cong., 1st Sess.

_____. *Report from the Mississippi River Commission.* H.D. 38. 49th Cong., 1st Sess.

_____. *Reports in Reference to Inundations of the Mississippi River.* S.D. 20. 32nd Cong., 1st Sess.

_____. *Report Intended to Illustrate a Map of the Hydrographical Basin of the Upper Mississippi River.* S.D. 380. 26th Cong., 2nd Sess.

_____. "Report of the Board of Engineers on the Ohio and Mississippi Rivers." H.D. 35. 17th Cong. 2nd Sess.

_____. *Report of Chief Engineer Relative to the Application of Appropriation for Removing Obstructions to the Navigation of the Ohio and Mississippi Rivers.* S.D. 14. 19th Cong. 1st Sess.

_____. "A report of the Chief of Engineers upon the proposed improvement of the Mississippi River from Alton to the Meramec River." S.D. 50. 41st Cong., 3rd Sess.

_____. *Report of Chief Topographical Engineer, 1841-1855.* 27th – 34th Congress.

_____. *Report of the Mississippi River Commission, 1880.* H.D. 95. 46th Cong., 3rd Sess.

_____. *Report of the Mississippi River Commission, Nov 25, 1881.* H.D. 10. 47th Cong. 1st Sess.

_____. "A Report of the Present Strength of the U.S. Army." H.D. 18. 15th Cong., 1st Sess.

_____. *Report on the Control of Floods of the Mississippi River by Means of Reservoirs.* House Flood Control Committee Doc. 2. 70th Cong., 1st Sess.

_____. *Report on the Meramec River.* HD 686. 71st Cong., 3rd Sess.

_____. *Reports on the Ohio and Mississippi Rivers.* House Flood Control Committee Doc. 17. 70th Cong., 1st Sess.

_____. *Roads and Canals*, S.D. 250 (10th Cong., 1st Sess.).

_____. *Salt River, Missouri.* H.D. 507. 87th Cong., 2nd Sess.

_____. "Sand Bar—Harbor of St. Louis." H.D. 124. 24th Cong., 2nd Sess.

_____. *Showing the Condition of the Military Establishment and Fortifications during the Year 1827.* H.D. 360. 20th Cong., 1st Sess.

_____. *St. Francis River, Mo. And Ark.* H.D. 159. 71st Cong., 2nd Sess.

_____. *St. Louis and Illinois Bridge across the Mississippi River.* H.D. 194. 43rd Cong., 1st Sess.

_____. *Supplement to the Annual Report of the Chief Engineer.* S.D. 125. 26th Cong., 1st Sess.

_____. *Survey of Mississippi River between Missouri River and Minneapolis.* H.D. 137, Pt. 1. 72nd Cong., 1st Sess.

_____. "United States Railroad Administration." S.D. 275. 65th Cong., 2nd Sess.

U.S. Congressional Budget Office. *Alton Locks and Dam: A Review of the Evidence.* Staff Working Paper. Washington, D.C.: Congressional Budget Office, 1976.

U.S. Congressional Office of Technology Assessment. *Wetlands: Their Use and Regulation* (Washington, D. C.: GPO 1984).

U.S. Congressional Research Service. 'The Supreme Court Addresses Corps of Engineers Jurisdiction over "Isolated Waters": The SWANCC Decision.' Washington, D.C.: GPO, 2001.

U.S. Government Accountability Office. *Wetlands Overview: Problems With Acreage Data Persist.* Washington, D.C.: GPO 1998.

U.S. Government Accountability Office. *Wetlands Protection.* Washington, D.C.: GPO, 2005.

Correspondence

Coalition for Environment to district. Letter. June 24, 1971. MVS Archives.

Cool, Don to Damon Manders. E-mail. Reservoir data. Apr. 26, 2011.

Delbridge, N.G. to Chief of Engineers. Memorandum. Ste. Genevieve, Missouri. Apr. 16, 1985. MVS Archives.

District Counsel to CELMS-PM-M (Sutton). Memorandum. Legal Opinion on the Mississippi River Navigation Project Dimensions, May 28, 1993. MVS Archives.

Elliott to Maj. J.H. Carruth, Memorandum. Nov. 25, 1929. MVS Archives.

Harloe, B.M. to Division Office, UMVD. Memorandum. Feb. 7, 1934. MVS Archives.

Heiberg, E.R. to Secretary of the Army. Memorandum. Aug. 20, 1986. MVS Archives.

Hoge, William E. to Division Engineer. Memorandum. Report on letter from Mr. H.N. Pharr. Mar. 15, 1935. MRC Archives.

Jackson, Thomas A. to Jadwin, Edgar. Memoranda. Abolishing the Northern District, Mississippi River Commission. Jul. 7, 1928; Field Reorganization. Jul. 13, 1928; Functions and Agencies of the Mississippi River Commission, July 27, 1928. MRC Archives.

Lewis, Meriwether and Clark, Lewis Expedition. Letters Nos. 86-124, 207. Sept. 8, 1803-June 3, 1804, Sept. 23, 1806. Jackson, Donald. Ed. *Letters of the Lewis and Clark Expedition with Related Documents, 1783-1854*. Urbana: University of Illinois Press, 1962.

L'Enfant, Pierre. Letter to Continental Congress, Dec. 15, 1784. Walker, Paul K. Ed. *Engineers of Independence: A Documentary History of the Army Engineers in the American Revolution, 1775-1783*. Washington: CEHO, 1981.

Letter to LMVD. Review of Corps Projects. Mar. 1, 1977. MVS Archives.

Lyman, AKB to Secretary of War. Memorandum. Transfers at Government expense. Oct. 22, 1929. MRC Archives.

Memorandum to Col. Kittrell. Meramec River Basin—Outline of Investigation. Apr. 19, 1949. MVS Archives.

Memorandum for Commander, Mississippi Valley Division. Implementation Plan for ER 5-1-11, Programs and Project Management. N.D. MVS archives.

Memorandum. CWA Jurisdiction Following the U.S. Supreme Court Decision in *Rapanos v. United States*. June 5, 2007. MVS Archives.

Memorandum. Meramec Park Lake Disposal Project. Oct. 17, 1983. MVS Archives.

Memorandum of Opinion. Integrated River Management; Mississippi River Navigation Project Dimensions. May 26, 1993; Mr. Martin. Low Water Reference Plane – St. Louis to Thebes. Dec. 20, 1972. MVS Archives.

Niemi, Jack. Memorandum. Remarks of Jack Niemi to LMVD. Apr. 14, 1975. MVS Archives.

Office of Chief of Engineers to Division Engineer, UMVD. Memorandum. Public Hearings on the Meramec Basin Reservoirs. Dec. 23, 1947. MVS Archives.

Paddock, Mark, to Col. Carroll LeTellier. Letter. June 24, 1971. MVS Archives.

Pike, Zebulon Expedition. Letters No. 39, 117, 121. Feb. 28, 1806. Jul 20, 1807. Aug. 12, 1807. Jackson, Donald. Ed. *Journals of Zebulon Montgomery Pike with Letters and Related Documents*. Vol. 1 and 2. Norman: University of Oklahoma Press, 1966.

Reinecke, P.S. Memorandum. Dams in the Meramec River Basin. Aug. 4, 1938. MVS Archives.

Robins, Thomas to Jackson. Memorandum. Reorganization of Engineer Department at Large. Oct. 7, 1929. MRC Archives.

Stark, James to Crear, Robert. Memorandum. ESF#3 Transition/Mission Close Out Plan – Hurricane Katrina. FEMA Louisiana Transitional Recovery Office: N.D. OH-MVD Files (electronic).

St. Louis Engineer Office to Chief of Engineers. Memorandum. Aug. 12, 1909. MVS Archives.

Court cases

Izaak Walton League of America, Et Al. v. John O. Marsh. 655 F.2d 346 (D.C. Cir. 1981).

Izaak Walton League of America, Et Al. and Atchison, Topeka, and Santa Fe Railway Company, et al. v. Clifford R. Alexander, et al. Civil Action No. 74-1190. (D.C. Cir. 1979).

Sierra Club v. Froehlke. Cause No. 72C584(3). U.S. Ct., East. Mo. Dist.

Solid Waste Agency of Northern Cook County v. U.S. Army Corps of Engineers. 99-1178. 531U.S. 159 (2001).

Thomas Gibbons vs. Aaron Ogden. 22 U.S. 9 Wheat. 1 (1824).

Litigation Report, *Sierra Club et. al. v. Robert F. Froehlke, et. al.*, Dec. 26, 1973 (MVS Archives).

Sierra Club v. Froehlke. Brief of Appellants, No. 75-1252 (8th Cir., 1975).

Litigation Report. *Lester Dill v. James R. Schlesinger.* Civil 74-246 C (2) (East. Mo. Dist. 1974).

Interviews

Beech, Gary D. By Michael Ruddy. July 11, 1985. MVS Archives.

Busse, David. By Jon Daly and Donna Zoeller. May 26 and July 26, 2010.

_____. By Damon Manders. July 11, 2011.

Carlock, M.F. By Rex Almsick. Mar. 19, 1979. MVS Archives.

Comfort, David. By Michael Ruddy. Mar. 17, 1980. MVS Archives.

Corbin, James. By Michael Ruddy. Jan. 4 and Nov. 3, 1989. Dec. 14, 1990. MVS Archives.

Craig, James. By Michael Ruddy. Nov. 20, 1991. MVS Archives.

_____. By Michael Ruddy. Sep. 2, 1992. MVS Archives.

Crear, Robert. By Damon Manders. May 29, 2007. TFH Electronic Archives.

Dace, Michael. By Michael Ruddy. Feb. 15, 1985. MVS Archives.

_____. By Jon Daly and Donna Zoeller. May 25 and June 10, 2010. MVS Archives.

Flippen, Daniel. By Michael Ruddy. September 3, 1984. MVS Archives.

Hatch, Henry J. By Alan Atkisson. *In Context* 32 (Summer 1992).

Huizinga, Elmer F. N.D. MVS Archives.

Jester, Guy. By James Towey. August 10, 1987. MVS Archives.

_____. By Michael Ruddy. June 7, 1983. MVS Archives.

Lamm, Max. By Rex Van Almsick. Mar. 2, 1979. MVS Archives.

Lawler, James. By Rex Van Almsick. May 15, 1979. MVS Archives.

McKinney, Leon. By Martin Towey. Aug. 11, 1987.

Meanor, James B. May 26, 1983. MVS Archives.

Meyer, Morton. By Michael Ruddy. Aug. 22, 1980. MVS Archives.

Niedernhofer, Tom. By Brian Rentfro. Sep. 19, 2011. MVS Archives.

Peterson, Thorwald. By Michael Ruddy. May 19, 1983. MVS Archives.

Setliff, Lewis. By David Tajkowski. May 11, 2007 and June 12, 2007. TFH Electronic Archives.

Strauser, Claude. By Jon Daly and Donna Zoeller. Jul. 28, 2010. MVS Archives.

Wilson, Daniel. By Michael Ruddy. November 13, 1988. MVS Archives.

_____. By Michael Ruddy. July 28, 1988. MVS Archives.

Laws

U.S. Congress. Act authorizing the construction of certain public works on rivers and harbors, and for other purposes. (*River and Harbor Act of 1909*). P.L. 60-317. 60th Cong., 1st Sess.

_____. *Act authorizing the construction of certain public works on rivers and harbors for flood control, and for other purposes.* (*Flood Control Act of 1936*). PL 74-738. 74th Cong., 2nd Sess.

_____. Act authorizing construction of certain public works on rivers and harbors for flood control, and other purposes. (*Flood Control Act of 1938*). PL 75-761. 75th Cong., 3rd Sess.

_____. Act authorizing construction of certain public works on rivers and harbors for flood control, and other purposes. (*Flood Control Act of 1944*). PL 78–534. 78th Cong., 2nd Sess.

_____. Act authorizing construction, repair, and preservation of certain public works on rivers and harbors for navigation, flood control, and for other purposes (*Water Resources Development Act of 1976*). PL 95-587. 94th Cong., 2nd Sess.

_____. *Act to provide for the appointment of a Mississippi River Commission for the improvement of said river from the Head of the Passes near its mouth to its headwaters.* PL 46-34. 46th Cong., 1st Sess.

_____. *Act to provide for the conservation and development of water and related resources. (Water Resources Development Act of 2007).* PL 110-114. 110th Cong., 1st Sess.

_____. *Act to provide for the protection of Native American graves, and for other purposes. (Native American Graves Protection and Repatriation Act).* PL 101-601. 101st Cong., 2nd Sess.

_____. *Act to provide uniform policies with respect to recreation and fish and wildlife benefits and costs of Federal multiple-purpose water resource projects, and for other purposes. (Federal Water Project Recreation Act of 1965).* PL 89-72. 89th Cong., 2nd Sess.

_____. *Act for the control of floods on the Mississippi River and its tributaries, and for other purposes. (Flood Control Act of 1928).* PL 70-391. 70th Cong., 1st Sess.

_____. *Act to improve the navigation of the Ohio and Mississippi rivers.* PL 18-89. 18th Cong., 1st Sess.

_____. *Act making appropriations for certain Internal Improvements for the year 1832.* 22nd Cong., 2nd Sess.

_____. *Act to provide for the control of the floods of the Mississippi River and of the Sacramento River, California, and for other purposes. (Flood Control Act of 1917).* PL 65-367. 65th Cong, 1st Sess.

_____. *Disaster Relief Act Amendments of 1974.* PL 93-288. 93rd Cong., 1st Sess.

The Federal Water Pollution Control Act Amendments of 1972 (Clean Water Act). P.L. 92-500. 92nd Cong., 2nd Sess.

_____. *Robert T. Stafford Disaster Relief and Emergency Assistance Act.* PL 100-707. 100th Cong., 2nd Sess.

Manuscripts

"Cooperative Studies." Draft. Oct. 3, 1947. MVS Archives.

Dyhouse, Gary. "Chronology of Levee Construction on the Middle Mississippi River." Manuscript. Dec. 2009. MVS Archives.

_____. "Comparing Flood Stage-Discharge Data – Be Careful." Draft paper. MVS Archives.

_____. "Levees at St. Louis – More Harm Than Good?" Draft paper. MVS Archives.

Johnson, Arthur. "St. Louis District Begins Design of Alton Locks," Prepared for American Society of Civil Engineers Annual Meeting, Oct. 18-22, 1971. MVS Archives.

"Mobilization of the Field (St. Louis District) Organization in World War II." Manuscript. MVS Archives.

Pursell Carroll, and Willingham, William. "Protecting the Nation's Waters: A History of the U.S. Army Corps of Engineers' Regulatory Responsibilities, 1899-1999." Manuscript. February 1999. Corps of Engineers History Office.

Ruddy, T. Michael. "Mobilizing for War: St. Louis and the Middle Mississippi during World War II." Manuscript. [1981]. MVS Archives.

Sheely, Jr., Horace J. "Lee Serves in the West." Research Report. Jefferson Expansion Memorial. MVS Archives.

Root, Clarence J. "Draining the American Bottoms." May 1911.

U.S. Army Corps of Engineers. "Chapter 6: Environmental Engineering." Manuscript. N.D. MVS archives.

Periodicals

Aquatic Resources News.

Armed Forces Press Service.

Baton Rouge, La., *Advocate.*

Belleville News-Democrat

Better Homes and Gardens Country Home.

Big Muddy News.

Boonville, Mo., *Daily News.*

Centralia, Ill., *Sentinel.*

Clinton County News

Crawford, Mo., *Mirror.*

Cuba Free Press.

Des Moines Register.

Domestic Commerce.

East St. Louis *Sunday Journal.*

Edwardsville, Ill., *Intelligencer.*

Engineer News Record.

Fortune.

Government Executive.

Illinois Issues.

Literary Digest.

Los Angeles Times.

McCall.

Macon, Mo., *Chronicle.*

Memphis, Tenn., *Commercial Appeal.*

Midwest Motorist.

Monthly Weather Review.

Moultrie County, Ill., *News.*

MSNBC.

New York Times.

The Military Engineer (TME).

New Orleans *Times-Picayune.*

New Athens, Ill., *Journal-Press.*

National Park Service *Museum Gazette.*

Plains Daily.

Potosi, Mo., *Independent-Journal.*

Rolla Daily News.

Southeast Missourian.

Southern Illinoisan.

St. Louis *Commerce.*

St. Louis *Globe-Democrat.*

The St. Louis Magazine.

St. Louis *Post-Dispatch.*

St. Louis District *Esprit.*

St. Louis District *Information Bulletin.*

Sullivan, Mo., *Independent News.*

Sullivan Tri-County News.

U.S. Army Corps of Engineers *Engineer Update.*

Washington Post.

Water Spectrum.

Waterways Journal.

Willow Springs, Mo., *News.*

Regulations

Engineering Regulation, 500-1-1.

Technical Reports

Allies Engineers and Architects. *The Master Plan for Restoration of Ste. Genevieve, Missouri*. St. Louis: Hellmuth, Obata, and Kasselbaum; Booker and Associates, 1966.

Big Load Afloat: U.S. Inland Water Transportation Resources. Wash.: American Waterways Operators, Inc., 1966.

Blake, Eric S.; Rappaport, Edward N.; and Landsea, Christopher W. *The deadliest, Costliest, and Most Intense United States Tropical Cyclones from 1851 to 2006 (and Other Frequently Requested Hurricane Facts)*. Miami: National Hurricane Center (NHC), 2007.

Calhoun, John C. "Report of the Secretary of War Relative to Roads and Canals." Washington: De Krafft, 1819.

The Clean Water Jurisdictional Handbook. Washington, D.C.: Environmental Law Institute, 2007.

Council on Environmental Quality. *A Citizen's Guide to the NEPA: Having Your Voice Heard*. Washington, D.C.: CEQ, Executive Office of the President, 2007.

Cushing, Jerome. *Maintenance of Locks and Dam 26 (Alton, Illinois)*. St. Louis: MVS, 1976.

Eads, James B. "Review of the U.S. Engineers' Report on the St. Louis Bridge," in McHenry, pp. 77-88;): 55-66. "Address at the Grand Opening of the St. Louis Bridge, July 4, 1874," in McHenry, p. 43.

The Flood of 1903. Chicago: Chicago and Alton Railway, N.D.

Garvey, James E. et al. *Responses of Fishes, Waterbirds, Invertebrates, Vegetation, and Water Quality to Environmental Pool Management: Mississippi River Pool 25*. Carbondale, Ill.: Southern Illinois University, 2003.

Gordon, David. "A Remedy for the Chronic Dredging Problem." *Engineer: Professional Bulletin for the Army Corps of Engineers*. Oct.-Dec. 2004.

Humphreys, Andrew A. and Abbot, Henry L. *Report upon the Physics and Hydraulics of the Mississippi River (Delta Survey)*. Washington, D.C.: GPO, 1876.

Humphreys, Benjamin G. *Floods and Levees of the Mississippi River*. Wash.: Mississippi River Association, 1914.

Impact of the War on the St. Louis Area: City of St. Louis and St. Louis County, Missouri, Madison and St. Clair Counties, Illinois. Wash.: DOL, BLS, 1944.

Institute of River Studies, University of Missouri-Rolla. *Fish Populations in Bendway Weir Fields, Results of the November 1996 Hydroacoustic Surveys Performed on the Middle Mississippi River*. St. Louis: MVS, 1997.

Institute of River Studies. *Meramec River Basin Water Supply Study*. St. Louis: University of Missouri-Rolla, 1979.

Institute for Water Resources. *Surviving the Drought: Corps of Engineers Response to Drought Conditions in 1988*. D.C.: USACE, 1989.

McNerny, Michael J. and Hoxie, R. David. *Final Report: Archaeological Resources Survey and Impact Assessment of the Ste. Genevieve Levee Project*. St. Louis: MVS, 1983.

Missouri Department of Natural Resources, Upper Mississippi River Basin Commission. *Out of Harm's Way: Lower Meramec Valley Flood Damage Reduction Study, Summary Report*. St. Louis: MVS, 1981.

National Research Council. *Inland Navigation System Planning: The Upper Mississippi River-Illinois Waterway*. Wash., D.C.: National Academy Press, 2001.

National Response Plan. N.P.: DHS, Dec. 2004.

North American Waterfowl Management Plan, Plan Committee. *1994 Update to the North American Waterfowl Management Plan: Expanding the Commitment*. 1994.

_____. *North American Waterfowl Management Plan, A Strategy for Cooperation*. May 1986.

Peterson, Thorwald. "Statement of Findings Locks and Dam No. 26 (Replacement), Upper Mississippi River Basin, Mississippi River, Alton Illinois." St. Louis: MVS, 1974. MVS Archives.

Red Cross. *The Mississippi Valley Flood Disaster of 1927: Official Report of Flood Operations*. Washington, D.C.: Red Cross, 1927.

Sugerman, Jerry M. "Report on the Meramec Heritage Riverway, and Other Alternatives To the Meramec Park Reservoir Project." St. Louis: Sierra Club, 1977. MVS Archives.

Thomas, E.J. "Flood of 1927." MRC Tech Files 2-2-23.

Ullman, Edward L.; Boyce, Ronald R.; and Volk, Donald J. *The Meramec Basin Water and Economic Development, Report of the Meramec Basin Research Project, Vol. I: Summary and a Program of Water Resource Development Proposals*. St. Louis: Washington UP, 1962.

Upper Mississippi River Basin Commission, *Replacement of Locks and Dam 26, Proceedings of Public Information Meetings* (Minneapolis: UMRBC, 1975).

Upper Mississippi River Basin Commission, *Comprehensive Master Plan for the Management of the Upper Mississippi River System* (Minneapolis: UMRBC, 1982).

U.S. Army Corps of Engineers. *1969 Floods*. St. Louis: MVS, 1969.

_____. *2004 Report to Congress, Upper Mississippi River System Environmental Management Program*. Rock Island, Ill.: MVR, 2004.

_____. *After Action Report: Midwest Flood of 1993*. St. Louis: MVS, 1994.

_____. *After Action Flood Report: Midwest Flood of 1995*. St. Louis: MVS, 1995.

_____. *Alton Navigation Pool, Mississippi and Illinois Rivers*. DM 2Cc1. St. Louis: MVS, 1962.

_____. *Annual Report to Congress for Flood Damage Reduction*. St. Louis: MVS, 2010.

_____. *Bendway Weirs on the Mississippi River*. St. Louis: MVS, 1992.

_____. *Clarksville Navigation Pool, Lock and Dam No. 24, Mississippi River*. DM 2. St. Louis: MVS, 1967.

_____. "Concrete Report: First Coffer Dam, Dam No. 26." St. Louis: MVS, 1936.

_____. *Design Memorandum No. 11, Formulation Evaluation Report, Locks and Dam No. 26 (Replacement)*. Vol. I. St. Louis: MVS, 1975.

_____. *Draft Supplement Environmental Statement, Locks and Dam No. 26 (Replacement), Volume I, Upper Mississippi River Basin, Mississippi River, Alton, Illinois*. St. Louis: MVS, 1975.

_____. *Draft Environmental Impact Statement, Second Lock at Locks and Dam No. 26 (Replacement), Mississippi River, Alton, Illinois and Missouri*. St. Louis: MVS, 1986.

_____. *Environmental Impact Statement, Meramec Park Lake*. MVS: November 6, 1970.

_____. *Environmental Pool Management*. St. Louis: MVS, 1998.

_____. *Environmental River Engineering on the Mississippi*. St. Louis: MVS, 1995.

_____. *Final Environmental Statement, Mississippi River, Alton, Illinois, Vol. I, to Accompany the Final Report of the Chief of Engineers*. St. Louis: MVS, 1976.

_____. *Final Environmental Impact Statement, Second Lock at Locks and Dam No. 26 (Replacement), Mississippi River, Alton, Illinois and Missouri*. St. Louis: MVS, 1988.

_____. *Floods and Flood Control on the Mississippi, 1973*. N.P.: USACE, [1974].

_____. *Flood Protection for City of St. Louis and Vicinity: Supplementary Detailed Cost Estimate*. St. Louis: MVS, 1954.

_____. *General Reevaluation Report: St. Louis Harbor Missouri and Illinois Project*. St. Louis: MVS, 2004.

_____. *Integrated Final Feasibility Report and Programmatic Environmental Impact Statement for the UMR-IWW System Navigation Feasibility Study*. N.P.: MRD, 2004.

_____. "Kaskaskia River Navigation." St. Louis: MVS, 1974.

_____. *Lake Shelbyville Master Plan*. St. Louis: MVS, 2004.

_____. "Locks and Dam No. 26, Mississippi River – Alton, Illinois." Report on failure. St. Louis: MVS, [1977].

_____. *Locks and Dam No. 26 (Replacement) Design Memorandum No. 2*. St. Louis: MVS, 1972.

_____. *Locks and Dam No. 26 (Replacement) Design Memorandum No. 7.* St. Louis: MVS, 1973.

_____. *Locks and Dam No. 26 (Replacement) Conference, 18-19 November 1971.* St. Louis: MVS, 1971.

_____. *Locks and Dam No. 26 (Replacement), Supplement No. 2 to Design Memorandum No. 2.* St. Louis: MVS, 1979.

_____. *The Master Plan, Design Memorandum No. 10 (Revised 1974, updated 1979, 1986, 1997) Carlyle Lake, Illinois.* St. Louis: MVS, 1997.

_____. *Master Plan. Design Memorandum No. 9, Clarence Cannon Dam and Mark Twain Lake.* St. Louis: MVS, 2004.

_____. *Meramec Basin Reservoirs Missouri: Digest of Preliminary Information.* St. Louis: MVS, 1959.

_____. *The Meramec River Basin: An Information Bulletin.* St. Louis: MVS, 1962.

_____. *Meramec River Basin Water Supply Study.* St. Louis: MVS, 1979.

_____. "Melvin Price Locks and Dam," (St. Louis: MVS Archives).

_____. *Mid-West Flood 2008 After Action Report.* St. Louis: MVS, 2008.

_____. *Mississippi Low Water Dam between St. Louis, Mo., and Lock and Dam No. 26.* GDM 2. St. Louis: MVS, 1958.

_____. *Mississippi River – Chain of Rocks Project.* St. Louis: MVS, 1947.

_____. *Mississippi River Spring Flood 2008 After Action Report.* St. Louis: MVS, 2008.

_____. *Mississippi River and Tributaries: Post-Flood Report, 1973.* Vicksburg: LMVD, [1974].

_____. "Navigation Project: Kaskaskia River, Illinois." St. Louis: USACE, 1968.

_____. *Performance Evaluation Status and Interim Results.* Vicksburg: IPET, Mar. 10, 2006.

_____. *Planning Guidance Notebook.* ER 1105-2-100. Washington, D.C.: USACE, April 22, 2000.

_____. *Plan of Study, Navigation Effects of the Second Locks, Melvin Price Locks and Dam.* St. Louis: MVS, 1991.

_____. *Post-Flood Report, 1973.* Vicksburg, MS: LMVD, 1973.

_____. *Project Review, Meramec Park Lake.* St. Louis: MVS, Mar. 8, 1977.

_____. *Recognizing Wetlands.* Washington, D.C.: HQUSACE, 1998.

_____. *Regulatory Program 2002-2008 Report.* Washington, D.C.: GPO 2008.

_____. "Report on April-May 1944 Flood in the St. Louis Missouri Engineer District." St. Louis: MVS, 1944.

_____. *Report on Replacement, Lock and Dam No. 26, Mississippi River, Alton, Illinois*. St. Louis: MVS, 1968.

_____. *Revised Draft Supplement Environmental Statement, Locks and Dam No. 26 (Replacement)*. Vol. I. St. Louis: MVS, 1976.

_____. *Rivers Project Master Plan*. St. Louis: MVS, 2001.

_____. *Rock Island, Report to Congress, An Evaluation of the Upper Mississippi River System Environmental Management Program*. Rock Island: MVR, 1997.

_____. *Salt River Basin, Missouri, Mark Twain Lake, Water Control Manual*. St. Louis: MVS, 1991.

_____. *Saving the Past from the Future: Archaeological Curation in the St. Louis District*. (MVS, 1991).

_____. "Shelbyville Dam Dedication After Action Review." St. Louis: MVS, 1970.

_____. *Ste. Genevieve – St. Marys, Missouri*. St. Louis: USACE, 1948.

_____. *Ste. Genevieve Survey Report*. St. Louis: USACE, 1979.

_____. *St. Louis District, Environmental Documentation*. St. Louis: MVS, 2006.

_____. *St. Louis Final Environmental Statement, Locks and Dam No. 26 (Replacement), Upper Mississippi River Basin, Mississippi River, Alton Illinois*. St. Louis: MVS, 1974.

_____. *St. Louis Final Environmental Statement, Locks and Dam No. 26 (Replacement), Upper Mississippi River Basin, Mississippi River, Alton Illinois*. St. Louis: MVS, 1974.

_____. *Summary Report of the Meramec Cooperative Investigation Filed Committee* (MVS archives).

_____. Upper Mississippi River Conservation Committee. *Fishes interaction with aquatic macrophytes with special reference to the Upper Mississippi River System*. Rock Island: MVR, 1988.

_____. *Upper Mississippi River Restoration Environmental Management Program, 2004 Report to Congress*. Rock Island: MVR, 2004.

_____. *Upper Mississippi River Restoration Environmental Management Program, 2010 Report to Congress*. Rock Island: MVR, 2010.

_____. *Upper Mississippi River Pool 8 Drawdown Results*. Water Level Management Task Force, 2007.

_____. *Water level Management Opportunities for Ecosystem Restoration on the Upper Mississippi River and Illinois Waterway*. Vicksburg: MVD, 2004.

_____. *Wetlands Delineation Manual*. Washington, D.C.: HQUSACE, 1987.

_____. *Winfield Navigation Pool, Lock and Dam No. 25, Mississippi River*. DM 2Cc1. St. Louis: MVS, 1963.

_____. *Wood River Levee and Drainage District, GDM No. 4*. St. Louis: USACE, 1958.

Wlosinski, Joseph H. et al. *Response of vegetation and fish during an experimental drawdown in three pools, Upper Mississippi River*. N.P.: USGS, Aug. 2000.

Travelogues

"Bradbury's Travels in the Interior of America, 1809-1811." Thwaits, Reuben G. *Early Western Travels, 1748-1846*. Vol. V. NY: AMS, 1966.

"Breckenridge's Journey up the Missouri, 1811." Thwaits, Reuben G. *Early Western Travels, 1748-1846*. Vol. VI. NY: AMS, 1966.

Jackson, Donald. Ed. *Journals of Zebulon Montgomery Pike with Letters and Related Documents*. Norman: University of Oklahoma Press, 1966.

James, Edwin. *Account of an Expedition from Pittsburg to the Rocky Mountains*. Vol. 1 and 2. Ann Arbor: University Microfilms, Inc., 1966.

Schoolcraft, Henry. *Journal of a Tour into the Interior of Missouri and Arkansas*. London: Richard Phillips, 1831.

Video

Video interview with Claude Strauser on annual Environmental Coordination Trip on the Mississippi River. *www.semissourian.com/gallery/1855/*, Jun. 30, 2011.

www.ingramcontent.com/pod-product-compliance
Lightning Source LLC
Chambersburg PA
CBHW080722300426
44114CB00019B/2461